W9-ASO-166

Department of Economic and Social Affairs

This document has been prepared by the Statistics Division, with assistance from the Division for the Advancement of Women, Department of Economic and Social Affairs of the United Nations Secretariat.

The Secretariat gratefully acknowledges the gracious contributions of the following bodies and Governments: the United Nations Children's Fund (UNICEF), the United Nations Development Fund for Women (UNIFEM), the United Nations Office for Project Services (UNOPS), the United Nations Population Fund (UNFPA), the World Food Programme (WFP), the World Health Organization (WHO), the Inter-Parliamentary Union and the Governments of Bahrain, Denmark, Finland, Germany, Iceland, Italy, Mexico, the Netherlands, Norway and the United Kingdom of Great Britain and Northern Ireland.

United Nations
New York 2000

ST/ESA/STAT/SER.K/16

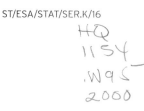

HQ
1154
.W95
2000

Social Statistics and Indicators Series K No. 16

THE WORLD'S WOMEN 2000
Trends and Statistics

United Nations
New York 2000

 KVCC KALAMAZOO VALLEY COMMUNITY COLLEGE LIBRARY

The designations used and the presentation of material in
this publication do not imply the expression of any opinion
whatsoever on the part of the Secretariat of the United
Nations concerning the legal status of any country, territory,
city or area or of its authorities, or concerning the delimitation of its frontiers or boundaries.

The term country as used in this publication also refers,
as appropriate, to territories or areas.

The designations "developed regions" and "developing
regions" are intended for statistical convenience and do not
necessarily express a judgement about the stage reached
by a particular country or area in the development process.

Symbols of United Nations documents are composed of
capital letters combined with figures.

ST/ESA/STAT/SER.K/16

United Nations Publication
Sales No. E.00.XVII.14
ISBN 92-1-161428-7

Copyright © United Nations 2000
All rights reserved
Manufactured in the United States of America

Cover photographs from United Nations archives and by
Richard Lord (top right, bottom left and bottom right).

Message from the Secretary-General

The United Nations is in a unique position to compile and analyse data on the realities of women's lives in countries around the world. A precise understanding of the economic and social roles of women and men in different societies is essential in designing policies and programmes at national and international levels to achieve gender equality. *The World's Women 2000: Trends and Statistics* is the only publication of its kind to present and interpret relevant statistics on how conditions are changing—or not changing—for women worldwide.

The World's Women: Trends and Statistics was first published by the United Nations in 1991. A new edition was requested for the 1995 Fourth World Conference on Women, held in Beijing. This third edition is timed to coincide with the twenty-third special session of the General Assembly, which is being held in New York from 5 to 9 June 2000 to review progress since the historic Beijing conference and to set in motion future actions for further implementation of the Beijing Platform for Action.

The World's Women 2000: Trends and Statistics presents new and updated statistics on population, the family, health, education and communication, work, and politics and human rights. As in previous editions, analysis is provided to increase awareness of the strides that have been made in bringing the world's women into the global community and the challenges that still lie before us. Statistics can—and must—play an important role in accomplishing these goals.

I urge Governments, non-governmental organizations, researchers, academics and activists around the world to make practical use of this information to help ensure that all women can enjoy their full human rights and dignity.

Kofi A. Annan
Secretary-General

■ CONTENTS

■ PREFACE

This third edition of *The World's Women: Trends and Statistics* provides an update of statistics and indicators on the situation of women and men around the world in several broad policy areas. *The World's Women* is a comprehensive and authoritative compilation of existing data and a source of gender-specific information. Non-technical language and a simple design have been employed to make the book accessible to a large audience and to respond to the needs of different users, including policy makers, planners, the media and all institutions concerned with gender issues.

A wide range of statistics from international and national sources was assembled for *The World's Women 2000* but many gaps remain—in coverage of important topics, in timeliness, in comparisons with men, in comparisons over time and in country coverage. The publication is, therefore, also intended to act as a guide for stimulating work by the international system and by national statistical agencies to address data gaps and revise methods of data collection and analysis, taking into account gender differences and the specific situations of women and men.

Much of the basic data presented in the publication are contained in much greater detail in the *Women's Indicators and Statistics Database (Wistat), Version 4,* CD-ROM (United Nations publication, Sales No. E.00.XVII.4), prepared by the United Nations Statistics Division.

The World's Women 2000 was prepared by the Statistics Division, with the assistance of the Division for the Advancement of Women, Department of Economic and Social Affairs of the United Nations Secretariat. Many United Nations bodies and organizations provided statistics, special studies and substantive guidance in their respective fields of expertise, including the Population Division of the Department of Economic and Social Affairs, the Office of the United Nations High Commissioner for Refugees, the Economic Commission for Latin America and the Caribbean, the International Labour Office (ILO), the United Nations Educational, Scientific and Cultural Organization (UNESCO), the United Nations Children's Fund (UNICEF) and the World Bank. The World Health Organization (WHO) prepared data and substantive inputs for the section entitled "Violence against women". In addition, the Inter-Parliamentary Union provided data and substantive inputs for the preparation of the section entitled "Women's participation in political decision-making".

Francesca Perucci was principal author of *The World's Women 2000* and Martha Riche provided substantive editing, as consultants to the United Nations.

Joann Vanek, Erlinda Go and Grace Bediako of the Gender Statistics Programme, United Nations Statistics Division, advised on the project and prepared the final draft. They were assisted by Ruth Cullen, Elizabeth Gould and Mary Jane G. Novenario-Reese, as consultants to the United Nations, and by Genene Zewge.

Other staff members of the United Nations Secretariat reviewed parts of the manuscript and provided substantive advice: Alice Clague, Jane Connors, Margarita Guerrero, Maria Hartl, Angela Me, Mary Beth Weinberger and Ibrahim Yansaneh.

The following individuals also provided substantive guidance: Elisabeth Aahman, WHO; Carla AbouZahr, WHO; Marcia Almey, Statistics Canada; Rosa Bravo, ECLAC; Teresa Castro Martin, Instituto de Economía y Geografía, Madrid; Marty Chen, Howard University; Monica Fong, World Bank; Claudia Garcia-Moreno, WHO; Howard Hayghe, United States Bureau of Labor Statistics; Birgitta Hedman, Statistics Sweden; Britta Hoem, Statistics Sweden; Bela Hovy, UNHCR; Joanna Jackson, ILO; Eric Jensen, Johns Hopkins University; Lawrence Johnson, ILO; Vasantha Kandiah, Population Division; Stefano Lazzari, UNAIDS; Cynthia Lloyd, Population Council; Alan López, WHO; Alain Marcoux, FAO; Madhu Bala Nath, UNIFEM; Keiko Osaki, Population Division; Christine Pintat, IPU; Detelina Radoeva, FAO; Mario Raviglione, WHO; Shahra Razavi, UNRISD; Torild Skard, Ministry of Foreign Affairs, Norway; Constance Sorrentino, United States Bureau of Labor Statistics; Iris Tetford, WHO; Manuela Tomei, ILO; Mukund Uplekar, WHO; Tessa Wardlaw, UNICEF; Peter Whitten, Eurostat; Derek Yach, WHO; Soon-Young Yoon, WHO; and Hania Zlotnik, Population Division.

Consulting assistance was provided by Robert Blackburn, assisted by Brad Brooks; Jacques Charmes; Gustavo De Santis; Margaret Gallagher; Catherine de Guibert-Lantoine; Andrew Harvey; Pamela Nichols Marcucci; Silvana Salvini, assisted by Lisa Francovich; and Muthu Subramanian.

Information on progress in generating gender statistics presented in "main findings and future directions" was provided by the following individuals: Rosa

PREFACE (cont'd)

Bravo, ECLAC; Carmelita Ericta, ESCAP; Guadalupe Espinosa, UNIFEM; Birgitta Hedman, Statistics Sweden; Ahmed Hussein, ESCWA; Yoichi Ito, Hosei University, Japan; Randi Kjeldstad, Central Bureau of Statistics, Norway; Lene Mikkelsen, ECE; Debbie Taylor, Community Agency for Social Enquiry, South Africa; Eeva-Sisko Veikkola, Statistics Finland; Sigridur Vilhjalmsdottir, Statistics Iceland; and Romulo Virola, National Statistical Coordination Board, Philippines.

Rocco Callari and Paul Kazarov of the United Nations Secretariat provided invaluable assistance.

The World's Women 2000 was designed by Cynthia Rhett/Shostak Studios Inc. ∎

■ ABOUT THE CHAPTERS

The *World's Women 2000* presents statistics and analyses in a format and language that non-specialists can readily understand. Each chapter covers a broad policy area, highlighting the main findings on the situation of women and men worldwide.

Statistical sources and reliability and timeliness of data

The statistics and indicators on women and men are compiled mainly from official national and international sources, as these are consistently authoritative and comprehensive, and allow for comparison among countries. Other sources and estimates that have been subjected to peer review are used to supplement official sources.

The World's Women 2000 is not intended for use as a primary source for the data presented, and every effort has been made to fully cite and document the sources drawn on. For specialized research and analyses in the fields covered, the reader is urged to consult the original sources.

The data sources used for most of the main tables and many of the charts are presented in the "Statistical sources" section at the end of the book. Most of these data are also contained in more detail in the *Women's Indicators and Statistics Database (Wistat), Version 4,* CD-ROM (United Nations publication, Sales No. E.00.XVII.4), prepared by the United Nations Statistics Division. The charts and graphs in *The World's Women 2000* also draw on a wide variety of more specialized studies, several of them undertaken especially for this publication. Since these studies are cited in the source notes that accompany each chart, reference notes are not included in discussions of information from charts in the text.

Timeliness of data is always a concern. Unfortunately, most international data often become available at least one to three years after the time period to which they refer.

In *The World's Women 2000,* some current-year estimates are incorporated but most series are based on census data, which in some cases are more than a decade old, or survey data that may be at least five or 10 years old. Surveys in specialized fields, such as illiteracy or cohabitation, may also be undertaken infrequently. Because internationally comparable data are often five to 10 years old, we have attempted to supplement them with recent data. However, the recent data are often available only for a small number of countries or for limited areas within a particular country. We have tried to describe these situations when they occur.

Countries, areas and geographical groupings

The basic grouping of countries is by continental region. While there is no United Nations standard for defining a country or area as developed or developing, these terms are applied for statistical and analytical purposes and do not express a judgement about the stage of development that a particular country or area has reached.

In general, the countries and areas covered are the same as those in the *Women's Indicators and Statistics Database (Wistat).* Included are 207 countries or areas, comprising all United Nations Member States, and countries and areas with a population greater than 50,000. For a full listing of regions, subregions and countries included, see Annex II.

When data are provided for any region in charts (for example, the listing of countries in which many households lack basic amenities), the only countries shown are those for which data are available. Such listings cannot, therefore, be considered exhaustive. In the main tables at the end of each chapter, two dots (..) indicate that data are not available for a country.

The designations employed and the form in which material is presented in *The World's Women 2000* do not in any way reflect or express the opinion of the Secretariat of the United Nations concerning the legal status of any country, territory, city or area, or that of its authorities, or concerning the delimitation of its frontiers or boundaries.

Presentation of data for regions and subregions

Regional and subregional averages are based on unweighted data for the countries and areas for which data are available. If country data were weighted by population, regional and subregional averages would mainly reflect the situation in one or two large countries. Use of unweighted data also allows for comparison with previous editions of *The World's Women.*

Statistical symbols and conventions

The following symbols are used to indicate reference periods of more than one year:
• A dash (-) between two consecutive years (e.g., 1994-1995) indicates coverage of the full period of two years;

• A dash between two years that are not consecutive (for example 1995–2000) indicates an average over the full period. This convention is used for many demographic indicators;

• A slash (/) between two consecutive years indicates a financial year, school year or crop year (for example 1994/1995);

• A slash between two years that are not consecutive indicates that the countries considered have data for one of the years in the interval (for example, 1990/1998 indicates that countries listed each have data for one of the survey years between 1990 and 1998).

The following symbols are used in the tables:
• A point (.) indicates decimals;
• A minus sign (-) before a number indicates a deficit or decrease, except as indicated;
• 0 or 0.0 indicates magnitude zero or less than half of unit employed;
• Two dots (..) indicate that data are not available or are not separately reported;
• Reference to dollars ($) indicates U.S. dollars, unless otherwise stated;
Details and percentages in tables do not necessarily add to totals because of rounding. ■

List of abbreviations and acronyms:

DHS	Demographic and Health Surveys	ISCO	International Standard Classification of Occupations	UNESCO	United Nations Educational, Scientific and Cultural Organization
ECA	Economic Commission for Africa				
ECLAC	Economic Commission for Latin America and the Caribbean	ISIC	International Standard Industrial Classification of All Economic Activities	UNFPA	United Nations Population Fund
				UNHCR	Office of the United Nations High Commissioner for Refugees
ECE	Economic Commission for Europe	NGO	non-governmental organization		
ESCAP	Economic and Social Commission for Asia and the Pacific	SNA	System of National Accounts	UNICEF	United Nations Children's Fund
		UNAIDS	Joint United Nations Programme on HIV/AIDS	UNIFEM	United Nations Development Fund for Women
ESCWA	Economic and Social Commission for Western Asia				
ILO	International Labour Office	UNDP	United Nations Development Programme	WHO	World Health Organization

■ MAIN FINDINGS AND FUTURE DIRECTIONS

In the Beijing Declaration adopted by the 1995 Fourth World Conference on Women, participating Governments "determined to advance the goals of equality, development and peace for all women everywhere in the interest of all humanity". The twenty-first century opens with this question: "Are these goals for women being met?" Some assert that progress for women is occurring rapidly, proclaiming that new technologies and globalization will benefit women and men equally. Others point out how, in some countries, the hard-won gains for women have been suddenly lost during dramatic economic and political transitions. Still others argue that while progress has been made, real change in the quality of women's lives—the achievement of social, economic and political equality and basic human rights—will take years to accomplish.

During the last decade, international conferences have sought to reshape a vision of women's lives. In Vienna, in 1993, the World Conference on Human Rights asserted that women's rights are human rights. In Cairo, in 1994, the International Conference on Population and Development (ICPD) built on this assertion and placed women's rights, empowerment and health, including reproductive health, at the centre of population and sustainable development policies and programmes. At the Beijing Conference, the world's Governments reached a consensus on a Platform for Action that "seeks to promote and protect the full enjoyment of all human rights and the fundamental freedoms of all women throughout their life cycle".

In the last seven years, Governments, institutions and non-governmental organizations have worked at every level to implement and incorporate the agendas of these conferences into national programmes for action. The success—or lack of success—of these efforts is the subject of The World's Women 2000: Trends and Statistics. The publication is also a response to a 1998 request to the Secretary-General from the United Nations General Assembly to provide a compilation of updated statistics and indicators on the situation of women and girls in countries around the world.

The World's Women 2000 is the third in a series of reports (the other two issued in 1991 and 1995) that look at the status of women through the lens of statistical data and analysis. The information and data in the present publication are intended to provide a "snapshot" of some of the more salient statistical findings since 1995, while also drawing out recent changes and long-term trends. As in the past two editions of The World's Women, the present edition compiles and analyses the data that are available from countries in the United Nations statistical system. While these data are essential for a comprehensive view, they do have a problem of timeliness. Data based on censuses are generally collected in a 10-year cycle and household surveys are often not collected on a regular basis. Furthermore, once these data are collected, tabulation and delivery to the international statistical services can take years, particularly in the developing regions where there are scant resources for statistical activities. As a result, analysts must rely on data that are often not current in preparing and producing reports, thus limiting assessment of the most recent trends.

In six chapters, The World's Women 2000 focuses on the status of women in six specific fields of concern: population, women and men in families, health, education and communication, work, and human rights and politics. Measuring women's progress in these and other areas is a new and evolving discipline—one that depends on the availability of basic demographic, social and economic data. It also depends on the ability of countries to meet the challenges of the increasing demand for data, following on the recommendations of the global conferences.

Even basic statistical series on women and men, such as literacy, health and causes of death, family status and economic activity, including income inequality, are not collected and tabulated routinely in many countries. Vital statistics registration systems, which compile data on births, deaths, marriages, divorces etc., do not exist in many countries of developing regions. Where data, including vital statistics, are collected and tabulated, countries often use different indicators or definitions of indicators, making cross-country analysis difficult and sometimes unreliable. In other areas, experience is limited on how data are to be collected and only a few countries have collected data on topics such as violence against women, time-use and school drop-outs.

The topics within each field of concern in The World's Women 2000 were shaped both by the availability of data and by the calls for action emerging from the global conferences. For example, the global conferences made certain life-stage categories—e.g., the girl and boy child, adolescent girls and boys, women and men in the reproductive years, and older women and men—central in setting priorities in policies and programmes. Reflecting these new priorities, emphasis has been placed in *The World's Women 2000* on specific age groups, especially in the chapters on population, women and men in families, health, and work.

Following on ICPD and its five-year review and the Beijing Conference, *The World's Women 2000* looks at statistical studies that take into account the rights and responsibilities of women and men to determine the size of their families, to have access to contraceptive services and products, and to have access to adequate maternal care.

Following up on the Beijing Platform for Action, the present publication takes a more comprehensive approach to work than earlier editions. In addition to data on paid employment, the chapter on work provides data on the informal sector, unpaid work in family enterprises and unpaid housework, as well as on economic activity in the formal sector. It also describes new efforts directed toward measurement of the overall contributions of women and men to national and regional economies.

Responding to calls from recent world conferences, *The World's Women 2000* also provides, in its chapter on human rights and political decision-making, new data on violence against women—including sexual violence, female genital mutilation and trafficking in women.

While each chapter in the present publication provides new findings in each of the subject areas, as well as up-to-date country and regional analysis of both new and earlier data, a number of cross-cutting themes emerge that point to changes—some positive, some negative—occurring in women's lives at the beginning of the twenty-first century.

A closing but persistent gender gap in education

The Framework for Action to implement the 1990 World Declaration on Education for All, the ICPD Programme of Action and the Beijing Platform for Action all place priority on the education of women as a human right. Women's equal access to education is seen as key to improving the health, nutrition and education of the family as a whole, as well as to empowering women to participate more fully in the development process. Among the targets set for Governments by the Beijing Platform for Action were: to close the gender gap in primary and secondary school education by the year 2005; to reduce the female illiteracy rate by, for example, providing universal access to the completion of primary education for girls by the year 2000; and to eliminate gender disparities in access to all areas of higher education.

The gender gap in enrolment in primary and secondary levels of schooling is closing. Enrolment has improved more for girls than for boys in regions where girls' enrolment was significantly lower than boys'—in Northern Africa, sub-Saharan Africa (excluding Southern Africa), Southern Asia and Western Asia. In South America and the Caribbean, enrolment ratios for girls and boys, which were at the same level in the past, improved more for girls than for boys, resulting in a gender gap now in favour of girls. In Eastern Asia, with slightly improved enrolment ratios for girls and declining ratios for boys, there are now more girls than boys enrolled. In Southern Africa, the gender gap in favour of girls in the past still exists but has narrowed because of a much larger improvement in boys' enrolment.

However, it is unlikely that the gender gap in education will be fully closed by the target date of 2005. In 22 countries of Africa and nine countries of Asia, the gap is still wide, with data showing enrolment ratios for girls less than 80 per cent that of boys. Furthermore, girls' access to and completion of primary and secondary education are still limited, particularly in rural areas, and girls are more likely than boys to drop out of school (except in the developed regions and in Latin America and the Caribbean).

Nearly two thirds of the illiterates in the world are women. Improvements in school enrolment over the years have resulted in generally higher literacy rates among younger adults but a large gender gap in favour of men continues to disadvantage women. The populations for which the gender gaps in enrolment and literacy are the widest—Southern Asia and sub-Saharan Africa—are also among the fastest growing. This suggests that there will continue to be enormous numbers of illiterate women in the world—many more than men. In fact, the United Nations Educational, Scientific and Cultural Organization (UNESCO) projects no decline in the gap in literacy between women and men over age 15 for the year 2025.

In higher education, women have made significant gains in enrolment in most regions of the world. Recently, for example, women's enrolment in higher education surpassed that of men in the Caribbean and Western Asia and is now equal to that of men in South America—although in all of these subregions, enrolment levels are still below 20 per 1,000 for women and for men. Enrolment ratios are higher for women than for men in many countries of Europe and in the United States and New Zealand. Enrolment in third-level education is the highest in the world in Australia, Canada and the United States. The lowest ratios of third-level education enrolments are found in many countries of sub-Saharan Africa—4 third-level students per 1,000 men and 2 or less per 1,000 women.

Women's lives shaped by decisions of the reproductive years

International conferences over the last decade have recognized women's right to quality reproductive health and reproductive services as an intrinsic component of their basic right to health and well-being. The ICPD Programme of Action, in particular, urged Governments to use their primary health-care systems to make reproductive health services available to all individuals throughout their reproductive years by 2015. Women's overall health, and especially their reproductive health, was recognized as being linked to their educational, economic and social status.

The Beijing Platform for Action considers that early marriage and early motherhood can severely curtail educational and employment opportunities for women and are likely to have a long-term adverse effects on their and their children's quality of life. Therefore, recent declines in early marriage and early childbearing in most regions of the world imply a significant change in the quality of women's lives. There are, however, exceptions to this overall pattern—for example, in 3 of 5 countries in Southern Asia and 11 of 30 countries in sub-Saharan Africa for which recent data are available, at least 30 per cent of young women aged 15 to 19 have been married.

Births to young women have also declined in some regions—for example, in Eastern Asia, Northern Africa and Western Europe, average birth rates declined by 50 per cent over the last two decades. However, fertility rates for young women have decreased only slightly or have stayed the same in Southern Asia, sub-Saharan Africa and the developed regions outside Europe.

The framework of the ICPD Programme of Action asserts the basic right of all couples and individuals to decide freely and responsibly the number, spacing and timing of their children and to have the information and means to do so. Monitoring childbearing under this broader concept of reproductive rights—in terms of desired family size, unmet need for contraception and the provision of maternal care—is now incorporated into the data-collection systems of many countries. The number of children desired (as expressed by women) has declined significantly in developing regions. The largest absolute decline is in some countries of sub-Saharan Africa, where women want, on average, two fewer children today than in the 1980s.

Whether women and men achieve their desired family size often depends on whether the demand for contraceptives is met. Unmet need for contraception is highest in sub-Saharan Africa, where nearly 30 per cent of women surveyed between 1988 and 1997, who either did not want another child or wanted to delay their next birth, had not been using contraception. In Asia and Northern Africa, unmet need was relatively low.

Contraceptive use has increased in most developing regions since 1980, and the trend continues in recent years. In most regions of the world, more than half of currently married women of reproductive age use contraceptives. However, in sub-Saharan Africa, levels of use are below 20 per cent. Low levels of use are also found in some countries in all other developing regions.

In all regions—and in almost all countries—fertility rates are declining, but the world's population is still increasing. The downward trend in overall levels of fertility has continued around the world and the upward trend observed during the 1980s in some developed countries—Finland, Sweden and the United States—has reversed. Although fertility has declined in most countries of sub-Saharan Africa, fertility in that region remains the highest in the world, at 5.4 births per woman.

Despite lower fertility rates, many women still lack access to reproductive health services. This situation has been universally recognized as a leading factor in maternal and infant morbidity and mortality. In developing countries, for example, maternal mortality continues to be a leading cause of death for women of reproductive age. The World Health Organization (WHO) and the United Nations Children's Fund (UNICEF) estimate that a woman's lifetime risk of dying from maternal causes is 1 in 16 in Africa, while a woman's risk is 1 in 1,400 in Europe. Furthermore, millions of women suffer from injuries and disabilities from maternal causes, often for the rest of their lives. WHO estimates that more than a quarter of all adult women in developing regions have pregnancy-related health problems.

Although new importance is being placed on women's reproductive health and "safe motherhood", data are not yet available to show whether the new concern with safe motherhood has been translated into improved maternal care. Recent data show that many women in developing countries receive little or no skilled prenatal or delivery care—services thought to play a major role in the reduction of maternal mortality and morbidity. For example, around half of pregnant women in most countries of Southern Asia and one third of women in many countries of Africa receive no prenatal care (WHO recommends a minimum of four prenatal consultations for a normal pregnancy). Moreover, in many countries of sub-Saharan Africa and in Southern Asia, about 60 per cent of women have no skilled attendant present at delivery, and even fewer women deliver in health facilities.

According to recent data, the timing of marriage is changing and the composition of the family continues to be diverse. For example, most people still marry but they marry later in life, especially women. In some countries of developing regions, consensual unions remain common, while polygynous unions are common in parts of Africa. In developed countries, marriages preceded by a period of cohabitation have increased and remarriage after divorce is more often postponed or never occurs.

In developed regions, since 1990, births outside marriage have increased greatly and lone-parent families (families in which children are raised by only one parent) are becoming more common. In addition, in developing regions, many children live away from their parents—for example, at least one third of girls and one fifth of boys aged 12 to 14 in some countries of sub-Saharan Africa.

Women still seeking influence

The Beijing Platform for Action recognized that without the active participation of women and the incorporation of women's perspectives at all levels of decision-making, the goals of equality, development and peace for women and men cannot be achieved. This recognition itself grew out of the active participation of women. Women, individually and as members and leaders of non-governmental organizations, have organized at the grass-roots, national and international levels to press Governments and international organizations to address issues central in the lives of women, including women's human rights, violence against women, reproductive health and unpaid work. They have engaged in education programmes to raise awareness, worked for legislation in these areas and lobbied for new data collection and analysis on topics of concern to women. The impact of their work is shown throughout the present publication.

With the support and encouragement of women's groups around the world, Governments were urged at the Beijing Conference to take measures to ensure women's access to, and full participation in, governance and leadership. However, in the years since the Conference, women's participation in the top levels of government and business has not markedly increased.

During the first part of 2000, only nine women were heads of State or Government. In 1998, 8 per cent of the world's cabinet ministers were women, compared to 6 per cent in 1994. Sweden is the only country with a majority of women ministers—55 per cent. Worldwide, more progress has been made in the appointment of women to sub-ministerial positions, particularly in the Caribbean and the developed regions outside of Europe, where women hold approximately 20 per cent of sub-ministerial positions.

Gender parity in parliamentary representation is also still far from being realized. In 1999, women represented 11 per cent of parliamentarians worldwide, compared to 9 per cent in 1987. Women's representation, on average, was highest in Western Europe (21 per cent) and in the developed regions outside Europe (18 per cent). Only the Nordic countries and the Netherlands have at least one third women parliamentarians.

Women are faring no better in the corporate world. For example, in 1999, women accounted for 11 to 12 per cent of corporate officers in the 500 largest corporations in the United States. While women accounted for 12 per cent of the corporate officers of the 560 largest corporations in Canada in 1999, they occupied only 3 per cent of the highest positions of those corporations. In Germany, in 1995, between 1 and 3 per cent of top executives and board directors in the 70,000 largest enterprises were women.

While women's share of administrative and managerial workers rose between 1980 and the early 1990s in every region of the world, except Southern Asia, the proportion of women in these positions is still low. For example, women's share at least doubled in sub-Saharan Africa (from 7 to 14 per cent) and in Western Asia (from 4 to 9 per cent). Even in developed regions outside Europe, women's share is only 35 per cent, although it has increased from 16 per cent since 1980.

The Beijing Platform for Action also highlights the potential of the new communications technologies to empower women and to advance their concerns. Girls, however, are much less likely than boys to enrol in mathematics and computer science courses, and, in a recent survey, men outnumbered women by about three to one among those planning careers in computer or information sciences. While, in some countries, women represent a rapidly increasing proportion of Internet users, they are more likely than men to lack the basic literacy and computer skills required for access to the emerging information and communications fields. Today, for the most part, a small minority of the population has access to the Internet, even in developed regions.

Toward a more comprehensive approach to work

As part of the Beijing Platform for Action, statisticians were called upon to develop a more comprehensive knowledge of all forms of work and employment. Efforts to improve measurement of women's participation and contribution to the economy and of the conditions of their work have been under way for some years and were strengthened by the Beijing Conference. Often, standard concepts and measurements inadequately represent the reality of women's work, however, and available statistics are still far from providing a strong basis for its assessment.

Over the past two decades, women's economic activity rates increased in all regions except sub-Saharan Africa, the transition economies of Eastern Europe and Central Asia, and Oceania. The largest increase occurred in South America, where rates rose from 26 to 45 per cent between 1980 and 1997. The lowest rates were found in Northern Africa and Western Asia, where less than one third of women were economically active.

An important aspect of these increasing rates of economic participation is that more women are in the labour force during their reproductive years. In Asia and Africa, women have always remained in the labour force until well beyond their reproductive period. But in other regions—in Latin America and the Caribbean, Europe, North America and Oceania—economic activity rates peaked for women in their early twenties throughout the 1970s. Now, according to regional data for 1990, labour force participation rates are high for women in their twenties, rise through their thirties and decline only after age 50. Increasingly, women remain in the labour force during their childbearing and child-rearing years because women now have fewer children and even those with young children are now likely to be employed.

Although the gender gap in rates of economic activity is narrowing, the nature of women's and men's participation in the labour force continues to be very different. Women still have to reconcile family responsibilities and market work and they work in different jobs and occupations than men, most often with lower status. Women have always engaged in the less formal types of work, working as unpaid workers in a family business, in the informal sector or in various types of household economic activities. They also continue to receive less pay than men. In manufacturing, for example, in 27 of the 39 countries with data available, women's wages were 20 to 50 per cent less than those of men. However, the limited data suggest that the differential between women's and men's earn-ings narrowed between 1990 and 1997 in the majority of these countries.

In many regions—in Africa, South America, Southern Asia and Eastern and Southern Europe, self-employment in non-agricultural activities, such as petty trading, service repairs, transport and small manufacturing, increased between 1970 and 1990. In these regions, women's self-employment as a proportion of the non-agricultural labour force has grown. The largest increase was in sub-Saharan Africa, where women's self-employment grew from 44 to 90 per cent between 1970 and 1990. There is also evidence that more self-employed women are becoming involved in the micro and small enterprise sector. For example, the number of women business owners and operators rose in nearly every Organisation for Economic Cooperation and Development (OECD) country during the last decade.

Close to half or more of the female non-agricultural labour force is in the informal sector in seven of the 10 Latin American countries for which data are available and in four Asian countries. In India and Indonesia, for example, nine out of every 10 women not working in agriculture are working in the informal sector.

Official statistics on home-based work—work performed in the home for an outside enterprise for wages or in-kind remuneration—are scarce and, even where they are collected, the statistics probably underestimate its prevalence. However, data available for the 1990s indicate that home-based work is an important and expanding source of employment worldwide, and that women predominate in this sector. The unsatisfactory conditions of home-based workers are also a source of concern. In 1996, the ILO International Convention on Home Work recognized the rights of home-based workers to treatment equal to that of other workers, and set a standard for minimum pay and working conditions.

Perhaps the major factor still influencing gender-based differentials in the labour market is the division of labour within the household—the time spent in the unpaid work of cleaning, caring for family members and preparing meals. Seven national studies undertaken between 1995 and 1999 in seven countries (mainly in the developed regions) show that women continue to spend substantially more time on unpaid work than men, even as they get old. Moreover, in most countries surveyed, the presence of small children requires women to allocate more time than men to unpaid work. It is difficult to tell from the data at hand if there has been any movement in recent years toward gender equality in unpaid work.

The toll of HIV/AIDS on the world's women

The HIV/AIDS pandemic continues to wreak havoc throughout the world and is of growing concern at every level of life: families are being decimated; social services are becoming overburdened; and the development prospects of entire countries are being threatened. Moreover, there is evidence to suggest that the toll of HIV/AIDS on women may be increasing.

According to recent Joint United Nations Programme on HIV/AIDS (UNAIDS) global estimates, women now account for almost half of the 32.4 million adults currently living with HIV/AIDS and of the 12.7 million adults who have died from the disease since the epidemic began. In 1999, 52 per cent of the 2.1 million adults who died from AIDS worldwide were women. The majority of these deaths occurred in sub-Saharan Africa, where women account for 55 per cent of those infected with HIV/AIDS—i.e., there are 12 African women currently infected with the virus for every 10 African men. Women's risk of becoming infected with HIV during unprotected sexual intercourse is also known to be two to four times higher than that of men.

The Beijing Platform for Action recognized that social and cultural factors often increase women's vulnerability to HIV and may determine the course that the infection takes in their lives. Women too often do not have the power to insist on safe and responsible sex practices and have little access to public health information and services, both of which have been found to be effective in preventing the disease and/or slowing its progress.

HIV/AIDS reaches beyond women's health to their roles as mothers and caregivers and their contributions to the economic support of their families. This requires that Governments continue to collect and analyze gender-disaggregated data on the prevalence and consequences of HIV/AIDS.

Progress in generating gender statistics

The production and dissemination of gender-sensitive data have increased with each of the world conferences on women, slowly at first but gaining new momentum by the time of the Fourth World Conference on Women in Beijing in 1995. While a great deal of work had been done on gender statistics before Beijing, there was much more left to be done, both in countries and by international agencies. The Beijing Platform for Action outlined a comprehensive set of actions to "generate and disseminate gender-disaggregated data and information for planning and evaluation" **(see annex 1, which reproduces strategic objective H.3 of the Platform for Action).**

Many of the actions required to implement the comprehensive mandates on gender statistics put forth by the Beijing Conference are under way. In addition to the data and analysis presented in *The World's Women 2000*, the following represent some of these efforts:

Some developments in disaggregated data collection

For many years, most national statistical agencies have had a policy of disaggregating data by sex and age whenever it is appropriate to do so. The Beijing Platform for Action also gave new importance to the reflection in statistics of all issues relating to women and men in society. These mandates have received support in legislative statements and in other directives. Some examples include:

• The Statistical Commission of the United Nations reported to its legislative body (the Economic and Social Council) that, as a basic working method, the Commission incorporates a gender perspective in its work by (a) advising countries to collect, compile and analyse statistics related to individuals disaggregated by sex; (b) ensuring that gender stereotypes are not implicit in country data-collection programmes and methods; and (c) ensuring that statistics reflect problems, issues and questions related to women and men in society;

• The South Africa Statistics Act of 1998 underlines the necessity of disaggregating statistics by sex;

• Republic Act 7192 in the Philippines—the Women in Development and Nation-Building Act—mandates all Government agencies to collect sex-disaggregated data and to include such data in their programmes;

• In Finland, a chapter on the improvement of statistics was included in the 1997 National Plan for Promoting Gender Equality;

• In Iceland, the 1998 Parliamentary resolution on a four-year action programme for gender equality requests that all ministries and official institutions present statistics by sex;

• In Sweden, the Ordinance of Official Statistics states that "official statistics related to individuals should—if no special contradictory reasons exist—be disaggregated by sex";

• In the United Kingdom in 1997, the Social Statistics Committee of the Government Statistical Service agreed on a statistical policy on the collection and dissemination of statistics disaggregated by sex;

• A 1999 expert meeting of the Economic Commission for Latin America and the Caribbean (ECLAC) agreed on a comprehensive plan for the development of gender statistics in the region.

Policy-oriented publications on gender statistics

The general approach in the development of gender statistics has involved efforts to promote dialogue and understanding between statisticians and the various users of statistics—policy makers, representatives of non-governmental organizations, activists and researchers. User-producer seminars and training workshops, which are the first step in the development of gender statistics, have been held in countries around the world over the past 15 years. In recent years, for example, training workshops were conducted in Arab, Central American, and Caribbean countries and in many countries in transition.

Some Governments and international organizations are making a concerted effort to produce statistical publications on gender that present and interpret topical data on women and men in a form suitable for a wide range of non-technical users.

Sweden has been at the forefront of producing publications on gender statistics. For example, *Women and Men in Sweden: Facts and Figures*, first published in 1985 by Statistics Sweden, has been a model for work supported by the Swedish International Development Authority (SIDA), in consultation with Statistics Sweden, in 35 countries in Africa, Asia, Central America, Europe, Latin America and transition countries in Eastern Europe and Central Asia. In addition, four publications were prepared for cities and regions in the Russian Federation. Sweden was also instrumental in the production of a regional publication, *Women and Men in East, Central and Southern Africa: Facts and Figures 1995*, as well as a training manual, *Engendering Statistics: A Tool for Change*, published in 1996, which is now available in four languages (Chinese, Japanese, Russian and Spanish).

Other efforts to produce statistical publications on gender include:
• Three editions of *The World's Women: Trends and Statistics*—in 1991, 1995 and 2000—produced by the United Nations Statistics Division. The Division also produced, in 1997, the *Handbook for Producing National Statistical Reports on Women and Men*, a guide to preparing national publications, based on the format of *The World's Women*;
• *Women and Men in the ESCAP Region*, a statistical profile, published in 1999, as well as profiles prepared according to the same format by national experts, published since 1995 in 16 countries in the Economic and Social Commission for Asia and the Pacific (ESCAP) region;
• Statistical profiles on men and women in the South Pacific islands of Kiribati and Palau, published in 1997;

• *Arab Women 1995: Trends, Statistics and Indicators*, produced for the Economic and Social Commission for Western Asia (ESCWA) region, as well as national reports being prepared in connection with gender-sensitive training activities in nine countries of Western Asia and Northern Africa;
• Efforts at the national and regional levels in the Economic Commission for Latin America and the Caribbean region, which focused on the development of socio-economic indicators for use in the formulation of public policies; and ongoing work that includes the development of a set of indicators to facilitate the accurate measurement of changes over time in women's situations and cross-country analysis within the region;
• *La mujer mexicana: un balance estadístico al final del siglo XX*, a statistical analysis of women and men, published in 1995 in the format of *The World's Women*.

Though few of these books are published on a regular basis, Finland, Iceland, Norway, the Philippines, Sweden, the Nordic Council and the Economic Commission for Europe (ECE) have each published at least two gender statistics publications.

Involving additional stakeholders

Responding to the Beijing Platform, centres for women's studies and research organizations, both at the national and international levels, are becoming more involved with statistical producers in developing and testing appropriate indicators and research methodologies to strengthen gender analysis, as well as in monitoring and evaluating the implementation of the goals of the Beijing Conference. Examples include:
• The United Nations Development Fund for Women (UNIFEM) publication, *Progress of the World's Women*, published in 2000, complements *The World's Women* series by focusing both on benchmarks for progress established at international conferences and on women's visions and ideas of "progress". The UNIFEM publication looks at ways of assessing women's progress using a variety of indicators and examines the issue of accountability, focusing, in particular, on how to measure the impact of Government policies and programmes on women and men.
• The Japan Statistics Research Institute of Hosei University has had an active role in the development of gender statistics in Japan. The Institute has translated various international documents on gender statistics into Japanese, introduced papers on gender statistics into sessions and journals of the Society of Economic Statistics in Japan and promoted the debate on the needs in the field of gender statistics in Japan;

• The International Food Policy Research Institute in Washington, D.C., continues research and analysis of data on the measurement of gender and poverty, as well as on the allocation of resources within households;

• Women in Informal Sector Globalizing and Organizing (WIEGO), a coalition representing international organizations, academic institutions and non-governmental organizations, is working with the ILO and the United Nations Statistics Division to improve statistics on the informal sector, homeworkers and street vendors (some of the findings of which are included in Chapter 5 of *The World's Women 2000*);

• The World Health Organization (WHO) is working with international experts and local women's organizations and institutions to improve methods for collection of data on violence against women.

Moving ahead on gender statistics

A review of progress in gender statistics shows that considerable work has been done and advances made in ways of presenting gender statistics effectively. Data users know much more today than they did 10 years ago about how women's and men's situations differ in terms of their social, political and economic life. Further, as reflected in the Beijing Platform for Action, users of data are asking more questions than ever, thus increasing the demand for statistics.

Much remains to be done, however, to provide the statistics necessary to understand what is happening with respect to the main issues related to gender and to meet the requirements of the global conferences. Some of the work required relates to new data on issues unique to women—for example, violence against women and maternal health. Other work is required for the development of new data on men, especially in the areas related to their roles and responsibilities in reproductive health, fatherhood and unpaid work. *The World's Women 2000* describes efforts initiated since the 1990s to collect data on these and other topics.

Much of what is needed to understand the situation of women and men requires that all countries improve the capacity of their national statistical sys-

tems to regularly collect basic data, including births, deaths, marriages, place of residence, household formation, employment and other aspects of work, health and economic status. The improvement of national statistical capacity—the ability to provide timely and reliable statistics from censuses, household surveys and administrative systems—is essential for improving the quality and timeliness of gender statistics.

The United Nations Economic and Social Council (ECOSOC) has recognized the importance of statistical capacity-building for the implementation and follow-up of the global conferences. The Council has urged countries, international and regional agencies and donors to work together to support national statistical capacity-building in developing countries.

The Beijing Platform asks Governments to appoint staff to strengthen gender statistics programmes, to ensure coordination, monitoring and linkage to all fields of statistical work, and to prepare output that integrates statistics from the various subject areas. Few countries have designated staff responsible for gender statistics and among those that have, the arrangement is generally for part-time work in connection with other work in social statistics. Whatever the specific arrangements, a necessary condition for carrying out work on national gender policy is leadership by the national statistical agencies, in order to develop the necessary databases, to undertake the analytic work and to develop the new concepts required to measure women's situations and their contributions to society.

Recent international conferences recognized that gender-based data collection and analysis are invaluable tools not only for understanding the situations and conditions of women's and men's lives but also for informing policies and practices to improve their lives. By recognizing and filling some of the gaps that exist in data collection and analysis, *The World's Women 2000* hopes to shed light on the progress made to date—and challenges still ahead—in achieving equity and equality for the world's women. ■

CHAPTER 1

Population

Some important findings:

- Women are having fewer children on average but with more women of reproductive age, world population continues to grow.

- Population of 1.15 billion adolescents, living mostly in developing countries, is largest in history.

- Population of people over 60 is expected to grow from 600 million to 1 billion in next 20 years, with many more older women than men.

- Populations around the world are ageing as fewer children are born and people live increasingly longer lives.

- Although women outnumber men in most regions, men outnumber women in parts of Asia.

- Women represent a large proportion of international migrants—an estimated 56 million women out of a total of 118 million migrants.

DEMOGRAPHIC CHANGES

Profound demographic changes are taking place around the world. The largest-ever generation of adolescents in countries with high fertility in the recent past is one population group that reflects these changes. Another is the rapidly growing group of older women and men in all countries, with the oldest populations in countries where fertility has been low for decades. Even more than for men, these and other demographic changes interact in complex ways with the fundamental components of women's lives: their families, their health, their education, their economic participation and their rights.

Most of world's children living in developing regions

Over the last three decades the world's population of children (persons under age 15) increased from about 1.4 to 1.8 billion.[1] It is projected that their numbers will start decreasing slowly around 2025.

The large majority of the world's children (88 per cent) live in the developing regions, with the largest share (60 per cent) in Asia. In Asia, however, fertility has declined, and the number of children is projected to decrease slightly—from 1.083 to 1.036 billion—between 2000 and 2020. Over the same period, the number of children will increase by 100 million in Africa, where fertility decline started later and has been slow. Latin America is expected to have a slight increase in the number of children over the next twenty years (chart 1.1).

Children represent a large share of the population in some parts of the world. In 66 countries, at least 40 per cent of the population consists of children; in several countries, almost half of the population is under age 15 (table 1.A).

In almost all countries, however, the share of children in the population is decreasing as fertility rates continue to decline and increasing numbers of people survive to middle and old age. Over the last five years, the share of the population under age 15 has declined by 2 or 3 percentage points in most regions (chart 1.2). Sub-Saharan Africa is one exception; the share of the population under age 15 has declined only slightly. Western Europe and developed countries outside Europe are other exceptions; the share of children has remained low as a result of low fertility levels over many years.

Largest number of adolescents in history

There are 1.15 billion adolescents (persons aged 10 to 19) in the world, a number still growing and projected to reach 1.19 billion by the year 2020. By far the largest increase will be in Africa, which is expected to add almost 80 million adolescents in the next twenty years. It is expected that more than one in five of the world's adolescents will live in this region in 2020 (chart 1.3).

Close to 1 billion adolescents live in the developing regions—over 700 million in Asia alone. Fourteen per cent of the adolescent population live in the developed regions. If current trends continue, 11 per cent will live in the developed regions by 2020.

Population estimates and projections

Data on demographic trends used in the present report are taken from *World Population Prospects: The 1998 Revision*.[a] These population estimates and projections provide a standard and consistent set of figures for the analysis of the current world situation and a plausible range for future population trends. The United Nations Population Division prepares three variants of projections (high, low and medium). The three variants differ in their assumptions regarding future fertility trends. The medium-fertility variant, adopted in the present report for all indicators presented, assumes that fertility in countries with high fertility will ultimately reach replacement level (about 2.1 children per woman), while fertility will remain below replacement level in countries where it is already below replacement.

[a] United Nations publication, Sales Nos. E.99.XIII.8 and E.99.XIII.9.

Older people

Different age groups are used to categorize older people, depending on the circumstances in a particular country, such as average retirement age and life expectancy. In international sources, the categories "age 60 or over" and "age 65 or over" refer to *all* older people, while the categories "age 75 or over" and "age 80 or over" refer to the oldest old.

For the present report, to allow comparison to other relevant international publications and to maintain continuity with previous editions, the following definitions are used:
• Age 60 or over to refer to older people;
• Age 80 or over to refer to oldest old.

In some regions, recent high fertility and improvements in maternal and child health have led to the growing numbers of children and adolescents in the population. At least one in five persons is an adolescent in most countries in Africa, Asia (except Eastern Asia) and Central America. On average, adolescents account for 23 per cent of the populations of Northern Africa, sub-Saharan Africa and Southern Asia **(chart 1.4)**.

In recent years, policy makers have begun to focus on the crucial period of adolescence. Adolescent girls in the developing world face limitations and obstacles that boys are generally spared. Many young women have restricted mobility, inadequate access to educa-

Chart 1.1:

The number of children is expected to increase in Africa
Population under age 15

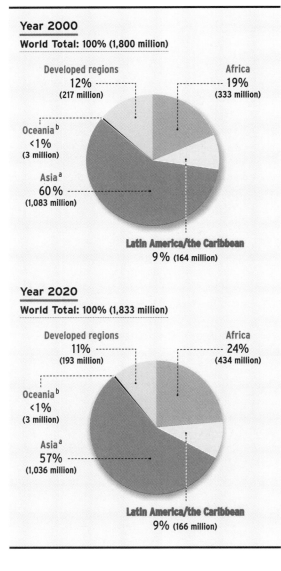

Year 2000
World Total: 100% (1,800 million)

Developed regions
12%
(217 million)

Africa
19%
(333 million)

Oceania[b]
<1%
(3 million)

Asia[a]
60%
(1,083 million)

Latin America/the Caribbean
9% (164 million)

Year 2020
World Total: 100% (1,833 million)

Developed regions
11%
(193 million)

Africa
24%
(434 million)

Oceania[b]
<1%
(3 million)

Asia[a]
57%
(1,036 million)

Latin America/the Caribbean
9% (166 million)

Source: Prepared by the Statistics Division of the United Nations Secretariat from *Women's Indicators and Statistics Database (Wistat), Version 4,* CD-ROM (United Nations publication, Sales No. E.00.XVII.4), based on Population Division of the United Nations Secretariat, *World Population Prospects: The 1998 Revision,* vol. II, *The Sex and Age Distribution of the World Population* (United Nations publication, Sales No. E.99.XIII.8).

[a] Excluding Japan, which is included in developed regions.

[b] Excluding Australia and New Zealand, which are included in developed regions.

tion and employment opportunities, and marry and have children while they are still adolescents. Boys, on the other hand, enjoy more autonomy and mobility, are offered more opportunities and rarely enter marriage during adolescence. Investing in education and employment opportunities for young women has the effect of delaying marriage and childbearing, which in turn is associated with smaller family size and improved quality of life **(see chap. 4)**.

Populations ageing rapidly
Older people

Populations all over the world are ageing. Although the number of older women and men is much smaller than the number of young people, it is increasing at a much faster rate. The population of older people (aged 60 or over) is expected to grow from slightly over 600 million to over 1 billion—a 67 per cent increase—between 2000 and 2020. In contrast, the population under age 15 will grow 2 per cent over the same period.[2]

Today, 11 per cent of the world's women and 9 per cent of the world's men are aged 60 or over. In 2020, 15 per cent of women and 12 per cent of men will be aged 60 or over. Older people will make up 14 per cent of the world population, while children will account for 24 per cent. If current assumptions are correct, older people will account for 22 per cent of the population in 2050, surpassing the share of children, which is expected to decline to 20 per cent.[3]

Until recently, the share of older women and men in the population was growing primarily in the developed regions. This growth was due to long-term declines in fertility, which reduce the share of younger people in the total population, and to increased life expectancy as a result of medical advances, increased availability of health care and improved health practices. The same conditions are now occurring in the developing regions. During the next two decades, the older population is expected to grow by 88 per cent in the developing regions, compared with 35 per cent in the developed regions.

Between 2000 and 2020, the proportion of older women in the population of South-eastern Asia is expected to increase from 7 to 13 per cent, and in Eastern Asia, from 11 to 19 per cent. It is also projected that populations will age rapidly in Southern and Western Asia, Oceania and the Caribbean. In these four regions, in the next two decades, the proportion of older women is predicted to increase by 50 per cent. Only in sub-Saharan Africa are the proportions of older women and older men expected to remain at their current levels (6 and 5 per cent, respectively) in 2020 **(chart 1.5)**.

Today, the oldest populations are in Western

Europe, where fertility has remained at very low levels for decades and life expectancy continues to increase. Older women represent about a quarter of all women in a number of countries in this region—as much as 27 per cent in Italy and Germany **(chart 1.6)**.

Projections based on current trends in fertility and mortality suggest that by 2020 over 30 per cent of women will be aged 60 or over in a number of developed countries. However, some demographers think that fertility rates in these countries might rise, as the fertility rates take into account later ages for childbearing.[4] This would mitigate the increase in the proportion of the population that is older. Still, the number—if not the share—of older people will continue to rise substantially because life expectancy is expected to continue to increase.

In Eastern Europe, on average, 21 per cent of women and 15 per cent of men are aged 60 or over **(chart 1.5)**. In some countries of the region, older women now represent almost a quarter of the female population and are expected to reach 30 per cent or more in 20 years.

In the rest of the developed countries, populations are relatively younger than in Europe, with 19 per cent of women and 16 per cent of men aged 60 or over. In the United States, for example, demographers think that the shift to delayed childbearing is almost complete and that fertility is near replacement level.

Chart 1.2+:
The proportion of children in the total population is declining and will continue to decline
Percentage of population under age 15

	1995	2000	2020
Africa			
Northern Africa	38	35	26
Sub-Saharan Africa	44	43	37
Latin America and the Caribbean			
Caribbean	30	27	21
Central America	40	38	28
South America	34	32	25
Asia			
Eastern Asia	27	25	18
South-eastern Asia	35	33	25
Southern Asia	40	38	30
Central Asia	38	36	26
Western Asia	36	34	28
Oceania	39	36	28
Developed regions			
Eastern Europe	22	19	16
Western Europe	18	18	15
Other developed regions	20	20	17

Source: Prepared by the Statistics Division of the United Nations Secretariat from *Women's Indicators and Statistics Database (Wistat), Version 4*, CD-ROM (United Nations publication, Sales No. E.00.XVII.4), based on Population Division of the United Nations Secretariat, *World Population Prospects: The 1998 Revision*, vol. II, *The Sex and Age Distribution of the World Population* (United Nations publication, Sales No. E.99.XIII.8).

+ In this and subsequent charts, regional and subregional averages are unweighted (i.e., the averages do not take into account the size of the individual countries' populations) and are based only upon available data for that region (see page xi for fuller explanation).

Chart 1.3:
The number of adolescents will keep growing in Africa
Population aged 10-19

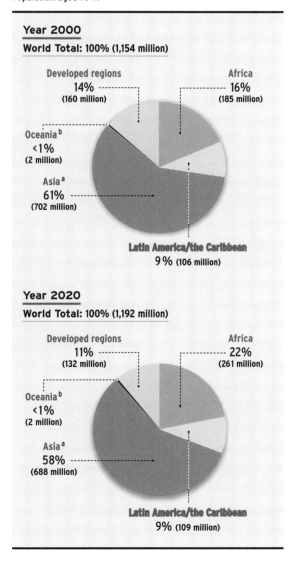

Year 2000
World Total: 100% (1,154 million)

Developed regions 14% (160 million)
Africa 16% (185 million)
Oceania[b] <1% (2 million)
Asia[a] 61% (702 million)
Latin America/the Caribbean 9% (106 million)

Year 2020
World Total: 100% (1,192 million)

Developed regions 11% (132 million)
Africa 22% (261 million)
Oceania[b] <1% (2 million)
Asia[a] 58% (688 million)
Latin America/the Caribbean 9% (109 million)

Source: Prepared by the Statistics Division of the United Nations Secretariat from *Women's Indicators and Statistics Database (Wistat), Version 4*, CD-ROM (United Nations publication, Sales No. E.00.XVII.4), based on Population Division of the United Nations Secretariat, *World Population Prospects: The 1998 Revision*, vol. II, *The Sex and Age Distribution of the World Population* (United Nations publication, Sales No. E.99.XIII.8).

[a] Excluding Japan, which is included in developed regions.

[b] Excluding Australia and New Zealand, which are included in developed regions.

Increases in the share of older people in the population are the direct result of continued decreases in mortality rates.[5]

The lowest proportion of older people is in sub-Saharan Africa and Southern Asia, where about 6 per cent of the population are aged 60 or over **(chart 1.5)**.

Since women generally live longer than men, they outnumber men at older ages, and this imbalance increases rapidly with age. Worldwide, there are 123 women for every 100 men aged 60 or over; 189 women for every 100 men aged 80 or over; and 385 women for every 100 men aged 100 or over.[6] There are more women than men in the older populations of every region. The widest gaps are in Eastern Europe, where there are 153 women per 100 men aged 60 or over, and in Central Asia, where there are 143 women per 100 men **(chart 1.7)**. These regions have the greatest sex differentials in mortality in the world **(see chap. 3)**.

In Western Europe, there are 134 women per 100 men aged 60 or over. In the other developed regions, the sex ratio (older women to older men) is 126, equal or close to the ratios in such developing regions as sub-Saharan Africa, South America, the Caribbean and Eastern Asia. The lowest sex ratios are in Southern Asia (102) and in Western Asia (107).

The ageing of the population, together with the increasing absolute number of older people in the population, presents both challenges and opportunities. Countries where older women and men represent an increasing share of the population face the challenge of adjusting existing—or developing altogether new—policies regarding pension, social welfare and health care to meet the needs of this growing population.

Older women are particularly vulnerable, as they are more likely than men to become widowed and to live alone, requiring continuing economic resources and/or support. Furthermore, as a result of life-long discrimination in the labour markets, women generally earn less than men and work more often in informal or unpaid activities, which do not provide social security or pensions. These circumstances, together with customs and laws (such as inheritance laws, which favour sons over daughters and children over wives), make women more likely than men to end up in poverty in old age **(see chap. 2)**. A study in six countries in transition found that the incidence of poverty is highest at older ages in all but one of the countries examined. The number of women in poverty exceeds the number of men in poverty at all ages, but the disparity is most pronounced at older ages.[7]

On the positive side, older people bring to their families and communities valuable resources, skills and knowledge gained over the years. In many countries, older persons work (in paid or unpaid activities), thereby helping to support themselves or fulfilling important voluntary functions—caring for their grandchildren, their spouses and often for their very old parents, or helping in schools and health and community centres. In the United States, for example, more than 3 million people aged 65 or over do volunteer work.[8]

In agricultural communities, where there is frequently no concept of retirement, women and men work until they are no longer able to carry out their tasks, which is often very late in life. In Africa, for example, as many as 32 per cent of women and 62 per cent of men aged 65 or over are economically active. These figures only reflect work captured by official statistics, and do not fully account for unpaid work for own-consumption or informal sector activities, where women represent a large proportion **(see chap. 5)**.

In the developed countries, where older people generally work only until retirement age, there is

Chart 1.4:

Adolescents are a large proportion of the population in most developing regions
Percentage of population aged 10-19 in 2000

Africa

Northern Africa	23
Sub-Saharan Africa	23

Latin America and the Caribbean

Caribbean	18
Central America	22
South America	20

Asia

Eastern Asia	17
South-eastern Asia	21
Southern Asia	23
Central Asia	22
Western Asia	21

Oceania

Oceania	21

Developed regions

Eastern Europe	15
Western Europe	12
Other developed regions	13

Source: Prepared by the Statistics Division of the United Nations Secretariat from *Women's Indicators and Statistics Database (Wistat)*, Version 4, CD-ROM (United Nations publication, Sales No. E.00.XVII.4), based on Population Division of the United Nations Secretariat, *World Population Prospects: The 1998 Revision*, vol. II, *The Sex and Age Distribution of the World Population* (United Nations publication, Sales No. E.99.XIII.8).

Chart 1.5:

Populations will grow older in almost all regions
Percentage aged 60 or over

	2000		2020	
	W	M	W	M
Africa				
Northern Africa	7	6	10	9
Sub-Saharan Africa	6	5	6	5
Latin America and the Caribbean				
Caribbean	12	10	18	15
Central America	7	6	10	9
South America	9	8	13	11
Asia				
Eastern Asia	11	8	19	17
South-eastern Asia	7	6	13	11
Southern Asia	6	6	9	8
Central Asia	9	7	12	9
Western Asia	8	7	12	13
Oceania	7	6	11	9
Developed regions				
Eastern Europe	21	15	27	20
Western Europe	23	18	29	24
Other developed regions	19	16	27	23

Source: Prepared by the Statistics Division of the United Nations Secretariat from *Women's Indicators and Statistics Database (Wistat)*, Version 4, CD-ROM (United Nations publication, Sales No. E.00.XVII.4), based on Population Division of the United Nations Secretariat, *World Population Prospects: The 1998 Revision*, vol. II, *The Sex and Age Distribution of the World Population* (United Nations publication, Sales No. E.99.XIII.8).

increasing recognition that women and men should work as long as they wish. Older people, irrespective of their status in the labour force, make innumerable contributions of both time and money to society.

The oldest old

Worldwide, there are some 70 million people aged 80 or over. Although this group has always represented—and still represents—a very small share of the population, it is the fastest-growing group. It is projected that the oldest old will number 132 million by the year 2020.[9]

In the developed regions, the population aged 80 or over rose from 2 per cent of the population in 1970 to about 3 per cent in 2000. If current assumptions about fertility and mortality trends are correct, this population will increase to 5 per cent of the total population by the year 2020.

The percentages of oldest old are highest in Western Europe and the other developed regions, and

Chart 1.6:

In some developed countries, at least one fourth of women and roughly one fifth of men are aged 60 or over

	Percentage aged 60 or over, 2000	
	W	M
Belgium	25	19
Germany	27	20
Greece	26	22
Italy	27	21
Japan	26	21
Sweden	25	20
Ukraine	25	16

And nearly one third of women and one fourth of men will be aged 60 or over in 2020

	Percentage aged 60 or over, 2020	
	W	M
Belgium	31	25
Czech Republic	31	24
Finland	32	26
Germany	32	26
Greece	32	27
Italy	34	28
Japan	35	29
Spain	31	25
Sweden	31	27

Source: Prepared by the Statistics Division of the United Nations Secretariat from *Women's Indicators and Statistics Database (Wistat), Version 4*, CD-ROM (United Nations publication, Sales No. E.00.XVII.4), based on Population Division of the United Nations Secretariat, *World Population Prospects: The 1998 Revision*, vol. II, *The Sex and Age Distribution of the World Population* (United Nations publication, Sales No. E.99.XIII.8).

A new understanding of population

Population growth has traditionally interested Governments and policy makers, especially in those countries where rapid growth was thought to hamper social and economic development. Today, research and programme experience have produced an international consensus—that population growth and its incumbent problems cannot be addressed solely by setting demographic targets and implementing family planning initiatives to meet those targets. Population policies and programmes must also take into account the powerful interrelationships that exist between population growth and sustainable development, while placing health, empowerment, gender equity and equality, and human rights for all at their centre.

This consensus was forged at the International Conference on Population and Development (ICPD) in Cairo in 1994. The ICPD Programme of Action, signed by 179 Governments, presents a 20-year plan for setting in place a broad range of policies and programmes, which aim to achieve a balance between the world's people and its resources by the year 2015. In 1999, at the five-year review of the ICPD, the Programme of Action was reaffirmed and extended in a "key actions" document, which came out of an extensive review process. As with the Programme of Action, the world's women form the centerpiece of these "key actions":

The Programme of Action emphasizes that everyone has the right to education, which shall be directed to the full development of human resources, and human dignity and potential, with particular attention to women and the girl child, and therefore everyone should be provided with the education necessary to meet basic human needs and to exercise human rights. It calls for the elimination of all practices that discriminate against women, and affirms that advancing gender equality and equity and the empowerment of women, and the elimination of all kinds of violence against women, and ensuring women's ability to control their own fertility are cornerstones of population and development-related programmes. It affirms that the human rights of women and the girl child are an inalienable, integral and indivisible part of universal human rights. It further affirms that reproductive rights embrace certain human rights that are already recognized in national laws, international human rights documents, and other consensus documents. These rights rest on the recognition of the basic right of all couples and individuals to decide freely and responsibly the number, spacing and timing of their children and to have the information and means to do so, and the right to attain the highest standard of sexual and reproductive health....The promotion of the responsible exercise of those rights for all people should be the fundamental basis for government- and community-supported policies and programmes in the area of reproductive health, including family planning.[a]

[a] Key actions for the further implementation of the Programme of Action of the International Conference on Population and Development (S-21/2, annex) Para. 3.

are also relatively large in Eastern Europe and the Caribbean **(chart 1.8)**.

Among the oldest old, there are 189 women per 100 men worldwide. The ratio of women to men is highest in Central Asia (281 women per 100 men), Eastern Asia (257 women per 100 men) and Eastern Europe (256 women per 100 men). Women-to-men ratios also exceed 200 in Southern Africa and Western Europe **(chart 1.9)**.

At these older ages, women are even more likely to live alone and to face economic hardship. Moreover, women in this age group are especially vulnerable to chronic and debilitating diseases, which may reduce their mobility, their ability to maintain social contacts and, therefore, their quality of life.

Many social and economic factors determine women's quality of life, and produce very different levels of functional capacity and health at older ages. Even at very old ages, a large number of women remain fit and able to care for themselves and others, including their grandchildren or other family members **(see chap. 3)**.

Fewer women than men in the world

There are slightly fewer women than men in the world—99 women per 100 men. On average, men outnumber women in most of Asia and in Northern Africa. The lowest average sex ratios are in Western Asia—92 women per 100 men—and in Oceania and Southern Asia, with average ratios of 95 and 96, respectively **(chart 1.10)**. Of 22 countries or areas in the world where there are 95 or fewer women per 100 men, all but one are in Asia and Oceania **(chart 1.11)**.

The deficit of women in Southern Asia may be in part the result of some forms of discrimination against women and girls. Discrimination and neglect can affect women's health and survival in many ways, most commonly through inferior nutrition and health care for girls, and poor nutrition and health care during pregnancy and breastfeeding **(see chap. 3)**.

In all other areas of the world, women outnumber men. By far the highest sex ratio is in Eastern Europe, where women outnumber men 108 to 100 **(chart 1.10)**. Starting in 1989, mortality rates rose considerably for men in the Baltic countries (Latvia, Lithuania and Estonia), the Russian Federation, Belarus and Ukraine, and have only recently levelled off. Today, these countries have sex ratios of 112 to 120 women per 100 men.

The sex ratio is also skewed considerably in countries where war or persecution has taken a particularly high toll on men. In Cambodia, for instance, an estimated one quarter of the population died—the majority men—between 1975 and 1979. As a result,

the sex ratio is particularly skewed—125 women for every 100 men—for people aged 25 or over.[10]

The ratio of women to men in the population is the result of differences in mortality and migration patterns between women and men, as well as sex ratios at birth. In a few countries, there is some evidence that the sex ratio at birth deviates from the norm in favour of male children, perhaps reflecting strong traditional preference for sons. Existing data from five countries show that the number of girls born falls below the biological ratio, which is normally 93 to 96 girls per 100 boys **(chart 1.12)**. These imbalances in the reported sex ratio at birth might be explained by increased availability of technologies that facilitate sex-selective abortion, underreporting of female births and female infanticides.

There are no official statistics on sex-selective abortion and female infanticide but studies by local non-governmental organizations, articles in the local

Chart 1.7:

At older ages, women outnumber men in all regions
Women per 100 men
aged 60 or over in 2000

Africa

Northern Africa	110
Sub-Saharan Africa	126

Latin America and the Caribbean

Caribbean	125
Central America	110
South America	125

Asia

Eastern Asia	125
South-eastern Asia	121
Southern Asia	102
Central Asia	143
Western Asia	107

Oceania 108

Developed regions

Eastern Europe	153
Western Europe	134
Other developed regions	126

Source: Prepared by the Statistics Division of the United Nations Secretariat from *Women's Indicators and Statistics Database (Wistat), Version 4*, CD-ROM (United Nations publication, Sales No. E.00.XVII.4), based on Population Division of the United Nations Secretariat, *World Population Prospects: The 1998 Revision*, vol. II, *The Sex and Age Distribution of the World Population* (United Nations publication, Sales No. E.99.XIII.8).

Chart 1.8:

The proportion of the population aged 80 or over will grow substantially
Percentage aged 80 or over

	2000		2020	
	W	M	W	M
Africa				
Northern Africa	0.5	0.4	0.9	0.6
Sub-Saharan Africa	0.5	0.3	0.6	0.4
Latin America and the Caribbean				
Caribbean	2.1	1.3	3.0	1.7
Central America	0.8	0.6	1.4	1.0
South America	1.2	0.7	2.0	1.1
Asia				
Eastern Asia	1.5	0.6	2.7	1.4
South-eastern Asia	0.7	0.4	1.4	0.8
Southern Asia	0.6	0.4	0.9	0.7
Central Asia	1.1	0.4	1.9	1.0
Western Asia	0.9	0.6	1.8	1.1
Oceania	0.3	0.1	1.4	0.6
Developed regions				
Eastern Europe	2.5	1.1	5.1	2.2
Western Europe	4.7	2.3	6.6	3.6
Other developed regions	4.1	2.1	5.7	3.3

Source: Prepared by the Statistics Division of the United Nations Secretariat from *Women's Indicators and Statistics Database (Wistat), Version 4*, CD-ROM (United Nations publication, Sales No. E.00.XVII.4), based on Population Division of the United Nations Secretariat, *World Population Prospects: The 1998 Revision*, vol. II, *The Sex and Age Distribution of the World Population* (United Nations publication, Sales No. E.99.XIII.8).

press and reports from health and social workers indicate that the practices exist.[11] It is estimated, for example, that almost 3,000 baby girls were killed in India's Tamil Nadu province between 1994 and 1997.[12] In India, social workers have reportedly attempted to dissuade parents from killing girl babies by offering parents consumer and other goods. A law was recently introduced in India that would ban abortion of healthy female foetuses.[13]

A review of Demographic Health Surveys (DHS) data for 44 countries surveyed between 1986 and 1995 indicates a strong preference for sons in Bangladesh, Egypt, India and Nepal. A distinct preference for sons is also evident in Jordan, Morocco, Pakistan, Sri Lanka, Tunisia and Turkey.[14] The study examines women's gender preferences, the extent to which these preferences influence reproductive behaviour and the differential treatment of daughters and sons, particularly in the first years of life. In some of the countries surveyed, gender-based discrimination is evident in education and health. One important finding is that mortality is higher for girls than for boys in Bangladesh, Egypt, India and Pakistan **(see chap. 3 for more extensive analysis of infant and child mortality by sex).**

There is some evidence that son preference is weakening, even in cultures where this preference traditionally has been strong. A recent study of Chinese provincial data used nine measures of modernization and women's status to examine preference for sons. Results showed that more modernized provinces and those where women had higher status tended to have lower degrees of son preference, and vice versa. Higher

Chart 1.9:
The ratio of women to men is highest among the oldest old
Women per 100 men aged 80 or over in 2000

Africa		Oceania	173
Northern Africa	123		
Southern Africa	243	**Developed regions**	
Rest of sub-Saharan Africa	149	Eastern Europe	256
		Western Europe	215
Latin America and the Caribbean		Other developed regions	195

Source: Prepared by the Statistics Division of the United Nations Secretariat from *Women's Indicators and Statistics Database (Wistat), Version 4,* CD-ROM (United Nations publication, Sales No. E.00.XVII.4), based on Population Division of the United Nations Secretariat, *World Population Prospects: The 1998 Revision,* vol. II, *The Sex and Age Distribution of the World Population* (United Nations publication, Sales No. E.99.XIII.8).

Latin America and the Caribbean	
Caribbean	162
Central America	136
South America	165

Asia	
Eastern Asia	257
South-eastern Asia	149
Southern Asia	113
Central Asia	281
Western Asia	147

Chart 1.10:
Women outnumber men in most regions
Women per 100 men in 2000

World total	98.6
Africa	
Northern Africa	98
Sub-Saharan Africa	102
Latin America and the Caribbean	
Caribbean	103
Central America	100
South America	102
Asia	
Eastern Asia	97
South-eastern Asia	99
Southern Asia	96
Central Asia	103
Western Asia	92
Oceania	95
Developed regions	
Eastern Europe	108
Western Europe	103
Other developed regions	103

Source: Prepared by the Statistics Division of the United Nations Secretariat from *Women's Indicators and Statistics Database (Wistat), Version 4,* CD-ROM (United Nations publication, Sales No. E.00.XVII.4), based on Population Division of the United Nations Secretariat, *World Population Prospects: The 1998 Revision,* vol. II, *The Sex and Age Distribution of the World Population* (United Nations publication, Sales No. E.99.XIII.8).

Adolescence: The need for new directions

Adolescence defined
Adolescence is generally viewed as the period of transition from childhood to adulthood, and its biological beginning is marked by puberty—the age at which a young person becomes capable of reproduction. Lacking a generally accepted marker for the end of adolescence, statistics commonly define adolescents as persons aged 10-19, although this range is not intended to cover a completely homogeneous population, socially or biologically.

Depending on the focus of the analysis and the policy relevance, children are usually defined as the population under age 15 or under 18; youth is defined as the population aged 15-24.

Data availability
Data about adolescents are scarce, especially in the developing countries. Researchers and policy makers have generally focused on small children and on young women's reproductive health and behaviours. Surveys often exclude young men and, to a lesser extent, young unmarried women.

As a result, there are few data on such important aspects of adolescence as access to educational and employment opportunities, the existence of exploitative living arrangements, discriminatory social and cultural norms in marriage and young women's needs and rights once they are married.[a]

Policy implications
This lack of data is reflected in policies that have failed to address adequately issues concerning adolescents. Policy concerns end with infant and child survival, and start again after young women become pregnant, with maternal and family planning programmes. Regardless of age, it is assumed that once a young woman is married, she is no longer a child in need of protection and services. The Convention on the Rights of the Child, however, establishes the age limit for children as 18 years. To classify a young woman as an adult only because she is married means depriving her of the rights, protections, services and opportunities offered to other people of the same age.[b]

---

[a] Barbara S. Mensch, Judith Bruce and Margaret E. Greene, *The Uncharted Passage: Girls' Adolescence in the Developing World* (New York, Population Council, 1998).

[b] Ibid.

degrees of son preference were associated with lower female/male sex ratios at birth, especially for births of a second child.[15]

Slower population growth

Women around the world are having fewer children than they were three decades ago, when the overall rate of population growth started to slow. In the early 1970s, the average birth rate worldwide was estimated at 4.5 children per woman, compared with an estimated 2.7 today.[16] The world's population, however, continues to expand because there are many more women having children today than there were 30 years ago, and because people are living longer.

In 1970, there were approximately 840 million women of reproductive age. Today, that number has nearly doubled to 1.53 billion; 80 per cent of these women live in the developing regions. Thus, despite a continuous decline in overall fertility, the number of children born has continued to rise—and will continue to do so for the foreseeable future. This fact, together with a longer life expectancy in most countries, has resulted in a net addition to the world population of close to 80 million people every year.

By far the fastest-growing population is in sub-Saharan Africa (with the exception of Southern Africa). Today, the population of this region is estimated at 594 million, and is projected to reach 942 million in 2020, a 59 per cent increase. It is expected that the population in Western Asia, currently 188 million, will reach 274 million in 2020 (chart 1.13).

By 2020, Asia will have added an estimated 865 million people to its current population. Although this number is large, it represents a relatively smaller growth rate than in other parts of the developing world. In all countries of Eastern Asia (except Mongolia), growth has slowed, with fertility below replacement level (approximately 2.1 children per woman). It is expected that the region's population will be 14 per cent larger in 2020 than it is today. In Southern Africa, where population growth has decelerated and is expected to slow further due in large part to the effects of acquired immunodeficiency syndrome (AIDS), the population in 2020 is projected to be 15 per cent larger than it is today.

The devastating number of deaths from AIDS has contributed to this deceleration, mainly in a number of countries of sub-Saharan Africa. Population growth in 34 countries is estimated to be far lower than it would have been in the absence of AIDS.[17] It is estimated that in the nine most affected countries—with human immunodeficiency virus (HIV) prevalence rates above 10 per cent—the total population in 2015 will be 15 per cent less than it would have been without the AIDS

pandemic. In Botswana, one of the countries most affected by HIV/AIDS, the annual population growth rate is expected to be 1.2 per cent between 2000 and 2005, compared to 2.9 per cent a decade earlier. In the absence of AIDS, Botswana's annual growth rate would have been 2.5 per cent; the population in 2025 would have been an estimated 23 per cent larger than now projected (see also chap. 3).

The populations of developed regions outside Europe will continue to grow slowly and will be 10 per cent larger in 2020. In contrast, the populations of Eastern and Western Europe have negative population growth; their populations are expected to decrease by 4 per cent and 1 per cent, respectively, by 2020.

Current population growth rates are negative in 20 countries or areas, most of them countries in transition in Eastern Europe and Asia (chart 1.14). As a by-product of economic uncertainty, fertility has decreased rapidly in these countries and mortality is either rising or holding steady, especially among men. Population growth rates are also negative in Italy, where fertility has been among the lowest in the world for many years, and in a few Caribbean islands, where the decline in population growth is thought to be the result of labour out-migration.

Women and their families generally benefit from slower population growth and reduced fertility. Where families are smaller, parents tend to invest more in their children's future, including girls, and women tend to have more opportunities outside the home. Research has shown that smaller families are linked to more favourable conditions for girls' and boys' education and nutrition, better health for families (particularly for women in the reduction of pregnancy-related illnesses and deaths) and improved opportunities for women to expand their roles in society.[18]

Research has also suggested that fertility reduction accompanies and may reinforce economic and social

Chart 1.11:

Men outnumber women in some countries or areas
Women per 100 men in 2000

Africa
Libyan Arab Jamahiriya	93

Asia
Afghanistan	95
Bahrain	76
Bangladesh	95
Brunei Darussalam	91
China[a]	94
Hong Kong SAR	89
East Timor	95
India	94
Jordan	94
Kuwait	90
Maldives	95
Oman	89
Pakistan	94
Qatar	54
Saudi Arabia	81
United Arab Emirates	58

Oceania
French Polynesia	94
Guam	90
Papua New Guinea	94
Samoa	91
Solomon Islands	95

Source: Prepared by the Statistics Division of the United Nations Secretariat from *Women's Indicators and Statistics Database (Wistat), Version 4,* CD-ROM (United Nations publication, Sales No. E.00.XVII.4), based on Population Division of the United Nations Secretariat, *World Population Prospects: The 1998 Revision,* vol. II, *The Sex and Age Distribution of the World Population* (United Nations publication, Sales No. E.99.XIII.8).

Note: Countries or areas listed are those where there are 95 or fewer women per 100 men.

[a] Data for China do not include Hong Kong Special Administrative Region (Hong Kong SAR) and Macao Special Administrative Region (Macao SAR).

Chart 1.12:

Fewer girls are born in countries where parents strongly prefer sons
Girls born per 100 boys

	1989/1993
China	88
Egypt	92
India	91
Pakistan	91
Republic of Korea	88[a]

Source: *Demographic Yearbook, 1997* (United Nations publication, Sales No. E/F.99.XIII.1); and *The World's Women 1995: Trends and Statistics* (United Nations publication, Sales No. E.95.XVII.2).
[a] For 1995.

development. In some parts of Asia, for instance, a sharp reduction in fertility has played a key role in the rapid economic transformation of countries. A study of some countries in Eastern and South-eastern Asia shows that slowing population growth has favoured educational expenditure per student and overall educational attainment.[19]

In countries where fertility is already particularly low, a woman's decision to have fewer children is believed to be influenced by unfavourable economic and social conditions for women, including inadequate social services, housing limitations and a lack of participation by men in household and parental responsibilities **(see chap. 2)**.[20] Moreover, in many developed countries, social policies have not always kept pace with women's changing circumstances.

Chart 1.13:

Population will continue to increase, except in Europe
Estimated and projected population (millions)

	1970	2000	2020
World total	3 696	6 055	7 502
Africa	357	784	1 187
Northern Africa	72	144	192
Southern Africa	25	47	54
Rest of sub-Saharan Africa	261	594	942
Latin America and the Caribbean	285	519	665
Caribbean	25	38	45
Central America	68	135	179
South America	192	346	440
Asia	2 043	3 556	4 421
Eastern Asia	882	1 359	1 547
South-eastern Asia	287	519	653
Southern Asia	754	1 435	1 879
Central Asia	33	56	69
Western Asia	86	188	274
Oceania	4	8	11
Developed regions	1 008	1 188	1 217
Eastern Europe	305	341	327
Western Europe	351	388	385
Other developed regions	351	459	505

Source: Prepared by the Statistics Division of the United Nations Secretariat from *Women's Indicators and Statistics Database (Wistat), Version 4*, CD-ROM (United Nations publication, Sales No. E.00.XVII.4), based on Population Division of the United Nations Secretariat, *World Population Prospects: The 1998 Revision*, vol. I, *Comprehensive Tables* (United Nations publication, Sales No. E.99.XIII.9).

WHERE WOMEN AND MEN LIVE

Today, the developed regions account for slightly less than 20 per cent of the world's population, down from 27 per cent in 1970 **(chart 1.15)**. In contrast, each of the other parts of the world represents a larger share of the world's population. In 1970, 55 per cent of the world's population lived in Asia, 10 per cent in Africa and 8 per cent in Latin America. Since then, the population of Asia has increased to 59 per cent of the world's population, while Africa has increased to 13 per cent and Latin America, 9 per cent. It is anticipated that in 2020 the populations of Africa and the developed regions will each represent 16 per cent of the world's population. In 2020, the populations of Asia and Latin America will have doubled relative to 1970, but they will still account for the same share of the world's population as they do today—59 and 9 per cent, respectively.

Urban population soon to surpass rural

Remarkable shifts in the distribution of women and men have occurred with respect to rural and urban living. The world's urban population has more than doubled since 1970 and now accounts for 47 per cent of the total, compared to 37 per cent in 1970. The United Nations Population Division estimates that by the year 2010 the urban population will have surpassed the rural population, and by 2020 urban residents will comprise 56 per cent of the total.[21] While the world's rural population will increase by about 4 per cent over the next two decades, the urban population is expected to grow by as much as 47 per cent, rising from 2.8 to 4.2 billion people.[22]

The most highly urbanized regions of the world are the developed regions outside Europe—where on average 84 per cent of the population live in urban areas—followed by Western Europe and Western Asia **(chart 1.16)**. Eastern Europe remains far less urbanized than the rest of Europe, and a few countries—Albania, Bosnia and Herzegovina, and the Republic of Moldova—still have predominantly rural populations **(table 1.A)**.

In countries of South America and Eastern Asia, on average almost three quarters of the population live in urban areas. Northern Africa and the Caribbean are also relatively highly urbanized.

In sub-Saharan Africa and in parts of Asia, the large majority of the population is still rural. The least urbanized part of the world is Southern Asia, where 27 per cent of the population live in urban areas. By 2020, Southern and Central Asia are expected to be the only regions where the majority of the population is still rural.

Recent data on urban population by sex are not available. However, United Nations estimates for 1995 indicate that, in Western Europe, developed

Chart 1.14:

Countries or areas where population growth rate is negative
Average annual rate of population growth (%), 1995 to 2000

Caribbean

Dominica	-0.06
Saint Kitts and Nevis	-0.78
US Virgin Islands	-0.85

Asia

Armenia	-0.31
Georgia	-1.10
Kazakhstan	-0.35

Europe

Albania	-0.40
Belarus	-0.30
Bulgaria	-0.66
Croatia	-0.09
Czech Republic	-0.16
Estonia	-1.24
Hungary	-0.38
Italy	-0.01
Latvia	-1.47
Lithuania	-0.30
Romania	-0.36
Russian Federation	-0.16
Slovenia	-0.05
Ukraine	-0.38

Source: *Women's Indicators and Statistics Database (Wistat), Version 4*, CD-ROM (United Nations publication, Sales No. E.00.XVII.4), based on Population Division of the United Nations Secretariat, *World Population Prospects: The 1998 Revision*, vol. I, *Comprehensive Tables* (United Nations publication, Sales No. E.99.XIII.9).

countries outside Europe, and Latin America and the Caribbean, the sex ratio of women to men is higher in urban areas than in rural areas. For example, in Latin America, there were 106 women per 100 men in urban areas, compared to 90 women per 100 men in rural areas.[23] In contrast, women tend to outnumber men in rural areas in sub-Saharan Africa and South-eastern Asia.

Chart 1.15:

Developing regions account for an increasing proportion of the world's population
Distribution of the world's population (%)

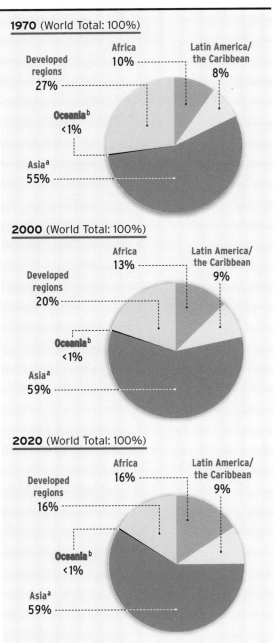

1970 (World Total: 100%)

Africa 10%
Latin America/the Caribbean 8%
Developed regions 27%
Oceania[b] <1%
Asia[a] 55%

2000 (World Total: 100%)

Africa 13%
Latin America/the Caribbean 9%
Developed regions 20%
Oceania[b] <1%
Asia[a] 59%

2020 (World Total: 100%)

Africa 16%
Latin America/the Caribbean 9%
Developed regions 16%
Oceania[b] <1%
Asia[a] 59%

Source: Prepared by the Statistics Division of the United Nations Secretariat from Population Division of the United Nations Secretariat, *World Population Prospects: The 1998 Revision*, vol. I, *Comprehensive Tables* (United Nations publication, Sales No. E.99.XIII.9).

[a] Excluding Japan, which is included in developed regions.

[b] Excluding Australia and New Zealand, which are included in developed regions.

Variations in sex ratios reflect different patterns of internal migration. In some countries, there are fewer women who migrate from rural to urban areas than men. This is in part due to the greater constraints placed upon women and to the fewer opportunities for employment for women in urban areas.[24]

It is usually assumed that cities offer women better educational and employment opportunities, and a wide range of indicators supports this assumption. Urban women are much more likely to be literate, and their fertility is much lower **(see chaps. 2 and 4)**. However, the dramatic increase in the number of women and men in urban areas has generally not been accompanied by concomitant improvements in services and infrastructure. Women in poor urban households may, in fact, face more problems than their counterparts in rural areas. Rural women, for example, are more likely to have a social network they can rely on than newly arrived urban migrants.[25]

Moreover, economic growth in large cities has not always been fast enough to absorb all rural migrants into the paid labour force. Nor has the availability of housing kept pace with urban population growth. According to data issued by Habitat,[26] at least 10 per cent of households are located in squatter settlements in 16 of 45 cities with data for 1993; percentages were as high as 50 per cent or more in four of those cities.

Women migrating as much as men

Migration between regions, between countries and between rural and urban areas is another important factor in redistributing population, and women have figured prominently in these migratory streams. An important issue in understanding both individual and family migration is the extent to which women migrate autonomously or as dependants, following husbands, fathers or other family members. Evidence from countries where data are available suggests that increasingly women are moving as autonomous migrants looking for employment. Consequently, the motivations, characteristics and needs of women migrants are receiving more attention in both developing and developed countries.

Internal migration

Data from the 1970 and 1980 rounds of censuses in selected developing countries generally show that women have been prominent in all types of internal migration.[27] More recent data, available for only a few countries, indicate that women may now outnumber men not only in rural-to-rural migration but also in rural-to-urban and urban-to-urban migration. In the Republic of Korea, for example, all three streams of migrants were 51 per cent female in 1995. In the

Philippines, 7.2 per cent of all women moved among municipalities between 1985 and 1990, compared to 6.5 per cent of all men.[28]

In five countries of Latin America and the Caribbean, 1990 census data on internal migrants by sex show that women make up about 51 per cent of migrants, including inter-state migration. In the island nations of Saint Lucia and Trinidad and Tobago, the proportions of female migrants are slightly higher—53 and 54 per cent, respectively.[29]

In Latin America, migration from impoverished rural areas is often a survival strategy for farm families. In this region, it is common for young women to leave rural areas to work as domestics in cities. Many women also migrate for seasonal work on plantations, industrial jobs or higher education in the city.[30] Some studies indicate that daughters who migrate can more often be relied on to send part of their earnings back to their families.

In Asia, there are generally four streams of women migrants to cities: women who migrate alone and join the informal sector as domestic workers, traders or prostitutes; unmarried, educated women seeking employment in the expanding formal sector; students seeking higher education; and dependants of other migrants.[31]

Women migrants, particularly those who migrate for work, have contributed substantially to the population growth of large cities. Manufacturing enterprises often prefer female employees because they are thought to be more suited to repetitive manufacturing tasks, less likely to engage in labour disputes, easier to hire and fire, and willing to accept lower wages.[32]

In some contexts, constraints on the mobility of young unmarried women can limit migration. However, as traditional attitudes change and economic needs increase, even young unmarried women are encouraged to seek work elsewhere to contribute to their families' survival. Women are more likely than men to migrate to cities by following siblings or other relatives or friends. These relatives and friends often provide support and protection to women migrants.[33]

Women who migrate from rural to urban areas generally have more children and are less likely to use modern contraceptives than long-term urban residents. DHS surveys in 22 countries found in nearly all the countries that rural-to-urban migrant women aged 30 to 34 had more children (born before and/or after migration) than non-migrant urban women.[34] However, the longer women migrants remain in the city, the more their reproductive behaviours come to resemble the behaviours of long-term city dwellers.

Chart 1.16:
The world's urban population will grow substantially
Percentage of population living in urban areas

	2000	2020
Africa		
Northern Africa	68	76
Sub-Saharan Africa	38	50
Latin America and the Caribbean		
Caribbean	61	69
Central America	53	63
South America	74	81
Asia		
Eastern Asia	73	79
South-eastern Asia	40	50
Southern Asia	27	37
Central Asia	40	45
Western Asia	76	82
Oceania	43	53
Developed regions		
Eastern Europe	61	68
Western Europe	78	82
Other developed regions	84	87

Source: Prepared by the Statistics Division of the United Nations Secretariat from Population Division of the United Nations Secretariat, *World Urbanization Prospects: The 1999 Revision*, "Percentage of the population living in urban areas", data in digital form (POP/DB/WUP/Rev.1999/1/F2).

International migration
In 1990, there were an estimated 118 million international migrants in the world. Of these, 56 million were women and 62 million were men—a global sex ratio of 91 women per 100 men.[35] In nine countries of Eastern Europe, however, there were on average 123 women immigrants for every 100 men immigrants in 1990 **(chart 1.17)**.

As a region, Western Europe has roughly equal numbers of women and men immigrants. However, in some countries of the region—notably Iceland and Italy—women immigrants outnumber men immigrants, 125 and 130 women per 100 men, respectively. In other countries, men immigrants outnumber women immigrants—generally in countries that are traditionally employment magnets for men: Austria, Belgium, Germany, Netherlands and Switzerland. During the last decade, some women migrants to Western European countries have been sex workers—mainly from Eastern Europe but also from other regions in the developing world.[36] In developed regions outside Europe, there are roughly equal numbers of women and men immigrants.

Chart 1.17:

Women immigrants equal or outnumber men in some parts of the world

Women per 100
men immigrants, 1990

Africa

Northern Africa	92
Southern Africa	69
Rest of sub-Saharan Africa	93

Latin America and the Caribbean

Caribbean	102
Central America	86
South America	97

Asia

Eastern Asia	88
South-eastern Asia	88
Southern Asia[a]	86
Western Asia	67

Oceania

Oceania	83

Developed regions

Eastern Europe	123
Western Europe	100
Other developed regions	102

Source: Prepared by the Statistics Division of the United Nations Secretariat from Population Division of the United Nations Secretariat, *Trends in Total Migrant Stock by Sex*, revision 4, data in digital form (POP/1B/DB/98/4).

[a] Excluding Nepal, where the number of women per 100 men immigrants is exceptionally high.

The ratio of women to men immigrants is lowest in Asia and Oceania but female migration to the region is growing rapidly, largely the result of women migrating on their own as contract workers. The earnings of these women migrants began to represent an important source of income for their families at home in the 1980s, and continues to do so today. Contract labour migration is the most rapidly increasing type of international migration in Asia, and women migrants are concentrated in such female-dominated occupations as domestic helpers, entertainers, sales persons, hotel and restaurant workers and assembly line workers.[37]

Women's contract work in the entertainment industry often involves prostitution.[38] Most women in the Asian entertainment industry come from the Philippines and Thailand but some also migrate from Indonesia, Myanmar, China and the Lao People's Democratic Republic. The size of this labour migration flow is probably underestimated because much of it is undocumented.

While Western Asia had an average of 67 women immigrants per 100 men in 1990, such countries as Bahrain, Lebanon, Qatar and Yemen reported fewer than 40 women immigrants per 100 men immigrants. In Southern Asia, ratios ranged from a low of 74 women per 100 men in Sri Lanka to 97 in Pakistan.

Migrants to Southern Africa are predominantly male, given the long-standing pattern of labour migration of men to work in the mines and urban centres of South Africa. Elsewhere in Africa, there are nearly as many immigrant women as men.

HOUSING CONDITIONS IN RURAL AND URBAN AREAS

Growing numbers without access to safe water

The United Nations Environment Programme (UNEP) estimates that 1.7 billion people lack access to safe water, and expects this number to reach 2.3 billion by 2025.[39] Polluted water is one of the most common causes of disease and death worldwide.[40] Such diseases

Chart 1.18:

Large numbers of households lack basic amenities, especially in rural areas

Country or area	% with piped water, 1990-1996		% within 15 min. walk from water source, 1990-1996		% with flush toilet, 1990-1996		% with electricity, 1990-1996	
	Urban	Rural	Urban	Rural	Urban	Rural	Urban	Rural
Northern Africa and Western Asia								
Egypt	97	69	96	86	97	71	99	92
Jordan	99	91	..	..	..	..	99	90
Morocco	94	18	91	41	90	18	85	16
Turkey	78	58	..	..	86	12	..	..
Yemen	87	24	88	39	54	2	91	34
Sub-Saharan Africa								
Benin	59	15	..	..	0	0	34	2
Burkina Faso	66	5	73	53	5	0	29	1
Cameroon	69	13	68	31	14	1	63	9
Central African Rep.	43	2	65	31	2	0	8	0
Comoros	74	41	70	36	8	2	52	20
Côte d'Ivoire	78	25	97	69	29	2	70	14
Ghana	76	13	80	36	16	1	75	6
Kenya	87	20	86	31	45	2	43	3
Madagascar	77	5	78	17	17	0	47	2
Malawi	82	18	76	41	14	1	20	1
Mali	49	3	88	75	3	0	22	0
Namibia	96	35	96	43	83	6	66	4
Niger	61	7	64	64	6	0	27	0
Nigeria	63	12	74	32	30	2	82	8
Rwanda	69	20	57	9	11	0	31	1
Senegal	84	20	90	62	25	2	59	2

Source: Mohamed Ayad, Bernard Barrère and James Otto, *Demographic and Socio-economic Characteristics of Households*, Demographic and Health Surveys, Comparative Studies, No. 26 (Calverton, Maryland, Macro International, 1997).

are acquired by the consumption of contaminated water, or indirectly via disease-carrying organisms (such as mosquitoes), which breed in water.

Inadequate sanitation facilities can also spread disease, especially if drinking water becomes contaminated with human waste. Water that is piped into the household is generally safer than water from wells or surface areas, such as ponds and lakes. DHS surveys in the 1990s, in 41 countries, found low percentages of rural households with piped water in sub-Saharan African countries (chart 1.18).[41] In Burkina Faso, Central African Republic, Madagascar, Mali and Uganda, piped water is virtually unknown in rural areas, and access is limited for urban households as well. Two of the 20 sub-Saharan countries surveyed had almost universal access to piped water. In nine countries, about a third or more of urban households had no piped water.

In three of five Northern African and Western Asian countries surveyed, piped water was available in nearly all urban households; in the other two countries, piped water was available in more than three quarters of all urban households. However, a large share of households in rural areas had no access to piped water. Similarly, in the Asian countries examined, access to safe water is a problem for many households in urban areas and for the great majority of households in rural areas.

Lack of adequate water facilities also affects a significant portion of both urban and rural households in the eight Latin American and Caribbean countries surveyed. In three countries, 30 per cent or more of urban households lacked piped water; in six countries, more than 50 per cent of rural households lacked piped water.

For households without piped water or wells, obtaining water for daily use can be time-consuming and arduous, especially in rural areas—and especially for women and children who are often burdened with the tasks of water and fuel collection.[42] In 14 of the 19 sub-Saharan African countries, water sources are more than a 15-minute walk from the majority of

Country or area	% with piped water, 1990–1996		% within 15 min. walk from water source, 1990–1996		% with flush toilet, 1990–1996		% with electricity, 1990–1996	
	Urban	Rural	Urban	Rural	Urban	Rural	Urban	Rural
Sub-Saharan Africa (cont'd)								
Uganda	45	1	47	9	9	0	40	2
United Rep. of Tanzania	78	25	69	28	5	1	36	2
Zambia	81	7	77	36	46	1	44	2
Zimbabwe	97	18	98	42	95	3	80	3
Latin America and the Caribbean								
Bolivia	89	33	91	59	54	4	93	27
Brazil	84	25	95	92	56	16	99	72
Colombia	98	57	98	74	96	46	99	74
Dominican Republic	81	44	73	45	63	9	97	48
Guatemala	70	61	75	78	65	11	89	40
Haiti	50	28	52	23	12	0	77	4
Paraguay	64	3	88	82	50	5	93	17
Peru	89	29	91	41	64	3	90	20
Asia								
Bangladesh	37	1	92	87	49	4	75	10
India	70	19	89	72	60	7	83	39
Indonesia	37	6	94	64	..	..	95	49
Kazakhstan	97	69	97	78	73	2	100	100
Nepal	57	29	87	59	17	0	78	12
Pakistan	79	14	93	69	73	6	95	45
Philippines	54	21	87	63	76	50	84	46
Uzbekistan	93	66	98	75	48	3	100	99

rural households. The same is true in five of the 19 countries surveyed in the other developing regions.

Flush toilets are common in only a few countries surveyed by DHS, and are virtually unknown in some countries, especially in rural areas. In sub-Saharan Africa, 18 of the 20 countries surveyed reported that less than 3 per cent of rural households had flush toilets (Namibia and Zimbabwe are exceptions) **(chart 1.18)**. In eight of the 20 sub-Saharan African countries, fewer than 10 per cent of urban households had flush toilets. Most rural households in Asian countries also lack flush toilets.

Access to electricity far from universal

The presence of electricity has been found to have a salutary effect on the health and well-being of family members, as well as to reflect the socio-economic status of the household. In both rural and urban areas, access to electricity enables household members to increase their productivity and to extend the hours that they are able to work. This is especially relevant for women, who must often juggle household responsibilities (including childcare) with economic activi-

ties carried out inside the home. Electricity also allows children to study after dark.

According to data from the 41 countries surveyed by DHS, virtually all households in rural sub-Saharan Africa are still without electricity **(chart 1.18)**. Access to electricity in urban households in sub-Saharan Africa is higher but still not universal— ranging from 8 per cent in the Central African Republic to 82 per cent in Nigeria. In the four countries of Northern Africa and Western Asia for which DHS reported data, nearly all urban households had electricity, with Egypt and Jordan reporting high levels of access in rural areas as well.

The eight Asian countries surveyed all reported that at least 75 per cent of urban households had electricity. In Kazakhstan and Uzbekistan, electricity is nearly universal in both urban and rural areas. In other Asian countries, however, less than 50 per cent of rural households had electricity.

Electricity is widely available in urban households in Latin America and the Caribbean. However, access varies considerably for rural households, ranging from 4 per cent in Haiti to 74 per cent in Colombia. ■

Notes

1 United Nations, *World Population Monitoring, 1999. Population Growth, Structure and Distribution* (United Nations publication, Sales No. E.00.XIII.4, forthcoming).

2 United Nations Statistics Division calculation, based on data from United Nations, *World Population Prospects: The 1998 Revision*, vol.II, *The Sex and Age Distribution of the World Population* (United Nations publication, Sales No. E.99.XIII.8).

3 United Nations, *World Population Monitoring, 1999...*

4 John C. Bongaarts, "Fertility decline in the developed world: where will it end?", in *American Economics Association Papers and Proceedings*, vol. 89, No. 2 (May 1999); and Jean-Claude Chenais, "Fertility, family and social policy in contemporary Western Europe", *Population and Development Review*, vol. 22, No. 4 (December 1996).

5 John Bongaarts, "Demographic consequences of declining fertility", *Science*, vol. 282 (October 1998).

6 United Nations, *World Population Monitoring, 1999...*

7 Christiann Groottaert and Jeanine Braithwaite, *Poverty Correlates and Indicator-based Targeting in Eastern Europe and the Former Soviet Union*, Policy Research Working Paper, No. 1942 (World Bank, 1998).

8 World Health Organization, "Ageing: exploding the myths; ageing and health programme", document WHO/HSC/AHE/99.1.

9 United Nations Statistics Division calculation, based on data from United Nations, *World Population Prospects: The 1998 Revision*, vol.II, *The Sex and Age Distribution of the World Population* (United Nations publication, Sales No. E.99.XIII.8).

10 Cambodia census results and analysis reported by The Associated Press on the Internet on 14 September 1999.

11 S. Sudha and S. Irudaya, "Female demographic disadvantage in India 1981-1991: sex selective abortions and female infanticide", *Development and Choice*, vol. 30, No. 3 (1999).

12 Gita Aravamudan, "Chilling deaths", *The Week*, 24 January 1999; and S.M. George, "Female infanticide in Tamil Nadu, India: from recognition back to denial?" *Reproductive Health Matters*, No. 10 (1997).

13 Ibid.

14 Fred Arnold, *Gender Preferences for Children*, Demographic and Health Surveys, Comparative Studies, No. 23 (Calverton, Maryland, Macro International, 1997).

15 Dudley L. Poston, Jr., Baochang Gu, Peihang Peggy Liu, and Terra McDaniel, "Son preference and the sex ratio at birth in China: a provincial level analysis", *Social Biology*, vol. 44 (1997).

16 United Nations, *World Population Monitoring, 1999...*

17 In the latest revision of the United Nations population estimates and projections, the potential demographic impact of AIDS is considered in 34 countries where estimated adult prevalence is 2 per cent or above and total population is one million or more. In addition, Brazil and India were considered because although prevalence in those countries has not yet reached 2 per cent, their large populations will mean a great absolute number of persons infected. See United Nations, *World Population Prospects: The 1998 Revision* (United Nations publication, Sales No. E.99.XIII.8); and report of a technical meeting between the United Nations Population Division and The Joint United Nations Programme on HIV/AIDS on the demographic impact of HIV/AIDS, New York, 10 November 1998.

18 United Nations, *World Population Monitoring, 1999...*

19 Dennis A. Ahlburg and Eric Jensen, *Education and the East Asian Miracle*, East-West Center Working Papers, Population Series, No. 88-3 (Honolulu, 1997).

20 Jean-Claude Chenais, "Fertility, family and social policy in contemporary Western Europe", *Population and Development Review*, vol. 22, No. 4 (December 1996).

21 United Nations, *World Urbanization Prospects: The 1999 Revision*, "Percentage of the population living in urban areas by major area, region and country, 1950-2030", data in digital form (POP/DB/WUP/Rev.1999/A1/File 2).

22 United Nations, *World Urbanization Prospects: The 1999 Revision*, "Urban and rural areas", data in digital form (POP/DB/WUP/Rev.1999/A1/File 3 and File 4).

23 United Nations, *The World's Women 1995: Trends and Statistics* (United Nations publication, Sales No. E.95.XVII.2).

24 Ibid.

25 United Nations, *Internal Migration of Women in Developing Countries* (United Nations publication, Sales No. E.94.XIII.3).

26 Habitat, *Urban Indicators Programme: Programme Activities, Analysis of Data and Global Urban Indicators Database*, part 2, table on housing tenure.

27 See, for instance, United Nations, *World Population Monitoring 1999...*

28 Graeme Hugo, "Gender and migrations in Asian countries", paper presented at the International Union for the Scientific Study of Population Seminar on Women in the Labour Market in Changing Economics: Demographic Issues, Rome, 22-24 September 1999.

29 United Nations, *World Population Monitoring, 1999...*

30 Sally Findley, "Women on the move: perspectives on gender changes in Latin America", *Gender in Population Studies* (International Union for the Scientific Study of Population, 1999).

31 Hugo, loc. cit.

32 Philip Guest, "The impact of population change on the growth of mega-cities", *Asia-Pacific Population Journal*, vol. 19, No. 1 (1994).

33 Lin Lean Lim, "The analysis of factors generating international migration: the processes generating the migration of women", paper presented at a United Nations Technical Symposium on International Migration and Development, The Hague, 29 June-3 July 1998.

Notes (cont'd)

[34] Robert Gardner and Richard Blackburn, *People Who Move: New Reproductive Health Focus*, Population Reports, Series J, No. 45 (Baltimore, Johns Hopkins School of Hygiene and Public Health, 1996).

[35] United Nations, *Trends in Total Migrant Stock*, Revision 4, data in digital form (POP/1B/DB/98/4).

[36] Lim, loc. cit.

[37] Ibid.

[38] Hugo, loc. cit.

[39] "World day for water", UNEP and United Nations University news release, 22 March 1999.

[40] UNEP, Global Environment Outlook (UNEP, 1997) and Global Environment Outlook 2000 (UNEP, 1999).

[41] Mohamed Ayad, Bernard Barrère and James Otto, *Demographic and Socioeconomic Characteristics of Households*, Demographic and Health Surveys, Comparative Studies, No. 26 (Calverton, Maryland, Macro International, 1997).

[42] United Nations, *The World's Women 1995...*

Table 1.A:
Population

Country or area	Population (thousands), 2000		Women/100 men, 2000	% aged 10-19, 2000	% under age 15, 2000	% aged 60 or over, 2000		Women/100 men, 2000		Annual population growth (%), 1995-2000	Urban population (%), 2000	Women/100 men int'l. migrants, 1990
Africa	**W** ■	**M**				**W** ■	**M**	**60+** ■	**80+** ■			
Algeria	15 544	15 927	98	23	37	6	5	115	106	2.3	60	122
Angola	6 511	6 367	102	23	47	5	4	120	157	3.2	34	94
Benin	3 091	3 005	103	25	46	4	4	108	100	2.7	42	95
Botswana	825	798	103	25	42	5	3	178	300	1.9	50	79
Burkina Faso	5 977	5 960	100	24	47	5	4	119	143	2.7	19	109
Burundi	3 418	3 277	104	24	46	5	3	155	200	1.7	9	107
Cameroon	7 585	7 500	101	23	43	6	5	118	141	2.7	49	81
Cape Verde	228	200	114	24	39	8	4	238	200	2.3	62	86
Central African Republic	1 857	1 758	106	24	43	7	5	133	200	1.9	41	99
Chad	3 867	3 783	102	23	46	6	5	122	142	2.6	24	86
Comoros	347	348	100	25	42	5	4	123	100	2.7	33	131
Congo	1 504	1 439	105	23	46	5	4	127	175	2.8	63	101
Côte d'Ivoire	7 266	7 520	97	26	43	5	5	92	109	1.8	46	81
Dem. Rep. of the Congo	26 088	25 567	102	23	48	5	4	129	165	2.6	30	93
Djibouti	326	312	104	23	41	6	5	113	100	1.2	83	111
Egypt	33 746	34 723	97	23	35	7	6	122	144	1.9	45	89
Equatorial Guinea	229	223	103	22	43	7	5	136	100	2.5	48	86
Eritrea	1 939	1 911	101	23	44	5	4	120	175	3.8	19	..
Ethiopia	31 168	31 397	99	23	46	5	4	118	176	2.5	18	108[a]
Gabon	620	606	102	20	40	9	8	119	150	2.6	81	75
Gambia	660	645	102	21	40	5	5	113	200	3.2	33	76
Ghana	10 152	10 060	101	24	43	5	5	116	139	2.7	38	85
Guinea	3 693	3 738	99	24	44	5	4	113	125	0.8	33	106
Guinea-Bissau	616	597	103	22	43	7	6	117	150	2.2	24	100
Kenya	15 005	15 076	100	26	43	5	4	118	146	2.0	33	103
Lesotho	1 092	1 061	103	22	40	7	6	131	200	2.2	28	69
Liberia	1 571	1 583	99	26	42	5	4	116	125	8.2	45	82
Libyan Arab Jamahiriya	2 703	2 902	93	25	38	5	5	84	150	2.4	88	44
Madagascar	8 028	7 914	101	21	44	5	4	121	124	3.0	30	62
Malawi	5 504	5 421	102	24	47	5	4	125	146	2.4	25	109
Mali	5 686	5 547	103	24	46	6	5	129	152	2.4	30	99
Mauritania	1 345	1 324	102	23	43	5	4	124	125	2.7	58	78
Mauritius	581	578	101	17	25	10	8	128	175	0.8	41	103
Morocco	14 161	14 190	100	22	33	7	6	123	118	1.8	56	97
Mozambique	9 957	9 724	102	23	45	5	5	121	146	2.5	40	133
Namibia	865	861	100	23	42	6	5	115	100	2.2	31	86
Niger	5 421	5 309	102	23	48	4	4	121	150	3.2	21	109
Nigeria	56 191	55 315	102	24	43	5	5	118	143	2.4	44	55
Reunion	358	342	105	18	27	12	8	159	300	1.3	71	80
Rwanda	3 914	3 819	102	25	45	4	3	125	200	7.7	6	95
Sao Tome and Principe	..	..	..	..	..	..	..	..	..	2.0	47	88
Senegal	4 753	4 728	101	23	45	5	4	123	100	2.6	47	85
Seychelles	..	..	..	..	..	..	..	..	..	1.1	64	85
Sierra Leone	2 472	2 383	104	22	44	5	4	124	160	3.0	37	32
Somalia	5 085	5 012	101	23	48	4	4	117	140	4.2	28	99

Table 1.A (cont'd):
Population

Country or area	Population (thousands), 2000		Women/ 100 men, 2000	% aged 10-19, 2000	% under age 15, 2000	% aged 60 or over, 2000		Women/100 men, 2000		Annual population growth (%), 1995-2000	Urban population (%), 2000	Women/100 men int'l. migrants, 1990
	W	**M**				**W**	**M**	**60+**	**80+**			
Africa (cont'd)												
South Africa	20 552	19 825	104	21	35	7	5	152	315	1.5	50	60
Sudan	14 705	14 785	99	24	39	5	5	108	109	2.1	36	100
Swaziland	522	486	107	23	43	5	4	119	300	2.9	26	53
Togo	2 333	2 296	102	24	46	5	4	121	157	2.6	33	107
Tunisia	4 744	4 842	98	22	30	8	8	101	98	1.4	66	99
Uganda	10 935	10 843	101	24	50	3	3	120	135	2.8	14	80
United Rep. of Tanzania	16 900	16 618	102	24	45	4	4	119	143	2.3	33	103
Western Sahara	147	146	101	22	38	5	5	114	..[b]	3.4	95	98
Zambia	4 630	4 539	102	26	47	4	3	120	110	2.3	40	99
Zimbabwe	5 874	5 795	101	26	41	4	4	114	138	1.4	35	82
Latin America and the Caribbean												
Antigua and Barbuda	..	..	..	..	..	..	..	..	..	0.6	37	108
Argentina	18 868	18 163	104	18	28	15	12	135	199	1.3	90	108
Aruba	..	..	..	..	..	..	..	..	..	4.6	..	126
Bahamas	156	151	103	18	31	8	7	118	200	1.8	89	93
Barbados	140	131	107	15	21	16	11	164	200	0.5	50	122
Belize	119	122	98	23	40	6	7	88	100	2.4	54	72
Bolivia	4 185	4 144	101	22	40	7	6	121	153	2.3	63	88
Brazil	86 113	84 003	103	20	29	9	7	125	154	1.3	81	87
Chile	7 680	7 531	102	18	28	11	9	132	188	1.4	86	97
Colombia	21 407	20 915	102	20	33	7	6	123	153	1.9	74	113
Costa Rica	1 983	2 040	97	21	32	8	7	111	138	2.5	48	73
Cuba	5 589	5 611	100	15	21	14	13	109	119	0.4	75	40
Dominica	..	..	..	..	..	..	..	..	..	-0.1	71	93
Dominican Republic	4 176	4 320	97	21	33	7	7	103	120	1.7	65	53
Ecuador	6 296	6 350	99	21	34	7	6	113	145	2.0	65	98
El Salvador	3 195	3 081	104	21	36	8	7	124	171	2.0	47	80
French Guyana	..	..	..	..	..	..	..	..	..	4.2	78	82
Grenada	..	..	..	..	..	..	..	..	..	0.3	38	102
Guadeloupe	233	223	104	15	24	14	10	139	200	1.4	100	101
Guatemala	5 645	5 741	98	24	44	5	5	106	118	2.6	40	102
Guyana	436	425	103	20	30	7	6	125	150	0.7	38	80
Haiti	4 183	4 039	104	26	41	6	5	125	138	1.7	36	131
Honduras	3 217	3 269	98	24	42	6	5	113	127	2.8	53	65
Jamaica	1 301	1 282	101	20	31	10	9	116	137	0.9	56	106
Martinique	204	192	106	15	23	16	13	128	200	0.9	95	102
Mexico	49 951	48 931	102	21	33	7	6	118	142	1.6	74	97
Netherlands Antilles	112	105	107	16	25	13	10	127	200	1.1	70	121
Nicaragua	2 551	2 523	101	24	43	5	4	120	175	2.7	56	109
Panama	1 415	1 441	98	20	31	8	8	104	115	1.6	56	88
Paraguay	2 725	2 772	98	23	40	6	5	126	150	2.6	56	90
Peru	12 935	12 726	102	21	33	8	7	115	142	1.7	73	107
Puerto Rico	2 004	1 864	108	16	24	15	13	129	143	0.8	75	106
Saint Kitts and Nevis	..	..	..	..	..	..	..	..	..	-0.8	34	102

Table 1.A (cont'd):
Population

Country or area	Population (thousands), 2000		Women/ 100 men, 2000	% aged 10-19, 2000	% under age 15, 2000	% aged 60 or over, 2000		Women/100 men, 2000		Annual population growth (%), 1995-2000	Urban population (%), 2000	Women/100 men int'l. migrants, 1990
	W	**M**				**W**	**M**	**60+**	**80+**			
Latin America and the Caribbean (cont'd)												
Saint Lucia	..	..	..	..	..	..	..	..	..	1.4	38	103
St. Vincent/Grenadines	..	..	..	..	..	..	..	..	..	0.7	55	106
Suriname	210	207	101	23	30	9	7	127	200	0.4	74	88
Trinidad and Tobago	651	644	101	21	25	10	9	118	125	0.5	74	104
Uruguay	1 718	1 619	106	16	25	19	15	139	187	0.7	91	119
US Virgin Islands	..	..	..	..	..	..	..	..	..	-0.9	46	114
Venezuela	12 009	12 161	99	21	34	7	6	116	152	2.0	87	97
Asia												
Afghanistan	11 063	11 658	95	20	44	5	5	103	119	2.9	22	86
Armenia	1 808	1 711	106	20	25	15	11	137	240	-0.3	70	..
Azerbaijan	3 946	3 788	104	20	29	12	9	144	305	0.5	57	..
Bahrain	266	351	76	18	30	5	5	82	100	2.0	92	39
Bangladesh	63 022	66 133	95	25	35	5	5	97	117	1.7	25	86
Bhutan	1 051	1 073	98	22	43	7	6	111	125	2.8	7	86
Brunei Darussalam	157	172	91	20	32	4	4	100	..[b]	2.2	72	73
Cambodia	5 748	5 420	106	24	41	6	4	178	141	2.3	16	90
China[c]	620 477	657 081	94	17	25	11	9	109	185	0.9	32	87[d]
Hong Kong SAR	3 260	3 666	89	14	17	15	13	104	165	2.1	100	95
Macao SAR	242	232	104	16	23	10	8	121	400	1.9	99	98
Cyprus	393	392	100	16	23	17	14	121	144	1.1	57	102
Dem. People's Rep. of Korea	11 986	12 053	99	15	28	10	6	155	288	1.6	60	90
East Timor	430	455	95	25	39	5	4	100	100	1.7	8	90
Georgia	2 593	2 375	109	16	22	21	15	148	274	-1.1	61	..
India	490 466	523 195	94	21	33	8	7	109	125	1.6	28	92
Indonesia	106 276	105 832	100	20	31	8	7	117	139	1.4	41	94
Iran (Islamic Rep. of)	33 358	34 345	97	26	36	6	6	98	109	1.7	62	81
Iraq	11 359	11 756	97	24	41	5	5	111	129	2.8	77	65
Israel	3 133	3 084	102	18	28	15	11	130	151	2.2	91	113
Jordan	3 225	3 445	94	23	42	5	4	104	100	3.0	74	109
Kazakhstan	8 327	7 895	105	20	28	14	9	164	361	-0.4	56	..
Kuwait	935	1 036	90	24	34	3	4	78	100	3.1	98	75
Kyrgyzstan	2 395	2 304	104	22	35	11	7	151	322	0.6	33	..
Lao People's Dem. Republic	2 696	2 737	99	23	44	6	5	110	125	2.6	24	90
Lebanon	1 676	1 606	104	20	33	9	8	119	130	1.7	90	39
Malaysia	10 971	11 273	97	20	34	7	6	111	129	2.0	57	93
Maldives	139	147	95	26	43	5	5	88	..[b]	2.8	26	86
Mongolia	1 327	1 335	99	24	35	6	5	121	220	1.7	64	90
Myanmar	22 907	22 704	101	21	28	8	7	115	120	1.2	28	86
Nepal	11 801	12 130	97	24	41	6	6	98	107	2.4	12	251
Occupied Palestinian Territory[e]	555	566	98	23	52	5	4	133	67	4.3	95	67[f]
Oman	1 195	1 346	89	24	44	4	4	94	133	3.3	84	50
Pakistan	75 753	80 731	94	23	42	5	5	101	94	2.8	37	97
Philippines	37 640	38 326	98	22	37	6	5	114	138	2.1	59	78

Table 1.A (cont'd):
Population

Country or area	Population (thousands), 2000		Women/ 100 men, 2000	% aged 10-19, 2000	% under age 15, 2000	% aged 60 or over, 2000		Women/100 men, 2000		Annual population growth (%), 1995-2000	Urban population (%), 2000	Women/100 men int'l. migrants, 1990
	W	M				W	M	60+	80+			
Asia (cont'd)												
Qatar	209	390	54	17	26	3	5	33	..b	1.8	93	35
Republic of Korea	23 220	23 624	98	15	21	13	9	142	284	0.8	82	71
Saudi Arabia	9 675	11 932	81	22	41	5	4	89	126	3.4	86	50
Singapore	1 770	1 796	99	13	22	11	10	116	167	1.4	100	111
Sri Lanka	9 514	9 313	102	20	26	10	9	110	108	1.0	24	74
Syrian Arab Republic	7 982	8 143	98	26	41	5	4	112	123	2.5	55	90
Tajikistan	3 105	3 083	101	24	40	8	6	128	207	1.5	28	..
Thailand	30 772	30 627	100	18	25	10	8	125	168	0.9	22	86
Turkey	32 966	33 624	98	19	28	9	8	115	151	1.7	75	99
Turkmenistan	2 252	2 207	102	23	38	7	5	139	271	1.8	45	..
United Arab Emirates	897	1 544	58	19	28	4	6	39	100	2.0	86	50
Uzbekistan	12 240	12 078	101	23	37	8	6	135	245	1.6	37	..
Viet Nam	40 405	39 426	102	22	33	9	6	145	262	1.6	20	72
Yemen	8 983	9 129	98	23	48	4	3	130	133	3.7	25	15
Oceania												
American Samoa	..	..	..	..	..	..	..	..	..	3.6	53	94
Fiji	402	415	97	22	31	8	7	111	300	1.2	49	98
French Polynesia	114	121	94	20	33	7	6	114	..b	1.8	53	68
Guam	79	88	90	17	33	8	7	100	..b	2.1	39	77
Kiribati	..	..	..	..	..	..	..	..	..	1.4	39	95
Marshall Islands	..	..	..	..	..	..	..	..	..	3.2	72	70
Micronesia (Fed. States of)	..	..	..	..	..	..	..	..	..	2.0	28	82
New Caledonia	105	109	96	17	30	9	6	129	..b	2.1	77	80
Palau	..	..	..	..	..	..	..	..	..	2.4	72	58
Papua New Guinea	2 330	2 476	94	22	39	5	5	111	120	2.2	17	81
Samoa	86	94	91	23	38	7	5	120	..b	1.4	22	88
Solomon Islands	216	228	95	24	43	5	5	100	100	3.1	20	79
Tonga	..	..	..	..	..	..	..	..	..	0.3	38	98
Vanuatu	95	95	100	24	42	4	5	80	..b	2.4	20	90
Developed regions												
Albania	1 522	1 592	96	19	29	10	8	114	180	-0.4	42	131
Andorra	..	..	..	..	..	..	..	..	..	3.9	93	87
Australia	9 506	9 380	101	14	21	18	15	120	183	1.0	85	97
Austria	4 158	4 052	103	12	17	24	17	146	260	0.5	65	77
Belarus	5 430	4 806	113	16	19	23	15	178	352	-0.3	71	..
Belgium	5 185	4 976	104	12	17	25	19	137	242	0.1	97	85
Bermuda	..	..	..	..	..	..	..	..	..	0.8	100	108
Bosnia and Herzegovina	2 007	1 965	102	16	19	17	13	133	200	3.0	43	..
Bulgaria	4 226	3 999	106	14	16	23	19	130	162	-0.7	70	131
Canada	15 734	15 413	102	13	19	19	15	126	191	1.0	77	104
Croatia	2 311	2 162	107	14	17	24	17	149	286	-0.1	58	..
Czech Republic	5 257	4 987	105	13	17	21	15	148	245	-0.2	75	147g
Denmark	2 675	2 618	102	11	18	23	18	131	203	0.3	85	97
Estonia	740	656	113	16	17	24	15	179	329	-1.2	69	..

Table 1.A (cont'd):
Population

Country or area	Population (thousands), 2000		Women/ 100 men, 2000	% aged 10-19, 2000	% under age 15, 2000	% aged 60 or over, 2000		Women/100 men, 2000		Annual population growth (%), 1995-2000	Urban population (%), 2000	Women/100 men int'l. migrants, 1990
Developed regions (cont'd)	W	M				W	M	60+	80+			
Finland	2 652	2 524	105	13	18	23	16	147	277	0.3	67	100
France	30 281	28 798	105	13	19	23	18	137	219	0.4	76	96
Germany	41 954	40 266	104	11	16	27	20	142	286	0.1	88	80
Greece	5 407	5 238	103	12	15	26	22	121	150	0.3	60	105
Hungary	5 239	4 796	109	13	17	23	16	158	229	-0.4	64	106
Iceland	140	141	99	15	23	16	14	115	133	0.9	93	125
Ireland	1 878	1 852	101	16	21	17	14	124	200	0.7	59	100
Italy	29 492	27 806	106	10	14	27	21	135	211	0.0	67	130
Japan	64 621	62 093	104	11	15	26	21	129	209	0.2	79	98
Latvia	1 288	1 069	120	15	18	25	15	194	382	-1.5	69	..
Liechtenstein	..	..	..	..	..	..	..	..	..	1.3	23	83
Lithuania	1 938	1 732	112	15	19	22	14	174	282	-0.3	68	..
Luxembourg	219	211	104	11	18	22	17	133	267	1.1	92	104
Malta	196	193	102	15	21	19	14	141	200	0.7	91	123
Monaco	..	..	..	..	..	..	..	..	..	1.1	100	115
Netherlands	7 968	7 817	102	12	18	21	16	132	228	0.4	89	71
New Zealand	1 959	1 903	103	15	23	17	14	123	195	1.0	86	101
Norway	2 252	2 213	102	12	20	22	17	132	198	0.5	76	100
Poland	19 929	18 836	106	16	19	19	13	152	265	0.1	66	117
Portugal	5 125	4 749	108	12	16	23	18	140	203	0.0	64	110
Republic of Moldova	2 283	2 097	109	18	23	17	12	155	222	0.0	46	..
Romania	11 369	10 958	104	15	18	21	17	131	177	-0.4	56	131
Russian Federation	78 260	68 674	114	16	18	23	14	189	422	-0.2	78	92[h]
San Marino	..	..	..	..	..	..	..	..	..	1.3	89	115
Slovakia	2 763	2 624	105	16	20	18	13	152	219	0.1	57	..
Slovenia	1 021	965	106	13	16	22	16	153	267	-0.1	50	..
Spain	20 253	19 376	105	11	15	24	19	133	201	0.0	78	107
Sweden	4 491	4 419	102	12	18	25	20	126	180	0.3	83	107
Switzerland	3 734	3 652	102	12	17	22	17	135	206	0.7	68	79
The FYR of Macedonia	1 013	1 011	100	16	23	16	13	119	130	0.6	62	..
Ukraine	26 955	23 501	115	15	18	25	16	175	345	-0.4	68	..
United Kingdom	29 944	28 886	104	13	19	23	19	130	212	0.2	90	107
United States	141 180	137 177	103	14	21	18	14	132	199	0.8	77	105
Yugoslavia	5 353	5 287	101	15	20	21	16	128	177	0.1	52	132[i]

Sources: Prepared by the Statistics Division of the United Nations Secretariat from the following compilations of the Population Division of the United Nations Secretariat: for population and all series pertaining to age-sex composition of the population, *World Population Prospects: The 1998 Revision*, "Sex and Age Quinquennial, 1950-2050", data set in digital form; for annual population growth rate, *World Population Prospects: The 1998 Revision*, vol. I, *Comprehensive Tables* (United Nations publication, Sales No. E.99.XIII.9); for urban population, *World Urbanization Prospects: The 1999 Revision*, "Percentage of the population living in urban areas", data set in digital form (POP/DB/WUP/Rev.1999/1/F4); for international migration, "Trends in Total Migrant Stock by Sex", revision 4, data set in digital form (POP/1B/DB/98/4).

Note: Two dots (..) indicate that data are not available or are not reported separately.

[a] Data refer to former Ethiopia, which inludes Eritrea.

[b] Not calculated because the small number of either men or women aged 80 or over rounds to zero thousand.

[c] For statistical purposes, data for China do not include Hong Kong and Macao Special Administrative Regions.

[d] Does not include Hong Kong Special Administrative Region or Taiwan Province of China.

[e] Unless otherwise noted, data refer to the Gaza Strip only.

[f] Data refer to the Gaza Strip and the West Bank.

[g] Data refer to former Czechoslovakia.

[h] Data refer to the former USSR.

[i] Data refer to former Yugoslavia.

Technical notes

Table 1.A presents data on female and male populations, the ratio of women to men, the percentages of total population aged 10-19 and under age 15, the percentages of women and men aged 60 or over, and the ratio of women to men aged 60 or over and aged 80 or over.

Data in table 1.A have been compiled from estimates and projections of population by age group and sex, prepared in 1998 by the Population Division of the United Nations Secretariat, for countries and areas with a population of at least 150,000 in 1995. The estimates were made by collecting, evaluating and adjusting, as necessary, all available data for the period 1950-1998. For the period 1995-2050, figures are mostly the result of projections from the year 1995, except for such cases where reliable, more recent data are available. These estimates and projections are also included in the *Women's Indicators and Statistics Database (Wistat)*.

Table 1.A also presents statistics on the annual rate of population growth, the percentage of urban population in the total population and the sex ratio of the international migrant population. Data on the annual rate of population growth were prepared in 1998 by the Population Division of the United Nations Secretariat and published in *World Population Prospects: The 1998 Revision*, vol. 1, *Comprehensive Tables* and are also available in *Wistat*.[a] Estimates of the urban population are also made by the Population Division and are published in *World Urbanization Prospects: The 1999 Revision*.[b]

The approach used in estimating rates of population growth assumes exponential growth. The growth rate shown is an annual average over the five-year period indicated.

Urban-rural classification of population follows the national census definition and varies from one country or area to another. National definitions are usually based on criteria that may include any of the following: size of population in a locality, population density, distance between built-up areas, predominant type of economic activity, legal or administrative boundaries, and such urban characteristics as specific services and facilities.

Estimates of the ratio of women to men among international migrants are taken from the database *Trends in Total Migrant Stock*, maintained by the Population Division. Estimates of migrant stock are based on the number of foreign-born or the foreign residents in a country enumerated by national population censuses and sample surveys, and complemented by the number of refugees in a country. Statistics on the foreign-born provide only a crude measure of the volume and composition of migration during an indefinite number of years prior to the census. International comparability of this indicator is affected, among other things, by the fact that some countries report data on non-citizens rather than on the foreign-born.

[a] United Nations publication, Sales No. E.00.XVII.4.

[b] United Nations publication, forthcoming.

CHAPTER 2

Women and men in families

Some important findings:

- Women are generally marrying later but more than a quarter of women aged 15 to 19 are married in 22 countries—all in developing regions.

- Informal unions are common in developed regions and in some countries of the developing regions.

- Birth rates continue to decline in all regions of the world.

- Births to unmarried women have increased dramatically in developed regions.

- More people are living alone in the developed regions, and the majority are women.

- In many countries of the developed regions, more than half of mothers with children under age 3 are employed.

Women's and men's roles in society are inseparable from their roles in the family. Major demographic and socioeconomic changes are influencing family formation and family life, simultaneously changing family composition and structure. Improved access to education, employment and reproductive health services is reshaping and expanding women's roles inside and outside the family, and re-defining roles and responsibilities for men. In the context of these changes, decisions regarding family life take on new meanings: whether and when to marry; whether and when to have children and how many to have; how to support a family and to combine parenthood with work; how to manage the dissolution of unions; and whether and how to form new unions and families.

The International Conference on Population and Development (ICPD) in 1994 recognized the family, however it is constituted, as the basic unit of society and, as such, the family should be strengthened and afforded comprehensive protection and support. The ICPD called for policies and programmes to take into account the diversity of family forms and to be particularly sensitive to the needs and rights of women and children.[1]

MARRIAGE AND OTHER UNIONS

For many people, marriage is the first step toward the formation of a new family. However, in many countries—under a variety of social, cultural, legal and political systems—less formal unions form the basis of family life. Included in the category of "other unions" are consensual unions, visiting unions, cohabitation and polygyny (the practice of a man tak-

ing more than one wife). This diversity of family forms presents researchers with both challenges and opportunities for understanding the mechanisms of how these unions come into being, how and if they are maintained and what happens upon their dissolution.

Early marriage has declined

While men tend to marry during adulthood, many women marry and have children while still adolescents, often curtailing education and limiting employment opportunities. In at least 22 countries where data are available for the 1990s, more than a quarter of women aged 15 to 19 are married (table 2.A).

The prevalence of early marriage for both women and men has declined in all regions (chart 2.1) but in most countries of Southern Asia and sub-Saharan Africa early marriage for women is still common. According to recent data, in three of five countries in Southern Asia and in 11 of 30 countries in sub-Saharan Africa, at least 30 per cent of young women aged 15 to 19 have been married (table 2.A). There are, however, substantial differences between Southern Africa and the rest of sub-Saharan Africa. For example, in all countries of Southern Africa with recent data, 10 per cent or fewer women aged 15 to 19 have been married.

In Eastern Asia, Western Europe and other developed countries, on average, 2 per cent of women and fewer than 1 per cent of men aged 15 to 19 have been married. The percentages of young adults who have been married range from 0 to 6 for young women and 0 to 2 for young men. The prevalence of early marriage among women is higher in countries in transi-

Age at first marriage

Calculation of the current average age at first marriage requires comprehensive vital registration data, seldom available in developing regions. The "singulate mean age at marriage" is thus often used instead. It is the mean age at first marriage among those who have ever been married in the age group 15-49. It is computed from the proportions never-married in each five-year age group, within the broad age group 15-49, usually from census and survey data. It therefore measures the average age at first marriage over the historical period covered by the age group 15-49, rather than the average age of those currently marrying for the first time.

tion in Eastern Europe and Central Asia—on average, 8 and 12 per cent, respectively **(chart 2.1)**.

The prevalence of early marriage varies widely in Latin America and the Caribbean, ranging from 1 per cent of women aged 15 to 19 in Jamaica to 29 per cent in the Dominican Republic. However, these figures may not include young women in consensual and visiting unions, which are often socially accepted and sanctioned contexts for bearing and rearing children **(see box on reporting marriages and unions)**.

Early marriage among men aged 15 to 19 is much less common than for women in all countries, rarely exceeding 10 per cent. Even in countries of sub-Saharan Africa, where many women marry young, the percentage of men aged 15 to 19 who are married seldom exceeds 5 per cent **(table 2.A)**.

Marriage age rising, albeit by little in developing regions

In general, women and men postpone marriage in countries where they enjoy higher social status and wider educational and employment opportunities. In Western Europe and other developed countries, for example, the average age at first marriage for women is

Chart 2.1✤:

The percentage of young women who are ever married has decreased in most regions
Percentage 15-19 ever married

	1975/1984		1985/1997	
	W	**M**	**W**	**M**
Africa				
Northern Africa	16	2	10	1
Sub-Saharan Africa	34	5	26	3
Latin America and the Caribbean				
Caribbean	7	2	8	2
Central America	23	5	18	3
South America	14	4	14	5
Asia				
Eastern Asia	3	1	2	1
South-eastern Asia	15	3	8	3
Southern Asia	44	10	32	5[a]
Central Asia	..	..	12	2[b]
Western Asia	22	4	14	3
Oceania	14	3	10	3
Developed regions				
Eastern Europe	14	2	8	2
Western Europe	4	1	2	<1
Other developed regions	5	1	2	1

✤ In this and subsequent charts, regional and subregional averages are unweighted (i.e., the averages do not take into account the size of the individual countries' populations) and are based only upon available data for that region (see page xi for fuller explanation).

well above 25, and sometimes close to or above 30 **(table 2.A)**. More recent data for some of the developed countries show a trend toward late marriage, especially in the Nordic countries, where the average age at first marriage is close to 30 for women and between 31 and 33 for men. In these countries, about a third of women and less than a fifth of men aged 25 to 29 are married.

In most of the other developed countries examined, less than 50 per cent of women and men aged 25 to 29 are married. The United States and Belgium are exceptions; over half of women aged 25 to 29, and close to a fourth of women aged 20 to 24, are married **(chart 2.2)**. Later marriages in developed countries reflect the large numbers of women who pursue education and career opportunities before marriage and the increasing number of young couples who cohabit without marrying.

In countries in transition in Eastern Europe and Central and Western Asia, the average age at first marriage has changed little since 1990. In these regions, marriages for both women and men occur at younger ages than in Western Europe. Women generally marry at age 22 or 23, and men between ages 24 and 27 **(chart 2.3)**.

The youngest average ages at first marriage for women are in Southern Asia and sub-Saharan Africa (except Southern Africa)—20 and 21 years, respectively. The average age at first marriage for women remains at 18 to 19 in two countries of Southern Asia and in most sub-Saharan African countries. In Southern Africa, however, the average ages at first marriage for both women and men are among the highest in the world—27 years for women and 30 for men **(chart 2.3)**. These higher ages at first marriage may reflect the prevalence of consensual unions and/or the postponement of marriage due to male migration.

In Asia (apart from the Southern region) women and men marry well into their twenties. In Eastern Asia, on average, women marry at age 25 and men at 28; in South-eastern Asia, on average, women marry at 24 and men at 27. The oldest average ages at marriage in South-eastern Asia are in Singapore—27 for women and almost 30 for men. In Western Asia, the average for all countries is 23 for women and 27 for men, with women in Oman and Yemen falling well below this average—age 19 in both countries.

In the Caribbean, on average, women marry at age 28 and men at 30. The prevalence of consensual

Source: Prepared by the Statistics Division of the United Nations Secretariat from *Women's Indicators and Statistics Database (Wistat), Version 4*, CD-ROM (United Nations publication, Sales No. E.00.XVII.4).

[a] Average for men based on data for only three countries.

[b] Average for men based on data for only two countries.

unions may account for later marriages in the countries of the Caribbean. In Latin America, the average age at first marriage for women is around 23.

Since 1980, the marriage age has risen almost everywhere, albeit by little in many developing regions. The greatest increase in age at first marriage is in the developed regions, with an average increase since 1980 of three years for both women and men in Western Europe, and three years for women and four for men in the developed regions outside Europe. In contrast, since 1980, there has been relatively little change in Northern Africa, sub-Saharan Africa (except Southern Africa), Latin America and the Caribbean and in most regions of Asia. In countries of Southern Africa, the average age at first marriage has increased by three years for women and two years for men. In Northern Africa and Eastern Asia, the age at first marriage for women increased by one year (chart 2.3).

Marriage and childbearing have a greater impact on women's lives than on men's lives, especially when women marry at a young age and/or their spouses are much older. A wide age gap between wife and husband often results in greater inequality between spouses. Many women who marry older men at a young age have little autonomy and may, as a result, be at a disadvantage in family decision-making, especially on issues concerning their reproductive behaviour.[2] Another disadvantage for women in such marriages is the possibility of being widowed at a relatively early age.

The widest differences between women and men in age at first marriage are in countries where women marry earliest. In Southern Asia and sub-Saharan Africa (except Southern Africa), for example, the average age at first marriage for women is five to six years lower than that for men. In Western Asia and Northern Africa, the average age at first marriage for women is four years lower than that for men, although women tend to marry later in these regions. In all other regions, differences between men and women in age at first marriage are between two and three years (chart 2.3).

There is some evidence that women who marry before age 20 are more likely to marry men who are several years older. In three countries—Colombia,

Chart 2.2:
Marriage is rare for young adults, particularly young men, in most developed countries
Percentage currently married, 1993/1998

	Ages 20-24		Ages 25-29	
	W	M	W	M
Western Europe				
Belgium	23	9	60	43
Denmark	9	3	32	19
Finland	10	4	34	23
France	10	3	39	26
Germany	14	5	39	23
Iceland	8	3	34	22
Ireland	7	3	41	27
Netherlands	13	4	42	25
Norway	8	3	32	18
Sweden	7	2	28	16
Switzerland	17	7	48	31
Other developed regions				
Australia	16	7	50	35
Japan	13	7	50	32
New Zealand	12	5	48[a]	39[a]
United States	27	16	55	44

Source: Compiled from regional and national sources by Catherine de Guibert-Lantoine as consultant to the Statistics Division of the United Nations Secretariat.

[a] Data refer to the age group 25-34.

Chart 2.3:
Average age at first marriage has risen for women and men in almost all regions
Singulate mean age at marriage

	1975/1984		1985/1997	
	W	M	W	M
Africa				
Northern Africa	22	27	23	27
Southern Africa	24	28	27	30
Rest of sub-Saharan Africa	20	26	21	27
Latin America and the Caribbean				
Caribbean	27	30	28	30
Central America	21	24	22	25
South America	23	26	23	26
Asia				
Eastern Asia	24	27	25	28
South-eastern Asia	23	26	24	27
Southern Asia	19	24	20	25
Central Asia	..	..	22	24
Western Asia	21	25	23	27
Oceania	22	26	24	27
Developed regions				
Eastern Europe	..	..	23	26
Western Europe	24	27	27	30
Other developed regions	24	26	27	30

Source: Prepared by the Statistics Division of the United Nations Secretariat from *Women's Indicators and Statistics Database (Wistat), Version 4*, CD-ROM (United Nations publication, Sales No. E.00.XVII.4), based mainly on *Demographic Yearbook 1995* (United Nations publication, Sales No. E/F.97.XIII.1) and compilations prepared by the Population Division of the United Nations Secretariat.

Egypt and Turkey—Demographic and Health Surveys (DHS) found that the age difference between spouses is much wider for women who marry before age 20 than for those who marry later. In Egypt, almost one quarter of women who marry before age 20 marry men who are at least 10 years older, compared to 12 per cent of women who marry after age 20.[3]

In some regions, early marriages are most often arranged by parents and other relatives. For example, in Egypt, 10 per cent of women who married before age 16 had chosen their husbands, compared to 40 per cent who married after age 25.[4]

Informal unions common in some developing countries

Marriage is not the only way in which families are formed. In countries where there are high percentages of never-married women and men, alternative family structures often exist. While informal unions are generally recognized by the societies in which they exist, they are not legally sanctioned and are often not registered as unions. As a result, many women and men in informal unions report themselves as "single" in censuses and are not included as "married" or "in unions" in data sets that look at marital status (see box on reporting marriages and unions).

In countries of Latin America and the Caribbean, informal unions are generally referred to as "consensual" unions. In the developed regions, the term "cohabitation" may also be used. Especially in the Caribbean, where 22 per cent of women and 19 per cent of men aged 45 or over have never married (chart 2.4), the number of consensual unions is generally high—for example, 28 per cent of women aged 15 to 49 in Haiti and 36 per cent in the Dominican Republic (chart 2.5). In a few sub-Saharan African countries, as well, high percentages of never-married women and men suggest a large number of consensual unions.

Data from DHS surveys conducted between 1992 and 1998 show that more than 10 per cent of women were in informal unions in half of the 12 African countries and all seven of the Latin American and Caribbean countries examined. In four of the Latin American and Caribbean countries, more than 25 per cent of women aged 15 to 49 surveyed were in consensual unions (chart 2.5). However, comparison of

Chart 2.4:

Significant proportions of women and men do not marry in some regions

Percentage 45+ who are never married, 1985/1997

	W	M
Africa		
Northern Africa	2	3
Sub-Saharan Africa	8	7
Latin America and the Caribbean		
Caribbean	22	19
Central America	12	11
South America	15	13
Asia		
Eastern Asia	2	4
South-eastern Asia	4	3
Southern Asia	1	2
Central Asia	1	1
Western Asia	3	2
Oceania	6	8
Developed regions		
Eastern Europe	5	4
Western Europe	9	9
Other developed	6	7

Source: Prepared by the Statistics Division of the United Nations Secretariat from *Women's Indicators and Statistics Database (Wistat), Version 4*, CD-ROM (United Nations publication, Sales No. E.00.XVII.4), based mainly on unpublished data from the Demographics Statistics Database maintained by the Statistics Division (as at January 1999).

Reporting marriages and unions

Gathering statistics on the relational status of couples presents a number of problems. Couples live in various types of unions, recognized by law or outside the legal framework, depending on the legislation and customs of the country. In practice, official statistics often fail to reflect all existing realities. Unions not sanctioned by law may be under-reported or may be classified in various ways in different countries. Moreover, classification of widowed, separated and divorced persons may change over time and among countries. Consequently, comparisons between separate data sources, whether within the same country or across countries and over time, should be made with caution.

Informal unions

Informal unions are relationships not sanctioned by a legal marriage. In Latin American countries, where these unions are common, such unions are generally referred to as "consensual unions", while in the developed regions the term "cohabitation" is often used.

Informal unions, by definition, are not reported and are therefore excluded from the civil registration system. Individuals living in informal unions are often reported as "single" in population censuses. Even when two separate categories ("legal marriages" and "other types of unions") are available, informal unions may be under-reported.

In some countries, persons in unions not sanctioned by legal documents are included in the "married" category; in these cases, "married" includes all individuals in legal marriages and all those in de facto unions. This presents two sets of problems: women and men in informal unions may fail to identify themselves as married; and it is impossible to distinguish the two types of unions, even though the distinction often has important policy implications.

Comparability across countries of statistics on marital status is affected not only by the marital status categories available to respondents but also by how respondents choose to report their marital status. This may depend on whether informal unions are socially accepted within a country.

Polygynous unions

Polygynous unions are those in which a man has two or more wives. These unions are rarely reflected in official statistics. The characteristics and conditions of polygynous unions and whether or not they are reported and registered vary across countries. A man may be legally married to the first wife and have consensual or visiting unions with one or more other wives, or—where acceptable—may be legally married to all wives. Partners may live in the same or different dwellings, even in different geographical areas. Second and higher-order wives, when not legally married, may report themselves as single. Data on these unions are often available only from surveys.

these data with earlier DHS surveys in African countries does not indicate a clear trend in the prevalence of consensual unions. Over a recent five- to 10-year period, in Cameroon, Ghana and Madagascar,[5] the proportion of consensual unions increased, while in Uganda, the United Republic of Tanzania and Zambia, the proportion decreased.

In Botswana, one of the African countries where consensual unions are common, the increase in the number of consensual unions is thought to be due, at least in part, to the disappearance of polygyny (the practice of a man having more than one wife) and to the shift from a rural to a cash economy. While polygyny was socially acceptable, many men took multiple partners. In the absence of sanctioned polygyny, sexual activity and childbearing outside marriage have become widespread. Men's migration for work to urban centres in Botswana and to South Africa has created shortages of men in villages.[6]

In Latin America and the Caribbean, women in consensual unions may be disadvantaged relative to women in legal marriages, with respect to financial commitments in cases of separation. Studies in these regions show that informal unions are more common among less educated women and among those living in rural areas.[7] Moreover, since informal unions are more common among poor women, the social and financial consequences of the dissolution of such unions are even more severe.

Informal unions (including cohabitation) have become common in some countries in the developed regions (chart 2.6). In six of the countries surveyed in 1992/1996 by the Fertility and Family Surveys of the Economic Commission for Europe (ECE), more than half the women aged 20 to 24 who were in unions were in cohabiting unions—in Sweden, more than three quarters. Cohabitation generally becomes less common with age, suggesting that many cohabitation relationships ultimately result in legal marriages. In some countries, however (especially where informal unions are socially accepted), cohabitation often continues after age 30. A significant proportion of women aged 30 to 34 who were in unions were in cohabiting unions—33 per cent in Sweden, 19 per cent in New Zealand, 18 per cent in France and more than 10 per cent in nine of the other countries surveyed.

Many women in polygynous unions in parts of Africa

Polygyny is common in some countries of sub-Saharan Africa and to a lesser degree in Northern Africa and in some countries of Southern and Western Asia. Data from DHS surveys conducted from 1992 to 1998 show that roughly half of married

Chart 2.5:

Consensual unions are common in some developing countries
Percentage of women 15-49 in consensual unions, 1992/1998

Sub-Saharan Africa		Dominican Republic	36
Benin	8	Haiti	28
Cameroon	10	Nicaragua	33
Comoros	1	Peru	24
Ghana	12	**Asia**	
Madagascar	15	Kazakhstan	3
Malawi	3	Kyrgyzstan	3
Mozambique	55	Philippines	6
Namibia	15	Uzbekistan	1
Rwanda	24		
Uganda	9	
United Republic of Tanzania	7	
Zambia	1	

Source: Demographic and Health Surveys country reports (Columbia and Calverton, Maryland, Macro International, 1992-98).

Note: For Africa and Asia, the data refer to unmarried women living together with a male partner.

Latin America and the Caribbean	
Bolivia	14
Brazil	13
Colombia	25

Chart 2.6:

Cohabitation is common in some developed countries
Percentage cohabiting among all women in unions, by age, 1992/1996

	20-24	25-29	30-34
Eastern Europe			
Estonia	33	19	14
Hungary	13	5	5
Latvia	20	16	9
Lithuania	5	4	4
Slovenia	36	17	11
Western Europe			
Austria	64	30	12
Belgium	27	13	6
Finland [a]	61	34	18
France	63	33	18
Germany			
Federal Rep. of Germany	39	22	12
former German Dem. Rep.	33	16	9
Italy	8	6	4
Netherlands	57	33	14
Norway [a]	57	33	15
Spain	22	8	5
Sweden	77	43	33
Switzerland	63	27	14
Other developed regions			
Canada [a]	46	24	16
New Zealand	67	30	19

Source: E. Klijzing and M. Macura, "Cohabitation and extra-marital childbearing: early FFS evidence", in *Proceedings of the International Population Conference, Beijing, 1997* (International Union for the Scientific Study of Population).

[a] Data shown for this country are for 1988/1990.

Chart 2.7:

A significant proportion of women are in polygynous unions in many countries of sub-Saharan Africa

Percentage currently married women 15–49 who are in polygynous unions, 1992/1998

Sub-Saharan Africa

Benin	50
Burkina Faso	51
Burundi	12[a]
Cameroon	33
Central African Republic	29
Chad	39
Comoros	25
Côte d'Ivoire	37
Ghana	28
Guinea	50
Kenya	16
Liberia	38[a]
Malawi	21
Mali	44
Mozambique	27
Namibia	13
Niger	38
Nigeria	41[a]
Rwanda	14
Senegal	46
Sudan	17
Togo	43
Uganda	30
United Republic of Tanzania	29
Zambia	17
Zimbabwe	19

Source: Sunita Kishor and Katherine Neitzel, *The Status of Women: Indicators for Twenty-Five Countries*, Demographic and Health Surveys, Comparative Studies, No. 21 (Calverton, Maryland, Macro International, 1996); and Demographic and Health Surveys country reports (Columbia and Calverton, Maryland, Macro International, 1993–1998).

Note: Countries listed are those where prevalence of polygyny is above 10 per cent. Levels of between 4 and 7 per cent have been found in Jordan, Morocco, Nepal, Pakistan and Yemen.

[a] Data refer to 1986/1990.

* Divorce statistics used in this section do not include the dissolution of informal unions. In addition, many couples end their marriages with separation agreements, which are not necessarily followed by legal divorce.

women aged 15 to 49 are in polygynous unions in Benin, Burkina Faso and Guinea. More than one third of married women of the same age group are in polygynous unions in six other sub-Saharan African countries (chart 2.7).

Polygynous unions are far more common among rural and less-educated women. In Burkina Faso, for example, 13 per cent of married women with secondary education are in such unions, compared to 55 per cent of married women with no education. Available data for 14 countries surveyed indicate that the proportion of women with secondary education who are in polygynous unions is half or less than half the proportion of women with no education. Polygynous unions are also more common among women who do not work and, among those who do work, polygynous unions are more prevalent for those engaged in unpaid work.[8]

Polygynous unions have important implications for the status of women, for the partners' relationships with their children and for many other aspects of women's lives. In sub-Saharan Africa, polygynous unions tend to be associated with wider age gaps between husbands and wives, often reinforcing patriarchal authority. These unions also lead to a proliferation of step-children and step-relatives. The effects of polygynous unions on women's lives differ according to the individual woman's rank among wives within the polygynous marriage and, overall, with the cultural and social circumstances in which the woman lives.[9]

THE DISSOLUTION OF UNIONS

Whether it is a marriage or an informal union that is dissolving, and whatever the reasons for the dissolution, the consequences are many and profound for both partners and for any children and/or other family members who are involved.

Although data on the occurrence of divorce and separation are scarce for most developing regions, an increase in the percentage of divorced or separated women and men can be seen almost everywhere. However, the proportions of divorced or separated persons remain low in most regions of Asia and Africa (chart 2.8).

Proportions divorced or separated among women aged 45 to 59 increased, on average, from 5 per cent in 1980 to 9 per cent in the 1990s in Europe and from 9 to 14 per cent in developed countries outside Europe over the same time period. In Latin America and the Caribbean, proportions increased from 7 to 10 per cent, on average. Divorce and separation have also become somewhat more common among women aged 45 to 59 in Western Asia (chart 2.8).

It is difficult to assess the extent to which informal unions dissolve. However, surveys in Latin America suggest that informal unions are more likely to dissolve than legal marriages.[10]

Divorce trends changing in developed regions

For many countries, including Belgium, Luxembourg, the Nordic countries, Switzerland and the United Kingdom, the divorce rate* is at least 40 divorces per 100 marriages. The highest divorce rate is in Sweden (51 divorces per 100 marriages).[11] The rate in the United States is almost as high.[12] In contrast, Greece, Italy, Portugal and Spain have fewer than 20 divorces per 100 marriages, on average.

In Eastern Europe, rates range from well below 20 divorces per 100 marriages in Bulgaria, Croatia, Poland and Slovenia to over 40 divorces per 100 marriages in most countries of the former USSR.

Chart 2.8:

Proportions of divorced and separated people have increased in some regions

Percentage 45-59 who are divorced/separated

	1975/1984		1985/1997	
	W	M	W	M
Africa				
Northern Africa	3	1	3	1
Sub-Saharan Africa	7	4	7	4
Latin America and the Caribbean				
Caribbean	8	5	10	8
Central America	7	3	10	5
South America	5	3	8	5
Asia				
Eastern Asia	1	1	2	2
South-eastern Asia	3	1	3	1
Southern Asia	1	<1	1	<1
Central Asia	..	..	8	4
Western Asia	3	1	5	1
Oceania	4	3	5	3
Developed regions				
Eastern Europe	5	3	9	6
Western Europe	5	4	9	8
Other developed regions	9	7	14	11

Source: Prepared by the Statistics Division of the United Nations Secretariat from *Women's Indicators and Statistics Database (Wistat), Version 4*, CD-ROM (United Nations publication, Sales No. E.00.XVII.4), based mainly on unpublished data from the Demographic Statistics Database maintained by the Statistics Division (as at January 1999).

The increase in the rate of divorce has slowed or even reversed in many developed countries, especially in Eastern Europe, the Nordic countries, Canada and the United States, where divorce has been socially accepted for decades or where traditionally rates have been high. In Canada, for example, the divorce rate decreased for the third straight year in 1997, reaching its lowest level since 1985.[13]

In contrast, in countries where divorce laws were liberalized more recently or where social attitudes are restrictive, divorce became common only recently, and is still on the rise. Examples of countries where divorce rates rose sharply from 1970 to 1980 and have risen steadily since then are Austria, Germany, Iceland, Luxembourg, Portugal and Switzerland.[14]

In most countries of the European Union, the tendency for marriages to end in divorce seems to have intensified with the younger generations. It is estimated that, of those couples who married in 1980, 27 per cent will be divorced, compared to 22 per cent of couples married in 1970 and 14 per cent of those married in 1960.[15]

Marriages are also ending sooner in countries of the European Union. Among the most recent marriage cohorts, the highest probability of divorce occurs after just four years of marriage. For these countries, the average duration of marriages that end in divorce has decreased by one or two years.[16]

In contrast, in Canada, not only have divorces become less common, but marriages are also lasting longer. Marriages that ended in 1997 lasted an average of 13.3 years, up from 12.3 years for marriages that ended in 1993.[17]

Remarriage rates decreasing in developed regions

Many women and men choose to remarry after divorce or widowhood. However, the interval between marriages seems to be lengthening, perhaps due to couples choosing to cohabit before committing to a new marriage.

In some countries, the absolute number of remarriages has been growing, to a large degree the result of the increase in the number of divorces. In addition, the proportion of marriages that are remarriages has been increasing, due not only to the increase in the number of divorces but also to the downward trend in first marriages. In much of the European Union, the number of remarriages has grown significantly. Remarriages are most prevalent in Denmark and the United Kingdom, where almost 30 per cent of marriages are second marriages for at least one partner. In contrast, remarriages are almost non-existent in Ireland and are relatively rare in Italy and Spain.[18]

Even with the increase in the number of remarriages, the rate of remarriage after divorce has been decreasing since the 1970s, following the same trend as first marriages. Today, many divorced people postpone remarriage or cohabit with a new partner without legalizing the union. In 1965, the probability of remarrying after divorce was around 60 to 70 per cent in Western Europe and 55 per cent in the Nordic countries. Twenty years later, these percentages had each decreased by at least 20 per cent.[19] In France, between 1980 and 1996, the rate of remarriage after divorce had decreased by 25 per cent. In Italy, the rate of remarriage after divorce decreased between 1980 and 1990, especially for men.[20]

A study in England and Wales found that a much higher proportion of divorced people were cohabiting in 1996 compared to 20 years earlier—slightly less than a quarter of divorced women and over a quarter of divorced men. In contrast, the proportion of divorced men and women who remarry was shown to have declined dramatically. In 1976, the rate of remarriage after divorce was around 180 remarriages per 1,000 divorces for men and 130 per 1,000 for women. In 1996, the rate was around 50 remarriages for men and 45 for women—a much lower rate and a much smaller difference between women and men than in 1976.[21]

Widowhood common among older women but not among older men

Most women and men marry and live with partners for at least part of their adult lives. However, higher mortality rates for men leave many women living alone in their later years, especially since most widowed women do not remarry. In contrast, older men generally live with a spouse.

Widowhood for women aged 60 or over is most prevalent in Northern Africa and Central Asia—59 and 58 per cent, respectively (chart 2.9). The prevalence is high in Northern Africa, probably because women tend to marry older men and because remarriage after the death of a spouse is less common than in other regions. In the countries of Central Asia, the high proportion of widowed women is largely due to high levels of male mortality. In all other parts of Asia, around half the women aged 60 or over are widowed, probably because young women tend to marry older men.

Older women in Latin America and the Caribbean have the lowest prevalence of widowhood—on average, about 36 per cent of women aged 60 or over. This is thought to be due, at least in part, to women in informal unions referring to themselves as "single" rather than "widowed" when they lose their partners.

Chart 2.9:

Older women are far more likely than older men to be widowed
Percentage 60+ who are widowed, 1985/1997

	W	M
Africa		
Northern Africa	59	8
Sub-Saharan Africa	44	7
Latin America and the Caribbean		
Caribbean	34	12
Central America	36	12
South America	37	13
Asia		
Eastern Asia	49	14
South-eastern Asia	49	14
Southern Asia	51	11
Central Asia	58	13
Western Asia	48	8
Oceania	44	15
Developed regions		
Eastern Europe	48	14
Western Europe	40	12
Other developed regions	39	11

Source: Prepared by the Statistics Division of the United Nations Secretariat from Women's *Indicators and Statistics Database (Wistat), Version 4*, CD-ROM (United Nations publication, Sales No. E.00.XVII.4), based mainly on unpublished data from the Demographic Statistics Database maintained by the Statistics Division (as at January 1999).

Chart 2.10:

Widowhood at younger ages is not uncommon for women in some regions

Percentage 45-59 who are widowed, 1985/1997

	W	M
Africa		
Northern Africa	19	1
Sub-Saharan Africa	16	2
Latin America and the Caribbean		
Caribbean	8	2
Central America	10	2
South America	10	3
Asia		
Eastern Asia	9	2
South-eastern Asia	16	2
Southern Asia	17	5
Central Asia	16	3
Western Asia	13	1
Oceania	13	3
Developed regions		
Eastern Europe	12	3
Western Europe	7	1
Other developed regions	5	1

Source: Prepared by the Statistics Division of the United Nations Secretariat from *Women's Indicators and Statistics Database (Wistat), Version 4*, CD-ROM (United Nations publication, Sales No. E.00.XVII.4), based mainly on unpublished data from the Demographic Statistics Database maintained by the Statistics Division (as at January 1999).

Widowhood among women aged 45 to 59 is relatively rare in Western Europe and the developed regions outside Europe (5 and 7 per cent, respectively). In contrast, in Africa and Southern, South-eastern and Central Asia, on average, between 16 and 19 per cent of women in this age group are widows **(chart 2.10)**.

The proportions widowed among older men are generally low and always much lower than among older women. The prevalence of widowhood for men aged 60 or over ranges from an average of 7 per cent in sub-Saharan Africa to roughly 14 per cent in Eastern Europe and parts of Asia **(chart 2.9)**.

Widowhood among middle-aged men is uncommon. Overall, percentages of 45- to 59-year-old men who are widowed range from 1 to 5, with the highest in Southern Asia. Low rates of widowhood among men are probably due to a combination of factors: they tend to marry younger women; they generally have higher mortality than women; and they are likely to remarry if they are widowed.[22]

PARENTHOOD

Women's and men's lives are greatly affected by the decision to have children, by the age at which they have children, and by how many children they have. Many factors determine how parenthood unfolds, including the educational and employment opportunities available to women and men, women's and men's knowledge of and access to family planning, the degree of gender equity and equality between partners, relationships within and outside the family, and the overall social and cultural context.

Widowhood in contemporary India[a]

About 10 per cent of women in India are widows, compared to only 3 per cent of men, according to the 1991 census. Fifty-four per cent of women aged 60 and over are widows, as are 12 per cent of women aged 35-59. Remarriage is the exception rather than the rule; only about 10 per cent of widows marry again.

According to a study based on qualitative information, widowers do not suffer the social stigma, restrictions and taboos associated with widows. They retain their economic resources and are much more likely to remarry. In contrast, the approximately 33 million Indian widows are expected to lead chaste, austere, ascetic lives. Meeting those expectations is possible only for women who come from households prosperous enough to care for a dependent widow. Reports describe brothers-in-law who usurp the widow's share of property and do not offer her a harvest share or daily maintenance; sons who live separately and do not support the widowed mother; and brothers who do not support the widowed sister although they inherited her share of the father's property.

Widows have a basic repertoire of strategies. They may try to exert their claims on male kin (if any). If not, widows may adopt a son or negotiate a daughter's marriage to a son-in-law willing to support them. Widows who own land are more likely than landless widows to be able to negotiate such arrangements. Widows may remarry or enter partnerships with men who offer support. They may continue to work in small-scale farming, trading or producing goods for sale, or they may enter the wage labour force. Others adopt a religious way of life, living from begging, chanting prayers or singing devotional songs. Still others become prostitutes or concubines to earn enough money to support themselves.

The sensational circumstances of small numbers of widows receive more attention than the less visible and quiet deprivations of millions. These deprivations do not show up in economic and social statistics, so the standard household-level analyses tell very little about widows and their well-being. Female-headed households are not reported by marital status, so widow-headed households cannot be compared with other households.

[a] Martha Alter Chen, *Perpetual Mourning: Widowhood in Rural India* (Oxford University Press, 2000).

Desired number of children declined in developing regions

Attitudes toward sexual and reproductive rights have changed considerably over the past three decades. Today, in many countries, women and men can choose when and whom to marry; whether to have children; and the number, timing and spacing of those children. Recent United Nations conferences in Cairo (1994) and Beijing (1995) established guidelines to protect and extend these reproductive rights, including the right of access to reproductive health information and services.

The 1994 International Conference on Population and Development (ICPD) held at Cairo was a catalyst for change on this front. The ICPD Programme of Action urged countries to develop and implement their own programmes and policies centred on the reproductive rights and health of women and men.

Since Cairo and Beijing, efforts to expand the availability of family planning services and to allow more women and men to control their own reproductive lives have been widespread.[23] However, according to the United Nations Population Fund (UNFPA), an estimated 120 to 150 million women who want to limit the number of children they have or to extend the period of time between pregnancies lack effective and safe means to do so. The large number of unwanted pregnancies often results in unsafe abortions or unwanted children, with serious consequences for the lives of the children and their parents.[24]

The number of children desired (as expressed by women) has declined significantly in developing countries, according to surveys undertaken in the 1980s and 1990s. The largest absolute decline is in sub-Saharan Africa, where women want, on average, two fewer children today than did women in the 1980s. However, women still want a large number of children—for example, in Cameroon, seven; and in Senegal, six.

In other regions, where family size has decreased considerably over the last several decades, women also say they want fewer children. Women in most of the countries surveyed in Asia and Northern Africa say they want between three and four children, down from between four and five in the 1980s (chart 2.11).

Whether women and men achieve their desired family size often depends on whether the demand for contraceptives is met. DHS data show the gap between supply and demand for contraceptive services. The unmet need is represented by the number of women who have a mistimed or unwanted pregnancy, or by the number of women who do not want a child, or want a child later, but are not using contraceptives.[25] Unmet need is highest in sub-Saharan Africa, where 29 per cent of women surveyed between 1988 and 1997, who either did not want another child or wanted to delay their next

birth, had not been using contraception. In Asia, unmet need is generally low. Wide variations are observed in Latin America and the Caribbean. Northern Africa had generally low levels of unmet need.[26]

The amount of time it takes for a woman to reach a facility offering contraceptive services and/or supplies is one indicator of family planning accessibility. DHS surveys show that it is more difficult for women in rural areas to get to family planning clinics. In the 22 countries in developing regions surveyed between 1990 and 1996, around 90 per cent of urban women had a family planning clinic within an hour of their homes; in rural areas in nine of those countries, less than 50 per cent of women interviewed lived within an hour of a family planning facility.[27]

Chart 2.11:

In developing regions, women today want fewer children than did women a decade ago
Number of children desired

	1980s	1990s
Northern Africa		
Egypt	4.1	2.9
Morocco	4.9	3.8
Tunisia	4.1	3.5
Sub-Saharan Africa		
Cameroon	8.0	6.8
Ghana	5.7	4.4
Kenya	6.8	3.7
Nigeria	8.3	5.8
Rwanda	6.0	4.2
Senegal	8.0	5.9
Latin America and the Caribbean		
Bolivia	2.6	2.5
Brazil (Northeast)	2.8	2.7
Colombia	3.5	2.6
Dominican Republic	4.3	3.1
Ecuador	3.5	3.0
Mexico	4.2	3.0
Paraguay	4.5	3.9
Peru	3.8	2.5
Asia		
Bangladesh	4.1	2.5
Indonesia	4.1	2.8
Jordan	6.3	4.4
Pakistan	4.2	4.1
Philippines	4.4	3.2

Source: Compiled from country reports of the World Fertility Surveys and the Demographic and Health Surveys by Silvana Salvini as a consultant to the Statistics Division of the United Nations Secretariat.

Fertility

Desired fertility is defined in DHS surveys for childless women as the number of children they would like if they could choose exactly the number to have in their lifetimes; and for women with children as the number of children they would like if they could go back to the time they did not have any children and choose exactly the number to have in their lifetimes.

Unwanted fertility is the proportion of births that women report as unwanted in the previous year. Women are asked about the planning status of births and choose among the categories "Wanted then", "wanted later", or "not wanted".

Unmet need for contraception is the proportion of women of reproductive age currently married or in a union who do not want a pregnancy immediately, but are not using any contraceptive. It includes the need for contraception to space births as well as to limit their number.

Total fertility rate is the number of children that will be born to each woman if all women survive to the end of their reproductive years and bear children at each age at the same rates as the ones observed in a given period. It is calculated as the sum of age-specific fertility rates for women aged between 15 and 49 years. The total fertility rate is said to be below replacement level when it is less than 2.1 births per woman.

Contraceptive use increasing in most developing regions

Contraceptive use has increased in most developing regions since 1980.[28] This trend has continued in recent years **(chart 2.12)**. Contraceptive use among currently married women (or women in informal unions) is high in Eastern Asia, with three quarters of women using some form of contraception. China reports the highest level of contraceptive use—83 per cent **(table 2.A)**. In South-eastern Asia, some countries show high levels of use (for example, Thailand, with 75 per cent use, and Indonesia, with 55 per cent use), while other countries have levels below 20 per cent (for example, the Lao People's Democratic Republic and Myanmar).

Use of contraceptives is also generally high in Western Asia and in Northern Africa, with nearly 50 per cent of women, on average, using some form of contraception **(chart 2.12)**. Contraceptive use, however, remains low in some countries in these regions, with the lowest levels reported in Yemen and Oman—19 and 22 per cent,

respectively **(table 2.A)**. Among the subregions of Asia, Southern Asia has the lowest level of contraceptive use—on average, 37 per cent. In some countries of sub-Saharan Africa (Ghana, Kenya, Malawi, Zambia and Zimbabwe), well over 20 per cent of women use contraception, while in other countries there is 5 to 10 per cent use.

Over 60 per cent of married women in South America use contraceptives, marking a moderate increase since 1990. In Central America and the Caribbean, most countries report contraceptive use well above 50 per cent. Exceptions are Haiti and Guatemala—18 and 31 per cent, respectively.

DHS surveys indicate that contraceptive use increases with women's level of education in all but one of the 22 countries examined. For example, in Cameroon, Madagascar, the Niger, Nigeria and the United Republic of Tanzania, women who have attended secondary school are at least 10 times more likely to use contraception than women with no education. In most other regions, educated women are twice as likely to use contraception as are women with little or no education.[29]

Chart 2.12:

The proportion of married women who use contraception has increased in most developing regions
Percentage currently married women of reproductive age using contraception

	1985/1992	1993/1997
Africa		
Northern Africa	47	50
Southern Africa	31	..
Rest of sub-Saharan Africa	15	18
Latin America and the Caribbean		
Caribbean	52	..
Central America	47	56
South America	57	62
Asia		
Eastern Asia	76	74 [a]
South-eastern Asia	47	49
Southern Asia	35	37
Central Asia	..	58
Western Asia	33	48
Oceania	29	..
Developed regions		
Eastern Europe	..	63
Western Europe	76	74
Other developed regions	71	70

Source: Prepared by the Statistics Division of the United Nations Secretariat from *Women's Indicators and Statistics Database (Wistat), Version 4*, CD-ROM (United Nations publication, Sales No. E.00.XVII.4).

[a] Average based on data for only two countries.

Contraceptives widely used in developed regions

In Western Europe and most developed countries outside Europe, at least 70 per cent of married women currently use some form of contraception. Japan is the exception, with 59 per cent contraceptive use. Eastern Europe also has a relatively low level of contraceptive use—63 per cent **(chart 2.12)**.

According to national surveys in North America, Japan and Europe, contraceptive preference varies widely among countries. For example, female sterilization is the preferred method of contraception in Canada, for 30 per cent of those surveyed. In Japan, 46 per cent of all married couples choose condoms as the preferred method.[30]

Abortion rates decreasing in some developed regions

The use of abortion to terminate an unwanted pregnancy varies widely among regions. Abortion rates have decreased significantly in all countries of North America and Western Europe. However, differences among countries remain substantial, ranging from a high of 30 abortions per 100 births in Denmark, Italy and Sweden to less than 20 per 100 births in Austria, Germany, Greece, the Netherlands, Spain and Switzerland.[31]

In countries where modern methods of contraception are not widely used—particularly in countries in transition—abortion is commonly used as a form of birth control. For example, throughout the 1990s, abortion rates were very high in the Russian Federation,

Gender relations and men's roles and responsibilities

Gender relations within and outside the family play a key role in determining fertility. Men's influence over women often extends to the realm of reproduction, determining decisions about sexual activity and contraceptive use. In addition, men often control access to reproductive health information and services, finances, transportation and other resources. Population and reproductive health programmes are beginning to take these roles into account in formulating ongoing policies and programmes.

Research has indicated that women and men who discuss family planning are more likely to use contraceptives, to use them effectively and, as a result, to have fewer children.[a] DHS surveys show wide variation among countries in the percentages of men who report having discussed family planning with their wives in the year preceding the survey. In seven countries of sub-Saharan Africa, for example, less than half of couples discussed contraception. In eight of 11 countries elsewhere in the developing regions, the majority of men reported that they had discussed issues of contraception with their partners.[b]

Men's reproductive roles and male fertility
Researchers and policy makers are increasingly interested in including men in studies of fertility and family planning.[c] At first, the focus was on improving men's support for women's use of contraceptives and increasing the commitment of male political, religious and community leaders to family planning programmes. More recently, attention has shifted to the importance of gender relations in reproductive behaviour and to understanding men's attitudes toward fertility, reproductive health and their own involvement in family planning.

Most modern contraceptive methods are, however, female methods, and family planning and reproductive health programmes are most often designed for women. Programmes designed to increase men's participation have been hampered by the lack of information about male attitudes and use of contraception. Until recently, the only data on men's reproductive roles were gathered by proxy from their partners, and little was known about men's sexual and reproductive health or the extent to which women and men share in reproductive decision-making and parental responsibilities.

DHS surveys began including men in 1987.

Since then, data have been gathered in 29 developing countries, with more than one DHS survey in eight of them. Data will soon become available for nine additional developing countries.[d] While the first surveys included only married men, more recent surveys also incorporate single men. New questionnaires address health-related behaviours such as drinking and smoking, fathers' participation in children's heath care and men's family life and reproductive preferences.

Men's use of contraception
The condom and vasectomy are male-controlled contraceptive methods. They are generally used much less frequently than female-controlled methods (the pill, injectables, the diaphragm, vaginal barrier methods, the IUD, hormonal implants and female sterilization). Condom use is low throughout most of sub-Saharan Africa, despite the fact that condom use has been shown to have a salutary effect in preventing the spread of HIV/AIDS. Condom use is also relatively low in Western Asia and Northern Africa.[e] Vasectomies are almost non-existent in Africa and popular in only a few Asian countries. Vasectomies are reported by 12 per cent of married couples in the Republic of Korea, by 10 per cent in China, by 5 per cent in Nepal and by 4 per cent in India. In Latin America and the Caribbean, Brazil, Costa Rica and Guatemala are the only countries to report some use.

Traditional contraceptive methods involving male cooperation—withdrawal and periodic abstinence—are not common in developing countries. However, DHS surveys indicate that the use of methods involving male cooperation has increased in several countries—for example, Ghana, Mali and Senegal.

Data from surveys regarding use of contraceptive methods involving men must be interpreted with caution, as women's and men's reports about use often disagree. Married men tend to report considerably higher levels of condom use than married women reporting on use of condoms by their husband. DHS surveys in Kenya found a difference of more than 20 percentage points between men's and women's reporting of overall contraceptive use.[f]

Male fertility
"Male fertility" refers to the number of children that a man fathers during his lifetime. Unlike female fertility, which has been well defined and studied, the determinants of male fertility have not been well developed. The determinants now used are usually linked to the use of contraception, age at first marriage (or union), age of spouse/partner and number of spouses/partners.

Male fertility and contraceptive use gained attention in the developing regions at the end of the 1980s, when it became clear that the family planning programmes of the 1960s and 1970s, which were focused on women, were less successful in lowering fertility than expected. Gender relations and decision-making between partners came to be seen as key elements in determining the success of family planning methods. Surveys conducted in several countries that included men found that men were interested in family planning but that they felt excluded, and that playing a role in determining the number of children they had was important to them.[g]

---

[a] M. Drennan, "New Perspectives on Men's Participation", *Population Reports*, Series J, No. 46 (Baltimore, Johns Hopkins School of Hygiene and Public Health, 1998).

[b] R. Gardner and R. Blackburn, "New reproductive health focus", *Population Reports*, Series J, No. 45 (Baltimore, Maryland, Johns Hopkins School of Hygiene and Public Health, 1998).

[c] Margaret E. Green and Ann E. Biddlecom, "Absent and Problematic Men: Demographic Accounts of Male Reproductive Roles", Population Council Working Paper, No.103 (New York, 1997).

[d] Drennan, op. cit.

[e] Demographic and Health Surveys country reports (Columbia and Calverton, Maryland, Macro International, 1988-1998).

[f] A.C. Ezeh and G. Mboup, "Gender differentials in contraceptive prevalence rates", *Studies in Family Planning*, vol. 28, No. 2 (1997).

[g] Margaret E. Green and Ann E. Biddlecom, "Absent and problematic men: demographic accounts of male reproductive roles", Population Council Working Paper, No.103 (New York, 1997); A. Noumbissi and J. P. Sanderson., "Does man actually decide in Africa?", paper presented at the International Union for the Scientific Study of Population (IUSSP) seminar on the theme "Men, family formation and reproduction", Buenos Aires, 13-15 May 1998; Nii-Amoo Dodoo, "Men matter: additive and interactive gendered preferences in reproductive behaviour in Kenya", *Demography*, vol. 35 , No. 2 (1998); and Mason K. Oppenheimer, H. L. Smith and P. S. Morgan, "The husband's role in determining whether contraception is used: the influence of gender context in five Asian countries", paper presented at a IUSSP seminar on the theme "Men, family formation and reproduction", Buenos Aires, 13-15 May 1998.

Belarus, Estonia and Romania (chart 2.13). In many countries of Eastern Europe, rates are higher today than they were before transition. In some Eastern European countries, there are more abortions than live births (for example, almost two abortions for every live birth in the Russian Federation). The prevalence of abortion in some of the countries in transition seems to be linked to the use of traditional, less-effective methods of contraception, given the limited availability of modern contraception.

Births declining everywhere

In all regions of the world—and in almost all countries—fertility rates are declining. The downward trend in overall levels of fertility has continued around the world, and the upward trend observed during the 1980s in some developed countries—Finland, Sweden and the United States—has reversed.

Between 1990–1995 and 1995–2000, fertility rates decreased by at least 10 per cent in all regions of Asia (except Southern Asia), Northern Africa, Eastern Europe and Central America. In the developed regions outside Eastern Europe and in sub-Saharan Africa, rates decreased by 5 and 7 per cent, respectively (chart 2.14).

In all countries of Eastern Asia (except Mongolia), fertility is now below replacement level (i.e., total fer-

tility rate of less than 2.1 births per woman). The average total fertility rate (TFR) for Eastern Asia is 1.8 births per woman—the lowest in Asia (chart 2.14). Of all Asian countries, those in Eastern Asia have the highest use of contraceptives and the highest age at first marriage, both factors linked to reductions in fertility rates.

The total fertility rate is 3.2 births per woman in South-eastern Asia. In two countries of South-eastern Asia—Singapore and Thailand—fertility levels are below replacement and are thought to be linked to better opportunities for women in education and employment. Other countries in South-eastern Asia have relatively higher levels of fertility (above 3 births per woman in five of 11 countries).

In Western Asia, the total fertility rate is 3.8 births per woman, with wide variations among countries within the region. Countries with rapid economic development have relatively low fertility rates—for example, Turkey (2.5) and Israel (2.7). Other countries have fertility rates between 4 and 5 births per woman (Jordan and the Syrian Arab Republic) or between 5 and 6 (Iraq, Oman and Saudi Arabia). Yemen and the Gaza Strip (within the Occupied Palestinian Territory)[32] have fertility rates among the highest in all of Asia—7 to 8 births per woman.

Southern Asia has the highest regional fertility in Asia—on average, 4.3 births per woman. However, fertility rates vary widely within the region, thought to be due in part to variations in levels of education, the availability of family planning services, and gender equity and equality. For example, in Bangladesh and India, where contraceptive use among women is high for the region (49 and 41 per cent, respectively), the fertility rates are around 3 births per woman; in Pakistan and Afghanistan, where there is less gender equity and equality in education and less access to family planning, the fertility rates are 5 and 7 births per woman, respectively (table 2.A).

Fertility rates in Latin America and the Caribbean range from an average of 2.3 births per woman in the Caribbean to 3.7 in Central America. The only countries with rates above 4 births per woman in these regions are Bolivia, Guatemala, Haiti, Honduras, Nicaragua and Paraguay (table 2.A).

Fertility in sub-Saharan Africa remains the highest in the world, at 5.4 births per woman. The majority of the world's high fertility countries (where women have more than six children) are in sub-Saharan Africa (table 2.A). Between 1990–1995 and 1995–2000, fertility rates have declined in all but three countries of the region.[33]

All Western European countries have fertility rates at or below replacement level. In some of the countries of Southern Europe and in Germany, fertility has reached unprecedented low levels. Fertility is also very

Chart 2.13:
Abortion rates remain high in many countries of Eastern Europe

	Abortions per 100 live births	
	1989	1996/1997
Eastern Europe		
Albania	30	41
Belarus	164	166
Bulgaria	118	135
Croatia	84[a]	18
Czech Republic	99	63
Estonia	116	152
Hungary	88	90
Latvia	126	116
Lithuania	90	60
Poland	15	1
Republic of Moldova	97	82
Romania	52	147
Russian Federation	205	198
Slovakia	70	47
Slovenia	68	54
The FYR of Macedonia	85	41
Ukraine	153	135
Yugoslavia	131	61

Source: United Nations Children's Fund, *Monitoring Eastern Europe*, MONEE Project database (Florence, International Child Development Centre, 1999).

[a] For 1990.

low in Eastern Europe—on average, 1.5 births per woman. Albania is the only country of the region with fertility above replacement level. Fertility levels are slightly higher in the rest of the developed regions. For example, in both New Zealand and the United States, the total fertility rate is 2 births per woman. Japan is the exception, with a total fertility rate of 1.4.

Reasons for low fertility
In low fertility countries, the overall declining trend in fertility is believed to derive from women's increased participation in economic activities, often made possible by private and public investments in higher education and career opportunities for young women. Women who take advantage of such opportunities tend to delay marriage and childbirth.

Declines in fertility levels, however, do not always reflect positive social factors. Adverse economic conditions, including high levels of unemployment, especially among young women, and housing shortages for young couples, may have caused women to post-

pone childbearing or to have fewer children.[34] Society's response to the changing needs of working women in terms of social policies and services has also been limited. In addition, in many countries, men have been slow to respond in terms of sharing the responsibilities of running a home and raising a family.[35] In Italy, for example, 54 per cent of women with children under age 3 spend more than 60 hours a week on paid work and household tasks, compared to 21 per cent of men with children of the same age.[36]

In Eastern Europe, low fertility seems linked to unfavourable social and economic conditions. Policies that encouraged women to have more children rarely succeeded, and the political and economic crisis of 1989-90 increased economic insecurity. Total fertility rates decreased significantly between 1990 and 1997 in most countries in Eastern Europe and Central Asia (chart 2.15).

The United Nations Children's Fund (UNICEF) reports that in countries in transition, couples are no longer having a second or third child, with economic insecurity being given as one of the underlying causes. In addition, the availability of childcare facilities has decreased, while childcare fees have increased. Between 1989 and 1997, enrolment rates in pre-school (for children up to 2 years of age) have fallen in all countries— for example, from 42 to 13 per cent in Latvia.[37]

Births to young women
The highest adolescent fertility rates are in countries of sub-Saharan Africa and Central America, with, on

Chart 2.14:
Fertility levels have declined around the world
Estimated total fertility rate (births per woman)

Africa	1990–1995	1995–2000
Northern Africa	3.9	3.4
Southern Africa	4.8	4.4
Rest of sub-Saharan Africa	5.9	5.5
Latin America and the Caribbean		
Caribbean	2.5	2.3
Central America	4.1	3.7
South America	3.2	2.9
Asia		
Eastern Asia	2.0	1.8
South-eastern Asia	3.6	3.2
Southern Asia	4.7	4.3
Central Asia	3.7	3.3
Western Asia	4.3	3.8
Oceania	4.0	3.7
Developed regions		
Eastern Europe	1.8	1.5
Western Europe	1.7	1.6
Other developed regions	1.9	1.8

Source: Prepared by the Statistics Division of the United Nations Secretariat from *Women's Indicators and Statistics Database (Wistat), Version 4*, CD-ROM (United Nations publication, Sales No. E.00.XVII.4), based on Population Division of the United Nations Secretariat, *World Population Prospects: The 1998 Revision*, vol. I, *Comprehensive Tables* (United Nations publication, Sales No. E.99.XIII.9).

Chart 2.15:
Fertility levels have declined substantially in virtually all transition countries since 1990
Total fertility rate (births per woman)

Eastern Europe	1990	1996/1997	Eastern Europe (cont'd)	1990	1996/1997
Albania	3.0	..	The FYR of Macedonia	2.1	1.9
Belarus	1.9	1.2	Ukraine	1.9	1.3
Bosnia and Herzegovina	1.7	..	Yugoslavia	2.1	1.7
Bulgaria	1.8	1.1	**Asia**		
Croatia	1.6	1.7			
Czech Republic	1.9	1.2	Armenia	2.6	1.5
Estonia	2.1	1.2	Azerbaijan	2.8	2.1
Hungary	1.8	1.4	Georgia	2.2	..
Latvia	2.0	1.1	Kazakhstan	2.7	2.0
Lithuania	2.0	1.4	Kyrgyzstan	3.7	2.8
Poland	2.0	1.5	Tajikistan	5.1	3.6
Republic of Moldova	2.4	1.7	Turkmenistan	4.2	2.9
Romania	1.8	1.3	Uzbekistan	4.1	3.2
Russian Federation	1.9	1.2			
Slovakia	2.1	1.4			
Slovenia	1.5	1.3			

Source: United Nations Children's Fund, *Monitoring Eastern Europe*, MONEE Project database (Florence, International Child Development Centre, 1999).

Chart 2.16:
Adolescent women have children in many parts of the world
Births per 1000 women aged 15-19, 1995–2000

Africa				
Northern Africa	44	South-eastern Asia	40	
Sub-Saharan Africa	130	Southern Asia	85	
		Central Asia	37	
Latin America and the Caribbean		Western Asia	54	
Caribbean	57	**Oceania**	62	
Central America	102			
South America	67	**Developed regions**		
		Eastern Europe	33	
Asia		Western Europe	13	
Eastern Asia	12	Other developed regions	28	

Source: Prepared by the Statistics Division of the United Nations Secretariat from *Women's Indicators and Statistics Database (Wistat), Version 4*, CD-ROM (United Nations publication, Sales No. E.00.XVII.4), based on Population Division of the United Nations Secretariat, *World Population Prospects, The 1998 Revision,* "Age patterns of fertility 1995–2050", data set in digital form.

observed in Eastern Asia and Western Europe, where there are, on average, 12 and 13 births per 1,000 women aged 15 to 19, respectively **(chart 2.16)**.

Births during adolescence are generally more common in the developed regions outside Europe, though rates vary—for example, 4 births per 1,000 young women in Japan and 59 per 1,000 in the United States. In the United States, high fertility levels among young women are linked to particularly high levels of sexual activity among adolescents and low levels of contraceptive use.[38]

Eastern Europe has, on average, 33 births per 1,000 women aged 15 to 19. The highest rates in the region are in Bulgaria and the Russian Federation—49 and 45 births, respectively. However, in Eastern Europe, adolescent births have been decreasing substantially since the onset of the economic transition, perhaps in part because contraceptives have recently become more widely available in some countries of the region.[39]

Data reported by countries in Eastern Asia, Northern Africa and Western Europe[40] indicate that adolescent fertility has declined sharply over the last two decades—average fertility rates are half of those observed in 1980. Births to young women have also decreased significantly in Eastern Europe, the

average, 130 and 102 births per 1,000 young women aged 15 to 19, respectively **(chart 2.16)**.

In Southern Asia, births to young women number 85 per 1,000, although there are wide variations among countries of the region. In Nepal, for example, the adolescent fertility rate is 120 births per 1,000, while in Sri Lanka, the rate is 20 **(table 2.A)**.

The lowest birth rates for young women are

Chart 2.17:
Births outside formal marriage have become more common in developed regions
Percentage of births to unmarried women

	1990	1994/1998		1990	1994/1998
Eastern Europe			**Western Europe** (cont'd)		
Belarus	9	16	Finland	25	37
Bosnia and Herzegovina	7	..	France	30	40[a]
Bulgaria	12	30	Germany	15	19
Croatia	7	7	Greece	2	4
Czech Republic	9	18[a]	Iceland	55	64[a]
Estonia	27	52	Ireland	15	30[a]
Hungary	13	25[a]	Italy	7	9[a]
Latvia	17	35	Luxembourg	13	18
Lithuania	7	17	Netherlands	11	21[a]
Poland	6	11	Norway	39	49[a]
Republic of Moldova	11	17	Portugal	15	20
Romania	4[b]	22[b]	Spain	10	12
Russia	15	25	Sweden	47	55
Slovakia	8	16[a]	Switzerland	6	9[a]
Slovenia	25	33	United Kingdom	28	38[a]
The FYR of Macedonia	7	9			
Ukraine	11	13	**Other developed regions**		
Yugoslavia	13	18	Australia	22	23
Western Europe			Canada	23	37
Austria	24	30	Japan	1	..
Belgium	12	18	New Zealand	34	41
Denmark	46	45	United States	28	32

Sources: Conseil de l'Europe, *Evolution démographique récente* (1998); Eurostat, *Demographic Statistics* (1998 and 1999); and A. Monnier, "La conjoncture démographique: L'Europe et les pays développés d'Outre-mer", *Population*, vol. 5 (1998).

[a] Provisional data.

[b] The sharp increase observed in Romania between 1990 and 1995 is due to an expansion of the definition, which in the past referred only to births from unknown fathers but now includes all births to unmarried women.

Caribbean and Western Asia. Birth rates for young women have decreased only slightly or have stayed the same in Southern Asia, sub-Saharan Africa and the developed regions outside Europe.

Contraceptive practices are important in determining if and when young women have children. In general, young women are much less likely to use contraceptives than are adult women. Adolescents who want to prevent pregnancies are often hindered by lack of access to contraceptive services and products, and family planning programmes are rarely tailored to their needs and circumstances.[41]

For young women, childbearing during adolescence often means the loss of important educational, vocational and social opportunities.[42] Young men are much less likely than young women to become parents during adolescence. Studies show that adolescent parenthood negatively affects young men in terms of educational and occupational opportunities, although the effects are not as severe as for young women.[43]

Births outside marriage
Between 1990 and 1994/1998, births outside marriage increased in all but two countries of the developed regions **(chart 2.17)**. In Eastern Europe, births outside marriage ranged from 7 per cent of all births in Croatia to 52 per cent in Estonia. In Western Europe, the proportion of births to unmarried women ranged from 4 per cent in Greece to 64 per cent in Iceland. In developed countries outside Europe, the proportion of births to unmarried women was 32 per cent in the United States and 37 per cent in Canada. In Japan, births outside marriage account for less than 1 per cent of all births.

Before cohabitation became common, births to unmarried women occurred mostly among women living without partners. Recent European data, however, suggest that many of these births now occur within cohabitation. Exceptions to this general pattern are the Federal Republic of Germany (not including the former German Democratic Republic), the Netherlands and Switzerland. Although cohabitation is reported to be widespread in these countries, the majority of women legalize their unions just before giving birth to their first child.[44]

In most developed countries, childbearing among unmarried, non-cohabiting women is thought to be less prevalent, although national experiences vary widely.[45] The circumstances of single motherhood are not fully understood but may correlate with individual characteristics and social contexts (e.g., societal norms and attitudes, contraceptive availability, socioeconomic status, etc.). In Austria and Germany, for example, the high level of births to single mothers might reflect societal norms. In Lithuania and Poland, high rates of childbearing among unmarried, non-cohabiting women are reported to be linked to limited availability and use of contraception.[46]

The above analysis covers only developed regions because data on the number of births outside marriage are not readily available for developing regions.

Many mothers employed
Throughout the world, women bear most of the responsibility for rearing children, and an increasing number of mothers are also in the labour force. More women are active in formal, paid employment before, during and after child-rearing. Attitudes toward employed mothers have changed profoundly during recent decades. In addition, the unpaid and/or informal work that women do in the home and community has begun to be more fully acknowledged.

Employed mothers in developed countries
Working mothers have many concerns about how to balance work and family responsibilities effectively and how to have men share those responsibilities.[47] The needs of working women have outpaced new accommodations made for women in the workplace and improvements in childcare. The availability and quality of childcare has become a crucial issue in many countries.

In many countries of the European Union (EU) and North America, more than half of all mothers with children under age 3 are employed **(chart 2.18)**.[48]

Chart 2.18:

Many women with young children are employed and their employment levels have increased
Employment/population ratio (per 100), of women with young children [a]

	1983	1992	1997
Western Europe			
Belgium	50	62	69
Denmark	..	43	45
France	48	52	51
Greece	27	42	45
Ireland	18	37	48
Italy	38	42	42
Luxembourg	34	37	46
Netherlands	18	42	59
Portugal	..	69	69
Spain	..	31	39
United Kingdom	21	45	55
Other developed regions			
Canada	42	54	62
United States	42	49	58

Source: Prepared by the Statistics Division of the United Nations Secretariat based on data provided by Eurostat from the European Labour Force Survey, and data provided by Statistics Canada and the United States Bureau of Labor Statistics.

[a] Children under 3 years of age

From the early 1980s to the late 1990s, their employment has increased in all the countries observed. The largest increases were in countries where employment of mothers with young children was particularly low in the 1980s—Ireland, the Netherlands and the United Kingdom. In these countries, employment levels of women with children under age 3 are now comparable to other countries in the EU.

The number of young children women have appears to influence employment levels. In 1997, in all European countries examined, employment levels of women with two or more children aged 5 or younger were substantially lower than those of women with only one young child. For the countries of the European Union, the employment-to-population ratio was 56 per cent for mothers of one child and 32 per cent for mothers of three or more children aged 5 or younger.[49]

Lone mothers (i.e., mothers raising children by themselves) with children under age 3 are, on average, less likely to be employed than all mothers of children under age 3, except in Austria, Italy, Luxembourg and Spain (chart 2.19). Differences across countries between employment of lone mothers and employment of all mothers are not fully understood. The differences may reflect the availability and quality of child-care services, the level of extended family support, the type and efficiency of the country's welfare system and/or the availability of compensation and benefits for working parents.

Data for countries of the European Union indicate that lone mothers have higher unemployment rates than mothers living with partners. In 1996, for the European Union as a whole, the unemployment rate of lone mothers was 17 per cent, compared to 11 per cent for mothers living with their partners, 10 per cent for lone fathers and 6 per cent for other heads of households with dependent children.[50] In Canada, a decrease in the employment of lone mothers was largely attributed to the economic recessions of early 1980s and early 1990s, but this trend was not observed among mothers who were living with a partner.[51]

Employed mothers in developing regions

Young children also influence women's working patterns in developing regions. In sub-Saharan Africa, women with children under age 5 tend to be a mi-

Chart 2.19:

In most countries in Western Europe, lone mothers with young children are less likely to be employed than all mothers with young childen
Employment/population ratio (per 100), women with young children[a], 1997

Western Europe	Lone mothers	All mothers
Austria	77	72
Belgium	51	69
Denmark	39	45
France	36	51
Greece	43	45
Ireland	26	48
Italy	60	42
Luxembourg	49	46
Netherlands	34	59
Portugal	52	69
Spain	53	39
United Kingdom	24	55

Source: Prepared by the Statistics Division of the United Nations Secretariat based on data provided by Eurostat from the European Labour Force Survey.

[a] Children under 3 years of age.

Chart 2.20:

In sub-Saharan Africa, women with young children tend to be a minority among women working for an employer but a majority among the self-employed
Percentage with young children[a], 1994/1998

	Among women working for an employer	Among self-employed women
Sub-Saharan Africa		
Benin	27	57
Central African Republic	31	51
Comoros	30	45
Kenya	40	58
Madagascar	40	62
Mali	43	66
Mozambique	51	60
Niger	44	67
Uganda	49	67
Zambia	41	64
Zimbabwe	37	59
Latin America and the Caribbean		
Dominican Republic	33	36
Guatemala	35	46
Haiti	49	35
Asia		
Jordan	69	64
Kyrgyzstan	29	30
Nepal	57	61
Uzbekistan	13	32
Yemen	70	67

Source: Compiled by the Statistics Division of the United Nations Secretariat from Demographic and Health Surveys country reports (Calverton, Maryland, Macro International, 1994-1998).

[a] Children under 6 years of age, except in Benin (under 3 years) and in Brazil and the Central African Republic (under 5 years).

nority among women working for an employer but a majority among those self-employed **(chart 2.20)**. Data on three countries in Latin America and the Caribbean indicate that women with young children represent a minority of both women who work for an employer and those who are self-employed. There are data for only a few countries in Asia, and the findings are mixed.

It is often assumed that in developing countries, employed mothers work mostly at home, where they can combine childcare with other work, paid or unpaid. However, data from 23 countries in Africa, Asia and Latin America and the Caribbean indicate that a majority of working women with children under age 5 work away from home. In all countries examined (except Bangladesh and Malawi), more than half of all working mothers work away from home.[52]

Data also show that women, lacking quality childcare, must take their children to work with them. In 10 of the 12 countries surveyed in sub-Saharan Africa, and in Pakistan and Peru, over 40 per cent of women have their small children with them when they work away from home.[53]

LIVING ARRANGEMENTS

Living arrangements for women, men and families are changing throughout the world. Families are becoming more dispersed as members are separating from one another. There are many possible arrangements: spouses or partners live separately, especially when one spouse migrates away from home for work; couples separate and/or divorce; children live away from one or both of their parents; young adults live apart from their families; and elderly people live alone instead of with close relatives.[54] In many parts of the world, these changes, together with an overall reduction in the number of children that women are having, are producing smaller households.

Lone-parent families becoming more common in developed regions

Lone-parent families (families in which children are raised by only one parent) are becoming more common in many developed countries **(chart 2.21)** and the lone parent is usually the mother. In the United States in 1998, of all families with children, a third—almost 12 million families—were lone-parent families, up from 28 per cent in 1990.[55] In Canada in 1996, there were 1.1 million lone-parent families—22 per cent of all families with children at home. Mothers account for over 80 per cent of lone-parent families in all these countries.

Lone-parent families are most often the result of separation, divorce or widowhood, or of unmarried,

non-cohabiting women giving birth. In the case of divorce, the partner who becomes the lone parent is most often the woman, as mothers are usually given custody of children. In Italy in 1997, for example, 90 per cent of children whose parents divorced stayed with their mothers; 6 per cent with their fathers; and the rest were in joint custody.[56]

Never-married women represent an increasingly significant proportion of lone mothers. In the United States in 1998, 42 per cent of lone mothers had never been married.[57] In Canada in 1996, 24 per cent of all lone mothers had never been married.[58]

The lone-parent family headed by the mother is arousing concern because its prevalence is growing and because it often places mothers and children in

Chart 2.21:
Lone-parent families in developed regions
Percentage of families with children[a] that are lone-parent families

	1988/1991	1995/1998
Eastern Europe		
Hungary	20 [b]	..
Poland	14	22
Former USSR	15 [b]	..
Western Europe		
Denmark	19 [c]	19
Finland	17 [c]	18
France	12	17
Germany	16	..
Iceland	20 [c]	..
Italy	14	..
Netherlands	18	..
Norway	20	22
Sweden	22	..
United Kingdom	15	..
Other developed regions		
Australia	17	20
Canada	19	22
Japan	5	..
United States	28	34

Sources: Institut national de la statistique et des études économiques, "Un parent seul dans une famille sur huit" (1994); for Canada: Statistics Canada, "1996 Census: marital status, common-law unions and families", *The Daily*, accessed on 14 October 1997 at: http://www.statcan.ca; for the United States: Lynne M. Casper and Ken Bryson, "Household and family characteristics: March 1998 (update)", in United States Bureau of the Census, *Current Population Reports*, accessed in October 1998 at: http://www.census.gov; for other countries, national statistical yearbooks, various years.

[a] Cut-off ages used to define children vary among countries.

[b] Data are for 1984/1985.

[c] Data are for 1994.

Household and family

According to the United Nations recommendations[a], a household is classified as either (a) a one-person household, in which one person makes provision for his or her own food or other essentials for living or (b) a multi-person household, defined as a group of two or more persons living together who make common provision for food or other essentials for living. The persons in the group may pool their incomes and have a common budget to a greater or lesser extent; they may be related or unrelated persons.

Many countries adopt an alternative concept, the so-called household-dwelling concept, where a household consists of all persons living together in a housing unit.

The United Nations recommendations define the family as those members of the household who are related, to a specified degree, through blood, adoption or marriage. In practice, most households consist of a family. However, these two concepts cannot be used interchangeably. A household may consist of only one person but a family must contain at least two members and the members of a multi-person household need not be related to each other, while the members of a family must be related.

The recommendations also define a family nucleus as a married couple living together without children, a married couple with one or more unmarried children, or a mother or father living with one or more unmarried children.

[a] See United Nations, *Principles and Recommendations for Population and Housing Censuses* (United Nations publication, Sales No. E.98.XVII.8)

economic need. Everywhere in the developed regions, lone mothers tend to be poorer than mothers who live with a partner, and even poorer in comparison to lone fathers.

In some countries, attention is turning toward lone fathers. In the United States, the number of lone fathers has been growing in recent years. While the number of lone mothers remained at 9.8 million from 1995 to 1998, the number of lone fathers increased nearly 25 per cent—from 1.7 million to 2.1 million—over the same period. Over half of these lone fathers are divorced or separated, while just over a third have never been married.[59] Of almost 40,000 Canadian divorces involving children in 1997, the father received sole custody in 11 per cent of the cases and joint custody in 28 per cent.[60]

Children of lone mothers often economically disadvantaged

There is some evidence that the number of children living with lone parents—either mothers or fathers—has been increasing. In the EU (excluding Denmark and Sweden), 10.7 million children were living with only one parent in 1996, representing 13 per cent of all dependent children. The percentage of children living with only one parent has been growing since 1983 and has more than doubled in Ireland and the United Kingdom.[61] In Canada, almost one in

five children lived in lone-parent families in 1996, up from one in six in 1991. In 1998, the United States had the highest proportion of children living in lone-parent families—28 per cent of children under 18, or a total of 19.8 million children.[62]

In the United States, children living with both parents usually have financial and educational advantages over those in lone-parent families. Children living with a divorced parent, however, generally fare better than those living with a never-married parent, who is more likely to have a low level of education and, as a result, fewer employment opportunities. Children who live with lone fathers have an economic advantage over those who live with lone mothers.[63] Nearly 60 per cent of children with lone mothers live near or below the poverty line—69 per cent of children with never-married mothers, as compared to 45 per cent of those with divorced mothers. In both cases, mothers are most often unemployed.[64]

In EU countries, too, there is evidence that children of lone mothers may be disadvantaged.[65] In 1996, 17 per cent of lone mothers in the EU were unemployed, compared to 11 per cent of mothers with partners, and 6 per cent of all other heads of families with dependent children. The adjusted income of lone-parent families in 1994 was 77 per cent that of other families.[66]

Chart 2.22:

In some developing countries, many children, particularly girls, do not live with either parent
Percentage of adolescents aged 12-14 living with neither parent, 1992/1996

	W	M		W	M
North Africa			**Sub-Saharan Africa** (cont'd)		
Morocco	8	9	Zambia	28	25
			Zimbabwe	27	24
Sub-Saharan Africa					
Benin	33	19	**Latin America and the Caribbean**		
Burkina Faso	21	16			
Cameroon[a]	26	24	Brazil	12	9
Central African Republic	28	25	Colombia	14	13
Comoros	28	23	Dominican Republic[a]	27	18
Côte d'Ivoire	36	25	Guatemala	9	8
Ghana	30	20	Haiti	36	26
Kenya	19	15	Paraguay[a]	17	12
Madagascar	22	21			
Mali	18	11	**Asia**		
Namibia	42	36	Indonesia	9	7
Niger[a]	26	16	Kazakhstan	10	5
Nigeria	22	16	Pakistan[a]	4	4
Senegal	21	20	Philippines	11	9
Uganda	31	27	Turkey	3	3
United Rep. of Tanzania	23	22	Uzbekistan	2	2

Source: Barbara S. Mensch, Judith Bruce and Margaret E. Greene, *The Uncharted Passage: Girls' Adolescence in the Developing World* (New York, Population Council, 1998).

[a] Data for this country refer to 1990/1991.

Many children living away from their parents in the developing regions

In developing regions, especially in sub-Saharan Africa and to a lesser extent in Latin America and the Caribbean, large numbers of adolescents do not live with their biological parents. For example, in Benin, Côte d'Ivoire, Haiti, Namibia and Uganda, at least one third of girls, and at least one fifth of boys, aged 12 to 14, do not live with their parents (chart 2.22).

In some of the sub-Saharan African countries considered—Benin, Côte d'Ivoire, Ghana, Mali, the Niger and Nigeria—and in the Dominican Republic, Haiti and Paraguay, considerably more girls than boys live away from their biological parents. In Asia and Northern Africa, it is much less common for children to live apart from their parents and sex differentials tend to be small (chart 2.22). Many of these children are placed in foster households because their biological parents think the children will have better access to education and work than they would if they stayed with their biological parents. Others are in foster households because their parents cannot afford to raise them (sometimes due to the number of children in the family) or are otherwise unable or unwilling to care for them. Still other children have been abandoned or orphaned. Large numbers of children have been orphaned because of acquired immunodeficiency syndrome (AIDS). Worldwide, more than 8 million children are estimated to have lost their mothers to AIDS, and 90 per cent of these children live in sub-Saharan Africa. In Uganda alone, 1.7 million children have lost one or both parents to AIDS since 1980.[67]

Foster households represent 20 per cent of all households in most of the African countries surveyed by DHS.[68] In the Latin American and Caribbean countries surveyed, at least 7 per cent of households included foster children. There is some evidence that fostered children work longer hours and have higher rates of morbidity and mortality than siblings who remain at home and that the younger the child when she or he is fostered away, the more detrimental it will be to the child's well-being.[69] AIDS orphans often face the additional problems of neglect and isolation because of the social stigma attached to the disease.

Other studies show that fostered children in sub-Saharan Africa, especially girls, are likely to end up as servants in the foster household. There is no evidence that fostered children enjoy better access to education. In fact, DHS data for 26 countries in sub-Saharan Africa, Latin America and the Caribbean and Central Asia (countries of the former USSR) show that enrolment of fostered children aged 12 to 14 is often lower than enrolment of children living with their parents.[70]

Women make up most of one-person households

In developed regions, one-person households are becoming more common, and these usually consist of unmarried elderly persons or young adults. Women comprise the majority of one-person households (chart 2.23).

Chart 2.23:
One-person households have increased in developed regions, and women comprise a majority of these households

	% households that are one-person		% women among one-person households, around 1990
	1970	1995/1998	
Eastern Europe			
Bulgaria	17	20[a]	57
Czech Republic	19	27	61
Hungary	17	26	64
Poland	16	20	65
Romania	14	17[a]	67
Slovakia	12	22	65
Slovenia	..	18[a]	67
The FYR of Macedonia	..	..	64
Yugoslavia	13	14[a]	..
Western Europe			
Austria	25	29	66
Belgium	19	27	59
Denmark	22	37	58
Finland	24	35	63
France	20	30	63
Germany	..	35	..
Greece	11	21	64
Ireland	13	23	53
Italy	13	23	66
Luxembourg	16	26[a]	61
Netherlands	17	32	58
Norway	21	45	54
Portugal	10	14	70
Spain	7	13	55
Sweden	25	40[a]	55
Switzerland	20	32[a]	59
United Kingdom	18	28	62
Other developed regions			
Australia	14	24	..
Canada	13	23[a]	58
Japan	20	26	44
New Zealand	..	20	58
United States	17	25	61

Sources: Eurostat, "Populations, ménages et logements en Europe: principaux recensements de 1990-91", Theme 3, Serie C; "Demographic trends and family in postcommunist countries" (1997); national statistical yearbooks.

[a] Data are for 1990/1993.

In Western European countries, the percentage of all households that are one-person households ranged from 7 to 25 per cent in 1970 and from 13 to 45 per cent in 1998. The percentage of one-person households also increased in all countries of Eastern Europe and in the developed regions outside Europe over the same period. One-person households now account for 14 to 27 per cent of all households in Eastern Europe, and for 20 to 26 per cent in the developed countries outside Europe.

In all developed countries except Japan, women make up the majority—55 to 70 per cent—of one-person households (chart 2.23), and many of these women are older persons. At older ages, many more women than men live alone. Among the member States of the European Union, for example, 39 per cent of women aged 60 or over lived alone, compared to 15 per cent of men in the same age group. By age 75 or over, 56 per cent of women are living alone, compared to 22 per cent of men.[71]

Older widows, in particular, tend to live alone. For example, in the United States, in 1998, 70 percent of widows aged 65 or over lived alone;[72] in Canada, in 1995, 75 per cent lived alone.[73]

Women-headed households common in some regions

Headship measures are not straightforward and data are not easily comparable. The designation of "headship" may depend on the culture, on prevalent living arrangements and on definitions and criteria adopted in data collection. Whether women perceive and report themselves as household heads varies across cultures, and is often dependent upon whether there is an adult male in the household. Moreover, a number of countries have substituted the concept of "reference person" for household head in their data-collection programmes. Use of a reference person as a substitute for household head rests on the assumption that the person so designated coincides with the person recognized by household members as head of household.

Since it is usually assumed that household heads have primary authority and responsibility for household affairs and in most cases are its chief economic support, available statistics on men and women heads of household considerably understate women's household responsibilities. However, these statistics do provide an indication of the number of households where women have sole responsibility for supporting the household.

Women are reported as household head or reference person in 9 to 42 per cent of households in all regions of the world (chart 2.24). The percentage of women-headed households is highest in Southern Africa and the Caribbean—42 and 36 per cent, respectively. The high percentages in these regions are thought to be due to the relatively late age at marriage for women and the prevalence of informal unions and of births outside marriage. Moreover, in countries of Southern Africa, where female headship is traditional, women are more likely to be listed as the household's head even when the household contains an adult male.

Female headship is also common in some sub-Saharan African countries (other than those in Southern Africa). For example, more than 30 per cent of households are headed by women in Botswana, Ghana, Kenya, Namibia, Swaziland and Zimbabwe (table 2.A). In sub-Saharan Africa, high rates of female headship may be linked to male migration and family dissolution, or to the matrilineal structure of kinship groups.[74]

In the developed regions, around 30 per cent of heads of household are women, although there are wide variations within the regions. In the Nordic countries[75], for example, almost 40 per cent of household heads are women, compared to around 20 per cent in Portugal and Greece. In the developed regions outside Europe, the percentage of women heads of household ranges from 17 in Japan to 37 in New Zealand.

In developed countries, a higher percentage of women-headed households reflects large numbers of both older widows and younger unmarried women living alone. This high percentage also suggests that it is easier in these countries for a woman to be recorded as head of household even when there is a man present.

In all regions, the percentage of heads of household who are aged 60 or over is higher among women than among men (chart 2.25). The highest percentage of women heads of household aged 60 or over is in Europe (46). By comparison, roughly 25 per cent of women heads of household are aged 60 or over in

Chart 2.24:

Women head a significant number of households in most regions

Percentage of household heads who are women, 1985/1997

Africa

Northern Africa	12
Southern Africa	42
Rest of sub-Saharan Africa	21

Latin America and the Caribbean

Caribbean	36
Central America	22
South America	22

Asia

Eastern Asia	22
South-eastern Asia	19
Southern Asia	9
Central Asia	24
Western Asia	10

Oceania	15

Developed regions

Eastern Europe	27
Western Europe	29
Other developed regions	31

Source: Prepared by the Statistics Division of the United Nations Secretariat from *Women's Indicators and Statistics Database (Wistat)*, *Version 4*, CD-ROM (United Nations publication, Sales No. E.00.XVII.4).

Note: Averages for some regions are based on a small number of countries.

Chart 2.25:

More than one fourth of women heads of household are aged 60 or over

Percentage of household heads aged 60+, 1985/1997

Region	W	M
Africa	24	18
Caribbean	26	20
Latin America	31	17
Asia	34	16
Europe	46	26
Other developed regions	32	22

Source: Prepared by the Statistics Division of the United Nations Secretariat from *Women's Indicators and Statistics Database (Wistat)*, *Version 4*, CD-ROM (United Nations publication, Sales No. E.00.XVII.4).

African and Caribbean countries. Female headship in these countries is less linked to widowhood and more to male migration for work, the prevalence of consensual and visiting unions or polygyny, or a traditional preference for matrilineal over conjugal ties.[76]

DHS surveys offer some insight into women-headed households. In general, women-headed households are smaller than male-headed households, probably because many of the former contain only one person. In addition, when a family unit with a female head is absorbed into a larger extended household, the male member of the extended household is most likely to be recognized as its head.[77] Differences in household size by sex of head of household are smallest in Latin America (five members, on average, when headed by men and four when headed by women) and in some sub-Saharan African countries. Differences are more pronounced in countries in Northern Africa and Western Asia (six members, on average, when headed by men and four members when headed by women).[78]

Women heads of household are more likely to be separated, divorced or widowed in Western Asia and Northern Africa (over 80 per cent in three of four countries surveyed) while fewer are separated, divorced or widowed in sub-Saharan Africa (between 44 and 72 per cent in the four countries considered). Studies generally show that separated, divorced or widowed women heads are more likely to be econom-ically disadvantaged than women who are still married and who often continue to receive remittance money from the absent husband.[79]

The limited data available seem to indicate a slightly upward trend in the number of women-headed households in some of the sub-Saharan African countries surveyed by DHS. In eight countries, the percentage of women-headed households increased, in one country it slightly decreased and in the three other countries it remained the same. In Latin America, the percentage of households headed by women increased in five of the six countries for which data are available. Data in the other regions are sparse and do not indicate any clear trend.[80]

Women-headed households are often used to assess the prevalence of households assumed to be especially vulnerable to poverty. This assumption may not always be valid: a women-headed household may consist of a woman living alone, a mother with children who receives adequate financial support from her partner, a lone mother solely responsible for the household or several other household types that merit investigation. Moreover, the relative vulnerability of women and those who depend on them for economic support is linked to such factors as the relative disadvantage that women face in accessing societal resources and the relative advantage that women may have in terms of accessing intra-familial support. ■

Notes

1 United Nations, *Population and Development–Programme of Action adopted at the International Conference on Population and Development, Cairo, 5-13 September 1994, Population Studies*, No. 149 (United Nations publication, Sales No. E.95.XIII.7).

2 Mead T. Cain, "Patriarchal structure and demographic change", in *Women's Position and Demographic Change*, Nora Federici, Karen O. Mason and Solvi Sogner, eds., (Oxford, England, Clarendon Press, 1993); and Barbara S. Mensch, Judith Bruce and Margaret E. Greene, *The Uncharted Passage: Girls' Adolescence in the Developing World* (New York, Population Council, 1998).

3 Mensch et al., op. cit.

4 Ibid.

5 A.E. Calves and D. Meekers, *Re-evaluating the Value of Children in sub-Saharan Africa: the Impact of Changing Forms of Marital Unions*, Population Research Institute Working Paper, No. AD95-05 (Pennsylvania State University, 1995).

6 See G. Letamo, "Modernization and premarital dyadic formations in Botswana", in *Proceedings of the International Population Conference, Montreal, 1993* (International Union for the Scientific Study of Population), vol. 1.

7 Teresa Castro Martin, "Marriages without papers in Latin America", in *Proceedings of the International Population Conference, Beijing, 1997* (International Union for the Scientific Study of Population).

8 Ian Timæus and Angela Reynar, "Polygynists and their wives in sub-Saharan Africa: an analysis of five Demographic and Health Surveys", *Population Studies*, vol. 52 (1998).

9 Ibid.

10 Castro Martin, loc. cit.

11 Statistics Canada, "Divorces", *The Daily*, accessed on 18 May 1999 at http://www.statcan.ca.

12 National Vital Statistics Reports, National Vital Statistics System, U.S. Department of Health and Human Services, July 6, 1999, Vol. 47, Number 21.

13 Statistics Canada, "Divorces"...

14 Conseil de l'Europe, *Evolution démographique récente*, 1998; Statistical Office of the European Communities (Eurostat), *Demographic Statistics* (1998 and 1999); A. Monnier, "La conjoncture démographique: L'Europe et les pays développés d'Outre-mer", *Population*, vol. 5 (1998).

15 Eurostat, "Un mariage sur quatre environ se termine par un divorce dans l'UE", *Divorce: Statistiques en Bref*, No. 14 (1997).

16 Ibid.

17 Statistics Canada, "Divorces"...

18 Eurostat, *Demographic Statistics* (1998 and 1999).

19 Data and analysis prepared by Catherine de Guibert-Lantoine, as consultant to the Statistics Division of the United Nations Secretariat.

20 Rosella Rettaroli, "Le seconde nozze", in Marzio Barbagli and Chiara Saraceno, *Lo stato delle famiglie in Italia* (Bologna, Societa' editrice il Mulino, 1997).

21 John Haskey, "Divorce and remarriage in England and Wales", *Population Trends* (Spring 1999).

22 United Nations, *World Population Monitoring, 2000: Population, Gender and Development* (United Nations publication, forthcoming).

23 United Nations, *Population and Development...*

24 United Nations Population Fund, *The State of the World Population 1997*.

25 C.F. Westoff and L. H. Ochoa, "Unmet need and the demand for family planning", Demographic and Health Surveys, Comparative Studies, No. 5 (Columbia, Maryland, Institute for Resource Development, 1991).

26 Data on percentages of currently married women or women in a union with unmet needs are from United Nations, *Women's Indicators and Statistics Database (Wistat), Version 4*, CD-ROM (United Nations publication, Sales No. E.00.XVII.4) and DHS country reports.

27 Based on data compiled in United Nations, *Women's Indicators and Statistics Database (Wistat), Version 4*, CD-ROM (United Nations publication, Sales No. E.00.XVII.4) from DHS Surveys.

28 United Nations, *World Population Monitoring, 1999: Population Growth, Structure and Distribution* (United Nations publication, Sales No. E.00.XIII.4).

29 S. L. Curtis and K. Neitzel, *Contraceptive Knowledge, Use and Sources*, Demographic and Health Surveys, Comparative Studies, No. 19 (Calverton, Maryland, Macro International, 1996).

30 United Nations, *Women's Indicators and Statistics Database...*

31 H.P. David and J. Rademakers, "Lessons from the Dutch abortion experience", *Studies in Family Planning*, vol. 27, No. 6; A Kulczycki, "Religious system and abortion: representation and reality", *Proceedings of the International Population Conference, Beijing, 1997* (International Union for the Scientific Study of Population); S.K. Henshaw, "Abortion incidence and services in the United States", *Family Planning Perspectives*, vol. 30, No. 6; and S. Salvini and D'Andrea S. Schifini, "Induced abortion in Italy: levels, trends and characteristics", *Family Planning Perspectives*, vol. 28, No. 6.

32 Estimates of total fertility rates are available only for Gaza Strip and not for all territories. Data reported by the Palestinian Central Bureau of Statistics indicate a total fertility rate for the Occupied Territories of 6 (5.8 in the West Bank and 7.8 in the Gaza Strip). See Palestinian Central Bureau of Statistics, *Women and Men in Palestine: Trends and Statistics, 1998*, (Ramallah, 1998).

33 United Nations, *Women's Indicators and Statistics Database...*

34 Britta Hoem and Jan M. Hoem, "Fertility trends in Sweden up to 1996", in United Nations, Expert Group on Below-Replacement Fertility, New York, 4-6 November 1997 (ESA/P/WP.140); UNICEF, *Women in Transition, 1999*, Regional Monitoring Report, No. 6 (Florence, 1999); and M. Delgado Perez and Massimo Livi-Bacci, "Fertility in Italy and Spain: the lowest in the world", *Family Planning Perspectives*, vol. 24, No. 4, 1992.

35 Hoem et al., loc. cit.; and Delgado Perez et al., loc. cit.

36 Based on data accessed at http://www.istat.it.

37 UNICEF, *Women in Transition, 1999*, Regional Monitoring Report, No. 6 (Florence, 1999).

38 D.M. Upchurch, L. Levy-Storms, C.A. Sucoff and C.S. Ansehensel, "Gender and ethnic differences in the timing of first sexual intercourse", *Family Planning Perspectives*, vol. 30, No. 3.

39 UNICEF, *Monitoring Eastern Europe*, MONEE Project database (Florence, International Child Development Centre, 1999).

40 Estimates of age-specific fertility rates for the period preceding 1995–2000 are not available in *World Population Prospects: The 1998 Revision*. The assessment of trends is based on actual data reported by countries and compiled also in *Women's Indicators and Statistics Database...*

41 A. K. Blanc and A. A. Way, "Sexual behavior, contraceptive knowledge and use", in J. Bongaarts and B. Cohen, eds., "Adolescent reproductive behavior in the developing world", *Studies in Family Planning*, vol. 29, No. 2 (1998).

42 Mensch et al., op. cit.

43 United Nations, *World Population Monitoring 2000....*

44 E. Klijzing and M. Macura, "Cohabitation and extra-marital childbearing: early FFS evidence", in *Proceedings of the International Population Conference, Beijing, 1997* (International Union for the Scientific Study of Population).

45 Ibid.

46 Ibid.

47 Eurostat, "Lone-parent families: a growing phenomenon", in *Statistics in Focus: Population and Social Conditions* (Luxembourg, 1998).

48 The analysis on working mothers is based mainly on data provided by Eurostat.

49 Data provided by Eurostat from European Labour Force Surveys.

50 Eurostat, "Lone-parent families: a growing phenomenon"...

51 Marcia Almey, "Labour force characteristics", in *Women in Canada: A Statistical Report* (Statistics Canada, 1995).

52 Sunita Kishor and Katherine Neitzel, *The Status of Women: Indicators for Twenty-five Countries*, DHS Comparative Studies, No. 21 (Calverton, Maryland, Macro International, 1996).

53 Ibid.

54 Judith Bruce, Cynthia B. Lloyd and Ann Leonard, *Families in Focus: New Perspectives on Mothers, Fathers and Children* (New York, Population Council, 1995).

55 Lynne M. Casper and Ken Bryson, "Household and family characteristics: March 1998 (update)", in United States Bureau of the Census, *Current Population Reports*, accessed in October 1998 at http://www.census.gov.

56 ISTAT, Italian National Statistical Office, accessed at http://www.istat.it.

57 Casper and Bryson, loc. cit.

58 Statistics Canada, "1996 Census: marital status, common-law unions and families", *The Daily*, accessed on 14 October 1997 at http://www.statcan.ca.

59 United States Bureau of the Census, "Father's Day 1999: June 20", press release, accessed on 10 June 1999 at http://www.census.gov.

60 Statistics Canada, "Divorces"...

61 Eurostat, "Lone-parent families: a growing phenomenon"...

62 Terry A. Lugaila, "Marital status and living arrangements: March 1998 (Update)", United States Bureau of the Census, *Current Population Reports*, accessed on 29 October 1998 at http://www.census.gov.

63 United States Bureau of the Census, "Census brief: children with single parents, how they fare", accessed in September 1997 at http://www.census.gov.

64 Ibid.

65 Eurostat, "Lone-parent families: a growing phenomenon"...

66 Ibid.

67 United Nations Children's Fund, *The Progress of Nations* (1999).

68 Demographic and Health Surveys, country reports (Calverton, Maryland, Macro International, 1995–1998).

69 Bruce et al., op. cit.

70 Mensch et al., op. cit.

71 United Nations, *World Population Monitoring 2000...*

72 United States Bureau of the Census, Economic and Statistics Administration data, and *Current Population Survey* (March 1998), main tables, accessed on 27 July 1998 at http://www.census.gov.

73 Bess Irwin, "Widows living alone", *Canadian Social Trends*, summer 1999, accessed at www.statcan.ca.

74 Mohamed Ayad, Bernard Barrère and James Otto, *Demographic and Socioeconomic Characteristics of Households*, Demographic and Health Surveys Comparative Studies, No. 26 (Calverton, Maryland, Macro International, 1997); and Kishor and Neitzel, op. cit.

75 Nordic countries include Denmark, Finland, Iceland, Norway, and Sweden; a recent figure for Iceland is not available and is therefore not included in the average.

76 Kishor and Neitzel, op. cit.

77 Ayad et al., op. cit.

78 Ibid.

79 Ayad et al., op. cit.

80 Kishor and Neitzel, op. cit.; Ayad et al., op. cit.; and data compiled by the Statistics Division of the United Nations Secretariat from Demographic and Health Surveys, country reports.

Table 2.A
Marriage, households and childbearing

Country or area	% 15-19 ever married, 1991/1998		Singulate mean age at at marriage, 1991/1997		% 60+ widowed, 1991/1997		Average household size, 1991/1994	% women-headed households, 1991/1997	Contraceptive use, currently married women (%), 1991/1998	Total fertility rate (births per woman)		Births per 1000 women aged 15-19, 1995-2000
	W	M	W	M	W	M				1990-1995	1995-2000	
Africa												
Algeria	10 a	1 a	24 a	28 a	55 a	6 a	7.0 a	11 a	52 b c	4.3	3.8	25
Angola	..	..	..	..	..	..	..	..	..	7.2	6.8	219
Benin	29	..	..	..	..	..	5.9	18	16	6.3	5.8	116
Botswana	6	3	27	31	45	9	4.8 a	47	33 a	4.9	4.4	78
Burkina Faso	45	..	19	28	37	6	6.2 a	7	8	7.1	6.6	157
Burundi	9 a	2 a	23 a	26 a	54 a	7 a	4.6 a	25 a	9 a	6.8	6.3	55
Cameroon	36	4	20	..	..	..	5.2 a	18	19	5.7	5.3	140
Cape Verde	7 a	1 a	26 a	28 a	26 a	8 a	5.0 a	38 a	..	3.9	3.6	79
Central African Republic	42	8	19 a	24 a	44 a	9 a	4.7 a	21	15	5.3	4.9	142
Chad	49	6	..	..	..	..	..	22	4	6.6	6.1	185
Comoros	12	3	22	29	23 d	3 d	6.2	25	21	5.4	4.8	83
Congo	..	..	..	..	..	..	..	..	..	6.3	6.1	141
Côte d'Ivoire	28	2	20 a	28 a	55 a	9 a	6.0 a	15	11	5.7	5.1	133
Dem. Rep. of the Congo	..	..	..	..	..	..	..	..	8	6.7	6.4	217
Djibouti	7 e	1 e	19 a	27 a	..	..	6.6	18	..	5.8	5.3	31
Egypt	14	..	22 a	26 a	60 a	12 a	4.9 a	13	47	3.8	3.4	65
Equatorial Guinea	..	..	..	..	..	..	..	..	..	5.9	5.6	178
Eritrea	38	2	..	..	..	..	..	31	5	6.1	5.7	119
Ethiopia	49 a f	8 a f			43 a f	6 a f	..	..	4 a c	6.6	6.3	152
Gabon	16	2	..	..	46	9	..	..	..	5.2	5.4	172
Gambia	..	..	..	..	..	..	..	..	12 a	5.6	5.2	155
Ghana	22	2	21 a	..	..	..	4.8 a	37	20	5.7	5.2	113
Guinea	49	..	..	..	..	..	7.2	7	2	6.0	5.5	193
Guinea-Bissau	..	..	..	..	..	..	7.9	..	..	6.0	5.8	190
Kenya	17	1	21 a	..	33 a	5 a	5.2 a	33	39	5.4	4.5	95
Lesotho	17 a e	2 a e	..	..	..	..	5.1 a	..	23 g	5.0	4.8	86
Liberia	46 a	..	20 a	..	..	..	5.0 a	19 a	6 a	6.8	6.3	213
Libyan Arab Jamahiriya	..	..	..	..	..	..	..	..	40	4.1	3.8	56
Madagascar	34	..	..	..	..	..	4.5	22	19	5.9	5.4	137
Malawi	45 a	9 a	19 a	24 a	40 a	6 a	4.3 a	26	22	7.2	6.8	162
Mali	50	5	19 a	28 a	46 a	5 a	5.6 a	8	7	7.1	6.6	181
Mauritania	..	..	23 a	30 a	..	..	..	..	3 a	5.9	5.5	135
Mauritius	11 a	1 a	24 a	28 a	71 a	13 a	4.4 a	18 a	75	2.3	1.9	37
Morocco	13	1	22 a	..	71	6	6.0 a	15	50	3.3	3.1	50
Mozambique	47	4	..	..	..	..	..	27	6	6.5	6.3	128
Namibia	7	3	..	..	30 h	5 h	5.2	39	29	5.3	4.9	105
Niger	62	4	17 a	23 a	64 a	5 a	6.4 a	10 a	8	7.4	6.8	199
Nigeria	36	7	..	..	46	5	5.4 a	14 a	6 a	5.7	5.2	121
Reunion	2 a	<1 a	28 a	30 a	45 a	12 a	3.8 a	..	67 a	2.4	2.1	20
Rwanda	10	..	..	..	..	..	4.7	25	21	6.6	6.2	56
Sao Tome and Principe	20	2	18	23	..	..	4.3	33	..	..	..	..
Senegal	29	..	20 a	29 a	54 a	5 a	8.8	18	13	6.1	5.6	119
Seychelles	6 a	1 a	24 a	26 a	27 a	9 a	4.5 a	..	..	..	..	..
Sierra Leone	..	..	18 a	27 a	..	..	5.7 a	11 a	4 a	6.5	6.1	202
Somalia	..	..	..	..	..	..	..	..	1 a	7.3	7.3	213

Table 2.A (cont'd):
Marriage, households and childbearing

Country or area	% 15-19 ever married, 1991/1998		Singulate mean age at at marriage, 1991/1997		% 60+ widowed, 1991/1997		Average household size, 1991/1994	% women-headed households, 1991/1997	Contraceptive use, currently married women (%), 1991/1998	Total fertility rate (births per woman)		Births per 1000 women aged 15-19, 1995-2000
	W	M	W	M	W	M				1990-1995	1995-2000	
Africa (cont'd)												
South Africa	4 [i]	1 [i]	27 [i]	29 [i]	49	12	5.8 [i]	..	50 [a]	3.6	3.3	68
Sudan	16 [aj]	..	24	..	..	..	6.3 [a]	13 [a]	10	5.0	4.6	52
Swaziland	10	2	26	29	25	2	..	40 [a]	20 [ak]	5.1	4.7	90
Togo	20	2	20 [a]	..	..	..	5.1 [a]	26 [a]	24	6.6	6.1	120
Tunisia	3	<1	25 [a]	..	49	7	5.4 [a]	11 [a]	60	3.1	2.6	13
Uganda	50	11	19	24	53	11	5.4 [a]	29	15	7.1	7.1	180
United Rep. of Tanzania	25	3	21	..	..	..	5.2 [a]	22	18	5.9	5.5	125
Western Sahara	..	..	..	..	..	..	..	..	..	4.5	4.0	53
Zambia	27	1	21 [a]	26 [a]	34 [ad]	4 [ad]	5.6	17 [a]	26	6.0	5.6	134
Zimbabwe	21	2	21	26	53	7	5.2 [a]	33	48	4.5	3.8	89
Latin America and the Caribbean												
Antigua and Barbuda	..	..	..	..	..	..	3.1	..	53 [a]	..	..	..
Argentina	12	8	23	26	44	30	3.7	22	74 [a]	2.8	2.6	65
Aruba	3	<1	26	29	37	13	3.4	..	..	..	..	..
Bahamas	4 [a]	1 [a]	27 [a]	29 [a]	43 [a]	14 [a]	4.1 [a]	36 [a]	62 [a]	2.6	2.6	69
Barbados	..	..	..	..	..	..	..	..	55 [a]	1.7	1.5	44
Belize	7 [l]	1 [l]	..	..	32	13	4.8	22	47	4.2	3.7	99
Bolivia	12	..	23	25	43 [a]	17 [a]	4.6 [a]	24	48	4.8	4.4	79
Brazil	17	..	..	..	42	11	4.2 [a]	18	77	2.5	2.3	72
Chile	12	5	23	26	39	13	4.0	25	..	2.5	2.4	49
Colombia	17	..	23 [a]	26 [a]	41	12	4.5	24	72	3.0	2.8	88
Costa Rica	6 [m]	1 [m]	..	..	34	11	4.3	20	75	3.0	2.8	85
Cuba	..	..	..	..	..	..	4.0 [a]	..	70 [a]	1.6	1.6	65
Dominica	..	..	..	..	..	..	..	..	50 [a]	..	..	..
Dominican Republic	29	..	..	..	..	..	4.5	25	64	3.1	2.8	89
Ecuador	20 [a]	7 [a]	22 [a]	25 [a]	31 [a]	12 [a]	4.8 [a]	..	57	3.5	3.1	72
El Salvador	16	4	22	25	35	13	4.1	27 [a]	53	3.5	3.2	95
French Guiana	1 [a]	<1 [a]	29 [a]	32 [a]	25 [a]	7 [a]	3.4 [a]	..	..	..	..	..
Grenada	..	..	..	..	..	..	..	..	54 [a]	..	..	..
Guadeloupe	1 [a]	<1 [a]	30 [a]	32 [a]	28 [a]	9 [a]	3.4 [a]	..	..	2.1	1.9	29
Guatemala	23	..	21 [a]	24 [a]	46 [a]	12 [a]	..	20	31	5.4	4.9	119
Guyana	..	..	..	..	..	..	..	..	..	2.6	2.3	58
Haiti	17	3	24 [a]	27 [a]	30	9	5.0	39	18	4.8	4.4	70
Honduras	..	..	..	..	..	..	5.4 [a]	20 [a]	50	4.9	4.3	115
Jamaica	1	1	..	..	31	12	..	38	67	2.8	2.5	91
Martinique	1 [a]	<1 [a]	31 [a]	33 [a]	30 [a]	11 [a]	3.3 [a]	..	..	1.9	1.8	27
Mexico	16 [a]	6 [a]	..	..	37 [a]	12 [a]	5.0 [a]	17 [a]	67	3.1	2.8	70
Netherlands Antilles	2	1	29	32	..	13	3.3	34	..	2.3	2.2	35
Nicaragua	34	..	..	..	..	..	..	28 [a]	60	4.9	4.4	152
Panama	21 [a]	5 [a]	22 [a]	25 [a]	32 [a]	11 [a]	4.4 [a]	22 [a]	..	2.9	2.6	82
Paraguay	17	3	22	26	30	11	4.7	21	56	4.6	4.2	76
Peru	13	..	..	..	..	..	5.2 [a]	23	64	3.4	3.0	58
Puerto Rico	15 [a]	6 [a]	24 [a]	26 [a]	40 [a]	13 [a]	3.9 [a]	32 [a]	..	2.2	2.1	70
Saint Kitts and Nevis	..	..	..	..	..	..	..	..	..	..	..	..

Table 2.A (cont'd):
Marriage, households and childbearing

Country or area	% 15-19 ever married, 1991/1998		Singulate mean age at marriage, 1991/1997		% 60+ widowed, 1991/1997		Average household size, 1991/1994	% women-headed households, 1991/1997	Contraceptive use, currently married women (%), 1991/1998	Total fertility rate (births per woman)		Births per 1000 women aged 15-19, 1995-2000
	W	M	W	M	W	M				1990-1995	1995-2000	
Latin America and the Caribbean (cont'd)												
Saint Lucia	..	..	..	..	..	..	4.0	..	47 [a]	..	..	..
St. Vincent/Grenadines	1	<1	31	35	25	14	..	..	58 [a]	..	..	..
Suriname	..	..	..	..	..	..	..	..	..	2.5	2.2	22
Trinidad and Tobago	11 [a]	5 [a]	..	..	41 [a]	16 [a]	4.1 [a]	..	53 [a]	2.1	1.7	40
Uruguay	13	3	23 [a]	25 [a]	42	10	3.3 [a]	23 [a]	..	2.5	2.4	70
US Virgin Islands	..	..	..	..	..	..	3.2 [a]	45 [a]	..	..	..	..
Venezuela	20 [a]	8 [a]	..	..	35 [a]	10 [a]	4.8 [a]	21 [a]	..	3.3	3.0	98
Asia												
Afghanistan	..	..	..	..	..	..	..	..	..	6.9	6.9	153
Armenia	15 [a,e]	2 [a,e]	23	27	..	..	4.4 [a]	..	..	2.2	1.7	41
Azerbaijan	9 [a,e]	1 [a,e]	23	27	..	..	4.5 [a]	..	..	2.6	2.0	17
Bahrain	7	<1	26	28	53	8	5.6	..	61	3.4	2.9	22
Bangladesh	50	..	18 [a]	26 [a]	56	4	5.5	9	49	3.4	3.1	115
Bhutan	..	..	..	..	..	..	..	..	19 [g]	5.8	5.5	71
Brunei Darussalam	8	1	25	27	43	13	5.8	..	..	3.1	2.8	33
Cambodia	..	..	..	..	..	..	..	..	..	4.9	4.6	14
China	2 [n]	1 [n]	22 [a,n]	24 [a,n]	45 [n]	19 [n]	4.0 [a,n]	..	83 [n]	1.9 [n]	1.8 [n]	5 [n]
Hong Kong SAR	2	1	28	30	43 [d]	11 [d]	3.4	27	86	1.3	1.3	7
Macao SAR	2	1	26	28	45	13	3.6	21	..	1.6	1.4	6
Cyprus	8	1	23	27	39	13	3.2 [o]	14 [o]	..	2.3	2.0	17
Dem. People's Rep. of Korea	..	..	..	..	..	..	..	..	62	2.2	2.1	2
East Timor	..	..	..	..	..	..	..	..	..	4.8	4.4	37
Georgia	17 [a,e]	3 [a,e]	25	28	..	..	3.7 [a]	..	..	2.1	1.9	47
India	39	..	..	..	54	15	5.5	9	41	3.6	3.1	112
Indonesia	14	2	22	25	57	12	4.5 [a]	13	57	2.9	2.6	58
Iran (Islamic Rep. of)	22	3	21	25	48	7	5.1 [a]	6	65	4.1	2.8	29
Iraq	28 [a]	15 [a]	22 [a]	26 [a]	45 [a]	8 [a]	7.3 [a]	..	14 [a]	5.7	5.3	45
Israel	5	<1	24	28	..	..	..	..	..	2.9	2.7	19
Jordan	9	1	25	28	50	7	6.9	..	50	5.6	4.9	43
Kazakhstan	13	..	22	25	59 [a]	14 [a]	3.6 [a]	..	59	2.5	2.3	54
Kuwait	13	1	25	30	51	4	6.5 [a]	5 [a]	35 [a]	3.2	2.9	34
Kyrgyzstan	14	..	22	25	59 [a]	12 [a]	4.7 [a]	26	60	3.6	3.2	40
Lao People's Dem. Rep.	..	..	..	..	..	..	..	..	19 [p]	6.3	5.8	104
Lebanon	..	..	..	..	..	..	..	..	59	3.1	2.7	26
Malaysia	8	1	..	..	51	12	4.8	18	48 [a]	3.6	3.2	25
Maldives	36 [a]	6 [a]	19 [a]	23 [a]	..	..	6.8 [a]	..	..	6.0	5.4	54
Mongolia	..	..	..	..	..	..	..	..	61 [g]	3.4	2.6	47
Myanmar	..	..	..	..	..	..	..	..	17	2.7	2.4	26
Nepal	44	..	..	..	48 [a]	18 [a]	5.6	13	29	4.9	4.5	120
Occ. Palestinian Territory	..	..	..	..	..	..	..	..	..	7.8 [q]	7.3 [q]	142 [q]
Oman	..	..	19 [a]	26 [a]	..	..	7.0	..	22	6.7	5.9	80
Pakistan	22	6	22 [a]	27 [a]	..	..	6.5 [a]	7 [a]	18	5.5	5.0	90
Philippines	10	3	24 [a]	26 [a]	41	14	5.3 [a]	11 [a]	47	4.0	3.6	43
Qatar	14 [a]	4 [a]	23 [a]	27 [a]	53 [a]	5 [a]	5.6 [a]	..	32 [a]	4.1	3.7	66

Table 2.A (cont'd):
Marriage, households and childbearing

Country or area	% 15-19 ever married, 1991/1998 W	% 15-19 ever married, 1991/1998 M	Singulate mean age at at marriage, 1991/1997 W	Singulate mean age at at marriage, 1991/1997 M	% 60+ widowed, 1991/1997 W	% 60+ widowed, 1991/1997 M	Average household size, 1991/1994	% women-headed households, 1991/1997	Contraceptive use, currently married women (%), 1991/1998	Total fertility rate (births per woman) 1990-1995	Total fertility rate (births per woman) 1995-2000	Births per 1000 women aged 15-19, 1995-2000
Asia (cont'd)												
Republic of Korea	1	<1	25 a	29 a	62	12	3.7 a	17	79	1.7	1.7	4
Saudi Arabia	16 a	1 a	22 a	26 a	..	..	7.4 a	..	..	6.4	5.8	113
Singapore	1 a	<1 a	27 a	30 a	54 a	16 a	4.2 a	..	..	1.8	1.7	7
Sri Lanka	7 a	..	..	..	..	..	..	..	66 r	2.2	2.1	20
Syrian Arab Republic	..	..	..	..	..	..	6.0	..	40	4.7	4.0	44
Tajikistan	12 a	2 a	21 a	23 a	56 a	14 a	5.7 a	..	..	4.5	4.2	35
Thailand	6	6	24 a	26 a	47 a	16 a	4.4 a	..	74	1.9	1.7	70
Turkey	14	..	22 a	25 a	45 a	11 a	5.0 a	10	63	2.7	2.5	44
Turkmenistan	6 a e	1 a e	24 a	..	..	..	5.2 a	..	..	4.0	3.6	20
United Arab Emirates	19 a	3 a	23 a	26 a	..	..	..	..	27	3.8	3.4	73
Uzbekistan	13	..	20	..	..	..	5.2 a	22	56	3.8	3.5	35
Viet Nam	11 a	5 a	23 a	24 a	53 a	15 a	4.8 a	32 a	65	3.3	2.6	27
Yemen	24	5	19 a s	23 a s	..	..	5.8 a s	12	19	7.6	7.6	102
Oceania												
American Samoa	5 a	2 a	26 a	28 a	46 a	11 a	7.0 a	..	..	..	..	..
Fiji	13 a	2 a	23 a	25 a	49 a	14 a	5.7 a	12 a	40 a	3.0	2.7	48
French Polynesia	3 a e	1 a e	28 a	30 a	..	..	4.7 a	18 a	..	3.1	2.9	68
Guam	6 a e	2 a e	24 a	27 a	..	..	4.0 a	21 a	..	3.5	3.4	96
Kiribati	16 a e	6 a e	22 a	25 a	..	..	6.4 a	..	37 a	..	..	..
Marshall Islands	23 a e	7 a e	..	..	..	..	8.7 a	..	..	..	..	..
Micronesia (Fed. States of)	10	4	..	..	..	..	7.5 a	..	..	..	..	..
New Caledonia	2 a	<1 a	28 a	31 a	46 a	15 a	4.0 a	16 a	25 a g	2.9	2.7	55
Palau	3 a e	1 a e	..	..	..	..	5.0 a	..	..	..	..	..
Papua New Guinea	21	..	21 a	25 a	..	..	..	8	26	5.1	4.6	24
Samoa	4 a e	1 a e	25 a	28 a	..	..	6.7 a	13 a	34 a	4.7	4.2	37
Solomon Islands	18 a e	3 a e	21 a	25 a	..	..	6.5 a	16 a	3 a g	5.4	4.9	94
Tonga	6 a	3 a	25 a	27 a	39 a	16 a	6.2 a	20 a	74 a	..	..	..
Vanuatu	13 a	3 a	23 a	25 a	38 a	17 a	5.0 a	..	15 g	4.7	4.3	74
Developed regions												
Albania	..	..	22	27	..	..	..	..	..	2.8	2.5	34
Andorra	..	..	..	..	..	..	..	..	..	..	..	..
Australia	2	1	27	29	38	11	3.0 a	..	76 a	1.9	1.8	20
Austria	3	1	26	29	47	13	..	..	..	1.5	1.4	18
Belarus	8 a	2 a	22	24	53 a	12 a	2.7 a	..	50	1.7	1.4	36
Belgium	2	<1	25	28	44	14	..	..	79	1.6	1.6	11
Bermuda	1	<1	29	31	38	11	2.6	34	..	..	..	..
Bosnia and Herzegovina	..	..	23 a	..	..	..	..	..	..	1.5	1.4	28
Bulgaria	16 a	3 a	23	27	43 a	17 a	3.0 a	18 a	..	1.5	1.2	49
Canada	1	<1	26	29	39	11	2.8	30	75	1.7	1.6	23
Croatia	5	1	25	28	48	12	3.1	..	..	1.6	1.6	19
Czech Republic	2	<1	23	26	50	13	2.5	26	69	1.7	1.2	23
Denmark	5	1	30 t	32 t	41	14	2.3 a	42	78 a u	1.8	1.7	9
Estonia	7 a e	2 a e	24	26	..	..	3.1 a	..	70 u	1.6	1.3	38
Finland	1	<1	29	32	41	11	2.5 a	42	..	1.8	1.7	10

Table 2.A (cont'd):
Marriage, households and childbearing

Country or area	% 15-19 ever married, 1991/1998 W	M	Singulate mean age at at marriage, 1991/1997 W	M	% 60+ widowed, 1991/1997 W	M	Average household size, 1991/1994	% women-headed households, 1991/1997	Contraceptive use, currently married women (%), 1991/1998	Total fertility rate (births per woman) 1990-1995	1995-2000	Births per 1000 women aged 15-19, 1995-2000
Developed regions (cont'd)												
France	1 [a]	<1 [a]	28 [a]	30 [a]	43 [a]	11 [a]	2.6 [a]	..	75	1.7	1.7	9
Germany	2	<1	28	30	46	13	2.3 [a v]	27 [a v]	75	1.3	1.3	11
Greece	6	1	25	29	42	10	3.0	20	..	1.4	1.3	13
Hungary	3	<1	24	27	52	16	2.7 [a]	35	73	1.7	1.4	28
Iceland	<1	<1	30	32	34	12	..	..	..	2.2	2.1	24
Ireland	<1	<1	28	29	41	12	3.3	26	..	2.0	1.9	19
Italy	..	..	27 [t]	30 [t]	..	..	2.9	..	..	1.3	1.2	7
Japan	1	1	27 [a]	30 [a]	41	10	3.0 [a]	17 [a]	59	1.5	1.4	4
Latvia	9 [a]	3 [a]	24	26	51 [a]	14 [a]	3.1 [a]	..	48	1.6	1.3	27
Liechtenstein	1 [a]	<1 [a]	26 [a]	29 [a]	41 [a]	8 [a]	..	..	..	..	..	..
Lithuania	7 [a]	3 [a]	23	25	50 [a]	13 [a]	3.2 [a]	..	59	1.8	1.4	37
Luxembourg	3 [a]	<1 [a]	26 [a]	28 [a]	23 [a]	14 [a]	2.7	26	..	1.7	1.7	12
Malta	3 [a]	<1 [a]	22 [a]	26 [a]	37 [a]	16 [a]	3.3 [a]	..	..	2.0	1.9	12
Monaco	..	..	..	..	..	..	..	..	..	..	..	..
Netherlands	1	<1	28	31	40	11	..	..	79	1.6	1.5	4
New Zealand	2	2	27	29	41	12	2.8	37	75	2.1	2.0	34
Norway	<1	<1	29	31	42	13	2.4 [a]	34 [a]	76 [a]	1.9	1.9	13
Poland	2	<1	23 [a]	26 [a]	45	20	3.1 [a]	31 [a]	..	1.9	1.5	23
Portugal	6	1	24	27	39	12	3.1	20	..	1.5	1.4	20
Republic of Moldova	14 [a e]	2 [a e]	22	24	..	..	3.4 [a]	..	74	2.2	1.8	32
Romania	7	<1	23	26	45	11	3.1	22	57	1.5	1.2	36
Russian Federation	11 [a]	3 [a]	23	25	55 [a]	12 [a]	2.8 [a]	..	..	1.5	1.3	45
San Marino	1	<1	27	29	41	10	2.8	19 [a]	..	..	..	..
Slovakia	7	1	21	24	53	15	2.9	23	74 [u]	1.9	1.4	32
Slovenia	2	1	26	29	45	12	3.1	44	..	1.4	1.3	17
Spain	3	1	26	28	38	11	..	..	59 [a]	1.3	1.2	8
Sweden	<1	<1	31	33	38	12	2.2 [a]	37 [a]	..	2.0	1.6	7
Switzerland	1	<1	27	30	38	11	2.4 [a]	28 [a]	..	1.5	1.5	4
The FYR of Macedonia	9	2	23 [a]	..	37	16	3.8	..	..	2.2	2.1	42
Ukraine	16 [a]	3 [a]	21 [a]	24 [a]	54 [a]	13 [a]	2.8 [a]	..	..	1.6	1.4	36
United Kingdom	1	<1	26 [a]	28 [a]	43	14	..	..	82 [w]	1.8	1.7	29
United States	4	2	25 [a t]	26 [a t]	34 [d]	10 [d]	2.6 [a]	36	74 [a]	2.1	2.0	59
Yugoslavia	12	3	24	28	41	14	3.6	22	..	2.0	1.8	39

Sources: *Women's Indicators and Statistics Database (Wistat), Version 4*, CD-ROM (United Nations publication, Sales No. E.00.XVII.4), based on various international and national sources, in particular the *Demographic Yearbook* (United Nations publication, various years up to 1997) and unpublished updates for statistics on marital status and household size; Population Division of the United Nations Secretariat, *World Population Prospects: The 1998 Revision*, vol. I, *Comprehensive Tables* (United Nations publication, Sales No. 99.XIII.9) for total fertility rate, and "Age Patterns of Fertility 1995-2050" (data set in digital form) for births per 1000 women aged 15-19.

[a] Data refer to a year between 1985 and 1990.

[b] Excluding sterilization.

[c] For all ever-married women of reproductive age.

[d] Data refer to the population aged 55+.

[e] Per cent currently married.

[f] Data shown are for former Ethiopia.

[g] For all women of reproductive age.

[h] Data refer to the population aged 50+.

[i] Excluding Bophuthatswana, Ciskei, Transkei and Venda.

[j] Data refer to urban and settled rural population only

[k] Including single women of reproductive age who have borne a child.

[l] Data refer to ages 14-19.

[m] Data refer to ages 9-19.

[n] For statistical purposes, data for China do not include Hong Kong and Macao Special Administrative Regions (SAR).

[o] Data refer to government controlled areas only.

[p] Not a nationally representative sample; national prevalence level probably lower than indicated.

[q] Data refer to the Gaza Strip only.

[r] Excluding several northern and eastern areas containing roughly 15 per cent of the population.

[s] Data shown are for the former Yemen Arab Republic.

[t] Average age at first marriage.

[u] For all sexually active women of reproductive age.

[v] Data shown are for the former Federal Republic of Germany.

[w] Excluding Northern Ireland.

Technical notes

The first six columns of **table 2.A** are indicators on the timing of first marriage and selected marital status of women and men at selected ages. The series on singulate mean age at marriage are those published in the 1995 *Demographic Yearbook*, supplemented by national sources and compilations prepared by the Population Division of the United Nations Secretariat from a worldwide review of the available information; for countries in transition, data were obtained from the MONEE Project database of the United Nations Children's Fund. The indicators % 15-19 ever married and % 60+ widowed were derived from statistics reported in the *Demographic Yearbook* and unpublished updates, and from the Demographic and Health Surveys country reports; these data are also available in *Women's Indicators and Statistics Database (Wistat)*.

Singulate mean age at first marriage, the average age at which women and men first marry, is an estimate of the average number of years lived prior to first marriage by a hypothetical cohort, if they marry before age 50. Singulate mean age at marriage is calculated on the basis of a single census or survey according to procedures described by Hajnal.[a] The definition and a further explanation of this indicator are provided in a sidebar on age at first marriage.

Statistics on marital status are derived from population censuses and demographic sample surveys. Two categories of marital status are included in table 2.A: ever married for the age group 15-19 and widowed for the age group 60 or over. All individuals who have ever been married are included in the first category, regardless of their current marital status.

Statistics on marital status may be affected by inaccurate responses to the question on marital status. For example, divorced persons may be erroneously reported as being single or married. Also, married males who are separated from their wives tend to report themselves as single, while their wives are more likely to report themselves correctly as married.

The next two columns of table 2.A present household size and percentage of households headed by women. These indicators are based mainly on population census results provided by national statistical services to the Statistics Division of the United Nations Secretariat for the *Demographic Yearbook*. They are supplemented by data from the Demographic and Health Surveys and other national reports. These data are also contained in *Wistat*.

The definition of household recommended by the United Nations for use in population and housing censuses is given in a sidebar in the chapter. In most censuses, persons not resident in a given household at the date of the census are not considered members of that household. However, a few national population censuses may include some categories of absent household members. In population censuses in most countries, the head of the household is defined as that person in the household or the family who is acknowledged as such by the other members. However, it is important to recognize that the procedures followed in applying the concept may distort the true picture, particularly with regard to women heads of households. Nonetheless, for most countries, this is the only practical way of identifying households for which women are responsible (see the section on women-headed households in the chapter).

The last four columns of table 2.A are indicators of contraceptive use and fertility. Data on contraceptive use among currently married women of reproductive age are drawn mainly from the compilation by the Population Division of the United Nations Secretariat and the Demographic and Health Surveys country reports. Statistics on contraceptive use are taken mainly from representative national sample surveys of women of reproductive age. Contraceptive use pertains to current use by currently married women or women currently in a union, unless otherwise indicated, and includes all contraceptive methods, traditional as well as modern. These data are also available in *Wistat*.

Indicators of fertility presented in table 2.A are estimates and projections prepared by the Population Division of the United Nations Secretariat in 1998 and are given as five-year averages. These data are also available in *Wistat*.

The total fertility rate is defined as the number of children that would be born to a woman if she were to live to the end of her childbearing years and bear children at each age in accordance with prevailing age-specific fertility rates. Births per 1,000 women aged 15-19 refers to the number of children born alive in one year per 1,000 women aged 15-19.

[a] J. Hajnal, "Age at marriage and proportions marrying", *Population Studies*, vol. 7, No. 2 (1953).

CHAPTER 3

Health

> ## Some important findings:
>
> - Life expectancy continues to increase for women and men in most developing regions but has decreased dramatically in Southern Africa as a result of AIDS.
>
> - Infant mortality is generally higher for boys than for girls, except in some countries in Asia where gender-based discrimination outweighs girls' biological advantage.
>
> - Where women are sexually active at a young age, they are at risk of suffering short- and long-term consequences of sexually transmitted infections (including HIV), early pregnancy and unsafe abortion.
>
> - Data on maternal mortality and other causes of death are often unavailable or, where available, are unreliable due to deficiencies in vital statistics registration systems.
>
> - Women now account for almost half of all cases of HIV/AIDS, and in countries with high HIV prevalence, young women are at higher risk of contracting HIV than young men.
>
> - New efforts are being made to measure health expectancy—not just life expectancy—of the world's ageing population.

Women's and men's health differ in significant ways, including how they are exposed to disease, how susceptible they are to diseases, how they are treated for diseases and what their outcomes are. These differences are often related to socio-economic and cultural factors that affect nutrition, lifestyle, access to health services and the overall health risks that women and men face throughout their lives. Recent global conferences have made the gender issues in health over the entire lifespan—birth, infancy, childhood, adolescence, the reproductive years and the older years—a focus for improved data collection and statistical analysis.

LIFE EXPECTANCY

Women are known to have an advantage over men in terms of life expectancy, an advantage thought to be linked to innate genetic and biological differences between the sexes. This advantage starts at birth and continues through the life of the individual, with men having greater vulnerability than women to diseases and injuries leading to death. Under normal circumstances, women can be expected to outlive men by several years. However, where women's life expectancy is only slightly higher, similar to or even lower than that of men, cultural, social, economic and/or environmental factors detrimental to women may have offset this "natural" advantage.[1]

Women live longer than men in all regions

Life expectancy is highest for both women and men in the developed countries outside Europe (on average, 81 years for women and 75 for men) and in Western Europe (80 and 74, respectively). Life expectancy is between 75 and 76 years for women in the Caribbean, Eastern Europe and Eastern Asia, and 70 years for men in the Caribbean and Eastern Asia (chart 3.1).

Life expectancy is lowest in sub-Saharan Africa (excluding Southern Africa)—on average, 51 years for women and 48 years for men. In Southern Africa, the dramatic increase in mortality due to acquired immunodeficiency syndrome (AIDS) has brought the average life expectancy down to 56 years for women and 52 years for men.

Women's advantage in life expectancy is six years in Western Europe, in developed regions outside Europe and in South America and the Caribbean. The largest gender gaps in life expectancy are in Eastern Europe and Central Asia, where women's life expectancy exceeds men's by eight years. Women survive men by as many as 10 years or more in several countries of the former USSR (table 3.A). In these transition countries, the life expectancy differential may be the result of war and civil unrest, economic uncertainty and substance abuse, which have taken a particularly high toll on the male population.[2]

Infant and child mortality rates

Infant mortality rate is the number of deaths in a given year of children less than one year old, divided by the total proportion of live births in the same year, multiplied by 1,000. It is an approximation of the proportion of children, per 1,000, who are born alive but die within one year of birth.

Child mortality rate is the number of deaths per 1,000 children aged 1 to 4. It is calculated as the number of deaths in a given year of children aged 1 to 4 years, divided by the mid-year population of the age group, multiplied by 1,000.

Where women's life expectancy is lower or only slightly higher than that of men, cultural factors are believed to adversely affect the situation and the status of women. In Bangladesh and India, for example, women's average life expectancy is about equal to that of men; in Nepal, it is lower.

Life expectancy decreasing dramatically in Southern Africa

Life expectancy has continued to increase for women and men in Asia, Northern Africa and Latin America and the Caribbean. The greatest gains in recent years were in Southern Asia, Northern Africa, and Central and South America, where life expectancy increased by about two years (chart 3.1).

In most countries of the developed regions, life expectancy—already high in the early 1990s—has remained high. At the same time, the negative trend in life expectancy observed in the past 20 years in transition countries, especially for men, has partly reversed.[3]

Estimates of life expectancy for women and men show a dramatic decrease in Southern Africa, where AIDS has contributed to a high mortality rate. Life expectancy is estimated to have declined by five years for women and men between 1990–1995 and 1995–2000 (chart 3.1).

Life expectancy is still below 60 years for women in 50 countries and for men in 57 countries (table 3.A). In 23 countries, life expectancy is below 50 years for women and below 48 years for men (chart 3.2).

In contrast, 22 countries report life expectancy for women of 80 years, compared to 14 countries reporting the same life expectancy for women five years ago. Nowhere in the world is men's life expectancy as high. The highest life expectancy for men is 77 years, in Iceland and Japan (table 3.A).

THE HEALTH OF CHILDREN AND ADOLESCENTS

Survey data indicate that mortality is consistently higher for newborn boys than girls during the first month of life, when perinatal conditions—conditions originating during pregnancy and labour and specific to the newborn—are most likely to be the cause of death. During the first years of life (excluding the first month), sex differentials in mortality tend to vary across countries and may reflect social and cultural factors. This differential varies even more widely between ages 1 and 5. While in most countries boys aged 1 to 5 have higher mortality than do girls, in some countries of the developing regions there is evidence of higher mortality for girls or of a significantly smaller advantage for girls over boys during these years (see section below on higher mortality for young girls).[4]

Ascertaining sex differentials in infant and child mortality is difficult because data are not widely available. Existing studies on sex differentials in infant and child mortality have generally relied on data obtained from demographic surveys, although there are problems with these data, including errors in the reporting of deaths and sampling errors.[5] Nevertheless, researchers and policy makers are interested in appraising gender differences in infant and child mortality, especially in countries where the girl child faces discrimination and where cultural preference for sons is strong.

Chart 3.1+:

Life expectancy has continued to increase for both women and men, except in Southern Africa

Life expectancy at birth

	1990-1995		1995-2000	
	W	**M**	**W**	**M**
Africa				
Northern Africa	67	64	69	66
Southern Africa	61	57	56	52
Rest of sub-Saharan Africa	51	47	51	48
Latin America and the Caribbean				
Caribbean	75	70	76	70
Central America	72	67	74	69
South America	71	65	73	67
Asia				
Eastern Asia	74	69	75	70
South-eastern Asia	65	61	66	62
Southern Asia	60	59	62	61
Central Asia	71	63	71	63
Western Asia	72	68	73	69
Oceania	71	66	72	68
Developed regions				
Eastern Europe	75	66	75	67
Western Europe	80	74	80	74
Other developed regions	81	75	81	75

✤ In this and subsequent charts, regional and subregional averages are unweighted (i.e., the averages do not take into account the size of the individual countries' populations) and are based only upon available data for that region (see page xi for fuller explanation).

Source: Prepared by the Statistics Division of the United Nations Secretariat from *Women's Indicators and Statistics Database (Wistat), Version 4,* CD-ROM (United Nations publication, Sales No. E.00.XVII.4), based on Population Division of the United Nations Secretariat, *World Population Prospects: The 1998 Revision,* vol. I, *Comprehensive Tables* (United Nations publication, Sales No. E.99.XIII.9).

Higher infant mortality among girls in some countries

The infant mortality rate declined dramatically between 1975 and 1995 and has continued to decline in all regions of the world. Although the gap in rates of infant mortality between developed and developing regions is narrowing, it is still wide.[6] Infant survival improved significantly in Northern Africa and Southern and South-eastern Asia—infant mortality rates for both girls and boys decreased by 8 or 9 deaths per 1,000 live births, on average, over the last five years (chart 3.3). Although the infant mortality rate also decreased by 8 deaths per 1,000 live births in sub-Saharan Africa, the region still has the highest infant mortality rate of all regions. In 1995-2000, on average, 86 girls and 98 boys died before age one for every 1,000 born in sub-Saharan Africa, compared to 41 girls and 48 boys, respectively, in Northern Africa.

In comparison, the infant mortality rate in Eastern Asia has declined from an average of 27 deaths per 1,000 live births for girls and 26 for boys in 1990-1995 to an average of 24 for girls and 23 for boys in 1995-2000. However, in the most populous countries of Southern Asia—Bangladesh, India and Pakistan—infant mortality rates range from 73 to 79 for girls and from 67 to 78 for boys (table 3.A), despite substantial declines in infant mortality in the region during the 1990s. In South America, infant mortality rates are, on average, 31 deaths per 1,000 live births for girls and 40 for boys, and in the Caribbean, 17 for girls and 22 for boys.

Every country in Western Europe, and every developed country outside Europe, has fewer than 10 infant deaths per 1,000 live births for both girls and boys, and many have an infant mortality rate of 7 or lower. Japan and Norway have the lowest infant mortality rates of all developed countries—4 deaths per 1,000 live births among girls and 5 among boys. In Eastern Europe, infant mortality rates range from 10 to 30 deaths per 1,000 in all countries except the Czech Republic and Slovenia, where they are below 10.

While infant mortality is generally higher for boys than for girls, in a few countries in Eastern, South-eastern and Southern Asia and in Oceania the biological advantage that girls have over boys seems to be outweighed by cultural and behavioural factors, such as gender-based discrimination.[7] In India, for example, there are 78 deaths among girls under age 1 for every 1,000 girls born alive, versus 67 deaths among boys. In China, the corresponding figures are 48 for girls and 35 for boys (chart 3.4).

Higher mortality for young girls linked to discriminatory practices

For many children, especially girls, childhood ushers in a relatively healthy stage of life, due largely to health

Chart 3.2:
Life expectancy for both women and men is below 50 years in many countries of sub-Saharan Africa
Life expectancy at birth, 1995-2000

Africa	W	M	Africa (cont'd)	W	M
Angola	48	45	United Rep. of Tanzania	49	47
Botswana	48	46	Zambia	41	40
Burkina Faso	45	44	Zimbabwe	41	40
Burundi	44	41			
Central African Republic	47	43	**Asia**		
Chad	49	46	Afghanistan	46	45
Côte d'Ivoire	47	46	East Timor	48	47
Ethiopia	44	42			
Gambia	49	45			
Guinea	47	46			
Guinea-Bissau	46	44			
Liberia	49	46			
Malawi	40	39			
Mozambique	47	44			
Rwanda	42	39			
Sierra Leone	39	36			
Somalia	49	45			
Uganda	40	39			

Source: *Women's Indicators and Statistics Database (Wistat)*, Version 4, CD-ROM (United Nations publication, Sales No. E.00.XVII.4), based on Population Division of the United Nations Secretariat, *World Population Prospects: The 1998 Revision*, vol. I, *Comprehensive Tables* (United Nations publication, Sales No. E.99.XIII.9).

Chart 3.3:
More infants are surviving and infant girls have an advantage over infant boys almost everywhere
Infant mortality rate (per 1000 live births)

	1990-1995		1995-2000	
	Girls	Boys	Girls	Boys
Africa				
Northern Africa	50	57	41	48
Sub-Saharan Africa	94	106	86	98
Latin America and the Caribbean				
Caribbean	19	25	17	22
Central America	33	39	28	34
South America	35	45	31	40
Asia				
Eastern Asia	27	26	24	23
South-eastern Asia	58	65	50	57
Southern Asia	79	78	70	69
Central Asia	41	51	41	51
Western Asia	33	39	27	33
Oceania	27	30	23	26
Developed regions				
Eastern Europe	16	21	14	20
Western Europe	6	8	6	7
Other developed regions	6	7	5	6

Source: Prepared by the Statistics Division of the United Nations Secretariat from Population Division of the United Nations Secretariat, *World Population Prospects: The 1998 Revision*, "Survivors to exact ages, 1990-2050", data set in digital form (POP/DB/WPP/Rev.1998/9).

advances of the last century. Child mortality rates are important indicators of this fact. There are, however, wide variations in levels of child mortality that raise important issues with respect to the differential treatment of girls and boys.

A United Nations study on gender and mortality in childhood notes that where infant mortality is lower for girls than for boys, it seems to be due to the biological and genetic advantage that girls have over boys in the first year of life (due to endogenous causes). At some point in childhood, usually between ages 1 and 5, cultural and behavioural factors come into play. These factors, which include discriminatory nutritional and health-care practices against the girl child, offset the biological advantage, resulting in excess mortality among girls. The regions where these higher mortality rates for girls have been documented and linked to discriminatory practices include some countries of Northern Africa and parts of Western, South-central and Eastern Asia, including China and the Republic of Korea.[8]

Based on available data, the lowest mortality rates in the developing regions are in Latin America and the Caribbean—rates of about 1 death per 1,000 for both girls and boys aged 1 to 5.

In Asia, data reported for 15 countries indicate wide variations among countries in levels of child mortality. The three countries with the highest reported child mortality rates—India, Bangladesh, and Pakistan—reverse the normal sex differential, with girls' mortality higher than that of boys. In India, mortality rates are highest by far, with 42 deaths per 1,000 for girls and 29 for boys in 1992-93 **(chart 3.5)**. The child mortality rate in Egypt is also higher for girls than for boys—6.6 per 1,000 versus 5.6.

In the developed regions, child mortality rates are less than 1 death per 1,000 children, and rates are lower for girls than for boys **(chart 3.5)**.

Child malnutrition prevalent in developing countries

Adequate nutrition is the key to the healthy development of children. Good nutrition increases children's resistance to disease and allows children to take full advantage of educational and social opportunities, thus laying the groundwork for a healthy adult life. Furthermore, the health of the girl child can affect the health of the next generation if and when young women become mothers.

Many of the world's children do not get adequate nutrition. As a result, many of these children are considered malnourished (i.e., they suffer from stunting or being underweight, or from wasting, a combination of the two). The consequences of stunting are permanent for children who are chronically malnourished

before they reach adolescence.[9] Stunting is almost as common among girls as among boys, and is prevalent in many developing countries.[10] At least 40 per cent of children under age 5 are stunted in countries as diverse as Bangladesh, Guatemala and Malawi. However, malnutrition is not confined to developing regions. United Nations Children's Fund (UNICEF) reports malnutrition in industrialized countries, as well, especially in some countries in transition, where widening income disparities have been accompanied by reductions in social protection.[11] For instance, in the Russian Federation in 1995, stunting was reported for 13 per cent of girls and 12 per cent of boys.[12]

Another indicator of malnutrition—being underweight—is known to delay children's development.[13] Most countries with a high prevalence of underweight children under age 5 are in sub-Saharan Africa and Southern and South-eastern Asia **(chart 3.6)**.

There is some evidence that children are more likely to suffer from malnutrition if they are born later in the birth order or if they are in families where children are born close together. For example, Demographic and Health Surveys (DHS) data show that in all countries examined, younger children in large families are more likely to exhibit symptoms of malnutrition. Moreover, children born two years or less after the

Chart 3.4:

The advantage of girls over boys in surviving the first year of life is reversed in some countries or areas
Infant mortality rate (per 1000 live births), 1995-2000

	Girls	Boys
Caribbean		
Barbados	13	12
Asia		
Bangladesh	79	78
Brunei Darussalam	10	9
China [a]	48	35
India	78	67
Iran (Islamic Republic of)	35	35
Maldives	58	43
Nepal	84	81
Oceania		
Guam	11	9
Papua New Guinea	64	59
Samoa	24	21

Source: Prepared by the Statistics Division of The United Nations Secretariat from Population Division of the United Nations Secretariat, *World Population Prospects: The 1998 Revision*, "Survivors to exact ages, 1990-2050", data set in digital form (POP/DB/WPP/Rev.1998/9).

[a] For statistical purposes, data for China do not include Hong Kong SAR and Macao SAR.

What constitutes malnutrition?

According to the World Health Organization, the most common nutritional disorders among infants and young children are protein-energy malnutrition, iodine deficiency, Vitamin A deficiency and iron-deficiency anaemia. In order to measure the severity of malnutrition among children, children are measured against a "reference population", which is assumed to be "well-nourished". Three indicators are commonly used to measure malnutrition: underweight, stunting and wasting. "Stunting" refers to a condition in which a child is shorter than "normal" for her/his age; "underweight" to a condition in which a child weighs less than "normal" for her/his age; and "wasting" to a condition in which a child weighs less than "normal" for her/his height.

Children who fall two standard deviations below the median value of the reference population are considered malnourished. Those children who fall three standard deviations below are considered severely malnourished.[a]

[a] UNICEF, "Child malnutrition: country profiles" (New York, 1993).

previous child were nutritionally disadvantaged in 75 per cent of the countries examined.[14]

Iron deficiency anaemia is another indicator of overall nutritional deficiency, and is common in developing countries. In some regions, anaemia affects about half of all children aged 5 to 14.[15] Iron deficiency anaemia can be the result of lack of iron in the diet, poor absorption of iron from food or hookworm infection. Girls may also lose iron through menstruation, and early pregnancy can further deplete iron in the body. Among the consequences of iron deficiency are susceptibility to disease because of impaired functioning of the immune system and lower levels of energy and productivity. Anaemia also increases women's risk of complications and even death during pregnancy and childbirth **(see section on prenatal care).**

Chart 3.5:

Child mortality rates are high in some developing countries relative to the developed regions
Child mortality rate (annual deaths per 1000 aged 1-4), 1990-1997

	Girls	Boys
Africa		
Egypt[a]	6.6	5.6
Latin America and the Caribbean[b]	1.1	1.3
Asia		
Armenia	1.2	1.3
Bangladesh	15.7	14.2
China		
Hong Kong SAR	0.2	0.2
India	42.0	29.4
Iran (Islamic Rep. of)	3.9	5.1
Israel	0.4	0.4
Kazakhstan	1.7	2.2
Kuwait[a]	0.7	1.0
Kyrgyzstan	3.2	3.3
Malaysia	0.6	0.8
Pakistan[a]	9.6	8.6
Philippines	2.5	2.8
Republic of Korea	0.6	0.7
Singapore[a]	0.5	0.4
Tajikistan	8.5	9.0
Developed regions[b]	0.5	0.6

Source: *Women's Indicators and Statistics Database (Wistat),* *Version 4,* CD-ROM (United Nations publication, Sales No. E.00.XVII.4), based mainly on *Demographic Yearbook* (United Nations publication, various years up to 1997).

[a] Data for this country refer to 1986/1989.

[b] Unweighted average for the region. Rates for countries in the region vary within a small range.

Grave health risks for sexually active adolescents, especially young women

Most adolescents are in good health **(box entitled "Do we know enough about adolescence?" in chap. 1).** Adolescents as a group (young people aged 10 to 19) have the lowest mortality rates of any age group in both developed and developing regions. Evidence suggests that serious risks for the health of adolescents, especially for the health of young women, arise when they become sexually active. The younger they are when they become sexually active, the more they risk contracting sexually transmitted infections (STIs), including human immunodeficiency virus (HIV). STIs have short- and long-term health consequences and can lead to death, particularly in the case of HIV/AIDS. Pregnancy and childbirth also carry severe health risks for some young women.[16]

Most young women and men become sexually active during adolescence.[17] For example, in nine of the 13 countries surveyed by DHS in sub-Saharan Africa, 80 per cent or more of women aged 20 to 24 had had sex before age 20. In the Latin American countries examined, the percentage of young women who reported being sexually active before age 20 ranged from 45 to 67 **(chart 3.7).**

Sexually transmitted infections
One of the most important health concerns is the high prevalence of STIs, including HIV, among young people. The World Health Organization (WHO) estimates that each year 1 in 20 adolescents contracts an STI (e.g., HIV/AIDS, gonorrhoea, syphilis, chlamydia and herpes).[18] A survey in the United States, for example, reported that women aged 15 to 19 had the highest incidence of gonorrhoea among all women, and men aged 15 to 19 had the second highest incidence among all men.[19]

Young women are particularly at risk of contracting STIs because pathogens penetrate the cervical mucus more easily in young women than in older women.[20] Young adults, in general, are also less likely to have access to information about STIs and to seek early treatment that might save them from the serious, and often chronic, health consequences of untreated infections.[21]

One of the most serious health consequences for adolescents is HIV/AIDS. It is estimated that in most parts of the world, half of all new HIV infections occurred in the age group 15 to 24, particularly among girls[22] **(see section on HIV infection and AIDS).**

Since the 1980s, policy makers and public education campaigns in many countries have promoted condom use—especially among adolescents—to prevent the spread of STIs, including HIV. As a result, condom use has increased. In the United States, the

Chart 3.6:

The proportion of underweight children is high in most developing regions
Percentage underweight among children aged 0-4, 1990/1997

	Girls	Boys
Africa		
Northern Africa	9	10
Sub-Saharan Africa	27	29
Latin America and the Caribbean		
Caribbean	12	12
Central America	15	16
South America	7	8
Asia		
Eastern Asia	15	15
South-eastern Asia	36	38
Southern Asia	42	41
Central Asia	11	15
Western Asia	14	14

Source: Prepared by the Statistics Division of the United Nations Secretariat from *Women's Indicators and Statistics Database (Wistat),* *Version 4,* CD-ROM (United Nations publication, Sales No. E.00.XVII.4).

Chart 3.7:

Many women become sexually active during adolescence

Percentage women aged 20-24 who had had sex before age 20, 1990/1994

Sub-Saharan Africa

Botswana	91[a]
Burkina Faso	89
Cameroon	93
Ghana	88
Kenya	79
Madagascar	80
Namibia	66
Niger	92
Nigeria	83
Rwanda	43
Senegal	70
United Republic of Tanzania	83
Zambia	87

Latin America and the Caribbean

Bolivia	57
Brazil (Northeast)	50
Colombia	50
Dominican Republic	49
Nicaragua	67
Paraguay	61
Peru	45

Asia

Indonesia	51
Philippines	30

Source: For all countries except Nicaragua: Demographic and Health Surveys, country reports (Columbia, Maryland, Macro International, 1990-1994); for Nicaragua: P. Stupp et al., "Encuesta sobre salud familiar Nicaragua 1992-93", final report.

[a] Data refer to 1988.

percentage of adolescent men who reported using condoms during sexual intercourse increased from 56 per cent in 1988 to 69 per cent in 1995.[23]

Consequences of early pregnancy

Early pregnancy is an important health risk for young women.[24] In many developing countries, at least 50 per cent of all women give birth before reaching age 20 **(see chap. 1, Population).** Young women who become pregnant before their bodies are fully developed, especially those under age 17, face a higher risk of diseases, injuries and death related to pregnancy, childbirth or abortion.

Young pregnant women, for example, have a higher risk than older pregnant women of hypertensive disease, which accounts for a large proportion of pregnancy-related deaths among women under age 20. Young women also suffer more often than older women from cephalopelvic disproportion (a condition in which a woman's pelvic opening is too small to allow the infant's head to pass during delivery). Cephalopelvic disproportion is common for very young women whose bodies have not fully developed, and may be aggravated by childhood stunting. The condition may lead to maternal and foetal death or to permanent damage for the mother, especially if her uterus ruptures during delivery. The consequent prolonged labour also increases a woman's risk of obstetric fistulae (tears between the vagina and the urinary tract or rectum) which, when not treated surgically, often leads to lifelong disability and pain.

Malnutrition and anaemia also contribute to the higher risk young women face during pregnancy and delivery. Young women need twice as much iron as adults of the same weight to avoid anaemia. Moreover, anaemia increases the risk of maternal mortality by as much as five times, because anaemic women are less able to resist infections and survive haemorrhage or other complications of labour and delivery.

The health risks of pregnancy for young women are further complicated by their lack of access to family planning information and modern contraceptives. Their pregnancies are often unwanted or mistimed, and, as a result, many young women have abortions, often performed under unsafe conditions. There is evidence, for example, that young unmarried women are more likely than older married women to seek abortions from untrained practitioners (even where abortion is legal), due to fear, shame, or lack of financial resources, reproductive health information and/or access to services. They are also more likely to perform abortions on themselves, and to delay seeking medical treatment if complications arise, often with tragic consequences for mother and child.

REPRODUCTIVE HEALTH

At the International Conference on Population and Development (ICPD) held at Cairo in 1994, 179 Governments agreed that everyone has the right to the enjoyment of the highest attainable standard of physical and mental health. Included under this umbrella of health was the concept of "reproductive health", which in the ICPD formulation refers to a state of complete physical, mental and social well-being and not merely the absence of disease or infirmity, in all matters relating to the reproductive system and to its functions and processes. All persons are to have access to a broad range of reproductive health services, as well as the freedom to exercise informed choice in determining the number and spacing of their children and the services needed to go safely through pregnancy and childbirth.[25]

Prenatal care and delivery care indicators of safe motherhood

"Safe motherhood" is the term used to refer to "a woman's ability to have a safe and healthy pregnancy and childbirth".[26] In 1987, the Safe Motherhood Initiative was launched by a coalition of international agencies and non-governmental organizations[27] to improve the services available to women during pregnancy and childbirth, to develop model programmes and to conduct research on strategies to improve maternal care in a wide range of countries and settings. The overall goal of the Safe Motherhood Initiative is to meet the targets agreed to at ICPD—reducing the number of maternal deaths by half by the year 2000 and by half again by the year 2015 **(see section on maternal morbidity and mortality).**[28]

Policy makers identified a set of integrated services that should be provided in order to ensure safe motherhood. Those services include: community education on safe motherhood; prenatal care and counseling, including the promotion of maternal nutrition; skilled assistance during childbirth; care for obstetric complications, including emergencies; postpartum care; management of abortion complications, post-abortion care and, where abortion is not against the law, safe services for the termination of pregnancy; family planning counseling, information and services; and reproductive health education and services for adolescents.[29]

Prenatal care

Prenatal care is essential for recognizing, diagnosing and promptly treating complications that may arise during pregnancy, as well as for advising pregnant women on ways to ensure the health and well-being of mother and child.[30]

According to the Safe Motherhood Initiative, adequate prenatal care requires a minimum of four visits to (or by) a skilled health attendant for healthy pregnant women, and more visits for women who develop complications.[31] A review by WHO of national data for 49 countries in developing regions found that between 70 and 90 per cent of pregnant women who had a first prenatal visit also had a second. The proportion of pregnant women having four visits or more, however, is considerably smaller.

While women's access to health care during pregnancy is almost universal in developed regions, it is estimated that 35 per cent of pregnant women—some 45 million pregnant women each year—receive no care at all in developing regions.[32] In the developing regions, prenatal care is highest in the Caribbean and in Eastern and Central Asia—90 per cent or more of pregnant women in these regions have at least one prenatal visit with skilled health personnel. Prenatal care is also relatively common in the rest of the Latin American region, where in most countries

70 per cent or more of pregnant women receive some prenatal care (chart 3.8).

In contrast, on average, 50 per cent or fewer of all pregnant women receive prenatal care in most countries of Southern Asia. In Afghanistan, for example, 8 per cent of pregnant women have at least one prenatal visit; in Nepal, 15 per cent. There is considerable variation within the other regions of Asia. In Western Asia, for example, the percentage of pregnant women receiving prenatal care (at least once during the pregnancy) ranges from 26 per cent in Yemen and 33 per cent in the Syrian Arab Republic to almost universal coverage in most other Arab countries, in Cyprus and in countries of the former USSR. In South-eastern Asia, coverage ranges from 25 per cent in the Lao People's Democratic Republic to almost universal coverage in Singapore and Brunei Darussalam.

In Southern Africa, on average, 86 per cent of women have at least one prenatal visit, while the per-

Reproductive rights as a basic human right

Reproductive rights and reproductive health are not new concepts. Since the International Conference on Human Rights held at Tehran in 1968, reproductive rights and reproductive health have been recognized as an intrinsic component of human rights. More recent international treaties and consensus documents have tried to define these concepts and to identify key actions and indicators to measure efforts and progress in securing these rights for women and men and their children.

In 1979, at the Convention on the Elimination of All Forms of Discrimination against Women, States Parties were urged to take positive steps to eliminate discrimination against women in the provision of health-care services, which included access to family planning services. The Convention also established the rights of women and men to decide freely the number and spacing of their children, as well as to the information, education and means to enable them to exercise these rights.

The 1993 Vienna Declaration adopted by the World Conference on Human Rights reaffirmed these basic reproductive rights by declaring, on the basis of equality between women and men, a woman's right to accessible and adequate health care and the widest rage of family planning services.[a]

The concept of reproductive rights as a basic human right was further strengthened at the ICPD in 1994 and at the five-year review of the implementation of the ICPD Programme of Action

in 1999. Women's equality with men and the sexual and reproductive rights and health of all were, for the first time, placed at the centre of an international document on population and sustainable development. Governments were urged to take all measures necessary to ensure universal access to health-care services, including those related to reproductive health care; access to safe, effective, affordable and acceptable methods of family planning; freedom from sexual violence; elimination of harmful traditional practices, including female genital mutilation; protection of the girl child; the right to health and education; and freedom from coercion within the family and society. The ICPD Programme of Action gave special attention to the needs and rights of adolescents and to the interaction between human sexuality, gender relations and reproductive health status.[b]

Women's right to health, and to reproductive health in particular, was also a central focus of the Fourth World Conference on Women held at Beijing in 1995. The Beijing Platform for Action addresses reproductive health in the broader context of gender equality and the status of women. It calls upon Governments to recognize that reproductive health eludes many due to inadequate levels of knowledge about human sexuality and inappropriate or poor-quality reproductive health information and services; the prevalence of high-risk sexual behaviour; dis-

criminatory social practices; negative attitudes toward women and girls; and the limited power many women and girls have over their sexual and reproductive lives.[c]

The Platform for Action further calls upon Governments to address the serious gaps that exist in the collection and analysis of statistical information on women and health, with particular focus on vulnerable and marginalized groups. It also encourages research on how social and economic factors affect the health of girls and women of all ages, about the provision of health services to girls and women and the patterns of their use of such services, and about the value of disease prevention and health promotion programmes for women. The Platform for Action calls for renewed efforts to research health problems that are unique to women or problems for which a gender-perspective would add critical—sometimes life-saving—new information.[d]

---

[a] UNFPA, *A Focus on Population and Human Rights* (New York, 1998).

[b] United Nations, *Report of the International Conference on Population and Development...*

[c] United Nations, *Report of the Fourth World Conference on Women, Beijing, 4-15 September 1995* (United Nations publication, Sales No. E.96.XIV.13), chap. I, resolution 1, annexes I and II.

[d] Ibid.

centage of coverage in the rest of Africa is, on average, 66. There is, however, wide variation among countries, ranging from 19 per cent in Eritrea to 100 per cent in Libyan Arab Jamahiriya.

Lower quality and frequency of prenatal visits and a delay in beginning prenatal care have been identified as key factors in the persistently high or increasing maternal mortality ratios in countries in transition. For example, in Bulgaria, 17 per cent of women lacked prenatal care in 1997.[33]

Delivery care

The presence of a skilled attendant who can recognize and manage obstetrical complications during delivery is essential in order to ensure that the birth proceeds

safely for mother and child. Also crucial is access to a health facility where the woman can receive emergency care and interventions as needed.

Receiving prenatal care does not ensure that a woman will have a trained health attendant during delivery. In some regions, the percentage of pregnant women attended by a skilled attendant at delivery is well below the percentage of those who received some prenatal care. In sub-Saharan Africa (excluding Southern Africa), for example, on average, 66 per cent of pregnant women received some prenatal care, but only 42 per cent of pregnant women were attended by skilled health personnel during delivery (chart 3.8). The percentage of women who were assisted by a skilled attendant at delivery was lowest in Southern Asia (on average, 39 per cent). In Southern Asia, the percentage of delivery coverage ranged from 8 in Afghanistan and Nepal to 94 in Sri Lanka (table 3.A).

On average, about two thirds of women received skilled delivery care in South-eastern Asia, Northern and Southern Africa, and Central America. Almost all women received skilled care at delivery in Eastern and Central Asia and in the Caribbean—except for Haiti, where, on average, only 20 per cent of women had skilled care at delivery.

Maternal morbidity and mortality urgent problems

Preventing and reducing maternal mortality is now recognized as an issue of social justice and human rights (see box on reproductive rights as a human right). Most Governments acknowledge—and international agreements support—the right of women to be protected from the risk of death or disability due to pregnancy and childbirth. The goal of reducing maternal mortality was first established at the 1987 Safe Motherhood Conference in Nairobi with the launching of the Safe Motherhood Initiative. Reduction of maternal mortality was one of the seven major goals of the 1990 World Summit for Children, and in 1994, the International Conference on Population and Development held at Cairo set a goal of reducing maternal mortality to half the levels of 1990 by 2000 and by half again by 2015.[34] In 1995, at the Fourth World Conference on Women held at Beijing, Governments agreed upon a set of key actions to reduce maternal mortality to the levels agreed upon in Cairo.[35]

Maternal mortality

According to estimates made by WHO and UNICEF, in 1990, there were 585,000 maternal deaths—i.e., deaths caused by complications during pregnancy, delivery or the puerperium (a period of 42 days

---

Monitoring maternal mortality

Monitoring maternal mortality is a first step toward developing policies and programmes to reduce and prevent its occurrence. Maternal mortality can be seen as an indicator of how well health systems are functioning in relation to women's needs; large numbers of maternal deaths signal that health systems, policies and programmes may be failing to address women's overall reproductive health needs.

Measuring maternal mortality and monitoring progress in its reduction are, however, difficult. Although countries are increasingly collecting data on maternal mortality, these data are often of poor quality and unreliable. Data provided by vital statistics registration systems are often deficient because of under-reporting and/or misclassification of maternal deaths as caused by other factors or vice versa. Measuring maternal mortality through household surveys is difficult, since maternal mortality is a relatively rare event and, therefore, requires a large sample size to record enough deaths to make prevalence estimates reliable. Even if Governments or institutions were to invest the resources needed to conduct such surveys, the results would have large margins of error.

Maternal mortality ratios presented in this report are provided by UNICEF and are compiled from data reported by countries, with no adjustments made for misclassifi-

cation and under-reporting. UNICEF regularly collects information on maternal mortality from countries and updates these figures every year. The country data may be from vital statistics registration systems or from direct or indirect estimates based on household surveys. As a result, these data have different levels of reliability and are not comparable.

Given the difficulty in measuring actual numbers of maternal deaths, alternative indicators, called process indicators, have been proposed for regular monitoring of progress.[a] Process indicators would allow producers of statistics on maternal mortality to substitute a set of indicators, based on conditions that have been found to reduce maternal deaths, for the actual prevalence of maternal deaths.

In their 1997 guidelines for monitoring the availability and use of obstetric services, UNICEF, WHO and UNFPA recommended a set of indicators. The percentage of births attended by skilled health personnel (doctors, nurses and midwives) is one process indicator that has been widely recommended for monitoring maternal mortality. While such process indicators do not necessarily capture the number of deaths due to maternal causes, they do provide data on progress in providing women with access to reproductive health services, which has been shown to reduce maternal mortality.

[a] Carla Abou Zahr and Tessa Wardlaw, "Maternal mortality at the end of the decade: what signs of progress?", unpublished.

immediately following the end of the pregnancy). Ninety-nine per cent of these deaths were in the developing regions. Maternal mortality ratios ranged from 190 maternal deaths per 100,000 live births in Latin America and the Caribbean to 870 maternal deaths per 100,000 live births in Africa. Ratios of over 1,000 maternal deaths per 100,000 live births were reported in Eastern and Western Africa.[36]

Moreover, WHO estimates that worldwide more than 15 million women a year suffer from injuries and disabilities related to pregnancy and child-birth—often for the rest of their lives.[37] Since women can suffer these injuries and disabilities each time they bear a child, the cumulative total number of women in the world today who have suffered or are suffering from these injuries is estimated at 300 million—more than a quarter of all adult women now alive in developing regions.[38]

A woman faces the risk of death every time she becomes pregnant. A woman's "lifetime risk" of dying from causes related to pregnancy is determined by the number of pregnancies a woman has, combined with the risk of maternal mortality for each pregnancy. There are large differences in lifetime risk of maternal mortality between developed and developing countries. For example, an African woman's lifetime risk of dying from pregnancy-related causes is 1 in 16, while a woman's lifetime risk of maternal mortality in Asia is 1 in 65, and in Europe, 1 in 1,400.[39]

Maternal mortality ratios vary widely across countries. Data reported by countries, although under-estimated in many cases, indicate that maternal mortality is still high in Africa, where 20 countries report maternal mortality ratios of 500 or more deaths per 100,000 live births (table 3.A). Among those countries with the highest maternal mortality ratios are the Central African Republic and Mozambique (1,100 maternal death per 100,000 live births) and Eritrea (1,000). Maternal mortality is also high in several countries of Southern and South-eastern Asia—the highest ratios are reported by the Lao People's Democratic Republic (650) and Nepal (540) (table 3.A). In many countries of Southern and South-eastern Asia, access to prenatal and delivery care is limited.

In other regions, maternal mortality is well below these levels. Most countries of Eastern, Central and Western Asia report maternal mortality ratios below 100 deaths per 100,000 live births. Yemen is one exception, with a reported maternal mortality ratio of 350. In Northern Africa, reported ratios range from 70 in Tunisia to 230 in Morocco.

The majority of Latin American and Caribbean countries report fewer than 200 deaths per 100,000

Chart 3.8:

Many women lack appropriate health care during pregnancy and delivery
Maternity care, around 1996

	% pregnant women receiving prenatal care[a]	% deliveries in health facilities	% deliveries attended by a skilled attendant
Africa			
Northern Africa	65	57	66
Southern Africa	86	64	67
Rest of sub-Saharan Africa	66	37	42
Latin America and the Caribbean			
Caribbean	95	86	88
Central America	75	62	70
South America	79	76	80
Asia			
Eastern Asia	93	89	95
South-eastern Asia	77	52	64
Southern Asia	49	28	39
Central Asia	90	92	93
Western Asia	82	79	82
Oceania	84	87	81
Developed regions	97	98	99

Source: Prepared by the Statistics Division of the United Nations Secretariat from *Women's Indicators and Statistics Database (Wistat), Version 4*, CD-ROM (United Nations publication, Sales No. E.00.XVII.4), based on WHO, "Coverage of maternity care: a listing of available information", fourth edition, 1996 (WHO/ RHT/MSM/96.28).

Note: See box below for definitions of maternity care indicators.

[a] Percentage of women attended at least once during pregnancy by skilled health personnel for reasons related to pregnancy.

Maternity care indicators

Among the essential services recommended by the Safe Motherhood Initiative to ensure that women have a safe and healthy pregnancy and delivery are: prenatal care; delivery care; and deliveries in health facilities.

Prenatal care coverage: Percentage of women attended by skilled health personnel at least once during pregnancy for reasons related to pregnancy. (While **chart 3.8** provides data on women receiving "at least one prenatal visit during pregnancy", WHO recommends at least four prenatal visits for a normal pregnancy, and more if there are complications.)

Deliveries attended by skilled health personnel: Percentage of deliveries attended by skilled health personnel, irrespective of outcome (live birth or foetal death). Skilled health personnel or skilled attendants are defined as doctors (specialists and non-specialists) and/or persons with midwifery skills who can diagnose and manage obstetrical complications as well as normal delivery. The term "skilled attendant" is used by WHO to emphasize the exclusion in this new definition of the category "trained traditional birth attendant".

Deliveries in health facilities: Percentage of deliveries in public and private hospitals, clinics and health centres, irrespective of who attended the delivery.

Source: WHO, "Coverage of maternity care: a listing of available information", fourth edition, 1996 (WHO/RHT/MSM/96.28).

live births, with the exceptions of Bolivia (390), the Dominican Republic (230), Honduras (220) and Peru (270).

In the developed regions, maternal mortality ratios are, on average, well below 50. Overall, the ratios range from 8 to 50 in Eastern Europe, compared to ratios of 8 or less in all but three countries in Western Europe and the developed regions outside Europe—Denmark and France (10) and New Zealand (15).

Among countries in transition, maternal mortality is particularly high in some countries of the former USSR—especially in Central Asia—and in Albania and Romania. According to a recent UNICEF study, high rates of maternal mortality may be linked to diminishing accessibility to, and deteriorating quality of, prenatal and delivery care. Moreover, it is estimated that unsafe abortion accounts for 20 to 25 per cent of all maternal deaths in countries in transition[40] **(see section on abortion).**

An estimated 80 per cent of maternal deaths are due to direct causes—obstetric complications, including severe bleeding, infections, hypertensive disorders and obstructed labour (e.g., eclampsia), and/or complications from unsafe abortion **(chart 3.9).** The remainder are due to pre-existing diseases or conditions, including anaemia, malaria, diabetes and hepatitis, which are aggravated by pregnancy.

In addition, women may experience long-term complications due to pregnancy and childbirth, with profound consequences for their quality of life. These include obstetric fistulae, severe anaemia, pelvic inflammatory disease, reproductive tract infections and infertility.[41]

Most maternal deaths are preventable. Haemorrhage, for example, which accounts for roughly 25 per cent of

maternal deaths, can be controlled by drugs and/or blood transfusions. Infections during delivery are often caused by untreated reproductive tract infections, which can usually be prevented or treated. Hypertensive disorders can be monitored during pregnancy and treated with drugs to prevent eclampsia. Obstructed labour, one of the possible consequences of female genital mutilation **(see section on female genital mutilation in chap. 6),** often requires emergency obstetrical intervention during delivery.[42]

Access to emergency obstetric care is considered one of the most important strategies for reducing maternal mortality. In Sri Lanka, for example, the extension of the health-care system and the improvement of midwifery skills have contributed to a decrease in maternal mortality. In Bangladesh, declines in maternal mortality have been achieved at least in part through pregnant women's use of midwives and community health workers and the increased availability of transportation for women who need emergency care during pregnancy and/or delivery.[43]

A mother's death has serious consequences for her family, particularly for her surviving children. The risk of death doubles or triples for children under age 5 who lose their mothers.[44]

Abortion a major public health problem

Abortion is permitted—sometimes under very limited circumstances—in most countries of the world **(chart 3.10).** According to recent estimates, 62 per cent of all women live in countries where abortion is permitted without restriction or under a wide set of conditions (i.e., upon request, to preserve the physical and/or mental health of the woman or for socioeconomic reasons). In most other countries of the world, abortion is legal only to save the life of the woman. Exceptions are Chile, El Salvador and Malta, where it is against the law under all circumstances.[45]

Both the ICPD Programme of Action and the Beijing Platform for Action recognized abortion, whether performed legally or illegally, as a major public health problem. The ICPD Programme of Action proposes that in countries where abortion is not against the law, such abortion should be safe and, further, that women should have access to quality health services for the management of complications arising from abortion.[46] The Beijing Platform for Action calls for research to better understand and address the consequences of induced abortion, including its effects on subsequent fertility; promotion of reproductive health practices; and research on complications of abortion and post-abortion care.[47]

WHO defines unsafe abortion as a procedure terminating an unwanted pregnancy performed by persons

Chart 3.9:

Medical causes of maternal mortality
Percentage distribution of maternal deaths by cause, 1997

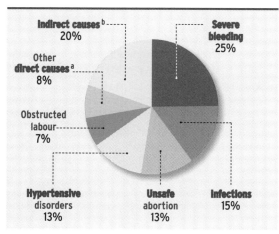

Source: WHO, *World Health Report 1998: Life in the Twenty-first Century: A Vision for All* (Geneva, 1998).

[a] Other direct causes include ectopic pregnancy, embolism and anaesthesia-related deaths.

[b] Indirect causes include anaemia, hepatitis, cardiovascular diseases, diabetes and malaria.

lacking the necessary skills or in a setting lacking minimal medical standards, or both. Of the 40 to 60 million abortions performed each year around the world, an estimated 20 million are unsafe and may have serious consequences on women's health and lives.[48]

In many countries of the developing regions, the overall risk of dying from an abortion is estimated at 1 in 250 procedures; in the developed regions, the risk is estimated at 1 in 3,700.[49] This translates to an estimated 70,000 to 80,000 maternal deaths each year, with many more women left with lifelong physical and/or mental health problems.[50]

Induced abortions are usually the consequence of unwanted pregnancies resulting from neglecting to use contraception or from contraceptive failure. A recent WHO study found that in Nepal, 95 per cent of induced abortions were the result of unplanned pregnancies and the majority of women who had abortions were not using contraceptives. However, abortions are performed everywhere, even where family planning information and education are accessible and contraceptive use is high. In China, for example, where family planning services are widely accessible, failure to use contraception was the primary reason given for unwanted pregnancy and consequent abortion. Contraceptive failures were the reported cause in 37 per cent of abortions in China.[51]

The prevalence of abortion is particularly high in countries in transition, where, on average, there are more abortions than live births. The high rates of abortion in these countries are largely due to a lack of information and education about reproductive health and contraception, as well as difficulty in obtaining affordable, effective contraceptives.[52] In transition countries, complications from abortions, together with sexually transmitted infections (STIs), are the leading causes of infertility (see section on infertility). In Ukraine, for example, 22 per cent of women who underwent abortions experienced complications leading to infertility.[53]

Fear of side effects affects women's use of contraceptives

Contraceptive use allows couples to avoid unwanted or mistimed pregnancies. The barrier methods of contraception also protect against the spread of STIs, including HIV, which have long-term, and possibly life-threatening, consequences for women and men and their children. There are, however, many reasons for non-use of contraceptives by both women and men, including lack of availability; lack of knowledge of different methods; high costs of some methods; social, cultural and religious constraints; and health concerns, including fear of side-effects.

Information and education about contraceptives and their side effects may lead to more effective use and dispel misconceptions about the various methods. In a number of countries surveyed by DHS, a substantial proportion of women reported not using contraception for fear of side effects—18 per cent in the Philippines, 16 per cent in the Dominican Republic and Nepal and 12 per cent in Indonesia and Yemen.[54]

In transition countries, fear of side effects and negative perceptions of modern contraceptives are cited as reasons for non-use. In the Russian Federation in 1991, for example, less than 20 per cent of women considered the contraceptive pill safe, reliable and convenient.[55] High cost and limited availability may also be factors.

It is difficult to assess the prevalence of health complications from contraceptive use. Women who discontinue the use of modern contraceptives for health reasons may have pre-existing health problems, or they may have inadequate information about the correct use and possible side effects. On the other hand, clinical studies may underestimate the number of women who experience complications, as doctors and health workers often dismiss certain symptoms as unimportant and women fail to report these symptoms unless they lead to serious complications.

According to DHS surveys, fear of side effects ranks right behind accidental pregnancy and the desire to have another child as reasons most frequently cited for discontinuing contraceptive use. In the Philippines, for example, 16 per cent of women said they stopped using their current method because they feared side effects. Fear of side effects was cited most often for injectables (45 per cent), the intrauterine device (IUD)(36 per cent) and the contraceptive pill (28 per cent).

In Egypt, 29 per cent of women cited fear of side effects as the reason for discontinuing contraceptive use, and an additional 10 per cent had concerns about possible effects of prolonged contraceptive use on their overall health. In Indonesia, health concerns and side effects were the most frequently mentioned reasons for discontinuing use of contraceptive implants and injectables.[56]

Infertility may have serious social consequences for women

Family planning refers not only to efforts made to help individuals avoid childbearing when they so choose (i.e., to provide individuals with the information and means to decide for themselves the number and spacing of their children) but also to efforts made to ensure that individuals who want to have children are able to do so. Infertility, broadly defined as the inability to have children, is, therefore, becoming an increasingly important component of family planning programmes.[57]

Infertility affects both women and men in all regions of the world. Infertility often has profound short- and long-term implications for the individuals involved and it may expose them to family and societal pressures. According to WHO estimates, between 8 and 12 per cent of all couples experience some form of infertility during their reproductive lives—50 to 80 million people worldwide.[58]

Primary infertility is defined as a woman's inability ever to conceive, despite exposure to pregnancy for a period of two years, while secondary infertility refers to a woman's inability to conceive though she has con-

ceived before and despite exposure to pregnancy for a period of two years.[59] Studies also indicate that primary infertility occurs naturally among all populations—generally at a level of about 3 per cent, in the absence of disease-based infertility.[60]

The majority—55 per cent—of cases of primary and secondary infertility are thought to be due to the consequences of untreated STIs (especially gonorrhoea and chlamydia, which lead to pelvic inflammatory disease) or to complications suffered after the birth of a child or after an abortion, especially illegally induced abortions.[61] WHO reports that

Chart 3.10:

Grounds on which abortion is allowed by countries
Information as of 1999

Under no condition					
Latin America and the Caribbean			**Developed Regions**		
Chile	El Salvador		Malta		

Only to save a woman's life					
Africa			**Asia and Oceania**		
Angola	Egypt—SA	Mauritius	Afghanistan	Kiribati	Solomon Islands
Benin	Gabon	Niger	Bangladesh	Lao People's Dem.	Sri Lanka
Central African	Guinea-Bissau	Sao Tome and	Bhutan	Rep.	Syrian Arab
Republic	Lesotho	Principe	Brunei	Lebanon	Republic—SA,PA
Chad	Libyan Arab	Senegal	Darussalam	Myanmar	Tonga
Congo	Jamahiriya—PA	Somalia	Indonesia	Nepal	United Arab
Côte d'Ivoire	Madagascar	Sudan—RI	Iran (Islamic	Oman	Emirates—SA,PA
Dem. Rep.	Malawi—SA	Swaziland	Rep. of)	Philippines	Yemen
of the Congo	Mali	Togo			
Djibouti	Mauritania				
Latin America and the Caribbean			**Developed Regions**		
Antigua and	Dominican Republic	Nicaragua—SA,PA	Andorra	Monaco	
Barbuda	Guatemala	Panama—PA,RI,FI	Ireland	San Marino	
Brazil—RI	Haiti	Paraguay			
Colombia	Honduras	Suriname			
Dominica	Mexico[a]—RI	Venezuela			

To preserve physical or mental health (also to save a woman's life)					
Africa			**Asia and Oceania**		
Algeria	Ethiopia	Nigeria[c]	Cyprus—RI,FI	Malaysia	Republic of Korea—
Botswana—RI,FI	Gambia	Rwanda	Fiji	Maldives—SA	SA,RI
Burkina Faso—	Ghana—RI,FI	Seychelles—	Iraq	Pakistan	Samoa
RI,FI	Guinea	RI,FI	Israel—RI,FI	Papua New Guinea	Saudi Arabia—SA,PA
Burundi	Kenya	Sierra Leone	Jordan	Qatar—SA,FI	Thailand—RI
Cameroon—RI	Liberia—RI,FI	Uganda	Kuwait—SA,PA,FI		Vanuatu
Comoros	Morocco—SA	United Rep. of			
Equatorial Guinea	Mozambique[b]	Tanzania			
Eritrea	Namibia—RI,FI	Zimbabwe—RI,FI			
Latin America and the Caribbean			**Developed Regions**		
Argentina—RI	Ecuador—RI	Saint Kitts and Nevis	Liechtenstein	Poland—PA,RI,FI	Portugal—PA
Bahamas	Grenada	Saint Lucia	New Zealand—	Switzerland	Spain
Bolivia—RI	Jamaica—PA	Trinidad and Tobago	RI,FI		
Costa Rica	Peru	Uruguay—RI			

untreated infections and pelvic inflammatory disease (PID) are the major causes of disease-related infertility, especially in countries with poor reproductive health care.[62]

In general, female factors are thought to cause infertility in 50 to 70 per cent of all infertile couples.[63] Female factors, however, might be overestimated because men are less likely than women to seek medical treatment for symptoms of infertility, clinical studies generally focus on women's reproductive systems and demographic surveys typically collect data only on women's reproductive histories.

In many developing countries, female infertility may have serious consequences for women. Where women's identity is closely linked to their reproductive role, the inability to fulfill the expectations of family and society may lead to divorce or abandonment by their husbands or partners, stigmatization and ostracism and, in some cases, violence at the hands of their partners.

Estimates of primary infertility are often derived from demographic data on childlessness. However, the existence of voluntary childlessness may confound any analysis of primary infertility based on data on child-

---

Economic or social reasons (also to save woman's life or to preserve health)

Africa

Zambia

Latin America and the Caribbean

Barbados—PA	Saint Vincent and
Belize	the Grenadines

Asia and Oceania

India—PA

Developed Regions

Finland	Luxembourg—PA
Iceland	United Kingdom
Japan—PA	

On request[d]

Africa

Cape Verde	South Africa	Tunisia

Latin America and the Caribbean

Cuba—PA	Guyana

Asia and Oceania

Armenia	Dem. People's Rep.	Singapore
Azerbaijan	of Korea	Tajikistan
Bahrain	Georgia	Turkey—SA,PA
Cambodia	Kazakhstan	Turkmenistan
China—PA	Kyrgyzstan	Uzbekistan
	Mongolia	Viet Nam

Developed Regions

Albania	Estonia	Romania
Australia[e]	France—PA	Russian
Austria	Germany	Federation
Belarus	Greece—PA	Slovakia—PA
Belgium	Hungary	Slovenia—PA
Bosnia and	Italy—PA	Sweden
Herzegovina—PA	Latvia	The FYR of
Bulgaria	Lithuania	Macedonia—PA
Canada	Netherlands	Ukraine
Croatia—PA	Norway—PA	United States—PA
Czech Republic—PA	Republic of	Yugoslavia—PA
Denmark—PA	Moldova	

Sources: Prepared by the Statistics Division of the United Nations Secretariat from Population Division of the United Nations Secretariat, *World Abortion Polices 1999*, wall chart (United Nations publication, Sales No. E99.XIII.5); spousal and parental authorization information taken from Center for Reproductive Law and Policy, *The World's Abortion Laws 1999*, wall chart.

Note: In addition to the grounds shown, many countries recognize the following grounds for abortion: rape or incest (indicated as **RI** next to the country name), foetal impairment (**FI**). Certain countries require spousal authorization (**SA**) or parental authorization/notification (**PA**) for abortion.

[a] Abortion law in Mexico is determined at the state level. The grounds shown refer to the Federal District; some states allow abortion on more liberal grounds.

[b] Abortions are also allowed in cases of contraceptive failure.

[c] The northern states only allow abortions to be performed to save the life of the woman.

[d] In most countries, the law governing abortion indicates a gestational limit within which abortion is allowed, generally ranging from 12 to 14 weeks.

[e] Abortion law in Australia is determined at the state level. The most restrictive laws allow abortion to be performed to save a woman's life or to preserve her physical or mental health; the most liberal allows abortion on request.

Definitions of RTIs and STIs[a]

Reproductive tract infections (RTIs) are viral, bacterial and protozoan infections of the lower and upper reproductive tract, transmitted through sexual intercourse, unsafe childbirth, abortion and other practices, including female genital mutilation.

Sexually transmitted infections (STIs) are reproductive tract infections that are transmitted mainly through sexual activity. The four major STIs are trichomoniasis, chlamydia, gonorrhoea and syphilis. Human immunodeficiency virus (HIV), which is the virus causing auto-immunodeficiency syndrome (AIDS), is often considered a sexually transmitted disease as it is most often spread through sexual contact. However, HIV is also transmitted non-sexually—through infected blood, blood supplies and needles or through breast milk **(see section on HIV infection and AIDS).**

[a] In order to be consistent with the new terminology recommended by WHO, in the present report the term "sexually transmitted diseases" has been replaced by "sexually transmitted infections". The new terminology reflects the fact that both symptomatic and asymptomatic infections need to be considered and treated. See WHO, "Sexually transmitted diseases or sexually transmitted infections?", accessed at http://www.who.int/ask/.

lessness. The measurement of infertility in demographic surveys is further complicated by reporting problems. For instance, having children is so highly valued in sub-Saharan Africa that women may hide the fact that they are infertile by either refusing to be interviewed or by claiming foster children as their own. The increasing prevalence of contraception also confounds infertility measures, since a woman's use of contraceptives may mask the fact that she is infertile.[64]

A study in sub-Saharan Africa indicates high infertility—especially in Central African countries—as a consequence of a high incidence of STIs and infections related to childbirth and abortion. The countries most affected were Cameroon, the Central African Republic, the Congo, Gabon, and the Democratic Republic of the Congo, where from 15 to 32 per cent of women were childless at the end of their childbearing years.[65] Recent data for Cameroon and the Central African Republic show a decline in childlessness. Still, these countries have higher levels of childlessness than other sub-Saharan African countries surveyed **(chart 3.11)**.

Infertility rates vary markedly within countries. Infertility is particularly prevalent in the northern region of Cameroon and in eastern parts of the Central African Republic, areas that are known to have had a high prevalence of STIs. Many of the women surveyed became infertile from disease-related causes after they had at least one child. Poor midwifery practices during the delivery of the first child are a possible cause, as are STIs. [66]

Two countries in other developing regions show proportions of childless married women above 4 per cent—Trinidad and Tobago (5) and Papua New Guinea (6).

In the developed regions, levels of childlessness may be a matter of choice rather than a couple's inability to have children. In addition, advances in reproductive health technologies may afford couples in these regions a better chance to treat infertility and bear children as desired.

Women more vulnerable to sexually transmitted infections, with more serious consequences

Sexually transmitted infections (STIs) are a major health concern worldwide and have serious health and social consequences for women and men and, often, for their children. The increased interest in and the new research on STIs derive from their serious health consequences —especially for women—and from their newly discovered role in facilitating the transmission of HIV.

The four major STIs (excluding HIV) are trichomoniasis, chlamydia, gonorrhoea and syphilis. Of the estimated 331 million new cases of these STIs in 1995, 167 million cases were reported in women. Trichomoniasis

is the most common STI, with an estimated 167 million new cases in 1995, 83 million cases of which were reported in women. The prevalence of trichomoniasis raises serious concern because trichomoniasis may facilitate the transmission of HIV to women.[67]

The prevalence of chlamydia and gonorrhoea—with 89 million and 62 million new cases, respectively, in 1995—is another health problem, especially in developing countries. Rates of gonorrhoeal and chlamydial infections have been found to be particularly high among pregnant women. For example, 44 per cent of pregnant women tested positive for chlamydia in El Salvador in 1991, as did almost 50 per cent of pregnant women in Botswana in 1990. From 1990 to 1993, rates of gonorrhoea among pregnant women were 14 per cent in Botswana, 12 per cent in Cameroon and 4 per cent in Côte d'Ivoire.[68]

Although the number of new syphilis infections in 1995 was far smaller—12 million cases—its prevalence is also cause for concern, especially in pregnant women, as it can result in foetal death. Syphilis is easily diagnosed with a simple and highly sensitive test, and may be successfully treated with antibiotics. However, WHO reports that the incidence of syphilis has been increasing since the 1960s, even in some developed countries.[69] In most countries in transition, for example, there has been a dramatic resurgence of syphilis, due in part to the deterioration of public health systems. In 11 countries in transition surveyed, the number of new cases of syphilis increased more than tenfold between 1990 and 1996. Young persons, especially young women, are particularly vulnerable. In Belarus, the incidence of syphilis is much higher among young women than among young men—984 cases per 100,000 young women compared to 300 per 100,000 young men. A similar or slightly wider gender gap in syphilis prevalence was observed in the Republic of Moldova, the Russian Federation and Ukraine.[70]

Epidemiological surveys have found that the incidence and prevalence of STIs vary widely between countries of different regions, within countries, and within population groups with similar characteristics. This indicates the strong influence of social, cultural, and economic factors, as well as different access to treatment, on the incidence and prevalence of STIs. For example, STIs tend to be more prevalent among people living in urban areas, among young adults and among unmarried individuals.[71]

Women are also biologically more likely than men to contract STIs.[72] Women, however, often do not experience early symptoms of STIs and, therefore, seek treatment late, resulting in more serious health consequences and long-term complications. It is reported, for example, that an estimated 70 to 75 per cent of women infected with chlamydia are symptom-free.[73] Women's delay in seeking treatment also contributes to the spread of STIs.

Untreated, gonorrhoea and chlamydia may lead to pelvic inflammatory disease, chronic pelvic pain, tubo-ovarian abscesses, ectopic pregnancies and infertility. Untreated STIs in pregnant women may also lead to low birth weight infants and/or infants with eye or lung problems, or result in foetal loss or stillbirth. WHO reports that two-thirds of pregnant women infected with early-stage syphilis pass the disease on to the foetus.[74]

HIV INFECTION AND AIDS

According to recent UNAIDS global estimates, there are 33.6 million people (including 1.2 million children under age 15) now living with HIV/AIDS.[75] Of these, 5.6 million (including 570,000 children) were newly infected with HIV in 1999. A total of 16.3 million people (including 3.6 million children) have died since the epidemic began.

Women account for 14.8 million—46 per cent—of the 32.4 million adults (aged 15 to 49) currently living with HIV/AIDS. In 1999, of the 5 million adults newly infected with HIV, 2.3 million—46 per cent—were women. Women also account for almost half (49 per cent) of the 12.7 million adults who have died since the epidemic began, and for 52 per cent of the 2.1 million adults who died of AIDS in 1999.

This last statistic suggests that women are bearing an increasingly large burden of the disease—a burden made even greater by the fact that women are also more likely than men to care for children who suffer from the disease.

Where HIV is spreading predominantly through heterosexual contact—for example, in a number of countries of sub-Saharan Africa and Asia—rates of infection are as high among women as among men. There is also evidence that it is spreading much faster among women. Where the spread of HIV occurs mostly through homosexual contact between men and through intravenous drug use—as in developed countries and in Latin America—the virus is now spreading beyond selected population groups to the heterosexual population, especially among young women and young men.

Wide regional differences in HIV prevalence

The overwhelming majority of people living with HIV/AIDS are in developing regions where health-care systems and economic resources are unable to keep pace with the spread of the disease. About 95 per cent of all people living with HIV/AIDS at the end of 1999 and 97 per cent of new infections in 1999 were in the developing regions.

Almost 70 per cent of the global total of HIV-positive people live in sub-Saharan Africa. As of the end of 1999, 23.3 million adults and children in the region—8 per cent of the population—were living with HIV/AIDS **(chart 3.12)**. The majority of AIDS deaths also occur in sub-Saharan Africa, where access to treatment is low and costs of treatment are prohibitive for most people. The highest adult HIV/AIDS prevalence rates were in Botswana and Zimbabwe—more than 25 per cent.

Among adults living with HIV/AIDS in sub-Saharan Africa, 55 per cent were women (i.e., there are 12 to 13 African women currently infected with the virus for every 10 African men).

In Asia, 6 million persons in Southern and South-eastern Asia, and a half million in Eastern Asia and the Pacific live with HIV/AIDS. Of these, 30 and 15 per cent, respectively, are women. The prevalence of HIV infection varies among countries, with rates in most countries of the region below 0.25 per cent. However, a number of countries have higher rates—Cambodia (2.4 per cent), Thailand (2.2 per cent), Myanmar (1.8 per cent) and India (0.8 per cent).

The HIV/AIDS epidemic started later in Asia than elsewhere in the world. This delay gave Governments an opportunity to set in motion prevention efforts. Nonetheless, rates of infection can increase quickly. For example, in Viet Nam, HIV prevalence among female sex workers increased five-fold between 1994 and 1998. Although the rates are not yet high in China, there is fear that they will increase with the growth of the sex industry. Surveys found that 50 per cent of sex workers in China had never used condoms, a proven method for preventing the spread of HIV/AIDS.

Chart 3.11:

Data on childlessness may suggest relatively high rates of infertility in some countries of Africa.

Percentage childless among women aged 40–44 who are currently married or in unions

Africa	
Cameroon	5
Central African Republic	7
Comoros	5
Liberia[a]	4
Madagascar	4
Niger	4
Nigeria	5
Sudan	3
Tunisia[a]	3

Latin America and the Caribbean	
Brazil	3
Dominican Republic	4
Paraguay	4
Trinidad and Tobago[a]	5

Asia	
Indonesia	3
Pakistan[a]	3

Oceania	
Papua New Guinea	6

Source: *Women's Indicators and Statistics Database (Wistat), Version 4,* CD-ROM (United Nations publication, Sales No. E.00.XVII.4), based mainly on Demographic and Health Surveys, country reports (Columbia and Calverton, Maryland, Macro International, 1990-1998).

Note: Only countries where at least 3 per cent of women currently married (or in union) are childless are shown.

[a] Data for this country refers to 1986/1989.

An estimated 1.4 million adults and children in Western Europe and North America are now living with HIV. In these regions, about 20 per cent of the adult population with HIV/AIDS are women **(chart 3.12)**.

In Latin America and the Caribbean, 1.7 million people are infected with HIV. The prevalence rate in the Caribbean is the highest after sub-Saharan Africa, with 2 per cent of the population infected **(chart 3.12)**. Prevalence rates are estimated at less than 1 per cent in most of the countries of Latin America, with women accounting for 20 per cent of all adults living with HIV/AIDS. In many countries of Latin America and the Caribbean, unprotected homosexual contact and intravenous drug use are seen as the focal points of infection. In Brazil, however, the share of women with HIV/AIDS is rising. In 1986, for example, the sex ratio of persons with HIV/AIDS was 16 men to 1 woman; in 1997, the ratio was 3 to 1.

Rates of HIV infection are increasing sharply in Eastern Europe and Central Asia. According to estimates, the number of people living with HIV rose by a third during 1999, reaching 360,000. Concern in these countries focuses on the increasing number of intravenous drug users and persons involved in high-risk sexual behaviours, which tend to increase the spread of the virus to other populations.

Women's risk of HIV infection from heterosexual contact at least twice that of men

Women's risk of becoming infected with HIV during unprotected sexual intercourse is two to four times higher than that of men. Women have a larger surface area exposed to their partner's sexual secretions than do men and there is a higher concentration of the virus in men's semen than in women's secretions. The risk is even higher for young women, as their genital tracts may not be fully developed.

Social and cultural factors also increase women's vulnerability to HIV. In some cultures, discriminatory practices limit women's access to reproductive health information that could protect them from disease and injury. Moreover, a power imbalance between women and men may inhibit women from exercising their rights and autonomy. For example, women often fail to require that their partners use condoms as a means of protecting both parties against HIV/AIDS (and other sexually transmitted infections), out of fear of retribution, abandonment and even violence.

Male promiscuity may also be responsible for the spread of HIV/AIDS and other STIs. Monogamous women may be infected by their partners without knowing about the potential risk. A study in India, for example, found that 91 per cent of the women attending an STI clinic reported having sex exclusively with their husband, yet all were infected with at least one STI and 14 per cent were infected with HIV.

Women living with HIV/AIDS may also face discrimination and violence. In India, a recent study found cases in which the husband of an HIV-infected woman dies and the woman's in-laws throw her out of her home and keep her children.

Sex workers are generally considered at high risk for contracting HIV, often lacking information and the means to protect themselves. Even when they understand the risks, they may find it difficult or impossible to practice safe sex. For example, young women driven into prostitution by sex traffickers often have little or no autonomy and are less able than other sex workers to protect themselves from HIV/AIDS and other STIs.

Chart 3.12:
Roughly 95 per cent of people living with HIV/AIDS are in the developing regions

	People living with HIV/AIDS at the end of 1999 (thousands)	% women among HIV-positive adults	Adult HIV prevalence rate (%)	New HIV infectiions in 1999 (thousands)
World	33 600	46	1.10	5 600
Sub-Saharan Africa	23 300	55	8.00	3 800
Northern Africa and Middle East	220	20	0.13	19
Southern and South-eastern Asia	6 000	30	0.69	1 300
Eastern Asia and the Pacific	530	15	0.07	120
Latin America	1 300	20	0.57	150
Caribbean	360	35	1.96	57
Eastern Europe/Central Asia	360	20	0.14	95
Western Europe	520	20	0.25	30
North America	920	20	0.56	44
Australia and New Zealand	12	10	0.10	0.5

Source: UNAIDS/WHO, "AIDS epidemic update: December 1999".

Note: The regional grouping shown is that used by UNAIDS/WHO for their estimates.

Where women work can also influence the course of their treatment for HIV/AIDS. For example, a recent study in Mexico found that HIV-positive women were less likely than HIV-positive men to receive the anti-retroviral drug regimen now recommended for the treatment of the virus; women work more often than men in the informal sector, where social security coverage is rare.[76]

Girls and young women at highest risk

Nearly half of all persons newly infected with HIV are aged 15 to 24. In the most affected countries, 60 per cent or more of newly infected people are in this age group. UNAIDS-sponsored studies in Western Kenya found that nearly 25 per cent of young women aged 15 to 19 are infected with HIV, compared to 4 per cent of young men. The rate of infection is three times higher for young women than for young men in Zambia.[77] Higher prevalence rates among young women relative to young men may reflect their greater biological vulnerability to infection.

Among the most vulnerable populations of young people are the homeless, refugees or displaced people, those living in urban slums, victims of sexual violence and abuse, young male homosexuals, sex workers and intravenous drug users.

Breastfeeding a dilemma
for HIV-infected mothers

According to UNAIDS, nearly 5 million children under age 15 have been infected with HIV since the pandemic began—570,000 children were infected in 1999 alone. Of the nearly 5 million children infected, some 3.6 million have already died of AIDS. The overwhelming majority acquired the virus from their mothers. Of these children, 90 per cent were born in Africa, although only 19 per cent of the world's children are estimated to live in this region. The high rates of HIV infection among children in sub-Saharan Africa are due in large part to high fertility rates combined with very high rates of infection among adults. In urban centres in several Southern African countries in 1998, for example, rates of HIV infection of 20 to 30 per cent were common among pregnant women tested at antenatal clinics. Rates of 59 per cent and even 70 per cent have been recorded in parts of Zimbabwe and between 34 and 43 per cent in Botswana.

Mother-to-child transmission (MTCT) of HIV has been identified as a serious and growing concern around the world. The risk of a baby acquiring the virus from an infected mother ranges from 15 to 25 per cent in developed regions and from 25 to 35 per cent in developing regions. Breastfeeding, which is more common and practiced over a longer period of

time in developing regions, is probably responsible for this difference. HIV may be transmitted to infants during pregnancy, childbirth or delivery. One third of infants who acquire the virus are believed to be infected while still in utero, most often during the last trimester of a woman's pregnancy. The rest are thought to be infected at the time of delivery. However, in populations where women breastfeed as a matter of course, one third of all infections may occur through infected breast milk.

The fact that breast milk has recently been shown to account for high rates of MTCT poses a serious dilemma for mothers, especially for poor women in developing regions. With the determination that breast milk is a leading vehicle for MTCT, breast milk substitutes were offered as an alternative to breast-feeding. This alternative, however, poses its own risks and obstacles: many women cannot afford the cost of infant formula; many women do not have access to clean water and fuel needed to prepare formulas safely; and for many women, the choice not to breastfeed may alert others to her HIV status and lead to discrimination, ostracism, violence and abandonment. For community health-care workers and policy makers, a decision to promote commercial formulas over breast milk for those at risk for MCTC also undermines efforts to encourage breastfeeding as the best means of preventing malnutrition for the overall population of infants. In the absence of a viable solution to this dilemma, policy makers are now promoting informed choice (including the provision of counseling and information) about the alternatives for women at risk of transmitting HIV to their infants.

Prevention measures and awareness
campaigns making a difference

According to UNAIDS, sex education encourages young people to postpone their first intercourse, thus helping to protect young people not only from early pregnancy but also from becoming infected with HIV and other STIs. In Uganda, for example, a public education campaign targeted mainly to young people has been successful in reducing the rate of new infections from 239,000 cases in 1987 to 57,000 in 1997. The campaign encourages the open discussion of HIV/AIDS, condom use, HIV testing and counseling services. As a result, many young Ugandans are postponing having sex for the first time, and many who are sexually active are taking fewer partners and practicing safe sex. HIV prevalence among pregnant women in urban areas has also dropped by 40 per cent.[78]

Strategies to reduce the spread of STIs could also reduce women's risk of contracting HIV. These strategies include development, production and marketing of female-controlled methods of contraception, including the female condom (a barrier-method of contraception that, when inserted, covers the vaginal wall, the cervix and the outer genitalia), and increasing research on microbicides (substances such as gels, creams, suppositories, or film that, when applied in the vagina or rectum, act as barriers against STIs, including HIV).[79]

An innovative programme was introduced among sex workers in a red-light district of Calcutta in 1992, aimed at protecting the rights of sex workers and increasing their knowledge of STIs, HIV and the practice of safe sex. By 1994, the district had a negative growth rate of HIV/AIDS, while rates of infection rose considerably in other red-light areas.[80]

OTHER DISEASES AND CAUSES OF DEATH

Data on morbidity and mortality are scarce in many countries. Not only is it difficult to obtain information on the prevalence of chronic or infectious disease but there are many countries in which the number of deaths resulting from such infectious diseases is incompletely measured **(see box on reporting problems with cause of death).** Where data are available—predominantly in the developed regions—analysis of prevalence and trends in morbidity and mortality can be made; however, in most developing countries, there is little or no data available. Nevertheless, WHO is able to provide some global and regional estimates of morbidity and mortality, which can inform policy and programmes.

Cancer claims more deaths among men than women

Cancer accounts for about one in seven deaths worldwide.[81] The most recent estimates on new cancer cases and cancer deaths, for 1990, were prepared by researchers at the International Agency for Research on Cancer from cancer registries, available mortality data by cause and information on cancer survival rates. These data were supplemented by model-based estimates to arrive at country, regional and global estimates of new cancer cases and deaths. According to this set of estimates, a total of 2.2 million cancer deaths occurred among women and close to 3 million among men in 1990. In developed regions, cancer was generally responsible for a smaller proportion of women's deaths than men's deaths but the range across countries was considerable. For instance, based on cause of death statistics reported by countries, cancer accounted for 10 or fewer per cent of all women's deaths in Albania and the Republic of Moldova in the 1990s, compared to 27 per cent in Canada and Iceland.[82]

Chart 3.13:

Women and men suffer from different types of cancer

	% distribution of new cases, 1990		% distribution of deaths, 1990	
	W	M	W	M
All sites	100.0	100.0	100.0	100.0
Lung	7.0	18.0	10.2	23.4
Stomach	7.6	11.9	10.3	13.4
Breast	21.0	–	14.1	–
Colorectal	10.1	9.4	9.7	7.5
Liver	3.2	7.4	5.4	10.3
Prostate	–	9.2	–	5.6
Mouth/pharynx	2.8	6.0	2.5	4.7
Esophagus	2.7	5.0	4.1	6.5
Cervical	9.8	–	8.5	–
Ovarian	4.4	–	4.5	–
Other sites	31.4	33.1	30.7	28.6

Source: D. Max Parkin, Paola Pisani and J. Ferlay, "Global cancer statistics", *CA: A Cancer Journal for Clinicians*, vol. 1, No. 49 (1999).

Reporting problems with cause of death

Data on mortality by cause and sex are important in studying gender differences in causes of death. The most reliable source of information on mortality by cause is a well-functioning vital registration system, which records information pertaining to the deceased, including age, sex and the date, time, place and cause of death. Cause of death is obtained from the statistical or medical portion of the death record. However, the degree of detail and the quality of the data on the cause of death vary considerably across countries, due to both the accuracy of the recorded cause of death and the completeness of registration.

In most developed countries, data on deaths by cause are available from a national vital registration system, which is usually relatively complete and accurate. In contrast, in most countries in the developing regions, death registration data are often unreliable due to non-registration of deaths, as well as to incomplete or inaccurate recording of information on the death record. The accuracy of the recorded cause of death is often questionable, especially when deaths are not attended and recorded by medically trained personnel. In both developed and developing countries, cause of death may also be misreported when social stigma is attached to the cause, such as in the case of AIDS or suicide.

In the absence of an accurate and complete vital registration system in a country, it is difficult to obtain an accurate number of deaths of women and men, let alone the diseases and conditions leading to those deaths.

Breast cancer accounted for 21 per cent of new cancer cases in women in the 1990s, more than double the second-leading type of female cancer (colorectal). Breast cancer was responsible for 14 per cent of cancer deaths and led to more deaths in women than any other cancer (chart 3.13). The estimated incidence of breast cancer had increased in most countries, especially in countries where it was previously low. Incidence rates of breast cancer were high in most developed regions, ranging from 67 cases per 100,000 population in Western Europe to 86 cases per 100,000 in North America. One exception is Japan, where stomach and colorectal cancers were more common. Breast cancer rates in most of sub-Saharan Africa and Asia were much lower—fewer than 30 cases per 100,000 population—with the lowest incidence in China (12 cases per 100,000). The prognosis for breast cancer was generally good in the developed regions, with survival rates ranging from 50 to 75 per cent.

Environmental exposure, reproductive factors and diet are thought to be risk factors for breast cancer, although the considerable variation in incidence among populations is not well understood.

For men, lung cancer (among all cancers) had the highest incidence and mortality rate, accounting for 18 per cent of all new cancer cases and 23 per cent of cancer deaths in 1990 (chart 3.13). The highest lung cancer rates were in North America and Europe. In regions where smoking is widespread, 90 per cent or more of lung cancer cases in men are thought to be tobacco-related. Incidence and mortality from lung cancer were still increasing for women (who took up smoking more recently than men), while for men, incidence rates had started to decline. Incidence was still increasing for both women and men in developing countries.

Worldwide, in 1990, cervical cancer was the third most common cancer in women, after breast and colorectal cancers. It accounted for about 10 per cent of all new cancer cases in women in 1990. Cervical cancer was much more common in developing countries, where it accounted for 15 per cent of all new cancer cases among women, compared to only 4 per cent in developed countries. Incidence rates were high among women in Latin America and the Caribbean, sub-Saharan Africa and Southern and South-eastern Asia. Low rates—below 6 cases per 100,000 population—however, were observed in China and Western Asia. The incidence and mortality rates of cervical cancer had declined substantially, especially in developed countries with screening programmes. A decline in incidence was also observed in some developing countries. In China, for example, incidence dropped from 18 cases per 100,000 population in 1985 to 5 cases per 100,000 in 1990. In some developing countries, breast cancer has replaced cervical cancer as the leading cancer in women.

Survival rates varied among regions but even in developing countries, where many cases were diagnosed at relatively advanced stages, about half the patients survived for five years.

Cardiovascular diseases kill more women than men

Cardiovascular diseases, which include coronary heart disease and cerebrovascular disease,[83] are the most common cause of death for adults.[84] According to WHO, globally, in 1998, these diseases accounted for more than 16 million deaths—31 per cent of all deaths—and many millions more were left disabled. While deaths due to cardiovascular diseases declined from 51 to 46 per cent of total deaths in developed regions between 1985 and 1997, cardiovascular diseases remain the leading cause of death in these regions. In the developing regions, cardiovascular

Chart 3.14:

Cardiovascular diseases account for most deaths in both women and men in developed regions

Percentage of total deaths due to cardiovascular disease, 1992/1995

	W	M		W	M
Eastern Europe			**Western Europe** (cont'd)		
Albania	38	34			
Belarus	51	41	Malta	46	42
Bulgaria	67	58	Netherlands	39	37
Croatia	57	43	Norway	45	44
Czech Republic	60	51	Portugal	48	37
Estonia	64	46	San Marino	54	48
Hungary	57	45	Spain	45	33
Latvia	58	42	Sweden	50	49
Lithuania	65	44	Switzerland	44	36
Poland	56	46	United Kingdom	46	45
Republic of Moldova	51	41			
Romania	69	55	**Other developed regions**		
Russian Federation	55	37			
Slovenia	49	36	Australia	47	40
The FYR of Macedonia	60	51	Bermuda	39	38
Ukraine	52	40	Canada	39	36
			Japan	39	30
Western Europe			New Zealand	44	42
Austria	59	47	United States	44	39
Belgium	40	34			
Denmark	39	38			
Finland	50	45			
France	36	28			
Germany	53	43			
Greece	57	46			
Iceland	45	48			
Ireland	46	45			
Italy	49	39			
Luxembourg	47	37			

Source: Prepared by the Statistics Division of the United Nations Secretariat from *Women's Indicators and Statistics Database (Wistat), Version 4*, CD-ROM (United Nations publication, Sales No. E.00.XVII.4), based on *Demographic Yearbook 1996* (United Nations publication, Sales No. E/F.98.XIII.1).

diseases are rapidly emerging as a major health concern, as well, as populations age and as individuals adopt unhealthy habits and behaviours. Deaths from cardiovascular diseases increased from 16 to 24 per cent of all deaths in the developing regions between 1985 and 1997.

The prevailing view that coronary heart disease and stroke are men's health problems has obscured their significance for women. In fact, cardiovascular diseases kill more women than men. Globally, 35 per cent of all female deaths (8.6 million deaths) were attributed to cardiovascular diseases in 1998, compared to 28 per cent of male deaths (8 million deaths).

In the developed regions, available data show that cardiovascular diseases account for nearly half of all female deaths and about 40 per cent of all male deaths, with considerable variation among countries (chart 3.14). In all developed countries (except Iceland), cardiovascular diseases account for a larger proportion of deaths for women than for men. The sex differential is largest in Eastern Europe, where deaths attributable to cardiovascular diseases account for more than half of all female deaths in the majority of countries.

Morbidity and mortality from stroke and other cerebrovascular diseases affect people under age 65 but occur mainly in the over-65 age group, in particular among ageing women. Although declines in death rates from heart disease and stroke have been greater for women than men in the majority of developed countries, it is expected that cardiovascular disease will continue to be a major health problem for older women.

Worldwide, there are more deaths annually from coronary heart disease (7.2 million) than stroke (4.6 million). The major risk factors are high blood pressure, cigarette smoking, unhealthy diet, high blood cholesterol level, lack of physical activity, diabetes and excess alcohol consumption. Cigarette smoking is the most readily preventable risk factor.

Chart 3.15:

Smoking is less prevalent among women than among men, and more prevalent in developed than developing regions

Smoking prevalence among persons aged 15 or over, 1988/1995

	W	M
Africa	7	41
Latin America and the Caribbean		
Caribbean[a]	14	44
Central America	15	37
South America	20	39
Asia		
Eastern Asia	7	56
South-eastern and Southern Asia	6	48
Central Asia[a]	1	33
Western Asia[a]	14	46
Oceania[a]	23	56
Developed regions		
Eastern Europe	22	50
Western Europe	26	35
Other developed regions	22	34

Source: *Women's Indicators and Statistics Database (Wistat), Version 4,* CD-ROM (United Nations publication, Sales No. E.00.XVII.4).

[a] Average shown for this region or subregion is based on only a few countries.

The Kobe Declaration[a]

The recent WHO International Conference on Tobacco and Health, held at Kobe, Japan in 1999, adopted a declaration that highlights grave concerns about the tobacco epidemic, particularly as it affects women and youth. The concerns expressed in the Declaration include:

- There are already over 200 million women smokers, and tobacco companies have launched aggressive campaigns to recruit women and girls worldwide. Tobacco undermines the principle of women and children's right to health as a basic human right;
- The scientific evidence has shown conclusively that both smoked and smokeless tobaccos contain toxins that cause multiple fatal and disabling health problems throughout the life cycle. Women who smoke have markedly increased risks of cancer, particularly lung cancer, heart disease, stroke, emphysema and other fatal diseases. Women experience gender-specific risks from tobacco and environmental tobacco smoke, such as negative impacts on their reproductive health and complications during pregnancy;
- Tobacco-related diseases lead to high morbidity rates worldwide, contrary to the goals of sustainable development and well-being for all;
- Transnational tobacco companies have implemented well-formulated and deliberate strategies to expand tobacco markets among women and children, particularly in populous and developing countries. The tobacco industry promotes the false association of tobacco with images of health, liberation, slimness and modernity.

The Kobe Declaration explicitly demands that the Framework Convention on Tobacco Control incorporate gender-specific concerns and perspectives and include a women's protocol. It also recommends a number of key interventions at national and international levels, including:

- A global ban on direct and indirect advertising, promotion and sponsorship by the tobacco industry across all media and in all forms of entertainment;
- Ensuring that gender equality in society becomes an integral part of tobacco control strategies and promoting women's leadership, which is essential to success;
- Monitoring the media to ensure accurate and balanced images of tobacco in reporting on women's health issues;
- Investing in overall education of women and girls as a mechanism for development of skills, empowerment and for improving their capacity to fight tobacco;
- Increasing public funding for counter-advertising that disconnects women's liberation and tobacco use and that reaches women and girls in all cultural contexts;
- Increasing public funding for research and advocacy on women and girls and tobacco;
- Improving dissemination of research results to the general public;
- Upholding the principle of women and children's right to health as a basic human right.

[a] WHO, "Making a difference to tobacco and health: avoiding the tobacco epidemic in women and youth", report submitted to the International Conference on Tobacco and Health, Kobe, Japan, 14–18 November 1999 (WHO/NCD/TFI/KOBE/99.6).

Tuberculosis a leading cause of death among young women worldwide

Tuberculosis is among the 10 leading causes of death for both women and men, and its incidence has risen over the last three decades. In 1993, WHO declared tuberculosis a global emergency.[85] Tuberculosis accounted for 1.5 million deaths in 1998—600,000 women and almost 900,000 men. In the same year, there were an estimated 7.4 million new cases worldwide. The majority of these cases and deaths were in Asia. Worldwide, women account for 40 per cent of deaths from tuberculosis.

Tuberculosis disproportionately affects poorer and younger people. WHO estimates that it causes 25 per cent of preventable deaths among young people in developing countries, and that it is a leading cause of death among young women worldwide. Investigators and policy makers increasingly recognize gender-relevant factors—such as gender-based differences in access to care and different treatment outcomes in women and men—as key variables to study for preventing and controlling the spread of the disease.[86]

Women and men infected with tuberculosis may later develop the disease. Patterns of infection and progress to disease, however, vary by age and between sexes. At young ages, the prevalence of infection is similar for girls and boys. After age 15, infection prevalence rates are higher among men. However, recent studies have indicated that the progression from infection to disease may be faster for women than for men during the reproductive years. Fatality rates may also be higher for women at younger ages (young to middle-aged).[87]

Health consequences of tobacco use may be worse for women than for men

Four million deaths each year are linked to tobacco use, a figure that is expected to rise to about 10 million by 2030. Smoking is expected to cause about one in three of all deaths to adults in 2020 (up from one in six in 1990), and 70 per cent of these deaths are expected to be in developing regions.[88] Men account for the vast majority of smokers and deaths due to smoking.[89] However, women are not spared from the health consequences of tobacco use. In almost all countries, female deaths due to tobacco use are also increasing.[90]

WHO estimates that of all adults in the world, one third—1.1 billion people—are smokers. Overall, women account for roughly one in five of the world's smokers, and it is estimated that the number of women smokers will triple over the next generation. In addition, women and children comprise the majority of "involuntary smokers" (those who often suffer diseases and conditions related to second-hand smoke). Women also comprise a growing population of "smokeless tobacco" users. In parts of Southern Asia, for example, 10 to 50 per cent of women of reproductive age are users of chewing tobacco, with its attendant health risks.[91]

Smoking among women is most prevalent in the developed regions—on average, 26 per cent of all women in Western Europe smoke, as do 22 per cent of all women in Eastern Europe and the developed regions outside Europe (chart 3.15). Prevalence rates among women of 30 per cent or higher are reported in the Czech Republic, Denmark, Fiji, Israel, Norway and the Russian Federation (chart 3.16). Some countries in Latin America and the Caribbean have almost as many women smokers, proportionately, as the developed regions.

In developed and developing regions alike, tobacco use is increasing rapidly among women, especially young women. This is particularly true in Denmark, Germany and the United States, where more women aged 14 to 19 now smoke. Similarly, in some countries of Asia, there is an increase in smoking among women aged 18 to 24, even though there is an overall decrease in smoking.[92]

In Asia and Africa, prevalence rates are considerably lower for women than for men. In these regions, smoking prevalence among women is, on average, less than 10 per cent. In Sri Lanka, for example, where smoking prevalence among women is among the world's lowest—1 per cent—tobacco companies are reported to use advertising and promotional strategies to reach women, including sponsoring events that attract women and hiring promoters to distribute free cigarettes.[93]

Diseases most often linked to tobacco use, especially in countries with long-term tobacco use, include lung cancer (90 per cent of all cases); other types of cancer (15 to 20 per cent of all cases); chronic lung diseases, including bronchitis and emphysema (75 per cent); and cardiovascular diseases for women and men aged 35 to 69 (25 per cent).[94]

During the last few years, evidence has mounted that the health consequences of smoking may be worse for women than for men. For instance, women develop lung cancer earlier than men despite starting to smoke later and smoking less. Smoking is also linked to premature menopause and osteoporosis, and to an increased risk of cervical cancer.[95]

A clear and widely studied relationship also exists between smoking during pregnancy and many prenatal and neonatal complications. For example, smoking has been associated with a higher risk of ectopic pregnancy and spontaneous abortion. Women who smoke or who are exposed to second-hand smoke may, in addition, be more likely than non-smokers to have low-birth-weight

Chart 3.16:

In many countries, 25 per cent or more of women smoke

Adult smoking prevalence (%), 1990/1994

	W	M
Latin America and the Caribbean		
Brazil[a]	25	40
Cuba	25	49
Chile	25	38
Uruguay	27	41
Asia and Oceania		
Fiji[a]	31	59
Israel[a]	30	45
Papua New Guinea	28	46
Eastern Europe		
Hungary[a]	27	40
Poland	29	51
Russian Federation	30	67
Czech Republic	31	43
Slovakia	26	43
Western Europe and other developed regions		
Austria	27	42
Canada	29	31
Denmark	37	37
France	27	40
Greece	28	46
Iceland	28	31
Ireland	28	29
Italy	26	38
Luxembourg	26	32
Netherlands	29	36
Norway	36	36
Spain	25	48
Switzerland	26	36
United Kingdom	26	28

Source: *Women's Indicators and Statistics Database (Wistat), Version 4,* CD-ROM (United Nations publication, Sales No. E.00.XVII.4).

[a] Data for this country refer to 1988/1989.

children. A study in India found that pregnant women who smoked were three times more likely to have low-weight births than were non-smokers.[96]

Gender roles and relations affect exposure to tropical diseases and access to treatment

Tropical diseases are a major cause of disability and death in many developing countries.[97] Malaria alone, with 273 million cases reported worldwide in 1998, accounted for 1.1 million deaths—87 per cent in Africa. Taken together, other tropical diseases were responsible for over 100,000 deaths—58,000 men and 48,000 women—all in developing countries. Among these tropical diseases are: leprosy; schistosomiasis (snail fever), which is endemic in 74 countries and affects 200 million people each year; lymphatic filariasis (elephantiasis), which affects over 120 million people in 73 countries; onchocerciasis (river blindness); African trypanosomiasis (sleeping sickness); trachoma, which has already affected some 152 million persons worldwide, of whom six million have been irreversibly blinded; Chagas' disease, a fatal disease affecting some 16 to 18 million people in 21 countries of Latin America; and leishmaniasis (kala azar or oriental sore).

WHO reports that sleeping sickness, after being almost eradicated, has reappeared, especially in Central Africa, where reported cases have more than doubled over the last few years. In contrast, the global prevalence of leprosy was reduced from 5.4 million reported cases in 1985 to 900,000 cases in 1997. Most cases today are in South-eastern Asia.

Although tropical diseases affect women and men alike, research has found that gender roles and relations affect exposure to disease and infection and influence access to health-care and prevention programmes. For example, a recent study in Nigeria found that the prevalence of schistosomiasis peaks at age 15, when young women are most likely to be engaged in water-related tasks in agriculture and domestic work.

Women's limited access to health services has been associated with their restricted mobility, lower level of education, lack of financial independence, limited access to information and transportation, and even to their husbands' refusal to grant them permission to seek medical attention. In cases of disfiguring diseases, including leprosy, filariasis, onchodermatitis and leishmaniasis, women may also delay or never seek the medical care they need due to the social stigma and shame attached to these diseases.[98]

Tropical diseases have additional health consequences for women. Malaria, for instance, is an important indirect cause of maternal mortality, spontaneous abortion and stillbirth, and may contribute to the development of chronic anaemia. Genital schisto-somiasis in women has been associated with infertility, spontaneous abortion, pre-term delivery and ectopic pregnancy, a life-threatening condition for women, particularly in developing regions.

THE HEALTH OF AN AGEING POPULATION

WHO has drawn the attention of policy makers to the quality of life of older people, particularly the effects of non-communicable diseases and their associated disabilities on quality of life. WHO has stressed that increased longevity without quality of life is an empty prize—that health expectancy is more important than life expectancy.[99] The Jakarta Declaration on Leading Health Promotion into the Twenty-first Century reaffirmed that the ultimate goal is to increase health expectancy and to narrow the gap in health expectancies between countries and groups.[100]

In most countries, life expectancy at age 60 is increasing for both women and men. According to estimates, women who reach age 60 can now expect to live an additional 20 years, while men can expect to live an additional 17 years. By 2020, these figures are expected to increase by another two years.[101]

Life expectancy at age 60 is highest in the developed countries outside Europe (24 years for women and 20 for men) and in Western Europe (23 years for women and 19 for men). Corresponding values for sub-Saharan Africa are 16 years for women and 14 years for men, and for Southern Asia, 17 years for women and 16 years for men (chart 3.17).

Women can expect to live two to four years longer than men in all regions of the world, except in Southern Asia, where women live one year longer. Globally, life expectancy at age 60 ranges from 12 years for men in Sierra Leone and four other African countries to 25 years for women in Japan (table 3.A).

Years of added life expectancy spent in good health or disability?

The number of years that women and men live after age 60 may be years spent in health, years spent with disabilities and/or impairments, or a combination of both. Given the scarcity of data on health and disability status of older populations, it is impossible to predict which of these alternatives will occur and in what proportions. Moreover, studies use different collection methods, different definitions (e.g., for "good health", "quality of life" and "disability") and often the data cannot be compared across countries and/or over time. However, a number of ongoing efforts should lead to improvements in the availability and the quality of the data and indicators, and thereby to improvements in our understanding of the health of ageing populations.

Chart 3.17:

Women's life expectancy at age 60 exceeds men's in every region

Life expectancy at age 60, 1995–2000

	W	M
Africa		
Northern Africa	18	16
Sub-Saharan Africa	16	14
Latin America and the Caribbean		
Caribbean	22	19
Central America	21	19
South America	20	17
Asia		
Eastern Asia	21	17
South-eastern Asia	18	16
Southern Asia	17	16
Central Asia	20	16
Western Asia	20	17
Oceania	19	16
Developed regions		
Eastern Europe	20	16
Western Europe	23	19
Other developed regions	24	20

Source: Prepared by the Statistics Division of the United Nations Secretariat from Population Division of the United Nations Secretariat, *World Population Prospects: The 1998 Revision,* "Supplementary tabulation, mortality indicators for older persons", data set in digital form.

Research based on the United States Health Interview surveys show that most years of increased life expectancy after age 60 were spent "without disability" in the 1980s, in contrast to almost all years in increased life expectancy spent "with disability" in the 1970s. While this outcome holds true for women and men, the increases in both total life expectancy and in life expectancy without disability were larger for men than for women.[102]

In Spain, results based on national surveys on self-assessed health status show that years spent in good health increased between 1986 and 1995 for both women and men. However, in 1995, women aged 65 or over were expected to live 12 years in "bad" rather than in "good" health, in contrast to men who were expected to live 9 years in bad health.[103]

REVES, an international network of researchers,[104] has compiled, for a number of countries, relevant data to estimate "health expectancy", which is defined as life expectancy in good health (i.e., the average number of years that an individual can expect to live without a long-term debilitating illness or without restrictions in the activities of daily living).[105]

Although currently available data cannot be used for rigorous cross-country comparisons, they can be used to ascertain the number of years spent in good health versus the number of years spent in disability. The data generally suggest that women's longer life expectancy relative to men extends both to years spent in good health and to years spent in disability.

Estimates of an indicator of health expectancy are available for women and men aged 65 or over in eight developing countries (six in Asia and two in North Africa). The indicator used, "independent life expectancy", refers to the average number of years an individual is expected to live without restrictions in the activities of daily living (including eating, caring for one's own well-being, shopping, cooking etc.). In those countries, women are expected to have 10 to 14 years of "independent" life after age 65, while men are expected to have 10 to 12 years.

REVES has also prepared estimates using another indicator of health expectancy for a few developed countries where data are available for two points in time. "Handicap-free life expectancy" refers to the average number of years an individual is expected to live without limitations that would prevent the fulfillment of an individual's social relationships and the enjoyment of economic self-sufficiency. In a few studies using this indicator in the 1980s and 1990s, older women not only had longer life expectancy than older men but they also enjoyed one to six more handicap-free years. However, given women's longer life expectancy, women generally spent from one to five years more than men with one or more handicaps. For most of the countries studied, older women spent more years with disability than older men. Studies suggest that the greater number of years lived with disability by women relative to men results from their higher survival rate after developing these disabilities.

By 2020, women over age 65 are estimated to account for 10 per cent of the world's women (22 per cent in developed regions); older men will be about 8 per cent of the world's men (16 per cent in developed regions). As a consequence, it is expected that even more women than men will live in poor health or with disability. If life expectancies continue to increase and disability rates also increase with age, disability prevalence rates are also likely to increase.

Social welfare and health-care policies and programmes must take this information into account, especially in those regions where the population of older people is growing rapidly and where many older people are living with disabilities. However, policy makers should also consider best ways to provide services to the growing numbers of older women and men who remain healthy late into life and who maintain active, independent and productive lives. ∎

Notes

1 Dominique Tabutin and Michel Willems, "Differential mortality by sex from birth to adolescence: the historical experience of the West (1750-1930)", in United Nations, *Too Young to Die: Genes or Gender?* (United Nations publication, Sales No. E.98.XIII.13).

2 UNICEF, "Crisis in mortality, health and nutrition, economies in transition studies", Regional Monitoring Report No. 2, (Florence, 1994); UNICEF, "Education for all?", Regional Monitoring Report No. 5, (Florence, 1998).

3 United Nations, *World Population Prospects: The 1998 Revision,* vol. I: *Comprehensive Tables* (United Nations publication, Sales No. E.99.XIII.9).

4 Ingrid Waldron, "Sex differences in infant and early childhood mortality: major causes of death and possible biological causes", in United Nations, *Too Young to Die...*

5 "Levels and trends in sex differentials in infant, child and under-five mortality", in United Nations, *Too Young to Die...*

6 Based on estimates of infant mortality rate for 1970–1975, 1990–1995 and 1995–2000, from United Nations, *World Population Prospects: The 1998 Revision...*

7 "Levels and trends in sex differentials...

8 Ibid.

9 WHO, *The World Health Report 1998: Life in the Twenty-first Century: A Vision for All* (Geneva, 1998).

10 *Women's Indicators and Statistics Database (Wistat), Version 4,* CD-ROM (United Nations publication, Sales No. E.00.XVII.4).

11 UNICEF, "The state of the world's children 1998", accessed at http://www.unicef.org/sowc98/feat03.htm, as of April 2000.

12 WHO, Global Database on Child Growth and Malnutrition, accessed at http://www.who.int/nutgrowthdb, as of April 1999.

13 WHO, *The World Health Report 1998.*

14 A. Elisabeth Sommerfelt and M. Kathryn Stewart, *Children's Nutritional Status,* Demographic and Health Surveys, Comparative Studies, No. 12 (Calverton, Maryland, Macro International, 1994).

15 WHO, *The World Health Report, 1998...*

16 "Meeting the needs of young adults", *Population Reports,* vol. XIII, No. 3 (October 1995).

17 Ibid.

18 WHO, *The World Health Report 1998...*

19 "Meeting the needs of young adults"...

20 Ibid.

21 WHO, *The World Health Report 1998...*

22 Ibid.

23 J. J. Murphy and S. Boggess, "Increased condom use among teenage males, 1988-1995: the role of attitudes", *Family Planning Perspectives,* vol. 30, No. 6 (1998).

24 This section is based on data contained in "Meeting the needs of young adults"...

25 United Nations, *Report of the International Conference on Population and Development, Cairo, 5-13 September 1994* (United Nations publication, Sales No. E.95.XIII.18), chap. I, resolution 1, annex.

26 The Safe Motherhood Initiative, "What is safe motherhood?" accessed at http://www.safemotherhood.org, as of April 2000.

27 Partners in the Safe Motherhood Initiative include: United Nations Children's Fund (UNICEF), United Nations Population Fund (UNFPA), World Bank, World Health Organization (WHO), International Federation of Gynaecology and Obstetrics (FIGO), International Confederation of Midwives, International Planned Parenthood Federation (IPPF), Population Council, Safe Motherhood Network Nepal, Regional Prevention of Maternal Mortality Programme (Africa) and Family Care International (FCI).

28 United Nations, *Report of the International Conference on Population and Development...*

29 The Safe Motherhood Initiative, loc. cit.

30 WHO, "Coverage of maternity care: a listing of available information", fourth edition, 1996 (WHO/RHT/MSM/96.28).

31 Ibid.

32 Ibid.

33 UNICEF, "Women in transition, 1999", Regional Monitoring Report, No.6 (Florence, 1999).

34 United Nations, *Report of the International Conference on Population and Development...*

35 United Nations, *Report of the Fourth World Conference on Women...*

36 WHO and UNICEF, "Revised 1990 estimates of maternal mortality: a new approach by WHO and UNICEF" (WHO/FRH/MSM/96.11/) and (UNICEF/PLN/96.1), April 1996.

37 Populations Reference Bureau, "Making pregnancy and childbirth safer", accessed at http://www.measurecommunication.org.

38 UNICEF, *The Progress of Nations 1996* (New York, 1996).

39 WHO, *The World Health Report 1998...*

40 UNICEF, "Women in transition 1999"...

41 United Nations, *The World's Women 1995: Trends and Statistics* (United Nations publication, Sales No. E.95.XVII.2).

42 WHO, *The World Health Report 1998...*

43 The World Bank, "Making motherhood safe", accessed at http://www.worldbank.org; and Population Reference Bureau, loc. cit.

44 Population Reference Bureau, loc. cit.

45 The Center for Reproductive Law and Policy, "The World's Abortion Laws 1999", wall chart (New York, 1999).

46 United Nations, *Report of the International Conference on Population and Development...*

47 United Nations, *Report of the Fourth World Conference on Women...*

48 WHO, "Abortion in the developing world", press release (WHO/28), 17 May 1999.

49 United Nations, *The World's Women 1995...*

50 WHO, *The World Health Report 1998...*

51 WHO, "Abortion in the developing world"...

52 UNICEF, "Women in transition 1999"...

53 Ibid.

54 Demographic and Health Surveys, country reports (Calverton, Maryland, Macro International, various years between 1994 and 1998).

55 UNICEF, "Women in transition 1999"...

56 Demographic and Health Surveys, op. cit.

57 United Nations, "World Population Monitoring, 1996: Selected Aspects of Reproductive Rights and Reproductive Health" (United Nations publication, Sales No. E.97.XIII.5).

58 WHO, "Infertility: a tabulation of available data on prevalence of primary and secondary infertility" (WHO/MCH/91.9).

59 Ibid.

60 John Bongaarts and Robert G. Potter, *Fertility, Biology and Behaviour: An Analysis of Proximate Determinants,* Academic Press (New York, 1983).

61 WHO, "Infertility: a tabulation...

62 United Nations, *World Population Monitoring, 1996...*

63 Ibid.

64 Ulla Larsen and Han Raggers, "Levels and trends in infertility in sub-Saharan Africa", paper presented at seminar on the theme "HIV, STDs and infertility: past trends and current monitoring", sponsored by UNAIDS, USAID and Measure Evaluation, 14 and 15 December 1998, Arlington, Virginia.

65 United Nations, *World Population Monitoring 1996...*

66 Larsen and Raggers, loc. cit.

67 C. G. Gerbase, Jane T. Rowley and Thierry E. Mertens, "Global epidemiology of sexually transmitted diseases", *Lancet,* vol. 351 (1998).

68 WHO, "An overview of selected curable sexually transmitted diseases", accessed at http://www.who.int//.

69 Ibid.

70 UNICEF, "Women in Transition 1999"...

71 Gerbase et al., loc. cit.

72 United Nations, *World Population Monitoring 1996...*

73 Ibid.

74 WHO, "An overview of selected curable sexually transmitted diseases...

75 Unless otherwise cited, this section is based on data from UNAIDS/WHO, "Report on the global HIV/AIDS epidemic, June 1998" (UNAIDS/98:10-WHO/EMC/VIR/98.2-WHO/ASD/98.2); UNAIDS/WHO, "AIDS epidemic update: December 1999" (UNAIDS/99.53E-WHO/CDS/CSR/EDC/99.9-WHO/FCH/HSI/99.6); and UNAIDS, "AIDS five years since ICPD: emerging issues and challenges for women, young people and infants", UNAIDS discussion document (UNAIDS/99.2).

76 UNIFEM, "Mexican women and the HIV/AIDS epidemic: the intersection of gender, power and HIV/AIDS in Mexico", unpublished.

77 UNICEF, *The Progress of Nations 1999* (New York, 1999).

78 Ibid.

79 UNAIDS, "Gender and HIV/AIDS: taking stock of research and programmes" (UNAIDS/99.16E).

80 Madu Bala Nath, "Women's health and HIV: experience from a sex-workers' project in Calcutta", *Gender and Development,* vol. 8, No. 1 (March 2000).

81 Unless otherwise cited, this section is based on data in D. Max Parkin et al., "Global cancer statistics", *CA: A Cancer Journal for Clinicians,* vol. 49, No. 1 (January-February 1999).

82 Calculated from cause of death statistics published in WHO, *World Health Statistics Annual 1995 and 1996* (Geneva, 1996 and 1998).

83 WHO lists the following under cardiovascular diseases: acute myocardial infarction, arteriosclerosis, arterial hypertension, atherosclerosis, cardiomyopathies, cerebrovascular disease, Chagas' disease, coronary heart disease, heart failure, high blood pressure, hypertension, ischaemic heart disease, myocardial infarction, peripheral vascular disease, rheumatic heart disease, stroke and thrombosis.

84 This section is based on data from WHO, *The World Health Report 1998...;* and WHO, *The World Health Report 1999, Making a Difference* (Geneva, 1999).

85 Unless otherwise cited, this section is based on data from WHO, *The World Health Report, 1998...;* and WHO, *The World Health Report 1999...*

86 WHO, "Gender and tuberculosis in Bangladesh, evidence for gender bias is tuberculosis case detection and proposal for further study" (WHO/CDS/CPC/TB/99.266), unpublished.

87 C. B. Holmes, H. Hausler and P. Nunn, "A review of sex differences in the epidemiology of tuberculosis", *International Journal of Tuberculosis and Lung Disease,* vol. 2, No. 2 (1998).

88 WHO, *The World Health Report 1999...*

89 WHO, "The tobacco epidemic: a global public health emergency", *Tobacco Alert,* paper for World No-tobacco Day 1996 (Geneva, 1996); and WHO, "Making a difference to tobacco and health: avoiding the tobacco epidemic in women and youth", report submitted to the International Conference on Tobacco and Health, Kobe, Japan, 14–18 November 1999 (WHO/NCD/TFI/KOBE/99.6).

90 WHO, "Making a difference to tobacco and health...

91 Ibid.

92 Ibid.

93 Garrett Mehl, "Women and tobacco smoking in Sri Lanka: preventing the inevitable", in Global Alliance on Women's Health, *Smoking and Women's Health: "Les Liaisons Dangereuses",* proceedings of a panel and discussion co-sponsored with WHO at the forty-third session of the Commission on the Status of Women (1999).

94 WHO, *The World Health Report 1999...*

95 Derek Yach and Olive Shisana, "Preface: World Health Organization", in Global Alliance on Women's Health, op. cit.

96 Paul Dolin, "Smoking and women's health: the adverse effects" in Global Alliance on Women's Health, op. cit.

Notes (cont'd)

97 Unless otherwise cited, this section is based on data from WHO, *The World Health Report 1998...;* and WHO, *The World Health Report 1999...*

98 WHO, "Gender and health: a technical paper" (Geneva, 1998).

99 WHO, *The World Health Report 1997: Conquering Suffering, Enriching Humanity* (Geneva, 1997).

100 Jakarta Declaration on Leading Health Promotion into the Twenty-first Century, adopted by the Fourth International Conference on Health Promotion, Jakarta, 21-25 July 1997 (WHO/HPR/HEP/41CHP/BR/97.4).

101 United Nations, *World Population Prospects: The 1998 Revision,* "Supplementary tabulation: mortality indicators for older persons", data set in digital form.

102 Eileen M. Crimmins, Yasuhiko Saito and Dominique Ingegneri, "Trends in disability-free life expectancy in the United States 1970-90", *Population and Development Review,* vol. 23, No. 3. (1997).

103 E. Regidor and J. L. Gutiérrez-Fisac, "Health indicator: fourth evaluation in Spain of the European regional health for all programme" (Madrid, Ministerio de Sanidad y Consumo, 1999).

104 The international network, Réseau espérance de vie en santé/ International Network on Health Expectancy and the Disability Process (REVES), launched in 1989, has brought together many researchers working on the methods of estimating health expectancy. The work of the network to develop indicators of health expectancies builds on the Classification of Impairments, Disabilities and Handicaps (ICIDH). Currently, a first estimate of health expectancy (mainly disability-free life expectancy) is available for at least 48 countries, mostly developed countries.

105 The results reported in the paragraphs that follow are based on Jean-Marie Robine and Isabelle Romieu, "Healthy active ageing: health expectancies at age 65 in the different parts of the world", REVES paper, No. 318 (May 1998).

Health

Country or area	Life expectancy at birth, 1995–2000		Life expectancy at age 60, 1995–2000		Infant mortality rate (per 1000 live births), 1995–2000		People with HIV/AIDS at the end of 1997		% pregnant women who received prenatal care[b], 1996	% deliveries attended by skilled attendant, 1996	Maternal mort. ratio, (per 100,000 live births), 1980 / 1998
	W	**M**	**W**	**M**	**Girls**	**Boys**	**Estimated number[a] (thousands)**	**% women among adults**			
Africa											
Algeria	70	68	18	17	39	48	..	..	58	77	220
Angola	48	45	15	14	115	134	110	52	25	17	..
Benin	55	52	17	15	81	94	54	50	60	38	500
Botswana	48	46	15	13	55	62	190	49	92	77	330
Burkina Faso	45	44	15	13	96	102	370	49	59	43	..
Burundi	44	41	14	13	112	125	260	50	88	24	..
Cameroon	56	53	17	16	70	78	320	48	73	58	430
Cape Verde	71	66	20	17	52	59	..	..	99	..	55
Central African Republic	47	43	15	14	88	108	180	50	67	46	1100
Chad	49	46	16	14	105	119	87	51	30	15	830
Comoros	60	57	16	15	70	82	..	..	69	24	500
Congo	51	46	16	14	78	100	100	49	55	50	..
Côte d'Ivoire	47	46	15	14	82	92	700	49	83	45	600
Dem. Rep. of the Congo	52	49	16	15	84	96	950	50	66	..	..
Djibouti	52	49	16	15	98	114	33	50	76	79	..
Egypt	68	65	17	15	47	53	..	10	53	46	170
Equatorial Guinea	52	48	16	15	99	116	2	48	37	5	..
Eritrea	52	49	16	14	86	97	..	..	19	6	1000
Ethiopia	44	42	15	14	109	121	2 600	48	20	8	..
Gabon	54	51	16	15	82	93	23	50	86	80	600
Gambia	49	45	15	14	112	131	13	48	91	44	..
Ghana	62	58	18	16	60	71	210	50	86	44	210
Guinea	47	46	15	14	120	128	74	50	59	31	670
Guinea-Bissau	46	44	15	14	123	138	12	52	50	..	910
Kenya	53	51	17	15	64	67	1 600	49	95	45	590
Lesotho	57	55	17	16	91	95	85	50	91	50	..
Liberia	49	46	15	13	109	123	44	50	83	58	..
Libyan Arab Jamahiriya	72	68	19	16	27	28	..	..	100	76	75
Madagascar	59	56	16	15	76	89	9	50	78	57	490
Malawi	40	39	14	13	136	140	710	49	90	55	620
Mali	55	52	21	20	111	124	89	50	25	24	580
Mauritania	55	52	16	15	85	99	6	49	49	40	550
Mauritius	75	68	20	16	12	19	..	..	99	97	50
Morocco	69	65	18	16	46	56	..	..	45	40	230
Mozambique	47	44	15	14	107	120	1 200	48	54	30	1100
Namibia	53	52	16	16	64	67	150	50	88	68	230
Niger	50	47	16	14	106	124	65	51	30	15	590
Nigeria	52	49	16	15	77	85	2 300	50	60	31	..
Reunion	80	71	23	17	8	10	..	..	95	97	..
Rwanda	42	39	14	13	117	131	370	49	94	26	..
Sao Tome and Principe	..	..	..	..	..	..	..	..	..	..	..
Senegal	54	51	14	12	59	67	75	50	74	47	560
Seychelles	..	..	..	..	..	..	..	..	..	..	..
Sierra Leone	39	36	14	12	160	179	68	50	30	25	..

Table 3.A (cont'd):
Health

Country or area	Life expectancy at birth, 1995–2000		Life expectancy at age 60, 1995–2000		Infant mortality rate (per 1000 live births), 1995–2000		People with HIV/AIDS at the end of 1997		% pregnant women who received prenatal care[b], 1996	% deliveries attended by skilled attendant, 1996	Maternal mort. ratio, (per 100,000 live births), 1980/1998
	W	M	W	M	Girls	Boys	Estimated number[a] (thousands)	% women among adults			
Africa (cont'd)											
Somalia	49	45	15	14	113	131	..	..	40	2	..
South Africa	58	52	16	12	51	67	2 900	50	89	82	..
Sudan	56	54	16	15	65	77	..	..	54	86	550
Swaziland	63	58	18	16	58	73	84	51	70	56	230
Togo	50	48	16	14	78	89	170	51	43	32	480
Tunisia	71	68	18	17	29	32	..	..	71	90	70
Uganda	40	39	13	12	101	112	930	49	87	38	510
United Rep. of Tanzania	49	47	15	14	77	86	1 400	49	92	44	530
Western Sahara	63	60	17	15	58	70	..	..	..	..	..
Zambia	41	40	13	12	81	84	770	51	92	51	650
Zimbabwe	45	44	14	13	65	73	1 500	51	93	69	400
Latin America and the Caribbean											
Antigua and Barbuda	..	..	..	..	..	..	..	..	..	..	150
Argentina	77	70	21	17	19	25	120	18	..	96	38
Aruba	..	..	..	..	..	..	..	..	..	..	..
Bahamas	77	71	22	19	13	18	6	34	100	100	..
Barbados	79	74	23	19	13	12	4	33	98	98	0
Belize	76	73	22	20	28	30	2	25	96	77	140
Bolivia	63	60	17	16	61	70	3	14	52	46	390
Brazil	71	63	19	16	36	48	580	23	74	73	160
Chile	78	72	22	19	12	14	16	18	91	98	23
Colombia	74	67	21	18	26	34	72	15	83	85	80
Costa Rica	79	74	22	19	11	14	10	26	95	97	29
Cuba	78	74	22	20	7	11	1	32	100	99	27
Dominica	..	..	..	..	..	..	..	..	..	..	65
Dominican Republic	73	69	20	18	29	38	83	33	97	90	230
Ecuador	73	67	21	19	40	51	18	14	75	64	160
El Salvador	73	67	21	18	29	35	18	24	69	87	160
French Guyana	..	..	..	..	..	..	..	..	..	..	..
Grenada	..	..	..	..	..	..	..	..	..	..	0
Guadeloupe	81	74	24	20	7	10	..	..	..	..	..
Guatemala	67	61	18	17	41	50	27	25	53	35	190
Guyana	68	61	18	16	48	67	10	33	95	93	190
Haiti	56	51	15	14	63	73	190	34	68	20	..
Honduras	72	68	21	19	30	40	43	24	73	47	220
Jamaica	77	73	22	20	20	23	14	31	98	92	120
Martinique	82	76	25	21	6	8	..	..	..	..	..
Mexico	76	70	22	19	29	33	180	12	71	69	48
Netherlands Antilles	78	73	22	18	11	17	..	..	95	95	..
Nicaragua	71	66	20	18	38	49	4	24	71	61	150
Panama	76	72	21	19	20	23	9	25	72	84	85
Paraguay	72	68	19	17	34	44	3	18	83	66	190
Peru	71	66	20	18	40	50	72	15	64	53	270

Table 3.A (cont'd):
Health

Country or area	Life expectancy at birth, 1995–2000		Life expectancy at age 60, 1995–2000		Infant mortality rate (per 1000 live births), 1995–2000		People with HIV/AIDS at the end of 1997		% pregnant women who received prenatal care[b], 1996	% deliveries attended by skilled attendant, 1996	Maternal mort. ratio, (per 100,000 live births), 1980/1998
	W	M	W	M	Girls	Boys	Estimated number[a] (thousands)	% women among adults			
Latin America and the Caribbean (cont'd)											
Puerto Rico	79	69	23	19	11	13	..	..	99	99	..
Saint Kitts and Nevis	..	..	..	..	..	..	..	..	..	..	130
Saint Lucia	..	..	..	..	..	..	..	..	..	..	30
St. Vincent/Grenadines	..	..	..	..	..	..	..	..	..	..	43
Suriname	73	68	19	17	24	34	3	33	100	91	110
Trinidad and Tobago	76	72	21	18	11	18	7	33	98	98	..
Uruguay	78	70	22	18	14	21	5	17	80	96	21
US Virgin Islands	..	..	..	..	..	..	..	..	..	..	..
Venezuela	76	70	21	18	18	24	82	15	74	97	65
Asia											
Afghanistan	46	45	14	14	146	156	..	..	8	8	..
Armenia	74	67	20	16	23	28	<1	..	95	95	35
Azerbaijan	74	66	21	17	31	41	<1	..	95	95	37
Bahrain	75	71	20	17	15	18	..	..	96	94	46
Bangladesh	58	58	16	15	79	78	21	15	23	14	440
Bhutan	62	60	18	17	59	66	..	..	51	12	380
Brunei Darussalam	78	73	21	18	10	9	..	..	100	98	0
Cambodia	55	52	16	14	97	108	130	50	52	21	470
China[c]	72	68	19	16	48	35	400	12	79	85	65
Hong Kong SAR	81	76	24	20	5	6	3	39	100	100	..
Macao SAR	80	75	23	19	9	10	..	..	..	..	..
Cyprus	80	76	23	20	8	9	..	..	100	98	0
Dem. People's Rep. of Korea	75	69	20	16	21	22	..	..	100	100	110
East Timor	48	47	15	13	127	142	..	..	..	..	..
Georgia	77	69	21	17	16	23	<1	..	95	95	70
India	63	62	17	16	78	67	4 100	24	62	35	410
Indonesia	67	63	17	16	43	54	52	25	82	36	450
Iran (Islamic Rep. of)	70	69	19	18	35	35	..	..	62	74	37
Iraq	64	61	19	17	94	97	..	..	59	54	..
Israel	80	76	23	20	8	9	..	..	90	99	5
Jordan	72	69	19	17	26	27	..	..	80	87	41
Kazakhstan	72	63	20	15	30	39	3	..	92	99	70
Kuwait	78	74	22	18	12	13	..	..	99	99	5
Kyrgyzstan	72	63	20	16	35	45	<1	..	90	95	65
Lao People's Dem. Rep.	55	52	16	15	88	99	1	52	25	30	650
Lebanon	72	68	18	17	25	33	..	..	85	45	100
Malaysia	74	70	19	17	10	13	68	20	90	98	39
Maldives	63	66	17	16	58	43	..	..	95	90	350
Mongolia	67	64	18	16	51	51	<1	..	90	97	150
Myanmar	62	59	16	15	72	85	440	21	80	52	230
Nepal	57	58	16	15	84	81	26	40	15	8	540
Occupied Palestinian Territory[d]	73	69	19	17	20	28	..	..	..	..	..
Oman	73	69	19	17	20	30	..	..	98	92	19

Table 3.A (cont'd):
Health

Country or area	Life expectancy at birth, 1995–2000		Life expectancy at age 60, 1995–2000		Infant mortality rate (per 1000 live births), 1995–2000		People with HIV/AIDS at the end of 1997		% pregnant women who received prenatal care[b], 1996	% deliveries attended by skilled attendant, 1996	Maternal mort. ratio, (per 100,000 live births), 1980/1998
	W	M	W	M	Girls	Boys	Estimated number[a] (thousands)	% women among adults			
Asia (cont'd)											
Pakistan	65	63	18	17	73	75	64	19	27	18	..
Philippines	70	67	18	16	31	40	24	30	83	53	170
Qatar	75	70	19	17	14	20	..	..	100	97	10
Republic of Korea	76	69	20	16	10	10	3	13	96	95	20
Saudi Arabia	73	70	19	17	20	26	..	..	87	90	..
Singapore	79	75	22	19	5	5	3	20	100	100	6
Sri Lanka	75	71	20	18	16	19	7	30	100	94	60
Syrian Arab Republic	71	67	18	16	27	39	..	..	33	67	110
Tajikistan	70	64	21	17	50	63	<1	..	90	92	65
Thailand	72	66	21	18	27	30	780	38	77	71	44
Turkey	72	67	19	17	39	51	..	..	62	76	130
Turkmenistan	69	62	19	15	49	61	<1	..	90	90	110
United Arab Emirates	77	74	20	18	15	17	..	..	95	96	3
Uzbekistan	71	64	20	17	39	49	<1	..	90	90	21
Viet Nam	70	65	20	16	38	38	88	20	78	79	160
Yemen	58	57	16	15	78	82	..	..	26	16	350
Oceania											
American Samoa	..	..	..	..	..	..	..	..	..	..	..
Fiji	75	71	19	17	15	24	<1	<1	100	100	38
French Polynesia	75	69	19	16	10	11	..	..	95	98	..
Guam	77	73	22	19	11	9	..	..	97	100	..
Kiribati	..	..	..	..	..	..	..	..	..	..	..
Marshall Islands	..	..	..	..	..	..	..	..	..	..	..
Micronesia (Fed. States of)	..	..	..	..	..	..	..	..	..	..	..
New Caledonia	76	69	21	16	10	11	..	..	98	98	..
Palau	..	..	..	..	..	..	..	..	..	..	..
Papua New Guinea	59	57	15	13	64	59	5	50	70	33	370
Samoa	74	69	20	16	24	21	..	..	52	52	..
Solomon Islands	74	70	19	17	18	27	..	..	71	85	550
Tonga	..	..	..	..	..	..	..	..	..	..	..
Vanuatu	70	66	18	16	33	44	..	..	90	79	..
Developed regions											
Albania	76	70	21	17	27	33	<1	..	..	..	..
Andorra	..	..	..	..	..	..	..	..	..	..	..
Australia	81	76	..	..	5	6	11	5	..	..	..
Austria	80	74	23	19	5	7	8	19	..	..	..
Belarus	74	62	20	15	16	29	9	..	..	..	22
Belgium	81	74	24	18	6	8	8	36	..	..	..
Bermuda	..	..	..	..	..	..	..	..	..	..	..
Bosnia and Herzegovina	76	71	20	17	13	17	..	..	..	..	10
Bulgaria	75	68	19	16	14	20	..	..	..	..	15
Canada	82	76	25	20	5	7	44	13	..	..	..
Croatia	77	69	20	16	9	11	..	..	..	..	12

Table 3.A (cont'd):
Health

Country or area	Life expectancy at birth, 1995–2000		Life expectancy at age 60, 1995–2000		Infant mortality rate (per 1000 live births), 1995–2000		People with HIV/AIDS at the end of 1997		% pregnant women who received prenatal care[b], 1996	% deliveries attended by skilled attendant, 1996	Maternal mort. ratio, (per 100,000 live births), 1980/1998
Developed regions (cont'd)	W	M	W	M	Girls	Boys	Estimated number[a] (thousands)	% women among adults			
Czech Republic	77	70	21	16	5	7	2	..	..	..	9
Denmark	78	73	22	18	6	8	3	25	..	..	10
Estonia	75	63	20	15	13	25	<1	..	..	..	50
Finland	81	73	23	18	5	6	1	20	..	..	6
France	82	74	25	20	6	7	110	..	..	..	10
Germany	80	74	23	19	5	6	35	19	..	..	8
Greece	81	76	23	20	7	8	8	..	..	..	1
Hungary	75	67	20	15	9	11	2	..	..	..	15
Iceland	81	77	24	20	5	5	<1	..	..	..	..
Ireland	79	74	22	18	6	8	2	..	..	..	6
Italy	81	75	24	19	7	7	90	30	..	..	7
Japan	83	77	25	21	4	5	7	6	..	..	8
Latvia	74	62	20	14	13	23	<1	..	..	..	45
Liechtenstein	..	..	..	..	..	..	..	..	..	..	..
Lithuania	76	64	21	16	17	24	<1	..	..	..	18
Luxembourg	80	73	23	18	7	8	<1	<1	..	..	0
Malta	79	75	22	19	7	9	<1	..	..	..	..
Monaco	..	..	..	..	..	..	..	..	..	..	..
Netherlands	81	75	24	19	5	6	14	..	..	..	7
New Zealand	80	74	23	19	7	7	1	15	..	..	15
Norway	81	75	24	19	4	5	1	..	..	..	6
Poland	77	68	21	16	13	17	12	..	..	..	8
Portugal	79	72	22	18	8	10	35	19	..	..	8
Republic of Moldova	72	64	18	15	23	34	3	..	..	..	42
Romania	74	66	19	16	18	27	5	..	..	..	41
Russian Federation	73	61	19	14	15	20	40	..	..	..	50
San Marino	..	..	..	..	..	..	..	..	..	..	..
Slovakia	77	69	21	16	10	12	<1	..	..	..	9
Slovenia	78	71	22	17	6	7	<1	..	..	..	11
Spain	82	75	24	20	6	7	120	21	..	..	6
Sweden	81	76	24	20	5	6	3	24	..	..	5
Switzerland	82	75	25	20	5	6	12	34	..	..	5
The FYR of Macedonia	75	71	20	17	22	25	<1	..	..	..	11
Ukraine	74	64	19	15	16	23	110	..	..	..	25
United Kingdom	80	75	23	19	6	8	25	..	..	..	7
United States	80	73	24	19	6	8	820	20	..	..	8
Yugoslavia	76	70	20	17	16	20	..	..	..	..	10

Sources: For life expectancy at birth: *Women's Indicators and Statistics Database (Wistat), Version 4,* CD-ROM (United Nations publication, Sales No. E.00.XVII.4), based on Population Division of the United Nations Secretariat, *World Population Prospects: The 1998 Revision,* vol. I, *Comprehensive Tables* (United Nations publication, Sales No. E.99.XIII.9); for life expectancy at age 60: *World Population Prospects: The 1998 Revision,* "Supplementary tabulation: mortality indicators for older persons", data set in digital form; for infant mortality rate: prepared by the Statistics Division of the United Nations Secretariat from *World Population Prospects: The 1998 Revision,* "Supple-

mentary tabulation: survivors to exact ages, 1990-2050", data set in digital form (POP/DB/WPP/Rev.1998/9); for people living with HIV/AIDS: *Wistat, Version 4,* CD-ROM, based on UNAIDS and WHO, *Report on the Global HIV/AIDS Epidemic,* June 1998 (WHO, 1998); for prenatal care and deliveries by skilled attendant: *Wistat, Version 4,* CD-ROM, based on WHO, "Coverage of maternity care: a listing of available information", fourth edition, 1996 (WHO/RHT/MSM/96.28); for maternal mortality ratio: United Nations Children's Fund, *The State of the World's Children 2000* (New York, Oxford University Press, 2000).

Note: Two dots (..) indicate that data are not available or are not reported separately.

[a] Adults and children.

[b] Percentage of women attended at least once during pregnancy by skilled health personnel for reasons related to pregnancy.

[c] For statistical purposes, the data for China do not include Hong Kong SAR and Macao SAR.

[d] Data refer to the Gaza Strip only.

Technical notes

Table 3.A presents statistics and indicators on health, including life expectancy at birth and at age 60, infant mortality rate, estimated number of people living with HIV/AIDS and the percentage of women among them, percentage of pregnant women receiving prenatal care, percentage of deliveries attended by a skilled attendant and maternal mortality ratio.

Life expectancy at birth is an overall estimate of the expected average number of years to be lived by a female or male newborn. Life expectancy at age 60 is the additional number of years expected to be lived by a woman or man who has survived to age 60. These indicators are obtained from the estimates and projections prepared every two years by the Population Division of the United Nations Secretariat. For many developing countries that lack complete and reliable statistics on births and deaths based on vital registration, various estimation techniques are used to calculate life expectancy using other sources of data, mainly population censuses and demographic surveys. Life expectancy at birth by sex gives a statistical summary of current differences in male and female mortality across all ages. However, trends and differentials in infant and child mortality rates are the predominant influence on trends and differentials in life expectancy at birth in most developing countries.

Infant mortality rate is the total number of deaths in a given year of female or male children less than one year of age, divided by the total number of female or male live births in the same year, multiplied by 1,000. It is an approximation of the number of deaths per 1,000 children born alive who die within one year of birth. This series is calculated from estimates and projections of the number of survivors at exact age 1 by sex prepared by the Population Division, based on a review of all available national sources. In most developing countries, where civil registration data are deficient, the most reliable sources are demographic surveys of households. Where these are not available, other sources and general estimates are made, which are necessarily of limited reliability.

The estimated number of people living with HIV/AIDS and the percentage of women among adults living with HIV/AIDS are obtained from a report prepared by UNAIDS and WHO in 1998. The data provided are summarized from the individual country 1997 epidemiological fact sheets, which are the collaborative efforts of UNAIDS, WHO and national AIDS programmes or other national authorities.

The estimated number of people living with HIV/AIDS includes all adults aged 15-49 and children under 15 infected with HIV, whether or not they have developed symptoms of AIDS, alive at the end of 1997. Percentage of women among those living with HIV/AIDS is calculated only for adults aged 15-49.

Table 3.A includes two basic indicators of maternity care during pregnancy and delivery: percentage of pregnant women receiving prenatal care and percentage of deliveries attended by a skilled attendant. The latter has been widely found to be a sensitive indicator in developing countries of access to maternal health services, which are essential to the survival and health of mothers and infants. Both indicators are estimated by WHO from a variety of national sources and are included in the *Women's Indicators and Statistics Database (Wistat)*.

Pregnant women receiving prenatal care refers to women attended at least once during pregnancy by skilled health personnel for reasons related to pregnancy. Number of live births, as a proxy for the total number of pregnancies, is used as the denominator in calculating the percentage of pregnant women receiving prenatal care. The percentage of deliveries attended by a skilled attendant is based on deliveries attended by skilled health personnel, irrespective of outcome (live birth or foetal death). Skilled attendant at delivery includes doctors (specialist or non-specialist) and/or persons with midwifery skills who can diagnose and manage obstetrical complications as well as normal deliveries. It excludes the category trained traditional birth attendant, even if the attendant has undergone extensive training and is subsequently integrated in the formal health-care system. The number of live births, as a proxy for the total number of pregnancies, is used as the denominator in calculating the percentage of deliveries attended by a skilled attendant.

Reliable national data on coverage of maternity care are not always available. Systematic national data-collection systems are often inadequate or absent. Estimates therefore rely on multiple sources, such as community-based studies, demographic and health surveys and other reports. The accuracy and precision of estimates depend upon the quality of the data on which they are based. Given the absence of standardized reporting systems, estimates given in this table should be interpreted with caution and viewed as indicating approximate orders of magnitude of coverage rather than precise figures. The estimates pertain to a period of time, rather than to a specific point in time. Furthermore, these estimates of maternity care do not take into account variation in the quality or impact of care.

Maternal mortality ratio is defined as the number of maternal deaths divided by the number of live births for a given year and is expressed per 100,000 live births. Maternal deaths are defined as those caused by deliveries and complications of pregnancy, child-birth and the puerperium. However, the exact definition varies from case to case and is not always clear in the original source, particularly regarding the inclusion of abortion-related deaths.

Maternal mortality ratio is compiled by the United Nations Children's Fund (UNICEF) and published annually in *The State of the World's Children*. Statistics on maternal mortality are based on national civil registration or demographic survey statistics on births and deaths calculated by national statistical services. The figures shown have not been adjusted for under-reporting or misclassification of cause of death. International comparability of maternal mortality statistics is hampered by varying and often undetermined degrees of misclassification or under-reporting of maternal deaths and different methods of data collection. WHO observes that most maternal deaths go unregistered in areas where maternal mortality rates are highest.

■ CHAPTER 4

Education and communication

Some important findings:

- The gender gap in primary and secondary schooling is closing but women still lag behind men in some countries of Africa and Southern Asia.

- Two thirds of the world's 876 million illiterates are women, and the number of illiterates is not expected to decrease significantly in the next twenty years.

- Women have made significant gains in higher education enrolment in most regions of the world; in some regions, women's enrolment now equals or surpasses that of men.

- More women than men lack the basic literacy and computer skills needed to enter "new media" professions.

- In many countries, women represent a rapidly increasing share of Internet users.

GENDER EQUALITY AND ACCESS TO EDUCATION

Access to primary and secondary education increasing

Enrolment in primary and secondary education has increased in almost all regions of the world. In some parts of the world, however, access to basic education has either stagnated or declined due to war, economic adjustments or cost shifting from government to families. This phenomenon dates back to the 1980s in some countries, notably in sub-Saharan Africa, where Governments have reduced spending on social services. It is a more recent phenomenon in many countries that are in transition from communism to a market economy. As these countries experience drastic reductions in government revenues, spending on education has decreased, school fees have been introduced and subsidies for school supplies and clothing have been reduced. This raises the cost of education to the family at the same time that family incomes are declining. As a result, enrolment in primary and secondary education has been decreasing for both girls and boys. The quality of education, once generally high, also seems to have declined, and inequality seems to be emerging, particularly for poor families, children in rural areas and ethnic minorities.[1]

In countries of the developed regions, excluding Eastern Europe, enrolment is nearly universal at both primary and secondary levels. The highest levels of enrolment outside the developed regions are in South America, the Caribbean[2] and Southern Africa. In these regions, more than 90 girls per 100 school-aged girls are enrolled (chart 4.1).

In Eastern Europe, Central Asia and Eastern Asia, most countries' primary/secondary gross enrolment ratios (see box on measuring education below) have declined to 90 or lower. The declines in enrolment are significant for both boys and girls in Central Asia and Eastern Europe, and for boys alone in Eastern Asia. In South-eastern Asia, Western Asia and Northern Africa, ratios are in general above 70 for girls and above 80 for boys. Enrolment ratios remain relatively low in only a few countries in these regions (chart 4.2).

Large increases in enrolment in primary and secondary education have taken place in Southern Asia and Africa, the regions with the lowest enrolment ratios in 1980. Despite these gains, enrolment remains low in most of the countries in these regions. Combined primary and secondary enrolment ratios are 47 for girls and 59 for boys in sub-Saharan African (excluding countries of Southern Africa), and 64 for girls and 77 for boys in Southern Asia. In Southern Asia, the regional average covers a wide spectrum: in Sri Lanka, for example, the enrolment ratio is 90 for girls and 87 for boys; in Afghanistan, it is 22 for girls and 49 for boys.

Closing the gender gap

Enrolment ratios have improved more for girls than for boys in those regions where girls' enrolment was significantly lower than boys' enrolment in the past—Northern Africa, sub-Saharan Africa (excluding Southern Africa), Southern Asia and Western Asia. As a result, the gender gap is closing in these regions, although it is still wide in many countries: in 22 African and 9 Asian countries, available data show enrolment ratios for girls to be less than 80 per cent those for boys (chart 4.2).

Levels of education

The United Nations Educational, Scientific and Cultural Organization (UNESCO) reports enrolment by level of education, based on the International Standard Classification of Education (ISCED). Data are generally reported for three levels: first-level (primary) education; second-level (secondary) education, including lower and upper secondary levels; and third-level (higher) education, including education not leading to a university degree, education corresponding to a university degree or equivalent and education leading to a research or higher degree.

Official school ages are generally as follows: primary education begins between ages 5 and 7 and lasts about five to six years; lower secondary education begins between ages 10 and 12 and lasts about three years; upper secondary education begins between ages 13 and 15 and lasts around three to five years; higher education begins between ages 17 and 19 and lasts for at least three or four years.

Literacy

UNESCO defines a *literate* person as one who can "with understanding both read and write a short simple statement on [her or] his everyday life", and an *illiterate* person as one who cannot "with understanding both read and write a short simple statement on [her or] his everyday life".

"*Literacy rate* refers in general to the proportion of the population who are literate, expressed as a percentage of the corresponding population. *Illiteracy rate* can be derived either by subtracting the corresponding literacy rate from 100 per cent, or taking the percentage of illiterates within the corresponding population".

It should be noted, however, that the gender gap is in favour of girls in certain regions. In South America and the Caribbean, for example, enrolment ratios for girls and boys, which were at the same levels in the past, improved more for girls than for boys, resulting in a gender gap now in favour of girls. In Eastern Asia, while the enrolment ratio for girls improved slightly, it declined for boys, resulting in an advantage for girls. In Southern Africa, the wide gender gap in favour of girls in the past still exists but has narrowed because of a much larger improvement in boys' enrolment.

Almost a third of the world's women live in Southern Asia and sub-Saharan Africa, where the gender gap in enrolment continues to be wide. The populations of these two regions are among the world's fastest growing, suggesting that the absolute number of illiterate women in these regions will continue to be enormous **(see the section below on illiteracy)**.

Less access for girls in rural areas

Girls are more likely than boys to suffer from limited access to education in rural areas. Demographic and Health Surveys (DHS) found that school attendance is much lower in rural than urban areas in 34 of 38 countries studied, and the imbalance tends to be much greater for girls. In the Niger, for instance, there are 80 girls for every 100 boys in school in urban areas, but only 41 girls per 100 boys in rural areas.[3]

These disparities reflect the unequal allocation of services, personnel and funds between urban and rural areas. They also reflect different demands on children's time—children are often kept away from school to help on family farms or in other family businesses—and different perceptions by parents of the value of education.

In addition, the distance that students must travel to school in rural areas tends to affect the enrolment of girls more than boys. Distance to school is a crucial factor in determining girls' attendance, especially in countries where families do not want girls exposed to boys in classrooms and to men on the way to and from school.[4] Girls' access to education is particularly low in Pakistan, for example, where schools are sex-segregated starting at the primary level, and where 21 per cent of girls in rural areas (compared to only 9 per cent of boys) do not have a school within 1 kilometre of their homes.

The quality of school facilities also influences enrolment levels. A study in Pakistan, for instance, indicates that girls' enrolment is positively influenced by the extent to which teachers live in the communities and by the amenities available to girls in the schools. Such factors appear to be less important for boys, perhaps because they often have more school choices and parents are less worried about sending them away from home.[5]

Boys stay in school longer than girls

Many children drop out of school before acquiring the necessary skills, which will enable them to continue to learn. In the developing countries, UNESCO

Chart 4.1+:

Enrolment ratios have increased in most of the developing world
Combined primary/secondary gross enrolment ratio

	1980		1990		1994/1996	
	Girls	Boys	Girls	Boys	Girls	Boys
Africa						
Northern Africa	58	80	67	82	76	86
Southern Africa	77	66	94	87	99	95
Rest of sub-Saharan Africa	36	53	40	53	47	59
Latin America and the Caribbean						
Caribbean	83	82	82	82	93	87
Central America	72	73	80	78	80	81
South America	84	85	86	86	91	89
Asia						
Eastern Asia	86	90	88	89	89	85
South-eastern Asia	71	76	75	79	77	82
Southern Asia	35	58	54	70	64[a]	77[a]
Central Asia	99	109	97	99	88	89
Western Asia	69	82	78	86	75	83
Oceania	63	68	76	77	75	78
Developed regions						
Eastern Europe	96	97	91	90	90	89
Western Europe	93	93	100	100	110	108
Other developed regions	95	94	98	98	107	107

✤ In this and subsequent charts, regional and subregional averages are unweighted (i.e., the averages do not take into account the size of the individual countries' populations) and are based only upon available data for that region (see page xi for fuller explanation).

Source: Prepared by the Statistics Division of the United Nations Secretariat from *Women's Indicators and Statistics Database (Wistat)*, *Version 4*, CD-ROM (United Nations publication, Sales No. E.00.XVII.4), based on United Nations Educational, Scientific and Cultural Organization, *Statistical Yearbook* (Paris, various years up to 1998).

[a] The average is based on only four countries.

estimates that only 74 of 100 girls (and only 76 of 100 boys) enrolled at grade 1 reach grade 5. Barely half of the children (52 per cent of girls and 59 per cent of boys) enrolled at primary level in countries that UNESCO classifies as "least developed" remain in school after grade 4.[6]

UNESCO reports that boys stay in school longer than girls in all regions except in the developed regions and in Latin America and the Caribbean. The reasons for leaving school differ for girls and boys, and for primary and secondary levels.

It is often assumed that pregnancy causes young women to leave school. However, in only one of 13 countries surveyed by DHS was "getting pregnant" most cited as the reason for leaving secondary school. In only five of those countries did more than 10 per cent of young women give pregnancy as their reason for leaving school. (In three of the countries, more than 20 per cent gave this reason.) [7]

At the primary level, girls in most countries frequently cited the following reasons for leaving school: "did not like school", "did not pass exams", "not able to pay fees", and "help needed in the family" (either on the farm or in business or because the family needed extra money).[8] The first two reasons may be associated with the low quality of teaching and teaching facilities, while the last two reasons may be linked to the family's financial situation. Girls' motivation may also be diminished when motherhood is the only role they see for themselves, or when role models and adequate curricula are lacking.

Illiteracy among women declining slowly

Nearly two thirds of the world's 876 million illiterates are women, according to UNESCO estimates.[9] In virtually every country where illiteracy is high, women are more likely than men to be illiterate. Despite significant gains in school enrolment, the number of illiterates is projected to decline by only about 10 million by 2005.[10] In some regions, the number of illiterate women will still be growing. In sub-Saharan Africa and Southern Asia, where many girls still do not go to school and populations are growing fast, the number of illiterate women is projected to rise from 87 to 91 million and from 256 to 285 million, respectively.

Improvements in school enrolment over the years show up in the generally lower illiteracy rates among younger adults. However, illiteracy rates are still high in those parts of the world where many girls and boys remain out of school or drop out too early to acquire the necessary skills to function as literate individuals. UNESCO estimates that in 2000, among children in the official school-age group for the primary level, 88 million children are not enrolled;

Chart 4.2:

Girls still have less access to education than boys in many countries
Combined primary/secondary gross enrolment ratio, 1994/1996

Northern Africa	W	M
Morocco	54	71

Sub-Saharan Africa	W	M
Benin	35	63
Burkina Faso	16[a]	26[a]
Central African Republic	26	43
Chad	23	47
Côte d'Ivoire	38	58
Dem. Rep. of the Congo	41	62
Djibouti	22	31
Ethiopia	20	33
Gambia	46	62
Ghana	50	64
Guinea	20	41
Guinea-Bissau	27[a]	50[a]
Mali	20	33
Mauritania	42	54
Mozambique	27	38
Niger	14	23
Nigeria	61	77

Sub-Saharan Africa (cont'd)	W	M
Senegal	37	48
Sierra Leone	29[a]	43[a]
Somalia	8[a]	16[a]
Togo	59	92

South-eastern Asia	W	M
Cambodia	68	86
Lao People's Dem. Rep.	63	80

Southern Asia	W	M
Afghanistan	22	49
Bangladesh	38[a]	49[a]
India	62	81
Nepal	53[a]	94[a]
Pakistan	26[a]	53[a]

Western Asia	W	M
Iraq	58	73
Yemen	34	90

Source: *Women's Indicators and Statistics Database (Wistat), Version 4*, CD-ROM (United Nations publication, Sales No. E.00.XVII.4), based on United Nations Educational, Scientific and Cultural Organization, *Statistical Yearbook* (Paris, various years up to 1998).

Note: Countries listed are those where enrolment ratio for girls is 80 per cent less than that of boys.

[a] Refers to a year around 1990.

Chart 4.3:

In some countries illiteracy is high even among young people, and particularly among young women
Illiteracy rate, persons aged 15-24, 1990 census round

Africa	W	M
Algeria	38	14
Benin	73	45
Burundi	52	40
Cameroon	29	15
Central African Republic	65	37
Côte d'Ivoire	62	40
Djibouti	62	38
Egypt	49	29
Malawi	51	30
Mali	81	62
Mauritania	62	43
Morocco	54	29
Niger	90	75

Africa (cont'd)	W	M
Senegal	72	51
Sudan	41	22
Tunisia	28	7
Uganda	37	23
Zambia	28	20

Latin America	W	M
Guatemala	29	18

Asia	W	M
Nepal	67	32
Yemen	64	17

Source: Prepared by the Statistics Division of the United Nations Secretariat from *Women's Indicators and Statistics Database (Wistat), Version 4*, CD-ROM (United Nations publication, Sales No. E.00.XVII.4), based on national data as published in United Nations Educational, Scientific and Cultural Organization, *Statistical Yearbook* (Paris, various years up to 1998).

Note: Countries listed are those where more than 25 per cent of women aged 15-24 are illiterate.

three out of five of those are girls. The widest gender gap is in Southern Asia, with 22 million girls and 13 million boys out of school.[11]

More than one in four women aged 15 to 24 are illiterate in 21 of the countries for which data are available from the 1990 round of censuses **(chart 4.3)**. On average, the highest percentages of illiterate young women are in Africa (except Southern Africa)—over 40 per cent of African women aged 15 to 24. Illiteracy is also high in Southern Asia (29 per cent of women

and 14 per cent of men) and in Central America (16 per cent of women and 14 per cent of men). In other parts of the world, the large majority of younger people are literate, although a gender gap (with women more likely than men to be illiterate) still persists even where illiteracy rates are low. The Caribbean is the most notable exception; at all ages, men are more likely than women to be illiterate **(chart 4.4)**.

UNESCO estimates of adult illiteracy show a clear improvement over the past two decades **(chart 4.5)**.[12]

Measuring education

Data on education come from one of three sources: population censuses, household surveys or records kept by education ministries. All three sources present problems for measuring education accurately. Censuses collect information on educational participation and attainment for the population, but they are usually conducted only once a decade and the results often do not become available until many years later. Household surveys are carried out more frequently, but surveys that measure such particular topics as literacy are rare. Most often, data available from international sources are derived from the records of education ministries, where record-keeping practices may differ.

Literacy
The ability to read is an ideal measure of education, especially for assessing gender differences and actual educational attainment. Attending a few years of school does not necessarily enable a person to master reading and writing, and many people acquire literacy outside the formal school system. However, given the sensitivity of questions regarding literacy, interviewers do not always succeed in capturing the reality.

In addition, countries do not always follow standard international definitions of illiteracy. They may identify illiterate persons as those with no schooling or they may change the definition between censuses. Criteria and practices for identifying illiterates also vary. Misreporting and biases in self-reporting can affect the reliability of literacy statistics. Finally, most available data on illiteracy, apart from UNESCO estimates, are derived from population censuses, which are usually conducted every ten years. As a result, the findings are often too old to assess recent trends.

School enrolment
The gross enrolment ratio (GER) is the total number of children enrolled at a specific level of edu-

cation, regardless of age, expressed as a percentage of the official school-age population corresponding to the same level of education in a given school-year. The GER is obtained by dividing the number of individuals enrolled at a given level of education, regardless of age, by the population of the age group that officially corresponds to the given level of education, and multiplying the result by 100.

A high GER generally indicates a high degree of educational participation, whether the pupils are in the official age group or not. A GER can exceed 100 because some enrollees (the numerator) may be older or younger than the official ages (the denominator). A GER value of 100 is therefore a necessary but not a sufficient condition for determining whether all eligible children are enrolled in school. For example, a recent study in a poor district in Kenya found 43 per cent of girls aged 16-18 in primary school, only 17 per cent in secondary school and the rest out of school. A similar situation was observed in Bangladesh, where a high percentage of girls aged 13-19 were in primary school.[a] A rigorous interpretation of a given GER requires additional information to assess the extent to which students repeat grades, enter school late, are absent from school, and drop out.

Higher education usually has no official ages for attendance. Gross enrolment ratios could be calculated for the five-year age group following the official secondary school-leaving age. However, the high level of drop-outs, frequent re-enrolment and the varying duration of third-level programmes make this ratio particularly uncertain. Consequently, higher education enrolment is generally measured in relation to the total population (per 1,000 or per 100,000).

The net enrolment ratio (NER) represents the number of children in the official age group

enrolled at a given level of education, divided by the total number of children of that age in a given school year, and multiplied by 100. It shows the extent of participation in a given level of education of children or youths belonging to the official age group. Consequently, the theoretical maximum value of the NER is 100. However, values up to 105 may be observed, reflecting inconsistencies in the enrolment and/or population data.

Neither the GER nor the NER provides a reliable measure of actual school attendance, particularly in developing regions, where absenteeism and dropping out are widespread. Moreover, since attendance may differ for girls and boys who are involved in household work at different levels and who drop out for different reasons, these ratios are not an accurate reflection of gender differentials.

Educational achievement
Measuring the effectiveness of the school system for both girls and boys ideally involves measuring educational achievement. This is especially important where the quality of education is low. Simple enrolment is not sufficient; children should actually learn at the appropriate level.

One way to measure achievement is to determine the number of years of schooling successfully completed (or the highest level attained). These data may be derived from population censuses and surveys but are not always compiled for international sources (data are available for some 80 countries). Moreover, data on educational attainment are generally gathered for the adult population (aged 25 or older), and therefore do not reflect recent trends in education. Finally, attainment does not measure the quality of the educational system or the actual skills learned by pupils. The only way to accomplish this is through "standardized tests", which are relatively rare, particularly in developing countries.

[a] Sajeda Amin, "Female education and fertility in Bangladesh: the influence of marriage and the family", in Roger Jeffery and Alaka M. Basu, eds., *Girls' Schooling, Women's Autonomy and Fertility Change in South Asia* (New Delhi, Sage Publications, 1996).

In some regions, estimated illiteracy rates for the year 2000 are half or less the levels of 20 years ago. Improvements are not as pronounced in sub-Saharan Africa and Southern Asia, where illiteracy rates in 2000 are 70 and 77 per cent, respectively, of their 1980 levels. Illiteracy is almost eradicated in the developed regions, and rates have declined rapidly in Eastern and South-eastern Asia, where illiteracy rates are down from 27 to 12 per cent for women and from 12 to 5 per cent for men.

Illiteracy is generally much higher in rural areas because educational opportunities are more limited and families make greater demands on children's time. The proportions of women who cannot read were two to three times higher in rural than in urban areas in 37 countries surveyed between 1990 and 1996.[13]

Enrolling in school is not enough to ensure that children will be able to function as literate adults in society, or to take advantage of opportunities for higher education and work. Recent DHS surveys found that large shares of women who attended or even completed primary school cannot read. In 15 of the 22 countries studied in Africa, and in three of the 16 countries studied in Asia and Latin America and the Caribbean, more than 20 per cent of women with some or complete primary education cannot read.[14]

Higher education lowers fertility

The extensive research on the relationship between education and fertility over the last 20 years has shown that just a few years of education or basic literacy alone has little effect in reducing the number of children a woman bears, and may even result in a slightly higher level of fertility. At higher levels of education, however, all countries show a clear inverse relationship between educational attainment and fertility.[15]

Fertility was much lower among women with secondary or higher levels of education than among women with no schooling in 28 countries with DHS surveys between 1990 and 1995. In contrast, fertility was only slightly lower among women with a primary education than among women with no education. In six countries, fertility of women with primary education was as high or even higher than fertility of women with no education.[16] The effects of education, especially limited education, on fertility are very much influenced by the national context. Factors that play a key role are the presence of mass schooling, the existence of family planning programmes and employment opportunities for women[17] **(see box on education and the fertility transition)**.

Fewer studies exist on the impact of men's education on fertility. DHS surveys that report both women's fertility and their husbands' level of educa-

Chart 4.4:

Illiteracy is lower among younger adults, but gender gaps in favour of men persist
Illiteracy rate, 1990 census round

	15-24 yrs		25 yrs or over	
	W	M	W	M
Africa				
Northern Africa	42	20	76	51
Southern Africa	11	15	41	37
Rest of sub-Saharan Africa	43	29	70	47
Latin America and the Caribbean				
Caribbean	4	7	10	11
Central America	16	14	33	26
South America	5	5	16	11
Asia				
South-eastern Asia	4	3	20	9
Southern Asia	29	14	51	33
Central Asia	<1	<1	5	2
Western Asia	12	6	32	18
Oceania	2	2	11	7
Developed regions				
Eastern Europe	<1	<1	5	1
Western Europe	<1	2	12	8

Source: Prepared by the Statistics Division of the United Nations Secretariat from *Women's Indicators and Statistics Database (Wistat)*, Version 4, CD-ROM (United Nations publication, Sales No. E.00.XVII.4) based on national data as published in United Nations Educational, Scientific and Cultural Organization, *Statistical Yearbook* (Paris, various years up to 1998).

Note: Averages are not shown for Eastern Asia because data are available for only one country. No data were available for "other developed regions".

Chart 4.5:

Illiteracy has decreased for women and men around the world
Estimated illiteracy rate, population 15 years or over

	1980		2000	
	W	M	W	M
Africa				
Northern Africa	74	43	48	25
Southern Africa	33	35	16	21
Rest of sub-Saharan Africa	73	51	51	33
Latin America and the Caribbean				
Caribbean	18	18	11	12
Central America	31	26	22	18
South America	18	12	9	6
Asia				
Eastern and South-eastern Asia	27	12	12	5
Southern Asia	65	44	50	30
Western Asia	48	27	25	13
Developed regions	8	4	3	1

Source: Prepared by the Statistics Division of the United Nations Secretariat from *Women's Indicators and Statistics Database (Wistat)*, Version 4, CD-ROM (United Nations publication, Sales No. E.00.XVII.4), based on literacy estimates and projections, 1970-2025, provided by United Nations Educational, Scientific and Cultural Organization in 1999.

Note: The data presented here are based on UNESCO estimates and may differ from rates derived from population censuses or sample surveys. Averages are not shown for Central Asia and Oceania because data are available for only one country.

Chart 4.6:

In some regions women's enrolment equals or surpasses men's

Third-level enrolment per 1000 population

	1980		1990		1994/1996	
	W	M	W	M	W	M
Africa						
Northern Africa	5	11	9	15	12	16
Southern Africa	2	3	4	5	7	8
Rest of sub-Saharan Africa	1	2	1	3	1	3
Latin America and the Caribbean						
Caribbean	5	6	14	12	16	14
Central America	10	14	13	15	12	14
South America	13	17	13	14	15	15
Asia						
Eastern Asia	11	15	15	22	20	25
South-eastern Asia	7	8	11	11	11	12
Southern Asia	1	4	3	6	7	11
Central Asia	..	..	20	22	18	21
Western Asia	13	16	16	16	19	16
Developed regions						
Eastern Europe	18	16	18	18	23	20
Western Europe	14	18	24	26	32	31
Other developed regions	33	38	43	40	51	47

tion provide some insights. In 16 of the 28 countries with data, fertility is significantly higher among women whose husbands have a primary-level education than among those whose husbands have no schooling at all. Women's fertility clearly decreases only when the husband has a secondary-level education, although not as much as when the wife has attained that level.[18]

Gender gap narrowing in higher education

The gender gap in higher education enrolment has disappeared in many parts of the world. In the Caribbean and Western Asia, women's enrolment has actually surpassed that of men (chart 4.6). In Western Europe, the former preponderance of men in higher education, still evident in the 1980s, has recently disappeared. Enrolment ratios are much

Source: Prepared by the Statistics Division of the United Nations Secretariat from *Women's Indicators and Statistics Database (Wistat), Version 4*, CD-ROM (United Nations publication, Sales No. E.00.XVII.4), based on United Nations Educational, Scientific and Cultural Organization, *Statistical Yearbook* (Paris, various years up to 1998).

Note: Two dots (..) indicate that data are not available or are not reported separately. Averages for Oceania are not presented because data are available for only a few countries.

Work keeps some children out of school[a]

The International Labour Organization (ILO) estimates that 250 million school-age children (aged 5-14) are engaged in economic activities. Of this number, 120 million are working full-time and 130 million are combining work with schooling.[b] Among schoolchildren, 42 per cent of girls and 33 per cent of boys are engaged in some form of part-time economic activity.

In general, more boys than girls are reported as economically active—on average, three boys to two girls. However, many girls not counted as working are engaged full- or part-time in unpaid economic activities within the household. Moreover, girls often work full-time in non-economic housework, taking care of younger siblings and doing household chores. One in three children who do not attend school report that housework is the main reason. The ILO estimates that if full-time housework were taken into account, the number of working girls would probably exceed that of boys.

Rural children are twice as likely as urban children to be economically active. This fact, together with limited school facilities, explains the wide gaps in schooling and literacy between rural

areas and urban centres. If the large numbers of children—especially girls—who engage in unpaid, generally under-enumerated activities are taken into account, the disparity is probably even wider.[c]

Rural children, in particular rural girls, begin to work at a very early age, closing off the opportunity to obtain even the lowest level of education. Based on surveys of several countries around the world, the ILO estimates that up to 20 per cent of working children in rural areas are only 5 to 9 years of age, compared to around 5 per cent in urban centres.

Child labour, to a great extent a consequence of poverty, is certainly a major obstacle to edu-

cation—the best means for escaping poverty. The International Labour Conference, at its eighty-seventh session in 1999, adopted a convention concerning the prohibition of, and immediate action for, the elimination of the worst forms of child labour. This convention recognizes the importance of education in eliminating the worst forms of child labour, and reinforces the 1996 ILO resolution on the elimination of child labour. That resolution recognized that child labour is to a great extent caused by poverty, and that the long-term solution lies in sustained economic growth leading to social progress, in particular poverty alleviation and universal education.[d]

[a] This box is based on Kebebew Ashagrie, *Statistics on Working Children and Hazardous Child Labour in Brief* (Geneva, ILO, 1998).

[b] The figures reported in this box are estimates prepared by the ILO on the basis of national household surveys. The surveys were carried out following a newly developed methodology for the measurement of child labour, as part of the ILO interdepartmental project on "the elimination of child labour", launched in 1992.

[c] The estimates reported consider the "currently active population", which is based on a short reference period. Figures on the "usually active population" are based on a longer reference period, e.g., 12 months, and also capture seasonal work. In the latter case, the ILO estimates that up to 40 per cent of children aged 5-14 are economically active.

[d] See ILO resolution concerning the elimination of child labour, International Labour Conference (eighty-fourth session), 1996.

higher for women than for men in many countries of Western Asia, Eastern and Western Europe and in the United States and New Zealand (see table 4.A). The United States Department of Education projects that this new gender gap in favour or women will increase dramatically in the United States by 2007, with only 6.9 million men enrolled compared to 9.2 million women.[19]

A significant gender gap in favour of men in higher education remains in those developed countries where a large gap already existed and where overall enrolment is much lower than in other developed countries. In Switzerland, Japan and Germany, fewer than 80 women per 100 men are enrolled in higher education. In Switzerland, 15 out of 1,000 women are enrolled in higher education, compared to 26 per 1,000 men (chart 4.7).

In Eastern Europe, women have traditionally had higher enrolment ratios than men and third-level education has become more common over the years for both women and men. Women now account for 55 per cent of enrollees in the region. The deterioration observed in basic education in countries in transition does not seem to have affected higher education in this region (see section above on access to basic education). In contrast, third-level enrolments have declined slightly in Central Asia over the last few years.

Overall, enrolment in third-level education is highest in the developed regions, especially outside Europe; on average, third-level enrolment ratios are 51 for women and 47 for men (chart 4.8). The exception is Japan, where ratios are only 27 for women and 36 for men.

Enrolment ratios are also relatively high in Eastern Asia and South-eastern Asia, but there is considerable variation within these regions. Cambodia, the Lao People's Democratic Republic, Sri Lanka and China have ratios among the lowest in the world. In contrast, enrolment ratios in the Republic of Korea, the Philippines and Singapore are similar to those of other countries where basic schooling is universal.

In Latin America and the Caribbean, a significant number of women and men take advantage of opportunities for higher education. Central America is the only part of the region where women's enrolment is lower than that of men.

Relatively few people have access to higher education in sub-Saharan Africa (2 per 1,000 women and 4 per 1,000 men) and in Southern Asia (7 per 1,000 women and 11 per 1,000 men). More people go on to third-level education in Northern Africa and

Education and the fertility transition

Demographers and social scientists have long studied the impact of women's schooling on the number of children they have. Few, however, have investigated the link between mass education (the near universal enrolment of children in primary schooling) and the fertility transition; that is, the immediate or short-term impact of education policies on family size.

A recent study on fertility and education, using DHS surveys rather than the international data commonly used, has examined this relationship.[a] The study focused on 17 African countries: Botswana, Burkina Faso, Cameroon, Côte d'Ivoire, Ghana, Kenya, Madagascar, Malawi, Mali, Namibia, Nigeria, Senegal, South Africa, Uganda, the United Republic of Tanzania, Zambia and Zimbabwe. Six of these countries have achieved mass education and are well into their fertility transition: Kenya, Zimbabwe, Botswana, Namibia, Zambia and South Africa.[b] Three more countries identified as having begun the fertility transition—Ghana, the United Republic of Tanzania and Cameroon—have already or have almost met at least one of the criteria used to identify mass education. The other countries are still far from achieving mass education.

The study also considered the hypothesis that mass education is effective in bringing about demographic changes only to the extent to which improvements are not confined to boys. It found that enrolment for girls has in fact increased and the gender gap has been narrowing in almost all the countries examined.

Addressing the wide gap between urban and rural settings in both fertility levels and educational opportunities, the study also suggested that where educational resources are unequally distributed between rural and urban areas, fertility will decline significantly only to the extent that urbanization takes place rapidly. Along the same lines, a study in 12 communities in Pakistan reported that contraceptive use was highest in settings with greater choice of schools, including schools for girls.[c]

[a] Cynthia B. Lloyd, Carol Kaufman and Paul Hewett, "The Spread of Primary Schooling in Sub-Saharan Africa: Implications for Fertility Change", forthcoming. An earlier version of the paper was presented at a seminar on reproductive change in sub-Saharan Africa, Nairobi, 2-4 November 1998.

[b] In the study, mass education was measured based on the following criteria: 90 per cent of 15-19 ever in school, 75 per cent of 15-19 completed four years or more and 60 per cent completed primary education.

[c] Zeba Sathar, Cynthia Lloyd, Minhaj ul Haque and Cem Mete, "Children's schooling and family building strategies: the case of rural Pakistan", paper presented at the annual meeting of the Population Association of America, New York, 25-27 March 1999.

Western Asia. However, there is a significant gender gap in favour of men in Northern African countries. Conversely, the gender gap in higher education is in favour of women in the Arab States, particularly in the United Arab Emirates.[20]

Some fields of study still dominated by men

Despite better access to higher education in most parts of the world, women do not always have access to fields of study traditionally dominated by men. Gender-based stereotypes survive, and role models that could lead young women to challenging, better-paid careers are scarce. In addition, the traditional view that women should engage in activities that are more suitable to their roles as mothers and caregivers discourages women from enrolling in fields traditionally occupied by men.

Liberal arts is the one field in which women predominate. In most regions, women represent two thirds or more of the total enrolled in this field.[21] Liberal arts is the field most frequently chosen by women in Asia, in sub-Saharan Africa and in the developed countries outside Europe **(chart 4.8)**. Many women also enrol in law and business schools in several regions: Latin America, Eastern Europe and Southern Africa.

Large proportions of women who continue into higher education enrol in "science and engineering", although men still tend to dominate this field. In all regions, science and engineering are the dominant fields of study for men; in Latin America and the Caribbean, in Northern Africa and Western Europe, these fields are also the dominant areas of study for women.

Enrolment is lowest for both women and men in agriculture. This is also the field where a gender gap is most apparent, with women often representing only one third of the total enrolment. Europe, Eastern Asia and the Caribbean are notable exceptions: in these regions over 40 per cent of agriculture students are women.[22]

TEACHERS AND EDUCATIONAL FACILITIES

Women under-represented in teaching at higher levels

Increasingly, primary and secondary teachers are women in most regions. Between 1985 and 1995, the global percentage of teachers who are women slightly increased from 55 to 56 per cent at the primary level and from 42 to 47 per cent at the secondary level.[23] Gains were largest in the Arab states,[24] and in Eastern and Southern Asia, where the share of women among teachers rose by 6 or 7 percentage points.

In most regions, the large majority of primary teachers are women. Percentages vary widely, ranging from an average of 87 per cent in Eastern Europe to 35 per cent in sub-Saharan Africa (excluding Southern Africa) and 47 per cent in Southern Asia **(chart 4.9)**. In some countries, women represent almost the totality of primary school teachers, but in others—14 in sub-Saharan Africa and two in Asia—fewer than 30 per cent of primary school teachers are women.

At higher educational levels, women are a lower percentage of teachers. At the secondary level, only 24 per cent of teachers are women in sub-Saharan Africa (excluding Southern Africa), and only 38 per cent in Southern Asia. At this level, women teachers outnumber men in Latin America and the Caribbean, Central and Western Asia, and most of the developed countries. Data for teachers at the third level are available for only 78 countries. In all but two of these countries,

Chart 4.7:

A large gender gap in favour of men in higher education persists in many countries or areas

Third-level enrolment per 1000 population, 1994/1996

Africa	W	M
Algeria	10.0	14.7
Benin	0.9	4.2
Burkina Faso	0.4	1.3
Burundi	0.4	1.1
Central African Republic	0.3	2.1
Chad	0.1	1.0
Côte d'Ivoire	2.1	6.0
Egypt	14.7	23.2
Eritrea	0.2	1.7
Ethiopia	0.2	1.0
Gambia	1.1	1.9
Guinea	0.2	1.9
Mauritania	1.3	6.2
Morocco	9.3	13.3
Swaziland	5.4	7.5
Togo	1.1	5.3
Uganda	1.0	2.2
Zimbabwe	3.7	9.1

Latin America and the Caribbean	W	M
Guatemala	3.6	11.5
Honduras	8.7	11.0
Jamaica	6.6	8.8

Asia	W	M
Cambodia	0.3	1.7
China	3.3	6.1
Hong Kong SAR	14.4	18.2
India	4.8	7.9
Indonesia	8.1	15.2
Iran (Islamic Republic of)	11.9	19.9
Lao People's Democratic Republic	1.5	3.6
Republic of Korea	41.8	70.1
Sri Lanka	3.9	5.6
Syrian Arab Republic	13.0	18.1
Tajikistan	11.9	25.4
Turkey	15.2	23.9
Yemen	1.1	7.3

Oceania	W	M
Papua New Guinea	2.1	4.2

Developed regions	W	M
Germany	22.9	29.9
Japan	27.2	35.8
Switzerland	15.4	26.0

Source: *Women's Indicators and Statistics Database (Wistat), Version 4*, CD-ROM (United Nations publication, Sales No. E.00.XVII.4).

Note: Countries or areas listed are those where third-level enrolment (per 1000 population) levels for women are less than 80 per cent of those for men; countries where enrolment levels are less than one student per 1000 population for both women and men are not shown.

Chart 4.8:

Many women are choosing fields traditionally dominated by men
Percentage distribution of third-level enrolment by field of study, 1994/1996

	Liberal arts		Law and business		Science and engineering		Agriculture	
	W	M	W	M	W	M	W	M
Africa								
Northern Africa	35	20	22	24	40	49	2	3
Southern Africa	41	37	24	20	24	34	1	2
Rest of sub-Saharan Africa	37	30	31	29	25	34	4	5
Latin America and the Caribbean								
Caribbean	31	14	8	5	59	76	2	3
Central America	24	14	32	25	40	58	1	2
South America	29	10	30	30	35	51	3	5
Asia								
Eastern Asia	45	23	17	21	30	45	3	4
South-eastern Asia	47	27	19	17	31	38	3	6
Southern Asia	44	30	15	22	38	45	3	4
Western Asia	45	26	17	24	33	44	2	2
Developed regions								
Eastern Europe	34	14	26	25	33	51	5	6
Western Europe	35	18	22	24	39	53	2	3
Other developed regions	36	16	25	30	25	40	1	3

Source: Prepared by the Statistics Division of the United Nations Secretariat from *Women's Indicators and Statistics Database (Wistat), Version 4,* CD-ROM (United Nations publication, Sales No. E.00.XVII.4), based on United Nations Educational, Scientific and Cultural Organization, *Statistical Yearbook* (Paris, various years up to 1998).

Note: Averages for Oceania and Central Asia are not presented because data are available for only very few countries.

Chart 4.9:

Women tend to teach at lower levels, men at higher levels
Percentage of teachers who are women, 1994/1996

	1st level	2nd level	3rd level		1st level	2nd level	3rd level
Africa				**Asia** (cont'd)			
Northern Africa	50	36	26	Central Asia	79	67	..
Southern Africa	75	50	35	Western Asia	66	52	28
Rest of sub-Saharan Africa	35	24	14	**Oceania**	58	42	..
Latin America and the Caribbean				**Developed regions**			
Caribbean	75	63	45	Eastern Europe	87	67	40
Central America	78	53	32	Western Europe	75	53	31
South America	73	54	31	Other developed regions	77	53	33
Asia							
Eastern Asia	69	48	31				
South-eastern Asia	53	47	23				
Southern Asia	47	38	23				

Source: Prepared by the Statistics Division of the United Nations Secretariat from *Women's Indicators and Statistics Database (Wistat), Version 4,* CD-ROM (United Nations publication, Sales No. E.00.XVII.4), based on United Nations Educational, Scientific and Cultural Organization, *Statistical Yearbook* (Paris, various years up to 1998).

Note: Two dots (..) indicate that data are not available.

men teachers largely outnumber women. Even in Eastern Europe, where women largely outnumber men in primary and secondary teaching, women are only 40 per cent of teachers in higher education.

Women are also under-represented in leadership and management roles in education. While the percentage of women in such posts as deputy vice-chancellor and academic head of department seems to be growing, there are relatively few women at the decision-making level (chart 4.10).

Although women represent the majority of the world's teachers, they outnumber men only among the lower-paid primary teachers and often have only primary education themselves. The 1998 UNESCO *World Education Report* suggests that teachers' salaries would be higher if teaching were a male profession.[25]

Education facilities found lacking

According to the UNESCO report, in most of the developed countries examined, more than 60 per cent of teachers are aged 40 or older. In the developing countries, this percentage is less than 40 and often as low as 20. In addition, teachers in poorer countries are considerably younger than elsewhere, usually have a much lower level of education and work in physically deteriorating facilities, with larger classes and scarce teaching materials.

Most of the world's teachers lack the resources and support that they need to work effectively. The UNESCO report shows that schools in the poorest countries face dire shortages of basic necessities, from water and electricity to textbooks. A 1995 UNESCO-United Nations Children's Fund (UNICEF) survey found that 90 per cent or more of primary school pupils in Bangladesh, Burkina Faso, Equatorial Guinea, Ethiopia, Nepal, Uganda, the United Republic of Tanzania and Zambia were in schools with no electricity. In 11 out of 14 countries sampled, over 90 per cent of pupils were in schools without a world map.[26]

In transition economies—in an overall context of reduced economic output and government spending—traditionally low teachers' salaries have further declined. Due to low pay scales and worsening condi-

Chart 4.10:
Few women hold decision-making positions in higher education

Organization	No. of member universities	% institutions led by women
Association of African Universities	120	5
Association of Arab Universities	103	2
Association of Commonwealth Universities	463	8 [a]
Association of European Universities	497	6-8
Association of French-speaking Universities	270	5-7
Association of Universities of Asia and the Pacific	140 [b]	5
Inter-American Organization for Higher Education	350	5 [c]
Union des Universidades de America Latina	177	27

Source: United Nations Educational, Scientific and Cultural Organization, "Higher education and women: issues and perspectives", paper prepared for the International Conference on Higher Education (Paris, 1998).

[a] 10% in non-ACU member universities.

[b] Founding member universities.

[c] 14% in Brazil.

Women on the web

The past few years have seen an explosion in women's on-line networking and Web sites around the world. Some sites are intended to widen women's network of contacts; others provide information in specific fields; and still others have an educational or mentoring component.

One of the most ambitious media-related Web projects so far has been the publication of the world's first virtual women's newspaper. Launched as a pilot in May 1999, *Worldwoman* is the initiative of a Scottish journalist. It aims to bring international news—selected, written and edited by women—to a global audience. It is also part of a strategy to encourage women to engage in the new information technology, which many still avoid.

A key global initiative to increase women's access to and use of new communication technologies is the Women's Programme of the Association for Progressive Communications (APC). Established in 1993, the programme aims to increase women's participation in computer communications so that they can redress gender inequities in the design, implementation and use of new technologies. The programme offers opportunities and support to women and women's organizations in all regions, and encourages information exchange, networking and other means of linking women who use information technologies.

Major regional initiatives, often directly linked with APC, are described below.

In West Africa, Environnement et développement du tiers monde—synérgie genre et développement (ENDA-SYNFEV) promotes electronic communication for women's groups as a tool for action, mainly in the fields of health and human rights. It organizes on-line conferences and technical training for women on the use of information and communication in francophone Africa.

In Southern Africa, Women's Net aims to make technology accessible to women by providing resources and information, organizing gender-sensitive training and creating strategic links between projects and organizations.

In Asia, the Asian Women's Resource Exchange (AWORC) was set up in 1998 to build electronic resource-sharing among women's information centres in Asia, and to promote Internet literacy and activism among individual women and women's organizations.

In Latin America, the Area Mujeres (Women's Programme) of the Latin American Information Agency (ALAI) was founded in 1989. It collaborates with organizations that share its electronic communication and networking goals. It also engages in advocacy, from a gender perspective, on the right to communicate.

tions, some teachers are resorting to informal sector activities to be able to make a living. In Georgia, for example, it is quite common to find women teachers among street vendors in the villages.[27]

INFORMATION AND COMMUNICATION

"New technologies" creating new challenges

Profound changes are occurring worldwide in the communications and information industries. Increasingly, these changes will affect women's and men's use of communication tools and information content.

The Internet is the fastest-growing communications medium in history. In 1999, it was estimated that over 201 million people worldwide had Internet access, up from 76 million in 1997. However, over one half of the users were in just two countries: the United States and Canada. North America and Europe accounted for almost 80 per cent of Internet users in 1999. In contrast, Africa, with 13 per cent of the world's population, had only 1.7 million Internet users, less than 1 per cent of the world total.[28] In mid-1999, the entire continent of Africa (population 780 million) had roughly the same number of computers connected to the Internet as Latvia (population 2.5 million).[29]

Disparities among countries in access to information technologies are acute (chart 4.11). In Southern Asia and sub-Saharan Africa, there are about 1.5 telephone lines per 100 people, compared to 64 per 100 in the United States. Although these technologies have become more widely available in the less-developed regions since 1990, the countries classified by UNESCO as least developed remain outside the information loop.

Women are more likely than men to lack basic literacy and computer skills, which would enable them to take advantage of the new global communication opportunities: women comprise 64 per cent of illiterate adults globally;[30] girls comprise two thirds of the school-age children in the developing world without access to basic education;[31] and girls are much less likely than boys to enrol in mathematics and computer science courses.[32]

On the other hand, in ways reminiscent of the "old" mass media, the "new media" are already targeting women as users: 70 per cent of all Internet advertising is now directed at women.[33] Women's access to the Internet is rising in most regions and is expected to reach 45 per cent globally in 2001.[34] As women in some countries begin to close the gender gap in access, the next fundamental challenge for women is to enter these new and powerful media as producers. If women do not participate in designing content and modes of use, they will be doubly excluded.

Women and men as "new media" users

Statistics on use of information and communication technologies are exceptionally scarce, and estimates of access to the Internet are at best inexact. Available data on Internet access show that the number of users is increasing rapidly everywhere, but access varies enormously around the world. More than 10 per cent of the population in the developed regions use the Internet in all countries for which data are available. At the other extreme, Internet use remains limited to a small minority in South Africa, in all the countries of Western Asia for which data exist and in China, the Philippines, Brazil and the Russian Federation. In most of these countries, fewer than 1 per cent of the total population use the Internet (chart 4.12).

In many countries, women are a rapidly increasing share of Internet users. In Japan, for instance, women accounted for 36 per cent of all Internet users in 1999, up from 1 per cent in 1997. However, although women constitute a sizeable proportion of Internet users in

Chart 4.11:

Access to media and information tools is lower in the developing regions
Access to media and information technologies (per 1000 persons)

	Telephone main lines[a]		Personal computers[b]	Internet hosts[c]
	1990	1997	1997	1997
World total	97	139	58	515
Developing regions	21	54	12	16
Sub-Saharan Africa	10	15	8	21
Arab States	33	55	10	5
Latin America and the Caribbean	61	107	31	49
Eastern Asia and Oceania	18	64	13	18
China	6	57	6	1
Southern Asia	7	22	2	1
India	6	18	2	1
Developed regions	466	554	274	3 411
North America	537	633	388	7 108
Asia and Oceania	441	482	223	1 357
Europe	424	521	204	1 336
Countries in transition	126	180	35	118

Source: United Nations Educational, Scientific and Cultural Organization (UNESCO), *World Education Report, 2000* (Paris, 2000).

Note: The country grouping used by UNESCO does not coincide with other groupings used in this report.

[a] Number of telephone lines per 1,000 inhabitants, that connect a customer's equipment to the switched network and that have a dedicated port on a telephone exchange.

[b] Estimated number of self-contained computers designed to be used by a single individual, per 1,000 inhabitants.

[c] Number of computers with active Internet Protocol (IP) addresses connected to the Internet, per 1,000 inhabitants.

most countries for which data are available, Internet users are a relatively small population in most countries. For instance, 43 per cent of Internet users in the Philippines are women but fewer than 1 per cent of the entire population have Internet access. In most cases, "on-line populations" are a tiny élite of high-income, urbanized citizens.

In much of Africa, Asia and Latin America, use of these new technologies is limited. Moreover, the "new" technologies in developing countries are of a far different order than "new" technologies in the developed world. In Nigeria, for example, most rural women's access to "new" technologies does not even include audio and video cassettes.[35] In India, a study of new information and communications technologies in five well-established women's development organizations found that three had no Internet connection and one had no computer.[36] In Bangladesh, the Grameen Phone project leases a cellular phone to Grameen Bank members (all of whom are women). The leasees serve as the village telephone operators, earning incomes, raising their status and increasing the community's access to information of various kinds.[37]

Practical obstacles often limit women's use of the Internet. A survey of women's groups and individual women around the world found that women often mentioned lack of training, the cost of equipment, and the cost of connectivity as obstacles to use.[38] Women in the developing regions and Eastern Europe listed poor infrastructure as the major barrier, while women in Northern Europe listed the lack of training. Women in Latin America, francophone and sub-Saharan Africa, and Eastern Europe listed other problems: the dominance of English on the Internet, privacy and security issues, the high cost of connectivity and difficulties in getting a phone line or repair personnel. Over half of the survey's respondents had received some kind of formal training; others were self-taught. For women in the Arab States, Africa and Latin America, the unavailability of training was a major issue.

Few women at top of communications pyramid
Careers in traditional mass media
In terms of education and training, women are a priori better equipped for careers in the traditional

Chart 4.12:

Women are a significant proportion of Internet users, especially where Internet use is common

	Internet users as % of total population		Women as % of all Internet users		Internet users as % of total population		Women as % of all Internet users
	1997	**Latest estimate[a]**	**Latest estimate[b]**		**1997**	**Latest estimate[a]**	**Latest estimate[b]**
Sub-Saharan Africa				**Western Europe** (cont'd)			
South Africa	1.6	3.7	19	Italy	0.7	7.9	30
South America				Netherlands	6.0	13.7	13
Brazil	0.6	2.1	25	Spain	3.2	8.7	19
				Sweden	21.3	40.9	46
Eastern and South-eastern Asia				United Kingdom	2.0	18.0	38
China	<0.1	0.3	8	**Other developed regions**			
Philippines	<0.1	<0.1	43	Australia	6.7	30.5	43
Western Asia[c]	0.4	0.8	4	Canada	15.3	25.4	38
				Japan	6.3	14.4	36
Eastern Europe				New Zealand	9.1	15.8	24
Croatia	..	12.0	42	United States	19.2	30.7	49
Czech Republic	1.9	2.6	12				
Russian Federation	0.4	0.8	15				
Slovakia	5.0	9.5	12				
Western Europe							
Belgium	2.3	16.0	38				
Estonia	..	10.0	38				
France	0.9	12.9	42				
Germany	4.7	10.0	35				
Ireland	2.9	13.5	31				

Sources: For all Internet users, Nua, "How many online?", accessed at: http://www.nua.ie/surveys; for women users in the Philippines, Belgium and Spain, based on CyberAtlas demographics, accessed at: http://www.cyberatlas.internet.com; for women Internet users in all other countries, based on Nua Internet surveys accessed at: http://www.nua.ie/surveys.

Note: Two dots (..) indicate that data are not available.

[a] Latest available estimates for all users refer to a period between January 1998 and June 1999.

[b] Latest available estimates for women users refer to a period between July 1997 and October 1999.

[c] Estimates for Western Asia are based on the following countries: Bahrain, Jordan, Kuwait, Lebanon, Oman, Qatar, Saudi Arabia and United Arab Emirates.

media than in the emerging communications industries. UNESCO data covering 83 countries show that in 53 countries, women account for at least 50 per cent of third-level graduates in journalism and other traditional communications fields (chart 4.13). However, women graduates in these fields are still a minority in some African and Asian countries.

Research has shown that the proportion of women finding employment in the mass media is by no means commensurate with their share of training. Nevertheless, the same research, covering 43 countries, found that women's share of middle-level cre-

Chart 4.13

Women are a large proportion of graduates in traditional media and information fields

Graduates in third-level mass communication and documentation studies, 1995/1997

	Total number	% women		Total number	% women
Northern Africa			**Asia** (cont'd)		
Algeria	220	79	Syrian Arab Republic	291	54
Egypt	248	68	Turkey	1 468	46[a]
Tunisia	325	75	Yemen	26	27[a]
Sub-Saharan Africa			**Eastern Europe**		
Botswana	67	63	Albania	32	50
Ethiopia	78	10	Bulgaria	548	90
Ghana	52	40[a]	Croatia	95	68
Mauritius	13	39[a]	Czech Republic	265	66
South Africa	4 026	56[a]	Estonia	200	94
Uganda	71	49	Poland	685	84[a]
			Romania	788	88
Latin America and the Caribbean			Russian Federation	9 651	76
			Slovakia	60	65
Brazil	7 381	67[a]	Slovenia	61	84
Cuba	72	71	The FYR of Macedonia	86	26
Honduras	17	59[a]			
Panama	198	80[a]	**Western Europe and other developed regions**		
Paraguay	50	60[a]	Australia	2 650	74
Asia			Austria	225	64
Afghanistan	75	63[a]	Belgium	1 836	68[a]
Armenia	73	78	Canada	3 419	66
China			Denmark	484	59
Hong Kong SAR	242	79[a]	Germany	1 310	64
Cyprus	48	69	Ireland	255	68
Indonesia	4 507	42	Italy	271	81
Iran (Islamic Rep. of)	703	34	Netherlands	1 222	68
Jordan	102	40	New Zealand	318	74
Lebanon	126	59	Norway	951	58
Macau	23	100	Portugal	1 558	73
Malaysia	307	57[a]	Spain	4 777	65
Mongolia	20	100	Sweden	409	72
Oman	51	33[a]	Switzerland	24	67[a]
Sri Lanka	87	36[a]	United States	62 354	56

Source: United Nations Educational, Scientific and Cultural Organization, *Statistical Yearbook* (Paris, 1998).

Note: Graduates refer to students who successfully completed their studies at the third level, including those who were awarded diplomas and certificates not equivalent to a first university degree; those who earned first university degrees or the equivalent; and those who earned postgraduate degrees or the equivalent. The International

Standard Classification of Education (ISCED) category of mass communication and documentation includes programmes in journalism, radio and television broadcasting, public relations, other communications arts and library science, library technician programmes, programmes for technicians in museums and similar repositories and programmes in documentation techniques.

[a] Data refer to 1990/1994.

ative professions, such as journalism and production, is over 30 per cent in most Latin American, Southern African and European countries.[39] Journalism in particular attracts substantial numbers of women **(chart 4.14)**. By the mid-1990s, women were almost as well represented as men among journalists in Finland and New Zealand, while longitudinal studies showed that women's share of senior editorial positions had increased in Canada and the United States since the 1980s.[40]

In Europe, too, periodic comparative studies show that the proportion of female middle and senior managers in radio and television increased from 11 per cent to 20 per cent between 1985 and 1995.[41] However, the senior-most positions still elude women. A 1999 study found that 13 of 18 major European broadcasting companies had no women in any senior creative decision-making positions. Across all companies, women held just 12 per cent of the top positions.[42]

Outside North America and Europe, several recent national studies show a similar media employment pyramid. For example, although women account for 33 per cent of all journalists in China, they hold only 8 per cent of higher decision-making positions and 18 per cent of middle/intermediate-level positions. In Nepal, women are 21 per cent of all employees at the national television organization (NTV) but are only 17 per cent of middle-level staff. There are no women in senior decision-making positions.[43]

Careers in new information and communications media
Entry into some of the new technology-based communications professions may be difficult for women, since they are less likely than men to have technical and computing skills. Women are a minority among third-level mathematics and computer science students in all but 16 of the 97 countries for which data are available. Eastern Europe and Western Asia have the largest share of women in these fields, where they often account for more than half the students **(chart 4.15)**. However, the proportion of women students seems to be falling in some Eastern European countries as men increase their enrolment in these fields faster than women do. This situation is echoed, albeit at a lower level, in almost every Western European country and in North America.[44] In some African countries, women are less than 5 per cent of mathematics and computer science students.

A European study of new media use by 6- to 17-year olds in 12 countries found that boys have more access at home than girls, and that boys are more

enthusiastic about computers. In the United Kingdom, for instance, 22 per cent of boys compared to 9 per cent of girls had the family's only personal computer (PC) in their bedrooms. Moreover, boys are twice as likely as girls to press their parents for computers and electronic games.[45]

The International Association for the Evaluation of Educational Achievement (IEA) found that in every country men outnumbered women by about three to one among those planning a career in computer or information sciences. In Sweden, for example, 16 per cent of boys and 1 per cent of girls planned to follow this career.[46]

Conflicting media images of women and girls
Traditional mass media
Assessing how the media portray women is hard to do across regions and across time. Studies looking at more than one country are rare. To date, the most extensive cross-national quantitative study of women's portrayal in the media—spanning newspapers, radio and television, and covering 71 countries—found that in 1995 only 17 per cent of the world's news "actors" (people interviewed, quoted or described in detail in the news) were women **(chart 4.16)**. The proportion of women

Chart 4.14:

Women account for between one fourth and one half of journalists in many countries or areas
Percentage of journalists who are women, 1991/1996

Northern Africa

Algeria	24

Latin America

Brazil	42
Chile	40
Ecuador	25
Mexico	25

Eastern Asia

China	33
Hong Kong SAR	35
Republic of Korea	14

Eastern Europe

Hungary	33

Western Europe

Finland	49
Germany	41
Spain	25
United Kingdom	25

Other developed regions

Australia	33
Canada	28
New Zealand	45
United States	34

Source: National studies reported in David H. Weaver, ed., *The Global Journalist: News People Around the World* (Cresskill, New Jersey, Hampton Press, 1998).

Chart 4.15:

Women are less likely than men to acquire skills needed for the new communications and media professions
Percentage women among students in third-level mathematics and computer science courses

	1990/1991	1994/1996
Africa		
Northern Africa	21	36
Sub-Saharan Africa	20	17
Latin America and the Caribbean		
Caribbean	..[a]	48
Central America	45	49
South America	..[a]	40
Asia and Oceania		
Eastern, South-eastern and Southern Asia and Oceania	32	42
Central and Western Asia	43	52
Developed regions		
Eastern Europe	37	43
Western Europe	30	27
Other developed regions	30	26

Source: United Nations Educational, Scientific and Cultural Organization, *Statistical Yearbook* (Paris, 1998).

[a] Average not shown because data are available for only one country.

news actors was lowest in Asia (14 per cent) and highest in North America (27 per cent).[47]

The study also looked at the extent to which news stories covered 10 broad issues of "particular concern to women" (e.g., violence against women, women's work and women's health). Overall, just 11 per cent of news stories dealt with such issues. According to the study, in the developing regions, newspapers are more likely to cover issues of particular concern to women, while television is less likely to cover such issues.

A second, more geographically limited, study was carried out in 1997 in Denmark, Finland, Germany, Netherlands, Norway and Sweden.[48] The global study covered all media (newspapers, radio and television) but considered only news; the European study covered only television but considered all types of prime-time content. Overall, 32 per cent of actors in television programmes were women. There was also a pronounced difference by age, with older women appearing less frequently: only 20 per cent of participants aged 50 or older were women.

Women were most often portrayed in roles equated with low social status: 47 per cent of "ordinary citizens" and 37 per cent of victims were women, whereas 72 per cent of politicians and 80 per cent of "experts" were men. This distribution is striking given that women's participation in decision-making and public life in these European countries is high. Women's representation in national parliaments, for example, ranges from 31 per cent in Germany to 43 per cent in Sweden.[49]

Other recent findings from national studies in Africa[50], Asia[51] and Latin America[52] confirm the broad pattern of gender portrayal in the media identified in both the global and European research.

Change in the media portrayal of women is very difficult to measure given the almost complete lack of longitudinal quantitative research in any country. A recent review of research since 1990 in 19 European countries concluded that the overall picture of gender portrayal is no longer monolithic stereotyping of the kind described in content studies of the 1970s and 1980s. However, although contemporary studies record greater diversity in images of women, they also find that new and highly sexist depictions of female characters coexist alongside more non-traditional roles for women.[53]

Media representations in general—and of women in particular—are deeply embedded in political and economic contexts. For instance, the media in many Asian countries have been transformed by the arrival of new commercial cable and satellite channels, and the privatization of old, state-run media has led to new market-oriented content. Studies from India and Singapore point to the often-contradictory ways in which the

media and advertising accommodate women's multiple identities.[54] Images of the "new woman" as an independent consumer and/or as a hard-headed individualist illustrate new stereotypes of women. Other research notes the emergence of new and highly sexualized images in the commercial media (e.g., in Cambodia and the Republic of Korea[55]), which are considered shocking and culturally intrusive.

New information and communications media
Sexism and pornography are central concerns in studies of how the media portray women. However, since most quantitative research focuses on the traditional media, there is relatively little information about the new communications media.

The picture that emerges from most analyses of new media content is still male-dominated, with representations that are frequently sexualized and often sexist. Online Computer Library Center (OCLC) research indicates that about 2 per cent of the public sites on the World Wide Web (a total of about 42,000 sites) contain sexually explicit content.[56]

Video games are one area that may be changing. Early research concluded that most games were strongly gender-stereotyped, with aggressive images

Chart 4.16:

Women are a distinct minority of people featured in the world's news media

News actors [a] in newspapers, television and radio, January 1995

	Total number	% who are women
All countries	21 037	17
Africa	720	19
Latin America and the Caribbean		
Central America and the Caribbean	940	24
South America	3 075	15
Asia		
Eastern, South-eastern and Southern Asia	3 538	14
Western Asia	998	14
Developed regions		
Eastern Europe	1 018	15
Western Europe	4 987	16
North America	4 056	27
Australia	1 273	22
Japan	132	30
New Zealand	147	13

Sources: Overall and for North America, Eastern Europe and Western Europe: "Women's participation in the news: global media monitoring project" (Toronto, MediaWatch, 1995); for Africa, Asia, Central America and the Caribbean, and Oceania: Margaret Gallagher and My von Euler, "Women's participation in the news: Africa" (London, WACC, 1996) (separate reports on Asia, Central America and the Caribbean, and Oceania); and for South America: Gloria Bonder, "La participación de las mujeres en las noticias: Sud América" (Buenos Aires, Satélite Eva, Centro de Estudios de la Mujer, 1996).

[a] News actors are people interviewed, quoted or described in detail in the news; newscasts were monitored in 71 countries in January 1995.

and violent themes that did not appeal to girls.[57] Market rather than equity factors seem to be changing this picture. In 1996, companies began developing computer games targeted to girls—games that emphasize relationships rather than competition and winning.[58] Research by Nintendo in 1999 found that 40 per cent of Gameboy owners were girls. Within weeks of its launch in October 1999, Gameboy's "girl-friendly" computer game "Pokémon" had become the company's fastest-selling game.[59]

A need for new data on "new media"

As this review of media, information and communications makes clear, statistics are scarce or absent in a number of key areas. New media are different from the established mass media in some important respects. New media, for example, blur the boundaries between genres and delivery systems and between producers and users. These and other differences in structure, production and use require that new approaches be developed to measure employment in and use of new media. For instance, because of the integration of different activities and tasks within new media, the classification now used in data collection on employment does not apply. It is necessary to design new systems and methods to collect employment data on the new media.

The Internet brings new opportunities but lack of access to these new technologies may broaden existing gaps between women and men, among different areas of the world and among different social groups. Therefore, it is important to measure access to the new information and communications technologies according to characteristics of individual users, including sex, age and education. Statistics also need to take into consideration the different contexts in which new media are used: in homes and offices, as well as in newer contexts, such as cybercafés, telecottages, new media/arts centres and libraries.

There are almost no data on gender portrayal in new media products. Studies are needed that look not only at the quantitative scope of such new phenomena as virtual pornography and on-line sexual harassment, but also at the content of new media products, including computer games, news groups and Internet broadcasts. This will require the development of relatively complex measurement instruments, because in the new media representations of women cannot be separated from constructions of identity, use of language and new styles of interaction. ■

Notes

1 In some of these countries, shifts in classification may have produced enrolment decreases at the secondary level, matched by
similar increases at the primary level. However, in other countries
of the region, the decrease is real. See also UNICEF *Education for
All?* Regional Monitoring Report, No. 5 (Florence, 1998).

2 Data for the Caribbean countries are sparse and the average for
the latest year available includes only four countries. It does not
include Haiti, where enrolment is very low: in 1990, the combined ratios for primary and secondary levels were 35 for girls
and 37 for boys.

3 Robert Gardner, *Education*, Demographic and Health Surveys,
Comparative Studies, No. 29 (Calverton, Maryland, Macro
International, 1998).

4 Marilyn I. Wilkinson, Wamucii Njogu and Noureddine
Abderrahim, *The Availability of Family Planning and Maternal
and Child Health Services*, Demographic and Health Surveys,
Comparative Studies, No. 7 (Columbia, Maryland, Macro
International, 1993); Shahrukh R. Khan, "South Asia", in
Elisabeth M. King and M. Anne Hill, eds., *Women's Education in
Developing Countries: Barriers, Benefits and Policies*
(Baltimore, Johns Hopkins University Press, 1993); Barbara
Mensch and Cynthia B. Lloyd, "Gender differences in the
schooling experiences of adolescents in low-income countries:
the case of Kenya", *Studies in Family Planning*, vol. 29, No. 2
(1998); Cynthia Lloyd, Barbara S. Mensch and Wesley Clark,
"The effects of primary school quality on the educational par-
ticipation and attainment of Kenyan girls and boys", paper presented at the annual meeting of the Population Association of
America, Chicago, 2-4 April 1998.

5 Zeba Sathar, Cynthia Lloyd, Minhaj ul Haque and Cem Mete,
"Children's schooling and family building strategies: the case of
rural Pakistan", paper presented at the annual meeting of the
Population Association of America, New York, 25-27 March 1999.

6 UNESCO, "Wasted opportunities: when schools fail", *Education
for All, Status and Trends* (1998).

7 Gardner, op. cit.

8 Ibid.

9 Data refer to the population 15 years and over; see UNESCO,
Statistical Yearbook, 1999.

10 UNESCO, *World Education Report, 1998: Teachers and
Teaching in a Changing World.*

11 UNESCO, *Estimates and Projections of the UNESCO Institute
for Statistics, 1999.*

12 The data reported here are the UNESCO estimates of illiteracy rates for the population 15 or over, as reported in UNESCO,
*Estimates and Projections of Adult Illiteracy, by Sex, 1980
and 2000.*

13 Gardner, op. cit.

14 Ibid.

15 See for instance, Caroline Bledsoe, J. B. Casterline,
J. A. Johnson-Kuhn and J. G. Haaga, eds., *Critical Perspectives
on Schooling and Fertility in the Developing World* (Washington,
D.C., National Academy Press, 1998).

16 Gora Mboup and Tulshi Saha, *Fertility Levels, Trends and
Differentials*, Demographic and Health Surveys, Comparative
Studies, No.28 (Calverton, Maryland, Macro International, 1998).

17 Ian Diamond, Margaret Newby and Sarah Varle, "Female education and fertility: examining the links", in Bledsoe et al., op. cit.

18 Mboup, op.cit.

19 Tamar Lewin, "American colleges begin to ask, where have all
the men gone?" *New York Times*, 6 December 1998.

20 In these countries, the favourable ratio of women to men is
probably due to a change in the sex and age structure of the
population, as a result of many men migrating to these countries to work in the oil industry; moreover, there is some evidence that men are more likely than women to attend universities abroad, which results in a relatively larger share of women
in local universities.

21 Data on share of women among students by fields of study are
not shown in **chart 4.8** and are from *Women's Indicators and
Statistics Database (Wistat), Version 4*, CD-ROM (United
Nations publication, Sales No., E.00.XVII.4).

22 Ibid.

23 UNESCO, *World Education Report 1998...*

24 In the UNESCO classification of countries, the Arab States
comprise Northern Africa, four countries in sub-Saharan Africa
(Djibouti, Mauritania, Somalia and the Sudan) and part of
Western Asia.

25 UNESCO, *World Education Report 1998...*

26 Ibid.

27 UNICEF, *Education for All?* Regional Monitoring Report, No. 5
(Florence, 1998).

28 "How many online?", Nua Internet Surveys, accessed in
September 1999 at http://www.nua.ie/surveys.

29 Mike Jensen, "Africa Internet Status", accessed in July 1999
at http://www3.sn.apc.org/africa/atstat.htm.

30 UNESCO, *Statistical Yearbook, 1998* (Paris, 1998).

31 UNICEF, *The State of the World's Children, 1999*
(New York, 1998).

32 C. Blurton, "New directions of ICT-use in education", paper prepared for UNESCO's *World Communication and Information
Report, 1999-2000*, accessed at http://www.unesco.org/educa-
tion/educprog/lwf/dl/edict.pdf.

33 Sally Burch, "ALAI: a Latin American experience in social networking", in Wendy Harcourt, ed., *Women @ Internet: Creating
New Cultures in Cyberspace* (London, Zed Books, 1999).

34 "Gender split nearly even by 2001", *CyberAtlas*, accessed on 7
June 1999 at http://cyberatlas.internet.com/big_picture/demo-
graphics.

35 Chinyere Stella Okunna, "Small participatory media technology
as an agent of social change in Nigeria: a non-existent
option?", *Media, Culture and Society*, vol. 17, No. 5 (1995).

36 Ila Joshi, "India: towards women-friendly communication tech-
nologies", in Ila Joshi, ed., *Asian Women in the Information Age:
New Communication Technology, Democracy and Women*
(Singapore, Asian Media Information and Communications
Centre, 1998).

37 Aasha Mehreen Amin, "Bangladesh: NCTs—helping hands for
women", in Joshi, op. cit.

Notes (cont'd)

38 Edie Farwell et al., "Global networking for change: experiences from the APC women's programme", in Harcourt, op. cit.

39 Margaret Gallagher, *An Unfinished Story: Gender Patterns in Media Employment* (Paris, UNESCO, 1995).

40 Gertrude J. Robinson and Armande Saint-Jean, "Canadian women journalists: the other half of the equation" and David Weaver and G. Cleveland Wilhoit, "Journalists in the United States", in David H. Weaver, ed., *The Global Journalist: News People Around the World* (Cresskill, New Jersey, Hampton Press, 1998).

41 Margaret Gallagher, *Employment Patterns in European Broadcasting: Prospects for Equality* (Brussels, European Commission, 1995).

42 "ERICArts: Women as Directors General or TV Programming Directors in EU public broadcasting companies", study prepared for the ERICArts project "Women in arts and media professions: European comparisons", accessed in January 1999 at http://www.ericarts.org/women.

43 Studies by the All-China Journalist Association and the China Academy of Sciences for UNESCO, 1995; and by Asmita Women's Media and Resource Organization for the World Association for Christian Communication, 1998.

44 Although data for the United States of America are not included in **chart 4.15**, the same trend is noted in a 1997 report by the Office of Technology Policy of the United States Department of Commerce; see Office of Technology Policy, *America's New Deficit: The Shortage of Information Technology Workers* (Washington, D.C., United States Department of Commerce, 1997), accessed at http://www.ta.doc.gov/reports/itsw/itsw.pdf.

45 Sonia Livingstone et al., "Children's changing media environments: overview of a European comparative study", in Ulla Carlsson and Cecilia von Feilitzen, eds., *Children and Media: Participation and Education–Yearbook from the UNESCO International Clearinghouse in Children and Violence on the Screen* (Goteborg, Sweden, Nordicom/UNESCO).

46 Ina V.S. Mullis et al., *Mathematics and Science Achievement in the Final Year of Secondary School* (Boston College, 1998).

47 MediaWatch, *Women's Participation in the News: Global Media Monitoring Project* (Toronto, MediaWatch, 1995). Regional data from the global study was further analysed for Africa, Asia, Caribbean/Central America and Latin America; see source note to **chart 4.16**.

48 Birgit Eie, "Who speaks on television?", Comparative study of female participation in European television programmes (Oslo, Norwegian Broadcasting Corporation, 1998).

49 1998 figures compiled by the Inter-Parliamentary Union.

50 Linda Goretti Nassanga, "Women, development and the media: the case for Uganda", *Media, Culture and Society*, vol. 19, No. 3 (1997); Dorothy A. Mbilinyi and Cuthbert Omari, eds., *Gender Relations and Women's Images in the Media* (Dar es Salaam University Press, 1996); Amna E. Badri and Shahira Osama, "Women and mass media: a critical and analytical study of the portrayal of Sudanese women in printed media", *The Ahfad Journal: Women and Change*, vol. 12, No. 1 (1995); Zureida Garda, "Women in the media in South Africa: challenging values", *Lolapress*, No. 11 (1999).

51 Arun K. Gupta and Nisha Jain, "Gender, mass media and social change: a case study of TV commercials", *Media Asia*, vol. 25, No. 1 (1998); Duncan Holaday et al., "Television and identity in Singapore: the Chinese majority", *Media Asia*, vol. 25, No. 2 (1998); Kung-Ja Lee, "Women and media in Korea: some issues and policies", paper presented to a WACC regional conference on gender and communication policy, Manila, 1997; Women's Media Centre of Cambodia, "Women in the media in Cambodia", "The portrayal of women in the Khmer press", first report of the Media Monitoring Group, and "How Cambodian TV portrays women", second report of the Media Monitoring Group, accessed at wmc@pactok.peg.apc.org; Lise Skov and Brian Moeran, eds., *Women, Media and Consumption in Japan* (Richmond, United Kingdom, Curzon Books, 1995).

52 Lilian Celiberti et al., *En El Medio de los Medios: Monitoreo realizado a los medios de comunicación* (Montevideo, Edición Cotidiano Mujer, 1998); Rosa María Alfaro and Helena Pinilla García, *Mujeres en los Medios: ¿Presencia o Protagonismo?* (Lima, Asociación de Comunicadores Sociales Calandria); Patricia Flores Palacios, *La Mirada Invisible: La Imagen de las Mujeres en los Medios de Comunicación de Bolivia* and *El Mundo y la Cotidianidad en Femenino y Masculino* (La Paz, Red de Trabajadores de la Información y Comunicación, 1999).

53 Ullamaija Kivikuru et al., *Images of Women in the Media: Report on Existing Research in the European Union* (Brussels, European Commission, 1999).

54 Lee Chun Wah, "Feminism in Singapore's advertising: a rising voice", *Media Asia*, vol. 25, No. 4 (1998); Shoma Munshi, "Wife/mother/daughter-in-law: multiple avatars of homemaker in 1990s Indian advertising", *Media, Culture and Society*, vol. 20, No. 4 (1998); Shailaja Bajpai, "Thoroughly modern misses: women on Indian television", *Women: A Cultural Review*, vol. 8, No. 3 (1997).

55 Women's Media Centre, "Women in the media in Cambodia", study for the International Federation of Journalists research project "Women and media in Asia", 1995, accessed at wmc@pactok.peg.apc.org; Myung-Jin Park, "Monitoring and advocacy: success and obstacles in Korea", paper presented to a WACC regional conference on gender and communication policy, Manila, 1997.

56 "OCLC research project measures scope of the web", OCLC news release, accessed on 8 September 1999 at http://www.oclc.org/.

57 Leslie Regan Shade and Gladys We, "The gender of cyberspace", *Internet Business Journal*, vol. 1, No. 2 (1993).

58 Mary J. Kelly, "Media use in the European household", in Denis McQuail and Karen Siune, eds., *Media Policy: Convergence, Concentration and Commerce* (London, Sage Publications, 1998).

59 Sarra Manning, "Computer games for girls", *The Guardian*, 20 October 1999.

Table 4.A:
Education and literacy

Country or area	Combined 1st/2nd-level gross enrolment ratio (per 100), 1992/1997		Girls' share of 2nd-level enrolment (%), 1992/1997	Percentage illiterate, 1985/1996				3rd-level students per 1000 population, 1992/1997		Women's share of 3rd-level enrolment (%), 1992/1997	% teachers who are women, 1992/1997	
				Ages 15-24		Ages 25+						
	W	M		W	M	W	M	W	M		2nd level	3rd level
Africa												
Algeria	82	90	48	37.8	13.8	79.5	50.2	10.0	14.7	..	..	..
Angola	..	..	..	..	..	..	..	..	..	..	45	..
Benin	35	63	..	73.1	44.8	88.0	67.3	0.9	4.2	19	..	..
Botswana	93	90	52	7.7	14.1	40.3	46.8	5.5	6.4	47	43	28
Burkina Faso	..	..	35	..	..	..	..	0.4	1.3	23	..	..
Burundi	..	..	39	51.6	40.2	81.8	57.1	0.4	1.1	27	20	11
Cameroon	53	63	..	29.0	15.0	68.0	43.0	..	..	..	..	..
Cape Verde	80	85	49	13.6	10.1	63.1	35.0	..	..	..	..	..
Central African Republic	26	43	29	65.1	37.4	87.2	59.6	0.3	2.1	15	..	..
Chad	23	47	20	..	..	..	..	0.1	1.0	13	4	..
Comoros	..	..	..	..	..	..	..	..	..	..	..	..
Congo	78	92	43	..	..	..	..	..	..	..	16	..
Côte d'Ivoire	38	58	32	62.2	40.1	85.3	63.5	2.1	6.0	25	..	..
Dem. Rep. of the Congo	41	62	31	..	..	..	..	..	..	..	17	..
Djibouti	22	31	41	62.0	38.0	87.0	63.0	0.2	0.3	44	..	..
Egypt	81	93	45	48.7	28.8	78.8	49.7	14.7	23.2	..	39	..
Equatorial Guinea	..	..	35	..	..	..	..	..	..	..	11	..
Eritrea	33	41	42	..	..	..	..	0.2	1.7	13	14	13
Ethiopia	20	33	43	..	..	..	..	0.2	1.0	19	10	6
Gabon	..	..	47	..	..	..	..	..	..	..	18	..
Gambia	46	62	38	..	..	..	..	1.1	1.9	36	17	23
Ghana	50	64	..	..	..	..	..	..	..	..	..	..
Guinea	20	41	26	..	..	..	..	0.2	1.9	11	..	3
Guinea-Bissau	..	..	..	..	..	..	..	..	..	..	..	..
Kenya	66	68	..	13.9	8.1	54.2	26.0	..	..	..	..	..
Lesotho	84	72	59	..	..	..	..	2.4	2.1	54	53	..
Liberia	..	..	..	..	..	..	..	..	..	..	..	..
Libyan Arab Jamahiriya	..	..	..	..	..	..	..	..	..	46	..	..
Madagascar	51	51	49	..	..	..	..	1.6	1.9	45	..	29
Malawi	94	106	18	50.9	29.5	74.5	37.2	0.3	0.8	30	..	..
Mali	20	33	34	81.0	62.0	91.0	76.0	..	..	..	..	..
Mauritania	42	54	34	61.8	43.1	82.7	59.3	1.3	6.2	18	11	..
Mauritius	84	82	50	8.3	9.3	31.4	16.9	5.8	6.1	51	45	..
Morocco	54	71	42	54.0	28.6	79.7	52.9	9.3	13.3	41	31	..
Mozambique	27	38	39	..	..	..	..	0.2	0.6	25	17	..
Namibia	108	103	54	9.6	14.3	35.0	26.8	8.9	5.8	61	46	..
Niger	14	23	35	90.1	74.8	97.2	86.8	..	..	..	14	..
Nigeria	61	77	46	..	..	..	..	..	..	..	36	..
Reunion	..	..	50	..	..	..	..	..	..	..	46	..
Rwanda	52	55	44	..	..	..	..	..	..	..	21	..
Sao Tome and Principe	..	..	..	8.1	4.2	54.1	21.1	..	..	..	..	..
Senegal	37	48	37	72.0	50.9	87.7	69.5	..	..	..	..	..
Seychelles	..	..	49	1.5	3.2	20.5	23.3	..	..	..	50	..
Sierra Leone	..	..	..	..	..	..	..	..	..	..	..	..
Somalia	..	..	..	..	..	..	..	..	..	..	..	..

Table 4.A (cont'd):
Education and literacy

Country or area	Combined 1st/2nd-level gross enrolment ratio (per 100), 1992/1997 W	M	Girls' share of 2nd-level enrolment (%), 1992/1997	Percentage illiterate, 1985/1996 Ages 15-24 W	M	Ages 25+ W	M	3rd-level students per 1000 population, 1992/1997 W	M	Women's share of 3rd-level enrolment (%), 1992/1997	% teachers who are women, 1992/1997 2nd level	3rd level
Africa (cont'd)												
South Africa	118	115	54	..	..	..	..	14.6	15.9	48	64	37
Sudan	40	47	47	40.5[a]	22.1[a]	74.1[a]	42.7[a]	..	..	..	45	..
Swaziland	92	96	51	15.7	16.9	46.2	38.4	5.4	7.5	44	43	40
Togo	59	92	27	..	..	..	..	1.1	5.3	17	12	8
Tunisia	86	91	48	27.8	7.4	67.8	42.2	12.0	14.6	45	38	26
Uganda	44	54	38	36.9	22.8	66.7	37.1	1.0	2.2	33	19	18
United Rep. of Tanzania	41	42	46	..	..	..	..	0.1	0.7	16	26	11
Western Sahara	..	..	..	..	..	..	..	..	..	..	..	..
Zambia	63	72	..	27.7	20.0	53.3	24.6	..	..	30	..	..
Zimbabwe	84	89	46	5.6	3.5	32.8[b]	16.7[b]	3.7	9.1	37	36	..
Latin America and the Caribbean												
Antigua and Barbuda	..	..	..	..	..	..	..	..	..	..	87	..
Argentina	99	97	52	1.5	1.9	4.9	4.4	..	..	..	66	..
Aruba	..	..	..	..	..	..	..	..	..	..	..	..
Bahamas	101	85	55	..	..	..	..	..	..	..	64	..
Barbados	..	..	..	..	..	..	..	29.7	21.5	..	..	..
Belize	97	99	52	20.2[c]	21.2[c]	32.6[d]	32.2[d]	..	..	..	46	..
Bolivia	..	..	..	8.3	3.7	36.5	15.7	..	..	..	..	..
Brazil	..	..	..	9.8	14.6	24.7	22.2	11.7	10.1	53	..	38
Chile	93	93	51	1.3	1.8	7.5	6.8	22.9	28.1	46	52	..
Colombia	89	87	51	3.9[e]	5.3[e]	11.7	11.1	18.2	17.1	52	48	28
Costa Rica	80	78	51	..	..	..	..	..	..	..	59	..
Cuba	96	93	52	..	..	..	..	12.2	8.0	60	57	45
Dominica	..	..	..	..	..	..	..	..	..	47	..	32
Dominican Republic	86	81	57	..	..	..	..	26.0	18.6	58	49	32
Ecuador	87	86	50	4.1	3.4	18.6	12.5	..	..	..	..	..
El Salvador	78	78	52	15.1	15.1	35.7	26.7	19.1	19.6	50	..	29
French Guiana	..	..	50	..	..	..	..	..	..	..	53	..
Grenada	..	..	54	..	..	..	..	..	..	..	..	..
Guadeloupe	..	..	52	..	..	..	..	..	..	..	..	..
Guatemala	56	63	47	29.3	18.3	49.9	33.6	3.6	11.5	..	..	..
Guyana	87	85	51	..	..	..	..	8.9	10.2	48	62	31
Haiti	..	..	..	..	..	..	..	..	..	..	..	..
Honduras	..	..	..	20.0	23.0	43.0	40.0	8.7	11.0	44	..	29
Jamaica	..	..	51	6.2	17.1	17.2	26.4	6.6	8.8	..	67	..
Martinique	..	..	51	..	..	..	..	..	..	..	54	..
Mexico	88	89	49	5.1	4.0	20.4	12.7	14.4	16.8	47	..	..
Netherlands Antilles	..	..	..	2.5	2.8	5.2	5.0	..	..	..	..	..
Nicaragua	80	76	53	5.2	4.6	14.8	13.4	12.6	12.0	51	..	36
Panama	..	..	..	..	..	..	..	32.2	21.6	..	..	..
Paraguay	80	81	51	4.6	4.1	14.4	9.7	11.0	10.0	55[f]	..	..
Peru	97	101	48	7.1[g]	3.3[g]	27.6[h]	10.4[h]	..	..	..	39	..
Puerto Rico	..	..	..	5.9	7.8	11.6	11.4	..	..	..	..	..

Table 4.A (cont'd):
Education and literacy

Country or area	Combined 1st/2nd-level gross enrolment ratio (per 100), 1992/1997		Girls' share of 2nd-level enrol-ment (%), 1992/1997	Percentage illiterate, 1985/1996				3rd-level students per 1000 population, 1992/1997		Women's share of 3rd-level enrol-ment (%), 1992/1997	% teachers who are women, 1992/1997	
				Ages 15-24		Ages 25+						
	W	M		W	M	W	M	W	M		2nd level	3rd level
Latin America and the Caribbean (cont'd)												
Saint Kitts and Nevis	..	..	51	..	..	..	..	..	..	55	59	61
Saint Lucia	..	..	63	..	..	..	..	..	..	72	63	49
St. Vincent/Grenadines	..	..	..	..	..	..	..	..	..	..	..	..
Suriname	..	..	53	..	..	..	..	..	..	53	60	..
Trinidad and Tobago	88	87	50	0.7	0.7	5.7	2.4	6.9	8.5	41	..	..
Uruguay	99	92	..	1.0	1.8	3.2	4.3	..	..	..	..	..
US Virgin Islands	..	..	50	..	..	..	..	..	..	74	..	48
Venezuela	85	80	57	3.6	5.3	14.1	10.9	..	..	..	53	..
Asia												
Afghanistan	22	49	25	..	..	..	..	..	..	..	34	..
Armenia	..	..	..	0.1	0.1	2.4	0.8	10.7	8.8	56	..	41
Azerbaijan	90	87	51	0.1	0.1	5.7	1.5	14.7	15.6	50	..	..
Bahrain	105	101	51	3.4	2.7	31.0	13.7	19.7	10.6	58	51	29
Bangladesh	..	..	..	..	..	..	..	..	..	..	..	..
Bhutan	..	..	..	..	..	..	..	..	..	..	..	..
Brunei Darussalam	93	90	52	1.9	1.9	24.2	9.7	6.4	4.1	57	47	17
Cambodia	68	86	36	..	..	..	..	0.3	1.7	16	27	17
China[i]	95	98	46	8.5	3.1	42.0	17.3	3.3	6.1	..	36	..
Hong Kong SAR	84	80	49	..	..	..	..	14.4	18.2	43	50	25
Macao SAR	89	86	53	..	..	..	..	16.3	17.7	49	..	30
Cyprus[j]	..	..	49	0.3	0.4	11.0	2.6	14.7	11.7	56	51	36
Dem. People's Rep. of Korea	..	..	..	..	..	..	..	..	..	..	..	..
East Timor	..	..	..	..	..	..	..	..	..	..	..	..
Georgia	80	82	49	0.1	0.2	1.8	0.6	29.7	30.4	51	71	..
India	62	81	38	..	..	..	..	4.8	7.9	36	..	..
Indonesia	79	85	45	4.9	2.6	33.5	15.8	8.1	15.2	35	37	..
Iran (Islamic Rep. of)	83	90	44	18.8	7.5	57.1	35.2	11.9	19.9	36[f]	44	18[f]
Iraq	58	73	38	19.6	11.5	53.3	31.4	..	..	..	56	..
Israel	..	..	50	1.2	0.6	9.2	3.7	35.4	32.8	..	65	..
Jordan[k]	..	..	50	3.5	1.9	40.7	14.7	19.4	21.0	47	48	18
Kazakhstan	94	88	52	0.2	0.3	4.9	1.2	30.3	25.7	55	..	..
Kuwait	68	69	49	15.9	9.3	38.9	25.6	25.9	19.3	62	54	..
Kyrgyzstan	91	87	..	0.3	0.3	6.1	1.9	11.5	10.8	52	67	..
Lao People's Dem. Rep.	63	80	39	..	..	..	..	1.5	3.6	30	38	29
Lebanon	95	93	..	..	..	..	..	26.1	28.2	49	..	33
Malaysia	84	78	57	5.0	4.4	..	..	..	..	..	60	..
Maldives	..	..	..	1.7	1.9	5.2	5.2	..	..	..	..	..
Mongolia	76	64	57	..	..	..	..	24.3	10.8	69	66	36
Myanmar	68	70	50	..	..	..	..	6.9	4.4	..	74	..
Nepal	..	..	32	66.9	31.6	89.2[l]	58.9[l]	..	..	..	12	..
Occupied Palestinian Territory	..	..	48	..	..	..	..	..	..	44	43	14
Oman	71	75	48	..	..	..	..	5.2	5.4	46	48	..

Table 4.A (cont'd):
Education and literacy

Country or area	Combined 1st/2nd-level gross enrolment ratio (per 100), 1992/1997 W	M	Girls' share of 2nd-level enrolment (%), 1992/1997	Percentage illiterate, 1985/1996 Ages 15-24 W	M	Ages 25+ W	M	3rd-level students per 1000 population, 1992/1997 W	M	Women's share of 3rd-level enrolment (%), 1992/1997	% teachers who are women, 1992/1997 2nd level	3rd level
Asia (cont'd)												
Pakistan	..	..	32	..	..	..	..	..	..	..	..	18^m
Philippines	..	..	..	3.1	3.7	8.7	7.2	34.0	25.6	57	..	..
Qatar	83	84	49	8.7	11.4	35.2	25.7	32.8	6.2	73	59	33
Republic of Korea	99	98	48	..	..	..	..	41.8	70.1	37	39	..
Saudi Arabia	67	71	46	18.9	6.0	55.3	24.9	15.3	14.0	47	50	30
Singapore	81	85	47	0.9	1.1	21.5	6.0	22.5	27.9	44	..	..
Sri Lanka	90	87	51			3.9	5.6	44	62	34		
Syrian Arab Republic	70	78	46	..	..	..	..	13.0	18.1	41	44	..
Tajikistan	82	88	..	0.3	0.2	4.9	1.6	11.9	25.4	33	..	..
Thailand	..	..	..	2.0	1.5	11.5	5.7	..	..	..	..	..
Turkey	69	84	39	11.6	3.4	40.2	13.2	15.2	23.9	38	40	33
Turkmenistan	..	..	..	0.3	0.2	4.8	1.7	..	..	..	..	..
United Arab Emirates	89	88	50	15.5	19.0	38.3	29.5	17.2	2.8	70	54	14
Uzbekistan	83	91	..	0.3	0.3	5.8	2.2	..	..	..	..	..
Viet Nam	..	..	..	6.6	5.9	22.1	7.6	..	..	..	..	31
Yemen	34	90	20	64.4	17.1	91.8	57.4	1.1	7.3	13	..	..
Oceania												
American Samoa	..	..	46	0.1	0.2	0.5	0.4	..	..	..	39	..
Fiji	98	97	49	2.6	2.4	22.6	13.5	..	..	..	46	33
French Polynesia	..	..	55	..	..	..	..	..	..	..	46	..
Guam	..	..	..	0.2	0.1	0.9	0.8	..	..	..	..	..
Kiribati	..	..	54	..	..	..	..	..	..	..	39	..
Marshall Islands	..	..	..	3.9	5.1	13.5	9.0	..	..	..	..	..
Micronesia (Fed. States of)	..	..	..	4.6	5.8	30.8	23.3	..	..	..	..	..
New Caledonia	102	99	52	1.1	1.3	10.9	7.9	..	..	..	42	..
Palau	..	..	..	0.7	0.5	4.3	2.1	..	..	..	..	..
Papua New Guinea	45	54	39	..	..	..	..	2.1	4.2	32	33	..
Samoa	87	86	50	0.8	1.1	2.3	2.8	..	..	..	47	..
Solomon Islands	58	69	38	..	..	..	..	..	..	..	..	..
Tonga	..	..	48	..	..	..	..	..	..	..	..	..
Vanuatu	58	64	43	..	..	..	..	..	..	..	..	..
Developed regions												
Albania	86	85	49	..	..	..	..	11.7	8.5	57	51	31
Andorra	..	..	..	..	..	..	..	..	..	..	..	18^m
Australia	122	123	49	..	..	..	..	56.1	55.0	51	..	31
Austria	102	104	47·	..	..	..	..	28.2	31.3	48	55	26
Belarus	95	94	..	0.2	0.2	3.7	0.7	33.2	30.1	55	..	..
Belgium	127	122	51	..	..	..	..	33.8	36.1	49	53	36
Bermuda	..	..	..	..	..	..	..	..	..	..	..	..
Bosnia and Herzegovina	..	..	..	..	..	..	..	..	..	..	..	..
Bulgaria	83	84	49	0.9	0.8	3.3	1.4	37.2	24.6	61	72	41
Canada	103	104	49	..	..	..	..	63.3	56.6	53	67	34
Croatia	84	83	49	0.4	0.3	6.1	1.4	18.7	19.4	51	64	34

Table 4.A (cont'd):
Education and literacy

Country or area	Combined 1st/2nd-level gross enrolment ratio (per 100), 1992/1997		Girls' share of 2nd-level enrolment (%), 1992/1997	Percentage illiterate, 1985/1996				3rd-level students per 1000 population, 1992/1997		Women's share of 3rd-level enrolment (%), 1992/1997	% teachers who are women, 1992/1997	
				Ages 15-24		Ages 25+						
	W	M		W	M	W	M	W	M		2nd level	3rd level
Developed regions (cont'd)												
Czech Republic	101	99	50	..	..	..	..	17.1	20.4	47	61	52
Denmark	112	111	49	..	..	..	..	34.7	29.0	55	52	30
Estonia	99	97	52	0.1	0.1	0.6	0.2	29.8	29.3	53	80	49
Finland	113	103	53	..	..	..	..	43.0	40.7	53	..	..
France	108	110	49	..	..	..	..	38.5	33.4	55	59	33
Germany	102	104	48	..	..	..	..	22.9	29.9	45	49	29
Greece	95	95	49	0.4	0.7	8.4	2.6	30.0	33.1	48	55	34
Hungary	100	99	50	..	..	..	..	19.7	18.8	53	66	33
Iceland	100	102	48	..	..	..	..	33.0	22.8	59	..	..
Ireland	112	108	50	..	..	..	..	36.6	35.8	51	54	37
Italy	96	97	49	..	..	..	..	32.0	30.0	53	64	32
Japan	103	103	49	..	..	..	..	27.2	35.8	44	33	22
Latvia	88	88	51	0.2	0.2	0.8	0.2	24.7	19.8	60	79	49
Liechtenstein	..	..	..	..	..	..	..	..	..	..	..	..
Lithuania	91	90	50	0.3	0.4	2.6	0.9	25.2	19.3	59	87	47
Luxembourg	..	..	49	..	..	..	..	..	..	..	..	..
Malta	92	96	47	1.6[n]	4.5[n]	15.4	16.3	15.2	16.7	48	45	17
Monaco	..	..	51	..	..	..	..	..	..	..	61	..
Netherlands	120	124	47	..	..	..	..	29.9	33.7	48	31	24
New Zealand	108	105	50	..	..	..	..	49.9	40.1	56	57	40
Norway	106	109	47	..	..	..	..	45.6	37.6	55	..	..
Poland	96	97	49	..	..	..	..	20.6	17.0	57	..	..
Portugal	117	115	51	0.7	0.9	18.8	10.5	33.4	27.5	57	..	..
Republic of Moldova	87	86	50	0.3	0.3	6.8	1.7	22.2	19.9	55	73	45
Romania	86	87	49	1.0	0.8	6.1	1.7	18.9	17.4	53	63	38
Russian Federation	95	91	..	0.3	0.3	3.8	0.6	31.5	28.2	56	..	..
San Marino	..	..	48	..	..	..	..	..	..	..	..	..
Slovakia	98	95	49	..	..	..	..	18.6	19.4	50	70	38
Slovenia	94	93	49	0.2	0.2	0.6	0.4	29.8	25.1	56	70	28
Spain	120	114	51	0.4	0.4	6.1	2.4	41.6	38.6	53	52	32
Sweden	126	115	53	..	..	..	..	32.5	26.9	55	58	36
Switzerland	97	100	47	..	..	..	..	15.4	26.0	38	..	41
The FYR of Macedonia	86	88	48	1.4	0.8	11.1	3.3	15.5	12.8	54	51	..
Ukraine	92	88	..	1.5	0.2	3.0	0.5	..	..	..	..	..
United Kingdom	131	119	52	..	..	..	..	31.0	31.7	51	55	30
United States	99	100	49	..	..	..	..	58.4	48.2	56	56	39
Yugoslavia	66	63	50	1.3	0.8	12.7	2.7	17.9	15.6	54	55	34

Source: United Nations, *Women's Indicators and Statistics Database (Wistat), Version 4*, CD-ROM, (United Nations publication, Sales No. E.00.XVII.4), based mainly on data provided by the United Nations Educational, Scientific and Cultural Organization.

Note: Two dots (..) indicate that data are not available or are not reported separately.

a Data refer to northern states only and do not include homeless and/or nomad populations.

b Data refer to ages 25-64.

c Data refer to ages 14-19.

d Data refer to ages 20+.

e Data refer to ages 18-24.

f Not including private universities.

g Data refer to ages 15-29.

h Data refer to ages 30+.

i For statistical purposes, data for China do not include Hong Kong Special Administrative Region (SAR) and Macao Special Administrative Region (SAR).

j All enrolment and teaching staff data exclude Turkish institutions.

k All enrolment and teaching staff data refer to the East Bank only.

l Data refer to ages 25-69.

m Not including teaching staff in arts and sciences colleges.

n Data refer to ages 20-24.

Technical notes

Table 4.A presents selected statistics on illiteracy, enrolment at the first, second and third levels of education, and women teachers at the second and third levels.

Indicators on enrolment have been prepared mainly from statistics published by the United Nations Educational, Scientific and Cultural Organization (UNESCO) in its *Statistical Yearbook*. UNESCO compiles enrolment statistics from data provided by national Governments in response to UNESCO questionnaires. Enrolment data are also included in *Women's Indicators and Statistics Database (Wistat)*.

ISCED classifies education at the first, second and third levels as follows: First-level education refers to schooling the main function of which is to provide the basic elements of education (e.g., at elementary school or primary school). The duration of first-level education varies considerably across countries (anywhere from four to nine years) but lasts for six years in most countries. Education at the second level is education provided at middle school, secondary school, high school, teacher-training school at this level, and schools of a vocational or technical nature. Second-level education follows at least four years' previous instruction at the first level, and provides general and/or specialized education. Education at the third level is that provided at university, teachers' college or higher professional school, and requires as a minimum condition of admission the successful completion of education at the second level. (See also sidebar to chapter 4 on levels of education.)

Enrolment data in table 4.A refer, in general, to the beginning of the school or academic year. While they offer an easy way of comparing the number of boys and girls enrolled in schools, these statistics do not reflect differences between boys and girls in rates of absenteeism, grade repetition and dropping out.

The combined first- and second-level gross enrolment ratio is defined as total first- and second-level enrolment, regardless of age, divided by the population of the age group that corresponds to these two levels of education. The ratio shown in the tables has been multiplied by 100 to make it less cumbersome to read. It should be noted that the numerator includes all pupils regardless of age, whereas the population used in the denominator is limited to the range of official school ages for the first and second levels. Therefore, for countries with almost universal education at these levels, the gross enrolment ratio may exceed 100 if the actual ages of the pupils do not coincide with official school ages (e.g., as a result of early age at enrolment or repetition of grades).

Rates of illiteracy are prepared from data published by UNESCO or the United Nations *Demographic Yearbook*, based on data from national population censuses or sample surveys. They are supplemented by published and unpublished data compiled from national sources by consultants in cooperation with the regional commissions of the United Nations Economic and Social Council. Data on illiteracy are also included in *Wistat*.

The definition of literacy is given in a sidebar to chapter 4. Persons able to read but not write, as well as those who can write but not read, are not considered to be literate. This definition of literacy is widely used in national population censuses and surveys, but its interpretation and application may vary to some extent among countries, depending on national, social and cultural circumstances. Furthermore, this concept of literacy includes persons who, although familiar with the basics of reading and writing, might still be considered functionally illiterate. Thus, a measure of functional illiteracy would also be useful, but such statistics are collected in only a few countries.

Illiteracy rates are shown separately for the age groups 15-24 and 25 or over. For young people in developing regions, literacy may be a better measure of education than enrolment since it usually reflects a minimal level of successfully completed schooling (see box on measuring education). It should be noted that data are lacking for a number of countries or areas in the developed regions. This is due to the fact that a question on literacy was not included in the population censuses, since illiteracy has been reduced to minimal levels through several decades of universal primary education.

Data on third-level students refer to the number of students enrolled in the third level of education per 1,000 population. The ratios have been calculated using the enrolment data provided by national Governments and the population figures provided by the Population Division of the United Nations.

The data on women teachers at the second and third levels of education are taken from the UNESCO *Statistical Yearbook*, and are also available in *Wistat*. In general, data refer to teaching staff in both private and public institutions, and as far as possible include both full-time and part-time teachers. They include, in principle, auxiliary teachers (assistants, demonstrators etc.) but exclude staff with no teaching duties (guidance personnel, librarians, administrators, laboratory technicians etc.).

■ CHAPTER 5

Work

Some important findings:

- Women now comprise an increasing share of the world's labour force—at least one third in all regions except in Northern Africa and Western Asia.

- Self-employment and part-time and home-based work have expanded opportunities for women's participation in the labour force but are characterized by lack of security, lack of benefits and low income.

- The informal sector is a larger source of employment for women than for men.

- More women than before are in the labour force throughout their reproductive years, though obstacles to combining family responsibilities with employment persist.

- Women, especially younger women, experience more unemployment than men and for a longer period of time than men.

- Women remain at the lower end of a segregated labour market and continue to be concentrated in a few occupations, to hold positions of little or no authority and to receive less pay than men.

- Available statistics are still far from providing a strong basis for assessing both quantitative and qualitative changes in women's employment.

WOMEN AND MEN IN THE LABOUR FORCE

Significant changes in the world economy, such as rapid globalization, fast-paced technological progress and a growing informalization of work, have, according to the International Labour Organization (ILO), greatly altered women's labour market status in recent years. While providing new opportunities for economic growth for national and global economies, these changes have generated major challenges—meeting the greater demand for skilled jobs, maintaining the employability of a large segment of the national labour force and containing the potential instability arising from such changes. Moreover, developments in recent years have rekindled concerns about the unfavourable global employment situation. For example, the Asian financial crisis of mid-1997 and the amount of excess labour in state and collective enterprises of countries in transition have led to persistently high levels of unemployment in spite of a growing labour force.

Among the groups most affected are the young, the old and the less skilled, and, as the ILO report states, there is "a bias against women in all these categories".[1] For instance, though women's entry into the labour force is increasing all over the world, their participation rates are still lower than men's. Also, women are disproportionately being engaged in non-standard forms of work, such as temporary and casual employment, part-time jobs, home-based work, self-employment and working in micro enterprises.

Women's share of the labour force increasing

Women comprise an increasing share of the labour force in almost all regions of the world **(chart 5.1)**. Their economic activity is growing, while men's is decreasing slightly **(see box on concepts related to the labour force)**.

The largest increase over the last two decades took place in Latin America. In 1980, little more than a quarter of the labour force was female in Central and South America; by 1997, women made up a third of the labour force in Central America and nearly two fifths in South America. From 1980 to 1997, the proportion of women in the labour force also grew in Western Europe and the other developed regions, but remained the same in Eastern Europe.

Women's share of the labour force also increased in regions where it has historically been small. In Northern Africa, women's share of the labour force rose from 20 per cent in 1980 to 26 per cent in 1997, and in Western Asia, from 23 to 27 per cent.

Toward a definition of work

There are many ways in which the term "work" may be understood. Work, in this chapter, refers to the participation of individuals in productive activities for which they either receive remuneration (in cash or in kind) for their participation or are unpaid because they are contributors to a family business enterprise. It also includes subsistence production of goods for their own households and non-economic activities such as domestic work, family and elder care, construction or repair of owner-occupied buildings, and volunteer work for which individuals receive no remuneration **(see box entitled "Toward a more comprehensive knowledge of all forms of work")**.

KVCC KALAMAZOO VALLEY COMMUNITY COLLEGE LIBRARY

Women's share of the labour force has remained almost the same in sub-Saharan Africa and in transition countries in Eastern Europe and Central Asia—where it already exceeded 40 per cent of the total—and has remained at 40 per cent in Southern Africa since 1980. The difference in labour force participation of women and men has historically been very small in transition countries, and has recently widened slightly in a few of them. The economic transition has been accompanied in these countries by a shift in national labour policy from a guaranteed right to employment to the simplification of lay-off procedures.[2] However, with weakened state support for families, family responsibilities are increasingly posing obstacles to women's employment.[3]

Women still represent a third or less of the labour force in Northern Africa, Western Asia, Southern Asia and Central America. However, in the developed regions, Eastern and South-eastern Asia, sub-Saharan Africa and the Caribbean, women's share of the labour force is approaching that of men (chart 5.1).

Gender gap in economic activity rate narrowing

Over the last two decades, the differential between women's and men's economic activity rate—i.e., the proportion of the working-age population in the labour force—has narrowed from region to region, as well as within regions.

Women's increased participation in the labour force is the result of several social and economic changes. Women have achieved more control over their fertility, thus expanding their opportunities for education and employment. In addition, attitudes toward employed women have changed, and public policies on family and childcare, part-time employment, maternity benefits, and parental and maternal leave are more favorable to the employment of women. Economic growth and the expansion of the service sector, which tends to employ large numbers of women, are also important factors in many regions and countries. Policies with respect to micro and small enterprises, including funding and credit programmes specifically designed to promote women's entrepreneurship, have played a role in some settings.[4]

Between 1980 and 1997, women's economic activity rate increased in all regions, except in Southern

Africa, Central Asia, Eastern Europe and Oceania, where it declined by 1 to 5 percentage points. Their participation in the labour force increased in Latin America and the Caribbean, with the largest increase in South America (from 29 to 45 per cent). It also increased in Eastern and South-eastern Asia (from 56 to 60 per cent and 59 to 62 per cent, respectively); as well as in the developed regions of Western Europe and outside Europe (from 42 to 49 per cent and 47 to 56 per cent, respectively). Although the rate increased in Northern Africa (from 21 per cent to 29 per cent) and in Western Asia (from 28 to 33 per cent), it remains relatively low (chart 5.2).

As women's economic activity rate increased, men's declined. Between 1980 and 1997, the rate declined for men in all regions except the Caribbean, where it remained the same. In most regions it declined at a slow pace, by less than 5 percentage points. The high-

Chart 5.1+:

Women's share of the labour force has increased almost everywhere

% of labour force who are women

	1980	1997
Africa		
Northern Africa	20	26
Sub-Saharan Africa	42	43
Southern Africa	40	40
Rest of sub-Saharan Africa	43	43
Latin America and the Caribbean		
Caribbean	38	43
Central America	27	33
South America	27	38
Asia		
Eastern Asia	40	43
South-eastern Asia	41	43
Southern Asia	31	33
Central Asia	47	46
Western Asia	23	27
Oceania[a]	35	38
Developed regions		
Eastern Europe	45	45
Western Europe	36	42
Other developed regions	39	44

Source: Prepared by the Statistics Division of the United Nations Secretariat from ILO, *Key Indicators of the Labour Market* (Geneva, 1999), table 1.

[a] Sparse data for this subregion; average should be interpreted with caution.

✤ In this and subsequent charts, regional and subregional averages are unweighted (i.e., the averages do not take into account the size of the individual countries' populations) and are based only upon available data for that region (see page xi for fuller explanation).

Chart 5.2:

Women's economic activity rates have increased in many regions, while men's have decreased

Economic activity rate (%)

	1980		1997	
	W	**M**	**W**	**M**
Africa				
Northern Africa	21	79	29	77
Sub-Saharan Africa	63	88	62	86
Southern Africa	52	85	47	77
Rest of sub-Saharan Africa	64	89	64	87
Latin America and the Caribbean				
Caribbean	44	75	53	75
Central America	31	85	39	83
South America	29	81	45	78
Asia				
Eastern Asia	57	83	60	80
South-eastern Asia	59	86	62	84
Southern Asia	44	88	45	84
Central Asia	63	76	59	75
Western Asia	28	80	33	78
Oceania[a]	58	88	57	83
Developed regions				
Eastern Europe	57	76	53	70
Western Europe	42	75	49	69
Other developed regions	47	78	55	74

Source: Prepared by the Statistics Division of the United Nations Secretariat from ILO, *Key Indicators of the Labour Market* (Geneva, 1999), table 1.

[a] Sparse data for this subregion; average should be interpreted with caution.

est decline for men was in Southern Africa, where the rate decreased by almost 8 percentage points.

In 1997, the economic activity rate of women ranged from below 10 per cent (Occupied Palestinian Territory) to more than 80 per cent (United Republic of Tanzania). More than 60 per cent of adult women were economically active in sub-Saharan Africa and Eastern and South-eastern Asia in 1997 (chart 5.2). In 14 countries of sub-Saharan Africa, three quarters or more of women are in the labour force (table 5.D). More than half of working-age (aged 15 or over) women were economically active in the Caribbean, Central Asia, the developed regions outside Europe, Eastern Europe and Oceania.

In Western Europe, women's economic activity rates were well below the levels of other developed countries. For example, in Greece, Italy, Luxembourg, Malta and Spain, less than 40 per cent of women were economically active (table 5.D).

Economic activity rates of women in 1997 were lowest in Northern Africa (29 per cent) and Western Asia (33 per cent). In these regions, the lowest recorded rates for women were in Arab countries, where cultural and social factors tend to discourage women's work outside the home.[5]

In 1997, activity rates of men varied within a much smaller range than those of women—from 69 per cent in Western Europe to 86 per cent in sub-Saharan Africa for men, compared with 29 per cent in Northern Africa to 62 per cent in sub-Saharan Africa and South-eastern Asia for women (chart 5.2).

More women in labour force during reproductive years

More and more, women all over the world are remaining in the labour force throughout their childbearing years. In the past, a "double peak" pattern was prevalent—most women entered the labour force in their early twenties, left after a few years to bear and raise children and reentered the labour force toward the end of their childbearing years. Recent age patterns indicate that women are finding ways to combine family responsibilities with market work.[6]

Through the 1970s, the double peak pattern in women's economic participation was most evident in the developed regions. According to the ILO, age patterns of activity rate for the developed regions (Europe, North America and Oceania) show that women's participation in the labour force was highest when women were in their early twenties, declined in their early thirties as they left to bear and rear children, and rose to a second but lower peak in their forties. In Latin America and the Caribbean, women's activity rate peaked at age 20 to 24 and declined gradually thereafter; unlike in the developed regions, there was

no sign of women reentering the labour force in the latter part of their reproductive period. In contrast, in Africa and Asia, women entered and remained in the labour force until well beyond their reproductive age. The age pattern for men was almost uniform across regions, with men joining the labour force at early ages and continuing until their retirement at older ages.[7]

In 1990, labour force participation rates were high for women in their twenties, rose through their thirties and forties, and declined only after age 50. Increasingly, women remain in the labour force during their childbearing and child-rearing years.

This change, from a pattern of withdrawal from the labour force at some point during the reproductive

---

Concepts related to the labour force[a]

The "economically active" population comprises all persons of either sex who (a) furnish or (b) are available to furnish the supply of labour for the production of goods and services, during a specified reference period. The reference period is either of "short" duration—one week or one day, which defines the current activity status of a person, or of "long" duration—one year, which defines the usual activity status of a person. As defined by the System of National Accounts (SNA), economic activity covers all production oriented to the market, some types of non-market production (including production and processing of primary products for own consumption), own-account construction and other production of fixed assets for own use. It excludes unpaid activities, such as unpaid domestic activities and volunteer community services.

The "currently active population", or labour force, comprises all persons above a specified minimum age who were either employed or unemployed during the specified reference period. The statistics on economic characteristics presented in this chapter refer to persons aged 15 or over, unless otherwise stated.

"Employed" comprises all persons above the age specified for measuring the economically active population who during the short reference period of one day or

one week (preferred) either worked for pay or profit, or contributed to a family business (or farm) without receiving any remuneration (i.e., were unpaid).

"Unemployed" comprises all persons above the age specified for measuring the economically active population who during a specified reference period:
- "did not have any work/job", i.e., were not employed;
- were "currently available for work", i.e., were available for paid employment or self-employment during the reference period;
- were "seeking work", i.e., had taken specific steps in a specified recent period to seek paid employment or self-employment (this condition is relaxed in situations where the conventional means of seeking employment is not relevant).

"Persons not in the labour force" (or "population not currently active") comprises all persons not classified as employed or unemployed during the reference period, as well as those below the age specified for measuring the economically active population (such as children and young people). A person may be inactive for the following reasons:
- attending an educational institution;
- engaging in household duties;
- retired or old age;
- other reasons, such as infirmity, disability, etc.

---

[a] R. Hussmans, F. Merhan and V. Verma, *Surveys of Economically Active Population, Employment, Unemployment and Underemployment: An ILO Manual on Concepts and Methods.* (Geneva, 1990), chapter 3.

years to a pattern of uninterrupted participation, is most visible in Europe and North America, where patterns of economic activity for women have come to resemble those of men. Trends for women in Latin America and the Caribbean parallel trends in the developed regions, but activity rates are generally lower. In Africa, where women's participation in economic activity has always been high throughout their lives—even during their childbearing years—little has changed. Asia's pattern is similar to Africa's, although in Asia the economic activity rates by age differ widely among countries.[8]

Still, some variations in the national patterns emerge in all regions **(chart 5.3)**, reflecting differing levels of economic development as well as cultural attitudes toward women's participation in economic activity.[9] In both Poland and Zimbabwe, women's activity rate is almost as high as men's at all ages and the age pattern resembles that of men. In Mexico and

Chart 5.3:
Age patterns of economic activity vary more for women than for men across countries, particularly during the reproductive years.

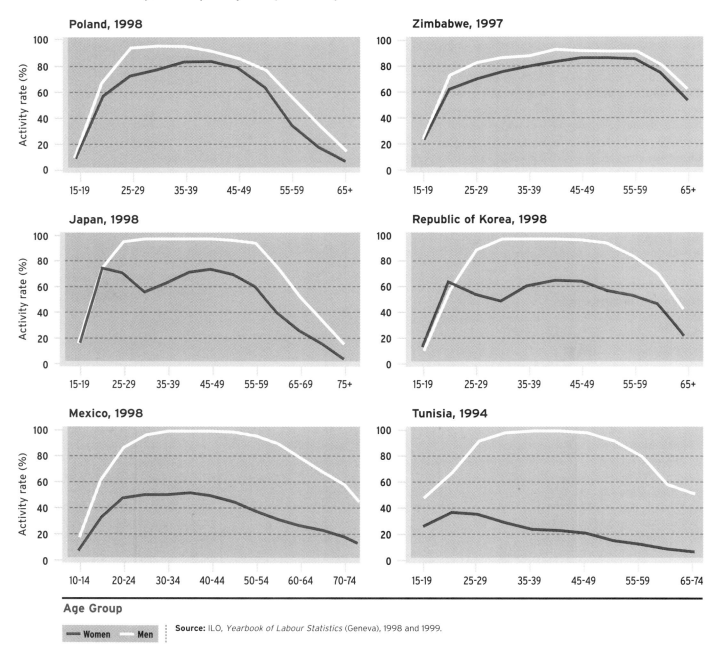

Source: ILO, *Yearbook of Labour Statistics* (Geneva), 1998 and 1999.

Tunisia, on the other hand, women's participation rate remains low compared with men's at all ages, and there is little indication of temporary withdrawal from the labour force by women. Women's participation rate, however, peaks at an earlier age in Tunisia (20 to 24 years) than in Mexico (35 to 39 years), and continues to decline gradually thereafter in both countries. In Japan and the Republic of Korea, the double peak pattern persists, with the first peak occurring at age 20 to 24 in both countries, and the second peak occurring at age 45 to 49 in Japan and earlier (age 40 to 44) in the Republic of Korea.

Economic activity rate declining for older men, varies for older women

Demographic changes, such as the decline in fertility rates, increase in life expectancy and the resulting ageing of populations (see chap. 1) are some of the factors affecting the age structure of the labour force. Having fewer children allows women to spend more of their adult years in the labour force, while the recorded increase in life expectancy implies that both women and men could retire later in life. However, in countries where pension plans provide economic security at older ages, there has been a steady decline in the average age of retirement from the labour market since 1950, for both men and women.[10] Many women and men, especially in developing countries where there are fewer pension plans offered, remain economically active until late in life (chart 5.4).

In all regions, fewer older women participate in the labour force than older men. This difference can be attributed in part to the fact that in some countries women qualify for a state pension two to five years earlier than men.[11]

Among regions, sub-Saharan Africa had the highest rate of economic activity for both women and men aged 65 or over—37 per cent and 65 per cent, respectively, in 1997. The economic activity rate for both women and men was also high in Oceania, with 31 per

Chart 5.4:[a]

Economic activity rates for older women and men have declined in most regions
Economic activity rate of persons aged 65 or over (%)

	1980		1997	
	W	M	W	M
Africa				
Northern Africa	10	41	6	31
Sub-Saharan Africa	37	71	35	65
Latin America and the Caribbean				
Caribbean	13	37	10	27
Central America	13	57	13	51
South America	8	44	12	34
Asia				
Eastern Asia	14	35	12	28
South-eastern Asia	23	53	22	46
Southern Asia	20	62	20	56
Central Asia	3	9	4	11
Western Asia	5	38	4	30
Oceania[a]	34	57	31	55
Developed regions				
Eastern Europe	8	22	7	15
Western Europe	5	15	4	9
Other developed regions	7	20	7	17

Source: Prepared by the Statistics Division of the United Nations Secretariat from ILO, *Key Indicators of the Labour Market* (Geneva, 1999), table 1.

[a] Sparse data for this subregion; average should be interpreted with caution.

New partnerships to improve data on paid and unpaid work

Measuring and valuing unpaid work in national statistics was one of the main issues at the Fourth World Conference on Women at Beijing in 1995, as at all previous global women's conferences. The Beijing Platform for Action recommended a detailed and ambitious agenda of actions to improve data on the full contribution of women and men to the economy. One of the key recommendations concerned the preparation of satellite accounts to value unpaid work in the framework of national accounts—work that is an important aspect of women's contribution to society. However, discussions with national statisticians made it clear that new accounting required new data, specifically time-use data.

Since 1995, and for the first time, many developing countries are undertaking time-use surveys as part of their official statistical activities. Nearly 20 pilot or full national surveys have either been undertaken or are in an advanced stage of planning, and plans are now underway for several more (see box on time-use surveys in developing countries).

Although time-use surveys are a regular part of the official statistical system in many developed countries, the United States has been a notable

exception. However, a proposal for a national time-use survey has now been made there.

The Beijing Platform for Action stressed the importance of collaboration between producers of statistics and user groups. To this end, the United Nations Statistics Division, the ILO and the United Nations Development Programme (UNDP) are working with Women in Informal Employment: Globalizing and Organizing (WIEGO)[a] to improve statistics on the informal sector, especially for women.

---

[a] WIEGO is a worldwide coalition of grass-roots organizations, academic and research institutions and international organizations concerned with improving policies, programmes, research and statistics in support of women in the informal sector of the economy.

cent of older women and 55 per cent of older men in the labour force. In the other regions, the economic activity rate of women was less than half that of older men. With the exception of Central and Western Asia, Northern Africa and the developed regions, the rate for older women was between 10 and 22 per cent, while that of older men was between 27 and 56 per cent. Fewer than 5 per cent of older women were economically active in the transition economies of Central Asia and in Western Asia and in Western Europe.

Between 1980 and 1997, the activity rate of women aged 65 or over has remained almost the same in all regions except Northern Africa, where it declined from 10 to 6 per cent, and South America, where it increased from 8 to 12 per cent. For men in the same age range, the activity rate declined in all regions except Central Asia and Oceania, where it remained almost the same.

The low economic activity rates of older women and men are of concern in many countries in the developed regions. The trend in these countries has been toward earlier retirement; the baby boom generation is reaching retirement and financing of retirement systems is in question, given that a declining economically active population has to support more and more non-economically active people.[11]

Services sector main source of employment for women and men

Over the last two decades, the global labour force has continued to evolve from a largely agricultural labour force to an industrial and a service labour force. An agricultural labour force is now characteristic of low-income countries, while a predominantly service-oriented labour force is a feature of the industrialized countries of Western Europe and other developed regions[12] **(see box on economic sectors).**

Women work primarily in the services sector in almost all regions. The only exceptions are sub-Saharan Africa and Southern Asia, where the agriculture sector has the highest proportion of women (65 to 66 per cent), and South-eastern and Central Asia, where women are almost equally represented in agriculture and services.

Men's pattern of distribution across economic sectors is similar to that of women in all regions except Central America and Eastern Europe. In Central America 40 per cent of men were in agriculture and 38 per cent were in services, and in Eastern Europe 44 per cent were in industry and 39 per cent were in services **(chart 5.5).**

Even when women and men are concentrated in the same sector, the degree of concentration in that sector is higher for women than for men. In services,

Chart 5.5:

In most regions, the employment of women and men is concentrated in the services sector
Percentage distribution of the labour force, each sex, 1990/1997

	Female labour force			Male labour force		
Africa	Agriculture	Industry	Services	Agriculture	Industry	Services
Northern Africa	30	21	48	17	31	52
Sub-Saharan Africa	65	7	28	57	16	27
Latin America and the Caribbean						
Caribbean	6	12	80	17	29	53
Central America	8	18	73	40	22	38
South America	5	13	81	12	31	56
Asia						
Eastern Asia	14	23	63	11	33	56
South-eastern Asia	46	13	41	45	20	35
Southern Asia	66	18	15	54	13	32
Central Asia	42	14	43	39	24	34
Western Asia	21	16	63	17	33	50
Developed regions						
Eastern Europe	16	29	55	17	44	39
Western Europe	5	16	79	7	38	55
Other developed regions	3	13	84	6	31	64

Source: Prepared by the Statistics Division of the United Nations Secretariat from ILO, *Key Indicators of the Labour Market* (Geneva, 1999), table 4.

where women and men are most concentrated (for example, in the Caribbean, South America, Eastern and Western Asia, and Western Europe), the proportion of women is 7 to 28 percentage points higher than that of men; in Northern Africa, the proportion of women in services is slightly lower than the proportion of men (48 and 52 per cent, respectively).

Women also differ from men in the degree of their participation in industry. Between 1990 and 1997, fewer than 20 per cent of economically active women were in this sector in all but three regions: Eastern Europe (29 per cent), Eastern Asia (23 per cent) and Northern Africa (21 per cent). In contrast, at least 20 per cent of men were in industry in all regions except sub-Saharan Africa (16 per cent) and Southern Asia (13 per cent).

In South America, the Caribbean, Eastern and Western Asia, Western Europe and the developed regions outside Europe, industry is the second major source of jobs for men after services; it is the main source in Eastern Europe.

Self-employment increasing, especially for women in some regions

The trend in labour markets around the world has been toward less formalized and more flexible forms of employment. In the developed regions, more people are modifying their involvement in the labour market by reducing the number of hours they work or by choosing self-employment.[13] For the developing countries, the limited job creation in the formal sector has led to a growing informal sector **(see box on elements of a definition of the informal sector)** and an increase in self-employment.[14] Many women with family responsibilities, in particular those who have no access to affordable childcare, often need flexibility in the timing, quantity and type of employment they engage in so as to maintain a reasonable balance between labour market work and household responsibilities.[15]

Paid employment

Employees represent the largest category of the labour force for both women and men, except in sub-Saharan Africa (excluding Southern Africa) and Southern Asia **(chart 5.6)**, where only about a third of economically active women are employees.[16] More than 50 per cent of women are in paid employment in all other regions. The patterns are similar for men. However, the proportion of employees among men is higher than among women, except in the Caribbean, Central America, the developed regions and Eastern Asia.

Chart 5.6

Wage and salaried work is the predominant form of employment for women and men in most regions
Percentage distribution of the labour force, each sex, 1990/1997

	Female labour force			Male labour force		
	Wage and salaried workers	Self-employed workers	Contributing family workers	Wage and salaried workers	Self-employed workers	Contributing family workers
Africa						
Northern Africa	62	10	25	65	26	7
Southern Africa	55	11	22	67	10	14
Rest of sub-Saharan Africa[a]	30	27	35	37	36	18
Latin America and the Caribbean						
Caribbean	81	15	2	71	24	2
Central America	63	28	7	61	32	6
South America	58	31	7	61	33	3
Asia						
Eastern Asia	81	10	8	77	21	1
South-eastern Asia	53	20	25	54	35	9
Southern Asia	36	20	40	40	41	11
Western Asia[a]	54	8	34	60	32	7
Developed regions						
Eastern Europe	84	10	6	79	17	4
Western Europe	85	11	4	79	20	1
Other developed regions	87	10	3	84	15	1

Source: Prepared by the Statistics Division of the United Nations Secretariat from ILO, *Key Indicators of the Labour Market* (Geneva, 1999), table 3.

[a] Sparse data for this subregion; average should be interpreted with caution.

Although the majority of economically active women are paid workers in Central and South America and Northern Africa, there are wide variations from country to country. In Egypt and Peru, for example, only about a third of women are paid workers, while more than three quarters of women are paid workers in Guatemala, Honduras and Morocco **(table 5.D)**.

The proportion of men working as paid employees varies much less across regions, ranging from 37 per cent to 84 per cent in the developed regions outside Europe. Men who are not paid employees tend to be self-employed rather than unpaid family workers.

Self-employment

According to the International Labour Office, paid employment is increasingly incorporating different forms of work arrangements that deviate from what used to be the dominant mode of employment —"stable, waged employment with clear-cut job descriptions"[17] **(see box on status in employment)**. Although these non-standard forms of employment for employees, such as part-time employment and temporary employment, have provided increased opportunities for employment, especially for women, they have also undermined both the stability of employment (including job tenure) and the quality of employment.[18]

All over the world, self-employment provides some women and men, especially those who have failed to secure paid jobs, with a means of contributing income to the family. Self-employment in turn can provide others with either regular or temporary jobs and can, therefore, help to ease unemployment. Sometimes self-employment makes it easier for women to combine family responsibilities and unpaid subsistence work with income-earning activities. On the other

hand, it can imply a high level of job insecurity and does carry with it a lack of such protections as maternity and parental leave.

In developing countries that have embarked on structural adjustment programmes, reduction in modern sector employment has compelled more women to seek income-earning opportunities to help maintain their families' living standards; increasing numbers of women are being reported as self-employed in those countries.

Regional averages indicate that women are less likely than men to be self-employed—either as own-account workers or employers **(chart 5.6)**. In Southern Africa, however, there is little difference. In Eastern and Southern Asia and Northern Africa, the proportion of self-employed, economically active men is at least twice as high as the proportion of women; in Western Asia it is four times as high. In Central and South America, the proportion of self-employed, economically active men is less than 2 per cent higher than that of women, and in the other regions, 30 to 80 per cent higher.

One in 10 economically active women is self-employed in the developed regions, Eastern Asia, Northern and Southern Africa, and the few countries of Western Asia for which data are reported. In contrast, 2 out of 10 economically active women are self-employed in South-eastern and Southern Asia, and about 3 out of 10 in sub-Saharan Africa (excluding Southern Africa) and in Latin America.

Among the self-employed, own-account workers generate employment for themselves and their families, while employers provide salaried jobs for those seeking work. Few countries, however, distinguish employers from own-account workers in data on self-employment. Proportionately more men than women are employers. Among both sexes (in all countries except Austria, Estonia and Germany) there are fewer employers than own-account workers **(chart 5.7)**.[19]

At the regional level, in Central and South America, Western Europe and the developed regions outside Europe, about 3 per cent of women and between 6 and 8 per cent of men are employers. In the Caribbean, Eastern Europe and South-eastern Asia, about 2 per cent of women and 4 to 6 per cent of men are employers.

Compared with employers, own-account workers represent a numerically important category of workers for both women and men. In the developed regions and in Latin America and the Caribbean, own-account workers represent from 6 to 32 per cent of the female labour force and from 11 to 27 per cent of the male labour force. In South America, which has the highest percentage of own-account workers, there are 10 times as many women own-account workers as

Economic sectors

The classification of individuals by economic sector is done in accordance with the main economic activity carried out where the work is performed. The three major economic sectors—agriculture, industry and services—are defined as follows: [a]
- Agriculture covers farming, animal husbandry, hunting, forestry and fishing.
- Industry comprises mining and quarrying (including oil production), manufacturing, electricity, gas and water supply, and construction.
- Services covers wholesale and retail trade; hotels and restaurants; transport, storage and communications; financial intermediation; real estate, renting and business activities; public administration, social security and defence; education; health and social work; and other community, social and personal services.[b]

---

[a] See United Nations, *The World's Women 1970-1990: Trends and Statistics* (United Nations publication, Sales No. E.90.XVII.3).

[b] United Nations, *International Standard Industrial Classification of all Economic Activities*, Revision 3 (United Nations publication, Sales No. E.90.XVII.11).

employers and three times as many men own-account workers as employers. Too few countries report in Asia and Africa for regional averages to be calculated.

Self-employment of the non-agricultural labour force

Self-employment in non-agricultural activities such as petty trading, service repairs, transport and small manufacturing activities increased in almost all regions between 1970 and 1990.

Between 1970 and 1990, the proportion of the non-agricultural labour force that was self-employed increased in all parts of Africa, South America, Southern Asia and Eastern and Southern Europe. The largest increase, from 31 to 75 per cent, was in sub-Saharan Africa (excluding Southern Africa). The proportion of self-employed non-agricultural workers also more than doubled in Eastern Europe (from 3 to 8 per cent) **(chart 5.8)**. In all the other regions, self-employment has remained almost the same among the non-agricultural labour force.

The proportion of self-employed among non-agricultural women workers doubled in sub-Saharan Africa (excluding Southern Africa)—from 44 per cent in 1970 to 90 per cent in 1990. The proportion also increased in Northern Africa, South America, Southern Asia and Eastern and Southern Europe—from 1 to 9 per cent in Poland and from 20 to 30 per cent in Italy.

Chart 5.7
Proportionately fewer women than men are employers

	Percentage in female labour force, 1990/1997		Percentage in male labour force, 1990/1997			Percentage in female labour force, 1990/1997		Percentage in male labour force, 1990/1997	
	Employers	Own-account workers	Employers	Own-account workers		Employers	Own-account workers	Employers	Own-account workers
Africa					**Asia** (cont'd)				
Tunisia	1	13	3	22	Pakistan	<1	13	1	46
					Singapore	2	3	8	9
Caribbean	2	15	4	20	Sri Lanka	1	15	3	31
Antigua and Barbuda	3	13	5	15	Thailand	1	20	4	40
Barbados	<1	9	1	15					
Dominican Republic	1	29	5	43	**Eastern Europe**	2	6	5	11
Grenada	2	10	5	12	Czech Republic	4	5	7	10
Jamaica	2	29	3	40	Estonia	1	1	4	4
Netherlands Antilles	1	3	4	6	Hungary	3	5	6	10
St. Kitts and Nevis	3	11	5	12	Latvia	2	9	5	10
S.t Vincent/Grenadines	3	15	7	20	Romania	1	16	2	24
Trinidad and Tobago	2	14	5	20	Slovakia	1	2	3	5
					Slovenia	2	6	4	12
Central America	3	25	7	27					
Belize	4	17	9	25	**Western Europe**	3	10	8	16
Costa Rica	4	18	9	20	Austria	3	5	7	5
El Salvador	3	38	7	24	Germany	4	3	6	7
Honduras	2	39	6	36	Greece	3	16	10	32
Mexico	2	22	6	26	Iceland	3	7	9	14
Panama	2	17	4	33	Ireland	3	5	7	20
					Portugal	4	22	8	20
South America	3	32	8	26	Spain	3	12	7	16
Bolivia	4	40	12	23					
Colombia	3	25	6	32	**Other developed regions**	3	8	6	12
Ecuador	5	28	10	28	Australia	3	8	5	12
Paraguay	2	23	5	15	Japan	1	7	4	10
Peru	3	42	8	32	New Zealand	4	8	10	15
Asia	2	11	4	30					
Bangladesh	<1	8	<1	43					
Israel	5	4	10	9					

Source: ILO, *Key Indicators of the Labour Market* (Geneva, 1999), table 3.

Women's self-employment outside the agricultural sector has declined in Central America, Eastern and South-eastern Asia, Western Asia, Northern and Western Europe and the developed regions outside Europe. In Eastern and South-eastern Asia, the decrease may be attributed to the industrialization process, during which many self-employed women became piece-rate home-workers or employees in other types of insecure and low-income jobs.

Contributing family workers

The self-employed, especially own-account workers who do not employ regular or permanent paid employees, often depend on family members for any additional labour the business may require. These family members are unpaid, and are referred to as "contributing family workers".[20] A larger proportion of women than men is classified as contributing family workers in each of the regions for which data are reported (chart 5.9).

At the regional level, the highest percentages of female contributing family workers are in Africa (between 22 and 35 per cent) and Asia (between 25 and 40 per cent); in Eastern Asia, however, 8 per cent of women are reported in this category. The percentage of contributing family workers among economically active women is as high as 77 per cent in Bangladesh, 65 per cent in Ethiopia and 62 per cent in Pakistan. In contrast, family workers represent 2 to 7 per cent of the female labour force (table 5.D) in the developed regions and in Latin America and the Caribbean.

Contributing family workers make up 1 to 7 per cent of the male labour force in all regions except Southern Africa and the rest of sub-Saharan Africa, South-eastern Asia and Southern Asia.

More women in small enterprise sector

The emergence of private enterprises such as those in transition countries of Central and Eastern Europe, as well as the Russian Federation, has played a key role in the development of market economies and has contributed to the creation of job opportunities in these countries.[21] For example, small enterprises—defined in Lithuania as enterprises having up to 50 employees and an annual gross income not exceeding 500,000 litas (approximately US$ 125,000)—comprised 34 per cent of all enterprises in 1997.[22]

According to the ILO, more self-employed women are becoming involved in the micro and small enterprise sector (see box on elements of a definition of micro and small enterprises). Such business enterprises are fostering economic growth and development worldwide, and their role is particularly critical in job creation and poverty reduction.[23] The number of women business owners, creators and operators rose in nearly every member country of the Organisation for Economic Cooperation and Development (OECD) during the last decade.[24] In the United States, between 1987 and 1996, the number of firms created and managed by women has grown twice as fast as the number of firms set up and managed by men.[25]

Unemployment higher for women than for men

Unemployment data are difficult to compare across countries because definitions and data sources vary. Even within a country, it is difficult to compare unemployment (or general labour force) data. Unemployment may lead to the depreciation of skills[26], especially in highly technical and fast-evolving fields such as information technology.

The unemployment rate—the percentage of people in the labour force who are unemployed—was higher for women than for men in 1997 in all regions for

Chart 5.8:

Women's self-employment has increased where self-employment as a proportion of the non-agricultural labour force has grown

	Percentage of total non-agricultural labour force who are self-employed		Percentage of female non-agricultural labour force who are self-employed	
	1970	1990	1970	1990
Africa				
Northern Africa	23	34	15	26
Southern Africa[a]	18	23	22	29
Rest of sub-Saharan Africa	31	75	44	90
Latin America and the Caribbean				
Caribbean[a]	43	..	43	..
Central America[a]	25	25	25	18
South America	29	41	28	36
Asia				
Eastern and South-eastern Asia	27	27	31	29
Southern Asia	33	44	31	35
Western Asia	24	25	20	18
Developed regions				
Eastern Europe	3	8	4	6
Southern Europe[b]	21	25	17	21
Northern and Western Europe[c]	11	10	9	7
Other developed regions	10	11	10	9

Source: Prepared by Jacques Charmes as consultant to the Statistics Division of the United Nations Secretariat.

[a] Sparse data for this subregion; average should be interpreted with caution.

[b] Southern Europe includes Greece, Italy, Portugal and Spain.

[c] Northern and Western Europe includes Austria, Belgium, Denmark, Finland, France, Germany, Ireland, the Netherlands, Norway, Sweden and the United Kingdom.

which data are available. Only in the developed regions outside Europe was the unemployment rate the same for women and men **(chart 5.10)**. In Greece, Italy and Spain, women's unemployment rate was about twice as high as that of men **(table 5.A)**. The same was true in the Dominican Republic, Guyana and Jamaica.

The lowest unemployment rates for women and for men were in Thailand and Uzbekistan (1 per cent), and the highest was in the Former Yugoslav Republic of Macedonia (46 per cent for women and 35 per cent for men).

Between 1990 and 1997, the unemployment rate for women increased by 2 to 5 percentage points in Northern Africa, Central and South America, and Eastern and Western Europe. The rate for men also increased in these regions, by 1 to 7 percentage points. The rate remained the same for men in South America and for both women and men in Asia **(chart 5.10)**.

Unemployment rates are generally lower for women and men with higher levels of education. Two notable exceptions are Eastern Europe, where rates are highest for women and men with secondary education, and the developed regions outside Europe, where rates for women do not vary according to the level of education. Generally, among workers with only a primary education the unemployment rate is higher for men. In contrast, among workers with a secondary or higher education more women than men are unemployed.[27]

Young people, especially young women, suffer from unemployment due to a variety of reasons: negative attitudes toward inexperienced young workers, lack of skills arising out of limited job experience, and their particular vulnerability to a poor economic environment.[28] The unemployment rate varied widely in the 1990s for both young men and women (aged 15 to 24 years)—from 5 per cent in Eastern Asia to 39 per cent in the Caribbean for younger women; and from 5 per

Status in employment[a]

Employment, as defined by the Thirteenth Conference of Labour Statisticians (Geneva, 1992), is comprised of two broad categories: "paid employment" and "self-employment".

Paid employment includes persons who during the reference period were either (a) "at work", i.e., performed some work for wage or salary, in cash or in kind, or (b) "with a job but did not work", i.e., were temporarily not at work but who had a formal attachment to their job, having already worked in their current job.

Self-employment includes persons who during the reference period either (a) were "at work", i.e., performed some work for profit or family gain, in cash or in kind, or (b) had an enterprise, such as a business or commercial enterprise, a farm or a service undertaking, but were temporarily not at work for any specific reason.

The International Classification of Status in Employment (ICSE), adopted in 1993, provides guidelines for classifying jobs in the labour market on the basis of the type of explicit or implicit contract of employment an individual has with his or her employer or other persons. Five major groups and a residual category are presented in ICSE-93: employees, employers, own-account workers, members of producer cooperatives and contributing family workers.

Employees are all those who hold paid employment jobs and are typically remunerated by wages and salaries, but may also be paid by commission from sales, or by piece-rates, bonuses or in-kind payments, such as food, housing or training.

Employers are those who, working on their own account or with one or several partners, hold self-employment jobs and have engaged on a continuous basis one or more persons to work for them in their businesses as employees.

Own-account workers are those workers who, working on their own account or with one or several partners, hold self-employment jobs and have not engaged any employees on a continuous basis.

Members of producers' cooperatives are workers who hold self-employment jobs in a cooperative producing goods and services, in which each member has equal say in decisions regarding production, sales, investments and distribution of proceeds.

Contributing family workers (referred to in previous classifications as unpaid family workers) hold a self-employment job in a market-oriented establishment (i.e., business or farm) operated by a relative living in the same household who cannot be regarded as partner because her/his degree of commitment to the operation of the establishment is not at a level comparable to that of the head of the establishment.

For analytical purposes, employers and own-account workers are sometimes combined and referred to as "self-employed". Workers in paid employment are referred to as "wage and salaried workers". The category of contributing family workers, though considered part of the group of "self-employment jobs", is usually analysed separately, since these jobs, unlike other self-employment jobs, are unpaid.

[a] ILO, *Yearbook of Labour Statistics 1998* (Geneva); see also ILO, *Bulletin of Labour Statistics*, 1993–2.

Chart 5.9

More women workers than men workers are unpaid

Percentage of labour force who are contributing family workers[a], 1990/1997

	W	M
Africa		
Northern Africa	25	7
Southern Africa	22	14
Rest of sub-Saharan Africa[b]	35	18
Latin America and the Caribbean		
Caribbean	2	2
Central America	7	6
South America	7	3
Asia		
Eastern Asia	8	1
South-eastern Asia	25	9
Southern Asia	40	11
Western Asia[b]	34	7
Developed regions		
Eastern Europe	6	4
Western Europe	4	1
Other developed regions	3	1

Source: Prepared by the Statistics Division of the United Nations Secretariat from ILO, *Key Indicators of the Labour Market* (Geneva, 1999), table 3.

[a] Sometimes referred to as "unpaid family workers".

[b] Sparse data for this subregion; average should be interpreted with caution.

Chart 5.10:

Women's unemployment rates remained higher than men's but the gap has narrowed in some regions

Unemployment rate (%)

	1990 W	1990 M	1997 W	1997 M
Africa				
Northern Africa	19	10	24	17
Latin America and the Caribbean				
Caribbean	20	13	17	12
Central America	9	7	11	8
South America	10	8	12	8
Asia	6	4	6	4
Developed regions				
Eastern Europe	10	7	12	11
Western Europe	8	5	10	7
Other developed regions	6	6	6	7

Source: Prepared by the Statistics Division of the United Nations Secretariat from ILO, *Key Indicators of the Labour Market* (Geneva, 1999), table 8a.

Chart 5.11:

Youths have more difficulty than adults in securing jobs, and young women have more difficulty than young men

	Youth unemployment rate (%), 1990/1997 W	Youth unemployment rate (%), 1990/1997 M	Ratio of youth unemployment rate to adult unemployment rate, 1990/1997 W	Ratio of youth unemployment rate to adult unemployment rate, 1990/1997 M
Africa				
Northern Africa	37	35	6	7
Sub-Saharan Africa	6	5	10	5
Latin America and the Caribbean				
Caribbean	39	24	3	3
Central America	18	12	4	3
South America	21	16	3	4
Asia				
Eastern Asia	5	9	3	4
South-eastern Asia	9	7	5	5
Southern Asia	25	14	2	4
Developed regions				
Eastern Europe	21	19	3	3
Western Europe	18	15	2	3
Other developed regions	12	13	2	3

Source: Prepared by the Statistics Division of the United Nations Secretariat from ILO, *Key Indicators of the Labour Market* (Geneva, 1999), table 9.

cent in sub-Saharan Africa to 35 per cent in Northern Africa for younger men. Unemployment rates for youth were more than twice the corresponding rates for the economically active adult population in all regions. The ratio of the youth unemployment rate to the adult rate was highest in Africa. In sub-Saharan Africa (excluding Southern Africa), young women's unemployment rate was 10 times that of adult women, while young men's unemployment rate was 5 times that of adult men **(chart 5.11)**.

Long-term unemployment

Long-term unemployment—defined as unemployment of a year or longer—is a significant portion of overall unemployment. In 1996/97, almost half of all unemployed women and men in Eastern Europe and about 40 per cent in Western Europe had been unemployed for a year or more. In the Caribbean, 38 and 27 per cent of unemployed women and men, respectively, were unemployed long-term, as were 25 and 21 per cent in Asia. In the developed regions outside Europe, 15 per cent and 22 per cent, respectively, of unemployed women and men in the labour force had been unemployed for a year or more.[29] Official statistics may tend to understate the level of long-term unemployment, since those affected are the most likely to become discouraged and therefore stop seeking employment. The groups considered most susceptible to long-term unemployment are those with a low level of education and older workers, as well as women, who are at greater risk of either not finding jobs or of losing their jobs.[30]

Gender differences in long-term unemployment rates and trends during the 1990s vary across regions. Long-term unemployment affects more men than women in the developed regions outside Europe. The rate is similar for men and women in Eastern Europe, while it is higher for women in Asia, the Caribbean and Western Europe. In Latin America, the rate for women was lower than for men between 1990 and 1993, but exceeded men's thereafter. In both Asia and Latin America, the gap between women's and men's long-term unemployment rates has increased since 1994 **(chart 5.12)**.

WORK IN THE INFORMAL SECTOR

The informal sector **(see box on elements of a definition of the informal sector)** accounts for a significant share of women's participation in the labour force. In the informal sector, women can create their own jobs, and in many countries it is their main source of employment.

The full extent of women and men's participation in the informal sector and the value of their contribution to production is still unknown. Until recently, the lack of both a standard definition of the sector and a common methodology for data collection rendered the informal economy largely invisible and hampered comparison across countries and between different sources of information. The 1993 adoption of an international definition of the informal sector [31] has made possible data collection and statistical estimation for this sector. However, due to its wide-ranging activities (from street-vending to small-scale manufacturing) and diverse modes of operation, the informal sector is characteristically difficult to measure.

Informal sector a larger source of employment for women than for men

Data on the composition of the non-agricultural labour force show the importance of the informal sector in many countries of the developing regions (chart 5.13). In some countries of sub-Saharan Africa, virtually all of the female non-agricultural labour force is in the informal sector—97 per cent in Benin and Chad and 96 per cent in Mali. Close to half or more of the female non-agricultural labour force is in

Chart 5.12:

The differences in long-term unemployment rates for women and men during the 1990s varied widely across regions

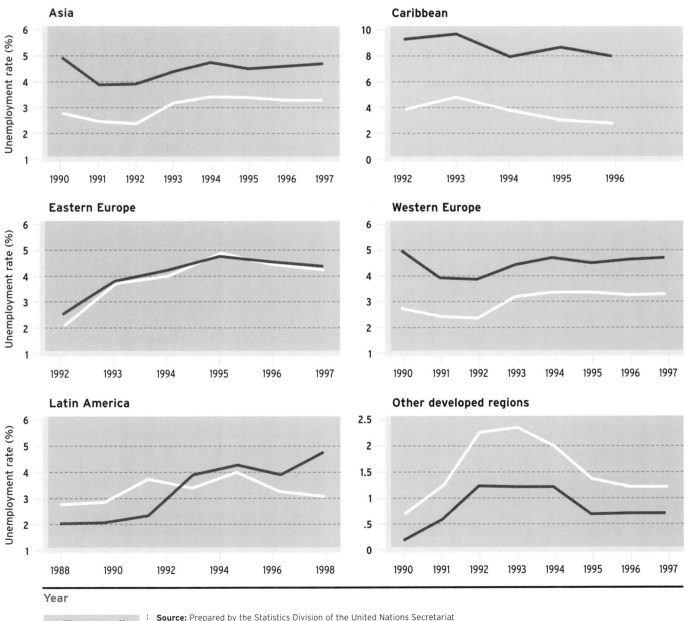

Source: Prepared by the Statistics Division of the United Nations Secretariat from ILO, *Key Indicators of the Labour Market*, (Geneva, 1999), table 10.

the informal sector in seven of the 10 Latin American countries for which data are available, and in four Asian countries. In India and Indonesia, the informal sector accounts for nine out of every 10 women working outside agriculture.

The informal sector is a larger source of employment for women than for men. The proportion of women non-agricultural workers in the informal sector exceeds that of men in most of the reporting countries. The exceptions are the Philippines and Tunisia, where the proportion of men exceeds that of women, and Venezuela, where the proportions are equal.

In nine countries, economically active women outnumber economically active men in the informal sector; i.e., their share of the informal sector is more than 50 per cent. In the other countries (except Guinea, India and Tunisia), women's share of the informal sector exceeds their share of the total labour force **(comparing chart 5.13 with table 5.D)**.

Characteristics of the informal sector vary across regions **(see box on gender-specific characteristics of enterprises)**. In some African countries, almost all women in the informal sector are either self-employed or contributing family workers **(chart 5.14)**. In nine out of 14 countries with data in Latin America and Asia, more than 20 per cent of women in the informal sector are wage workers. In every reporting country except Guinea, the percentage of employees in the informal sector is higher for men than for women. Moreover, in most countries with data, more than 20 per cent of men in the informal sector are employees (exceptions are Benin, Chad, Guinea and Mali). In countries where wage workers are a small minority, the informal sector mainly generates employment for the owners of the businesses and their immediate family members. The larger percentages of informal workers who are employees in Asia and Latin America suggest that the "micro enterprise"—employing a few employees on a continuous basis—segment of the informal sector is larger in these regions.

Detailed 1996/1997 data available for Latin America show that self-employed women and female contributing family workers make up a large majority of the informal sector. In addition, among the self-employed, own-account work provides for more than 80 per cent of women's employment. Though the proportion of self-employed men in the informal sector who are own-account workers is substantial, it is smaller than that of women **(charts 5.14 and 5.15)**.

Women's contribution to informal sector GDP significant

National economic and product accounts have historically underestimated informal sector activities. Before 1993, when the revised System of National Accounts provided a framework for distinguishing the informal sector within the household sector, few countries had estimated the value of informal sector production within the gross domestic product (GDP). The SNA does not, however, provide specific guidelines for compiling separate independent estimates for the informal sector. In the absence of such guidelines, there have been few attempts to derive national estimates of informal sector production.[32]

Among the eight countries for which data have been reported, women's share in the informal sector GDP was comparable to men's in Benin, Burkina Faso and Chad in 1992/1993. Their share of informal sector production matches or exceeds their share of informal sector employment **(chart 5.16)**, except in Benin and Kenya, where it is 9 per cent and 14 per cent lower, respectively.

Chart 5.13

The informal sector comprises a higher proportion of the female labour force than of the male labour force

	Percentage of non-agricultural labour force that is in the informal sector, 1991/1997		Women's share of the informal sector in the non-agricultural labour force, 1991/1997
	Women	**Men**	
Africa			
Benin	97	83	62
Chad	97	59	53
Guinea	84	61	37
Kenya	83	59	60
Mali	96	91	59
South Africa	30	14	61
Tunisia	39	52	18
Latin America			
Bolivia	74	55	51
Brazil	67	55	47
Chile	44	31	46
Colombia	44	42	50
Costa Rica	48	46	40
El Salvador	69	47	58
Honduras	65	51	56
Mexico	55	44	44
Panama	41	35	44
Venezuela	47	47	38
Asia			
India	91	70	23
Indonesia	88	69	43
Philippines	64	66	46
Thailand	54	49	47

Source: Data on Africa and Asia prepared by Jacques Charmes as consultant to the Statistics Division of the United Nations Secretariat; data on Latin America prepared by the Statistics Division of the United Nations Secretariat from statistics provided by the Statistics Division of ECLAC.

Women's employment in home-based work increasing

Official statistics on home-based work are scarce; even where they are collected, they underestimate this type of work (see box on measuring home-based workers). There is, however, some evidence that home-based work is an important and expanding source of employment worldwide, especially for women, and the conditions of these low-paid and unprotected workers are a growing concern.[33] In 1996, the ILO adopted the International Convention on Home Work, which recognizes the rights of home-based workers to treatment equal to that of other workers, and sets a standard for minimum pay and working conditions.[34]

Existing data for 1991 to 1999 show that in Benin, 66 per cent of the non-agricultural labour force is home-based. The corresponding figures are 14 per cent in the Philippines and 15 per cent in Kenya. In Brazil, Chile, Peru, Thailand and Tunisia, home-workers account for only 2 to 5 per cent of non-agricultural labour.[35]

These data also indicate that women predominate in home-based work. In six of the eight countries reporting data for 1991 to 1999, women account for 70 to 80

Source: Data on Africa and Asia prepared by Jacques Charmes as consultant to the Statistics Division of the United Nations Secretariat; data on Latin America prepared by the Statistics Division of the United Nations Secretariat from statistics provided by the Statistics Division of ECLAC.

Note: In Latin American countries, the self-employed category includes domestic employees.

Chart 5.14:
Wage-employment in the informal sector is considerably smaller for women than for men

	Percentage of the informal sector labour force that is self-employed or contributing family workers, 1991/1997		Percentage of the informal sector labour force that is paid employees, 1991/1997	
Africa	**W**	**M**	**W**	**M**
Benin	98	95	2	5
Chad	98	97	2	3
Guinea	97	100	3	0
Kenya	94	66	6	34
Mali	92	85	8	15
South Africa	86	62	14	38
Tunisia	100	77	..	23
Latin America				
Bolivia	91	71	9	29
Brazil	63	52	37	48
Chile	78	65	22	35
Colombia	47	40	53	60
Costa Rica	77	61	23	39
El Salvador	88	58	12	42
Honduras	93	66	7	34
Mexico	79	56	21	44
Panama	85	79	15	21
Venezuela	86	74	14	26
Asia				
India	46	49	54	51
Indonesia	68	63	32	37
Philippines	63	45	37	55
Thailand	68	60	32	40

Elements of a definition of micro and small enterprises

Different definitions of micro and small enterprises are used in different contexts and countries, generally applying one or more of the following criteria: the number of persons employed, the volume of output or sales, the value of assets, and the use of energy. The number of persons employed is the most common criterion, although the ILO notes that it may be misleading. For instance, a highly capitalized or technologically sophisticated enterprise may employ only a few people, whereas a small food-processing unit may use a large number of employees during the harvest season.[a] In addition, economic sector and geographical context play a role in the definition, as what is small by manufacturing firm standards may be considered large by retail firm standards, and what would be considered a small enterprise in Europe may be classified as a medium-sized enterprise in a developing country. In the Philippines, for example, micro and small enterprises are defined as those with capital assets of less than 15 million pesos (approximately US$ 0.5 million).[b]

Statistical information on women- and men-owned enterprises is lacking in most countries, and the little information available is often anecdotal and without clear indication of how qualifications such as "small" are defined.[c]

Data on micro and small-scale enterprises are not being collected or compiled on a routine basis. When data on enterprises are collected, they are generally not classified by the size of the enterprise (number of employees) or by the gender of the owner. In addition, the lack of a standard definition makes data comparisons difficult both within and between countries.[d]

[a] ILO, "General conditions to stimulate job creation in small and medium-sized enterprises", International Labour Conference, eighty-fifth session, 1997, report V(1).

[b] Gordon G. Zenaida, "SMEs in the Philippines", in OECD, *Women Entrepreneurs in Small and Medium Enterprises* (Paris, 1997).

[c] See for example Sherrye Henry, "The Office of Women's Business Ownership in the US Small Business Administration: A case study", in OECD, *Women Entrepreneurs in Small and Medium Enterprises*, (Paris, 1997).

[d] See for example, OECD, *Women Entrepreneurs in Small and Medium Enterprises...*

per cent of home-based workers **(chart 5. 17)**. In Kenya and Peru, women account for 35 per cent of home-based workers. In four out of the five countries that report data by status in employment, the majority of women home-based workers are own-account workers: Kenya (62 per cent), Tunisia (64 per cent), Brazil (91 per cent) and Peru (100 per cent). In Thailand, women home-based workers are mostly employees (81 per cent), or contributing family workers (18 per cent).[36]

Chart 5.16
In the informal sector, women's share of production is comparable to their share of employment
Women's share (%), 1992/1998

	Informal sector GDP	Informal sector employment
Africa		
Benin	51	60
Burkina Faso	61	42
Chad	62	53
Kenya	46	60
Tunisia	16	18
Asia		
India[a]	22	23
Indonesia	39	43
Philippines	44	46

Source: Prepared by Jacques Charmes as consultant to the Statistics Division of the United Nations Secretariat from official national accounts and labour force statistics.

[a] For India, the distribution of women in informal sector employment is assumed to be the same as their distribution in non-agricultural labour force (excluding public administration).

TIME USE
Most women and men divide their time between paid and unpaid work—either caring for their families or producing subsistence goods. Unpaid work is generally invisible in official statistics. However, statisticians and advocates of gender equality have been seeking ways to reflect all kinds of work in labour force statistics, and many countries have made efforts to improve official statistics. Improved definitions and data collection tools have increased the coverage of women's unpaid economic activities in labour force statistics, although not in all countries and not to the same extent. Other statistical tools—such as time-use surveys—provide a means to increase the coverage of both unpaid economic work and unpaid activities considered outside the boundaries of the

Chart 5.17:
Most home-based workers are women
Percentage women among home-based workers

	1991/1999
Benin	74
Brazil	79
Chile	82
Kenya	35
Peru	35
Philippines	79
Thailand	80
Tunisia	71

Source: Compiled by Jacques Charmes as consultant to the Statistics Division of the United Nations Secretariat from survey data contained in national reports.

Chart 5.15
Among the self-employed, women are more likely than men to be own-account workers

Own-account workers as a percentage of self-employed, 1996/1997

	W	M
Latin America		
Bolivia	96	78
Brazil	93	90
Chile	90	88
Colombia	92	87
Costa Rica	85	71
El Salvador	94	76
Honduras	95	76
Mexico	93	75
Panama	94	89
Venezuela	96	86

Source: Compiled by the Statistics Division of the United Nations Secretariat from data provided by the Statistics Division of ECLAC.

Gender-specific characteristics of enterprises [a]

In both developed and developing countries, women's enterprises are more often based in the home than men's, due to women's need to juggle their various roles as income-earners, mothers and home-makers or due to sociocultural norms and attitudes that limit their mobility. Women frequently build on traditional skills that they already know. Women's access to technology and scientific knowledge has historically been limited, due to cultural factors and biases in the educational system that have favoured men.

Women often have less time than men to pursue larger markets and, in some cases, are limited by taboos against dealing with men who are not family members. Women invest fewer resources in equipment than men. They spread their risk over a number of economic activities, while men tend to invest in a single business. Women's businesses are often at the lower end of the spectrum of productive economic activities. The smaller the microenterprise, the more likely it is to have a woman proprietor.

Women tend to concentrate in the less remunerative sectors or subsectors. Although they are present in all sectors, in developed countries they tend to concentrate in commerce and services. In developing countries, they are frequently involved in artisan activities, agriculture and production derived from agriculture. Women tend to predominate in enterprises with few barriers to entry (food and craft production), which, due to fierce competition, have low profitability and limited opportunities for growth.

[a] OECD, Proceedings of an OECD conference on women entrepreneurs in small and medium-sized enterprises, Paris, 16-18 April 1997.

System of National Accounts **(see box on new partnerships to improve data on paid and unpaid work).**

Time-use surveys measure what women and men do over the course of the day, and provide data for estimating their unpaid as well as paid work. In developed countries, time-use statistics are increasingly used to acquire insight into women's and men's allocation of time to a variety of activities, not just work, as a basis for formulating policy in such areas as education, childcare, and cultural or leisure activities.

Time-use surveys were initially implemented in developed countries. More recently, national statistical offices in developing countries have relied on

time-use surveys to improve the measurement of women's and men's unpaid work **(see box on time-use surveys in developing countries).** These surveys have only recently been implemented, and results are not yet widely available. Few countries have repeated time-use surveys and surveys were undertaken in differ-

Chart 5.18:

Women spend considerably more time than men on upaid work but much less on paid work
Time spent (hours per week), 1995/1999

Source: Prepared by Andrew Harvey as consultant to the Statistics Division of the United Nations Secretariat from the Multinational Time Budget Archive database, micro-data from country studies and other published national reports.

Note: Paid work refers to actual work time plus all associated time, such as work breaks and travel; unpaid work refers to housework and voluntary activities; leisure time refers to organizational activities, sports attendance, media activities and similar activities; basic needs refer to sleeping, washing, eating, medical self-care etc.

| | Work | | | | | | Leisure | | Basic needs | |
| | Total | | Paid | | Unpaid | | | | | |
	W	M	W	M	W	M	W	M	W	M
Australia	51	49	15	30	35	18	35	38	78	77
France	46	42	15	26	31	17	29	34	85	84
Japan	46	42	20	39	26	3	42	44	75	73
Latvia	62	56	22	32	40	24	28	33	75	76
Netherlands	36	37	10	25	26	11	47	48	76	74
New Zealand	49	49	16	29	33	19	32	33	82	80
Republic of Korea	40	38	23	36	17	2	30	37	79	79

Measuring poverty

Conventional measures of poverty have generally been based on income and consumption levels, with the understanding that "a person is considered poor if his or her consumption or income level falls below some minimum level necessary to meet basic needs".[a] Two broad concepts of poverty have been defined[b]:

- "absolute poverty" refers to the inability to attain even the minimum set of resources a person needs for survival;
- "relative poverty" refers to the conditions of one part of the population in relation to the rest of the society.

The conventional conceptualization and measurement of poverty generally emphasize income and consumption over other dimensions of poverty.[c] Increasingly, however, poverty is seen as a multi-dimensional phenomenon, one that includes not only market-based consumption but also the public provision of goods and services, access to common property resources and the intangible dimensions of a satisfactory life, such as clean air, dignity, autonomy and low levels of diseases and crime.[d] This broader definition extends beyond income criteria and considers different aspects of living conditions, including health and nutrition, education, hous-

ing, social services and mortality levels. It is more instrumental in understanding and measuring poverty from a gender perspective and uncovering gender biases and their causes.[e]

Another concern is the extent to which gender relations affect intra-household distribution and use of resources.[f] An analysis of data from four countries, for instance, suggests that individuals within the household have different preferences and do not pool their income. Moreover, assets controlled by women have a more positive and significant effect on expenditures for children, such as education and clothing, than those

controlled by men.[g]

Current efforts to analyze poverty from a gender perspective both determine the numbers of female and male poor and assess whether poverty affects women (or women-headed households) and men (or men-headed households) differently.[h] In order for poverty statistics to inform policy, it is not only necessary to assess the number of those in need; the conditions of social and economic deprivation and the ways in which "gender differentiates the social processes leading to poverty"[i] must also be considered.

[a] Simon Schwartzman, "Poverty statistics: The issues", presented at an expert group on poverty statistics, Rio De Janeiro, 1998.

[b] Ibid.

[c] Nilufer Cagatay, "Macroeconomic policy and poverty reduction: the gender perspective", based on UNDP research, in UNRISD, Gender Poverty and Well-Being: Indicators and Strategies, report of the UNRISD, UNDP and CDS International Workshop, Kerala, 24-27 November 1997 (Geneva, 1999).

[d] Shahra Razavi, "Gendered Poverty and Well-being: Introduction", *Development and Change*, vol. 30, No. 3 (July 1999).

[e] Marcoux Alain, "The feminization of poverty: claims, facts and data needs", *Population and Development Review*, vol. 24, No. 1 (March 1998).

[f] Ruhi Saith and Barbara Harriss-White, "Gender sensitivity of well-being indicators", United Nations Research Institute for Social Development, Discussion Paper No. 95, September 1998.

[g] Agnes R. Quisumbing and John A. Maluccio, "Intra-household allocation and gender relations: New empirical evidence" (IFPRI, September 1999).

[h] Razavi, op.cit.; Alain, op.cit.

[i] Razavi, op.cit.

ent years, so it is difficult to discern trends. However, while trends in paid work vary across countries, the number of hours spent on unpaid work in all the regions seems to be slowly increasing for men and decreasing for women.[37]

Women work more hours than men

Few studies on time use have been conducted since 1995.[38] In the seven countries for which recent data have been reported between 1995 and 1999, both women and men work between 35 and 50 hours a week, except in Latvia, where they work more than 50 hours on average (62 for women and 56 for men) (chart 5.18). Women's total time worked exceeded men's by two hours or more in all countries except the Netherlands and New Zealand, where the difference in the total time worked by women and men was less than one hour.

More than half of women's total work time is spent on unpaid work, except in the Republic of Korea, where 42 per cent of women's work time is devoted to unpaid work. In contrast, men spend between 30 and 42 per cent of their work time on unpaid work, except in Japan and the Republic of Korea, where unpaid work constitutes 7 and 6 per cent, respectively, of their total work time. Women spend 50 to 70 per cent as much time as men on paid work, but almost twice as much or more time as men on unpaid work. Differences are most pronounced in Japan and the Republic of Korea, where women's unpaid work is about eight times that of men (chart 5.18).

Men spend 1 to 7 hours more per week on leisure than do women, but women spend up to 2.5 hours more than men on basic needs.

Chart 5.19

The presence of small children increases unpaid work substantially more for women than for men

Time spent (hours per week), 1995/1999

	Unpaid Work				Paid Work			
	No children[a]		With child(ren)[a]		No children[a]		With child(ren)[a]	
	W	M	W	M	W	M	W	M
Australia[b]	40	22	49	22	14	30	16	43
Netherlands	36	18	47	23	12	29	9	34
New Zealand	34	23	50	23	20	29	11	41

Source: Prepared by Andrew Harvey as consultant to the Statistics Division of the United Nations Secretariat from the Multinational Time Budget Archive database, micro-data from country studies and other published national reports.

[a] Refers to children under age 5.

[b] Australia used the categories "without dependent or non-dependent children" and "with dependent or non-dependent children".

Elements of a definition of the informal sector

The first internationally accepted framework for defining and measuring the informal sector was the Resolution on Statistics of Employment in the Informal Sector, adopted by the Fifteenth International Conference of Labour Statisticians in 1993.[a]

The ILO resolution recommended that the concept and measurement of the informal sector be confined to non-agricultural and market-oriented activities.

The informal sector is broadly characterized as consisting of units engaged in the production of goods or services with the primary objective of generating employment and incomes to the persons concerned. Production units in this sector operate at a low level of organization, with little or no division between capital and labour as factors of production, and on a small scale, and have the characteristic features of household enterprises, in which owners must raise the necessary funds at their own risk. In addition, expenditure for production is often indistinguishable from household expenditure.

For statistical purposes, the informal sector is regarded as a group of production units that, according to definitions and classifications provided in the System of National Accounts, form part of the household sector as household enterprises or unincorporated enterprises owned by households.

Within the household sector, the informal sector comprises (a) informal own-account enterprises, which may employ contributing family workers and employees on an occasional basis; and (b) enterprises of informal employers, which employ one or more employees on a continuous basis. For operational purposes, informal own-account enterprises may comprise either all such enterprises or only those that are not registered under specific forms of national legislation. The enterprises of informal employers must fulfill one or both of the following criteria: size of unit below a specified level of employment, and non-registration of the enterprise or its employees.

The framework proposed by the ILO resolution allows countries to adapt the basic operational definition and criteria to their specific circumstances. In particular, flexibility is allowed with respect to the upper limit on the size of employment; the introduction of additional criteria such as non-registration of either the enterprise or its employees; and the inclusion or exclusion of professionals or domestic employees.

It is still difficult to collect accurate and consistent information on the informal sector. Therefore, different national sources are usually combined to derive statistics on this sector. The data presented in this chapter were compiled on the basis of data from national informal sector surveys (Kenya, Mali and Niger) and (b) labour force surveys in which information about the characteristics of the workplace was collected (Thailand and countries in Latin America). For all other countries the estimates were derived from a combination of sources, including labour force surveys and registered employment in formal sector.

[a] ILO, *Report of the Fifteenth International Conference of Labour Statisticians*, Geneva, 1993; see also resolution concerning statistics of employment in the informal sector, in ILO, *Bulletin of Labour Statistics* 1993–2 (Geneva), annex II, paras. 5–9.

Small children greatly increase women's unpaid work, not men's

Three out of seven countries report data on the time use of women and men with small children (children under age 5) (chart 5.19). In these countries, women with small children spend less time on paid work and more time on unpaid work. They spend at least 20 per cent less time on paid work than women with no small children in the Netherlands and 40 per cent less time in New Zealand, but 10 per cent more time in Australia. Men with small children spend more time on paid work than those without small children by about 40 per cent in Australia and New Zealand and 20 per cent in the Netherlands.

Men with children under age 5 spend at least five more hours on paid work than men with no small children. There is, however, little difference in the amount of time spent by either of these groups on unpaid work, except in the Netherlands, where they devote 18 and 23 hours, respectively, to unpaid work. In contrast, women's allocation of time both to paid and unpaid work is affected by the presence of small children—particularly in New Zealand, where women with small children spend nine hours less time on paid work but 16 hours more time on unpaid work than those with no small children.

The responsibility for childcare lies mainly with women, who spend more than twice as much time as men do on childcare. (Childcare includes all direct physical care, reading to and playing with children, but excludes secondary childcare—for example, watching children while engaged in other activities.) With the exception of the Republic of Korea, where, on average, both women and men spend less than one hour per week on childcare, women everywhere spend between two and five hours per week on childcare compared with less than two hours for men.[39]

Time spent on work diminishes with age

Time-use data for a few industrialized countries provide some insight into how older women and men spend their time.

At older ages, women spend more time working than men, mostly due to the difference in time they spend on unpaid work (chart 5.20). There is, however, a wide variation across countries in the amount of time women and men allocate to paid work. Women aged 60 to 64 spend two hours a week on paid work in the Netherlands, compared with slightly more than 10 hours in Norway. Men of this age spend seven hours a week on paid work in the Netherlands, compared with 27 hours a week in Norway. Paid work decreases after age 65, declining by about half for

both women and men aged 65 to 69. By age 75 to 79, paid work is reduced to just under four hours for men and less than an hour for women.

Unpaid work, on the other hand, continues to take up a considerable amount of time for both men and women at older ages. Women perform between 28 and 44 hours a week of unpaid work, on average, between the ages of 60 and 65, and 28 to 33 hours a week at ages 75 to 79. Men put in 14 to 28 hours a week of unpaid work at ages 60 to 65, and 13 to 30 hours a week at ages 75 to 79.

Chart 5.20

As women and men age, less time is spent on work and more time on basic needs and leisure

Time spent (hours per week)

	Paid work		Unpaid work		Basic needs		Leisure	
	W	M	W	M	W	M	W	M
Austria, 1991								
60-64	4	15	41	21	82	85	36	43
65-69	2	7	39	21	84	88	38	47
70-74	1	7	36	20	87	89	40	47
75-79	1	3	31	17	90	93	41	50
Canada, 1998								
60-64	7	17	35	25	78	75	48	51
65-69	4	6	35	26	77	79	52	57
70-74	1	3	31	25	81	82	55	58
75-79	0	1	28	28	85	83	54	56
Germany, 1991/92								
60-64	4	13	44	28	81	83	39	43
65-69	1	5	39	29	83	85	43	48
Italy, 1989								
60-64	3	15	44	14	83	87	34	46
65-69	2	9	41	15	86	89	37	49
70-74	1	6	39	15	89	93	37	50
75-79	<1	4	33	13	92	86	40	52
Netherlands, 1995								
60-64	2	7	36	27	72	75	50	49
65-69	<1	2	36	27	73	75	52	56
70-74	1	2	36	28	74	75	50	56
75-79	0	<1	33	30	76	79	54	52
Norway, 1991								
60-64	10	27	28	15	77	77	47	43
65-69	5	12	29	22	79	79	51	48
70-74	2	4	33	19	76	84	51	56
75-79	<1	2	28	21	86	82	51	57

Source: Prepared by Andrew Harvey as a consultant to the Statistics Division of the United Nations Secretariat from the Multinational Time Budget Archive database, micro-data from country studies and other published national reports.

WORKING CONDITIONS AND OPPORTUNITIES

The 165 countries that have ratified the Convention on the Elimination of All Forms of Discrimination against Women have assumed the obligation of taking appropriate measures to eliminate employment discrimination against women. In particular, these countries have committed to ensure "the right to the same employment opportunities, including the application of the same criteria for selection...;the right to free choice of profession and employment, the right to promotion, job security and all benefits and conditions of service and the right to receive vocational training and retraining...;the right to equal remuneration...and to equal treatment in respect to work of equal value".[40] In addition, the labour legislation of many countries now incorporates principles of gender equality. However, while women's participation in the labour force has increased worldwide, their working conditions have not improved commensurately.[41]

Gender-based segregation of occupations persisting in all regions

Gender-based segregation of occupations has been a longstanding and enduring characteristic of the labour market. It extends to all regions and countries irrespective of the level of economic development, the political system, or the religious, social or cultural environment.[42] Segregation of occupations can be either horizontal (the tendency for women and men to be employed in different occupations across occupational structure) or vertical (the tendency for women and men to be employed in different positions within the same occupation).

In the Nordic countries for which data are available (Finland, Norway and Sweden), 55 per cent of women are in occupations where at least 80 per cent of workers are women and 40 per cent are in occupations where they comprise 90 per cent of workers.

In occupations in which women are concentrated, such as teaching, they are usually in lower hierarchical positions. For example, in Finland 96 per cent of pre-primary school teachers and directors are women, but only 34 per cent of the teaching staff at universities are women.[43]

An ILO study[44] indicates that there is a preponderance of male occupations over female occupations—defined as an occupation in which either men or women, respectively, comprise at least 80 per cent of workers. The study reports that there are approximately seven times as many "male" as "female" non-agricultural occupations. The study also finds high levels of occupational segregation in the non-agricultural occupations. The levels of segregation differ widely among regions, although within regions there are similarities among countries. The lowest level of segregation is in Asia and the highest is in the Middle East and Northern Africa.

Occupational segregation can have undesirable effects on the labour market, such as limiting the economic efficiency of that market. Segregation excludes a majority of workers from a majority of occupations and may thus lead to waste; it also reduces the flexibility of the labour market and of the economy as a whole.[45] Moreover, occupational segregation is more detrimental to women than to men, especially given the characteristics of the typically female occupations. Female occupations are "relatively low paid, have relatively little employment security and have relatively little authority or career opportunities",[46] and are also undervalued in terms of social status.[47]

Patterns of concentration

Women are in fewer occupations than men and have fewer job opportunities available to them due to differences in education and experience.[48] Moreover, most of women's occupations are service oriented[49] or associated with stereotypes about women (e.g., caring, docile or home-based).

Women make up less than 30 per cent of any occupational group, except for agriculture in sub-Saharan Africa, excluding Southern Africa (64 per

---

Measuring home-based workers

Home-based workers (sometimes referred to as out-workers) are defined in the 1993 International Classification of Status in Employment (ICSE)[a] as those who work for an enterprise to supply goods or services by prior arrangement with that enterprise, and whose place of work is not within any of the enterprise's establishments.[b] Home-based workers may be classified as paid or self-employed, according to the specific terms of their contracts. They are paid employees when they receive remuneration independent of the enterprise's profits and based on the goods and services provided.

Because it is performed at home and because it can be a secondary activity, home-based work is difficult to measure.

Only a few national household surveys (and population censuses) have sought to collect information on home-based work, and these efforts were largely experimental. In the Philippines, for instance, a 1993 survey focused on home-workers under subcontracting arrangements, but excluded own-account workers; and in Thailand, a national survey of home-workers was conducted in 1999 but it did not cover own-account workers. Other types of surveys have rarely had national coverage or even comparable geographical representation. One way to improve the measurement of home-based work would be to collect information on the "place of work" in national labour force surveys.

[a] ILO, Report of the Fifteenth International Conference of Labour Statisticians (Geneva, 1993).

[b] ILO, Bulletin of Labour Statistics, 1993–2.

---

cent) and Southern Asia (47 per cent) **(chart 5.21)**. More than 30 per cent of men are in production-related jobs, except in sub-Saharan Africa (excluding Southern Africa), Southern Asia and Oceania. In these regions, men are predominantly employed in agriculture (60 per cent, 42 per cent and 37 per cent, respectively).

The concentration of women is almost the same in two or three occupational groups in Southern Africa (service, agricultural and production-related workers), South-eastern Asia (agricultural and production-related workers) and the Caribbean (service and production-related workers).

The professional and technical group is the second largest occupational group for women in Western Asia, Western Europe and other developed regions (21, 19 and 17 per cent, respectively). In Northern Africa, more women are employed in this group than in any other (21 per cent).

The occupational group with the smallest percentages of economically active women and men is that of the administrative and managerial workers—5 per cent or less in all regions except Western Europe (7 per cent of men) and the developed regions outside Europe (9 per cent of women and 12 per cent of men). In the developed regions outside Europe, agricultural workers are the smallest occupational group (3 per cent of women and 6 per cent of men).

Women professionals and managers

Not only do women and men have different occupations, they also have very different positions in the occupational hierarchy. Even in occupations dominated by women, men generally occupy better-paid and more powerful positions.

In many regions, women have reached educational levels comparable to or higher than men, increased their participation in the labour force, and

Chart 5.21:

Distribution of the labour force by major occupational groups
Percentage distribution of the labour force by occupational group, each sex, 1985/1997

	Professional, technical and related workers		Administrative and managerial workers		Clerical and related workers		Sales Workers		Service workers		Agricultural and other workers[a]		Production and related workers[b]	
	W	M	W	M	W	M	W	M	W	M	W	M	W	M
Africa														
Northern Africa	21	10	1	1	12	6	2	7	8	7	19	23	15	32
Southern Africa	11	7	1	2	9	4	8	4	17	7	18	23	17	35
Rest of sub-Saharan Africa	3	4	0	1	3	3	11	6	5	5	64	60	8	17
Latin America and the Caribbean														
Caribbean	12	8	5	5	15	5	15	7	18	10	7	17	18	38
Central America	14	7	3	3	13	4	21	9	23	8	6	33	20	34
South America	15	8	3	5	15	8	18	12	26	7	7	16	11	35
Asia														
Eastern Asia	9	8	1	5	19	10	13	13	15	9	23	20	22	35
South-eastern Asia	10	9	2	4	12	6	19	10	11	7	22	26	23	35
Southern Asia	13	5	0	1	5	4	2	10	5	7	47	42	20	26
Western Asia	21	10	1	3	15	12	4	8	28	13	17	11	6	39
Oceania	13	9	2	4	14	5	8	4	11	6	27	37	10	25
Developed regions														
Eastern Europe	13	10	5	5	15	6	9	4	10	4	12	11	25	49
Western Europe	19	14	5	7	23	11	12	8	18	7	5	7	13	41
Other developed regions	17	15	9	12	26	8	14	9	16	9	3	6	12	40

Source: Prepared by the Statistics Division of the United Nations Secretariat from *Women's Indicators and Statistics Database (Wistat)*, *Version 4*, CD-ROM (United Nations publication, Sales No. E.00.XVII.4), based on ILO, *Yearbook of Labour Statistics* (Geneva), 1985-1992 and LABORSTA database (as at 1998), national census and survey reports and national statistical yearbooks.

[a] Agricultural, animal husbandry and forestry workers, fishermen and hunters.

[b] Production and related workers, transport equipment operators and labourers.

expanded their opportunities by delaying marriage and limiting childbearing. However, they are still under-represented in senior management and other management positions that entail higher responsibility, status and pay.

Women make up 29 to 51 per cent of the professional and technical workers group, although they tend to be concentrated in the lower status and less well-paid occupations. For instance, the ILO reports that in the United States in 1991, almost half the women in this group were nurses and teachers. In Japan, 47 per cent of women professionals were nurses or teachers in 1990. In India, the corresponding figure was over 80 per cent.[50]

In contrast, women make up less than 30 per cent of the administrative and managerial labour force in all regions except the Caribbean (39 per cent), Eastern Europe (40 per cent) and the developed regions outside Europe (35 per cent). In all regions, women's share of this occupational group is less than their share of the labour market. This indicates that

few women are in occupations that entail decision-making authority and responsibility.

The share of women in the professional and technical group equals or exceeds their share in the labour force in all regions except sub-Saharan Africa (excluding Southern Africa) **(charts 5.22 and 5.1)**.

Since 1975/1984, women's share of professional and technical jobs has changed only slightly in most parts of the developing and developed regions. In Northern Africa, Latin America, Eastern and Western Asia, women's share increased by 4 to 9 percentage points. In Eastern Europe, where opportunities for women have decreased in parts of the public sector and their access to the new private sector jobs has been limited, their share of professional and technical jobs has declined by 9 percentage points.[51]

Between 1975/1984 and 1985/1997, women's share of administrative and managerial workers increased in every region of the world except Southern Asia **(chart 5.22)**. Over the same time period, their share doubled in sub-Saharan Africa, Central America, Western Asia and the developed regions outside Europe and increased by 30 to 90 per cent everywhere else.

There is a wide variation in the social status and pay levels of occupations within the professional and technical group. Even in countries where these occupations are not particularly desirable in terms of pay and social status, they are still dominated by men in most regions. Women in Northern Africa, sub-Saharan Africa (excluding Southern Africa) and Southern and Western Asia represent one third or less of these occupations.

Women at the top of large corporations
Although it is hard to compare figures across countries on the most senior jobs—as terms and definitions vary widely—the picture that does emerge from the available information shows that women are still a minority of senior management staff, especially in large corporations. The 1999 census of the 500 largest corporations in the United States shows, for instance, that women held just 11 per cent of all corporate officer positions and 5 per cent of the most senior of those positions, including four presidents and chief executives.[52] In Canada, a census of the 560 largest corporations in 1999 found that women held 12 per cent of all corporate officer positions and only 3 per cent of the highest positions (including 12 presidents and chief executive officers).[53]

In Brazil, a 1991 ILO survey found that less than 4 per cent of top executives were women in the 300 largest private companies, less than 1 per cent in the 40 largest state-owned companies, and less than 1 per cent in the 40 largest foreign-owned companies.

Chart 5.22:
Women continue to be a minority among administrative and managerial workers

	Women's share of administrative and managerial workers (%)		Women's share of professional, technical and related workers (%)	
	1975/1984	1985/1997	1975/1984	1985/1997
Africa				
Northern Africa	7	10	24	29
Southern Africa	12	23	53	51
Rest of sub-Saharan Africa	7	14	28	30
Latin America and the Caribbean				
Caribbean	22	39	51	50
Central America	14	29	45	49
South America	17	24	48	52
Asia				
Eastern Asia	7	12	35	44
South-eastern Asia	13	24	42	44
Southern Asia	8	8	30	28
Western Asia	4	9	30	34
Oceania	11	15	41	40
Developed regions				
Eastern Europe	22	40	54	45
Western Europe	16	26	42	45
Other developed regions	16	35	46	47

Source: Prepared by the Statistics Division of the United Nations Secretariat from *Women's Indicators and Statistics Database (Wistat), Version 4*, CD-ROM (United Nations publication, Sales No. E.00.XVII.4), based on ILO, *Yearbook of Labour Statistics* (Geneva), 1985-1992 and LABORSTA database (as at 1998), national census and survey reports and national statistical yearbooks.

In the United Kingdom, in 1995, 3 per cent of board members in more than 300 surveyed enterprises were women. A survey in Germany in 1995 found that between 1 and 3 per cent of top executives and board directors in the 70,000 largest enterprises were women.[54]

According to the ILO, one of the main obstacles to women's participation in high-level professional and managerial work is their responsibility for rearing children and managing the household, a responsibility still seldom shared with their partners in many parts of the world. Women in part-time work are often excluded from career advancement. Even women who work full time have difficulties in advancing to the higher levels if they also carry family responsibilities. A survey among managers in Germany in 1997 found that 43 per cent of women managers were unmarried, compared to only 4 per cent of men managers. A similar survey in the United Kingdom found that 88 per cent of men managers were married, compared to 69 per cent of women in the same positions.

Women in banking

Women's presence in the financial world has increased slightly. Their share of financial management positions increased from 20 to 24 per cent in Colombia between 1990 and 1996, and from 45 to 50 per cent in the United States between 1990 and 1995.[55]

A recent survey of 63 commercial banks in the European Union found that between 1990 and 1995, the share of women increased from 25 to 27 per cent in lower management, from 13 to 18 per cent in middle management, and from 6 to 8 per cent in higher management. Decision-making still appears to be largely male-dominated, however. The survey also found that women accounted for almost half of all employees but only 8 per cent of the highest-level managers. Only 3 per cent of executive committee members were women.[56]

Family obligations represent the main obstacle for women trying to reach management levels in this sector as well. In the same European Union survey, more than 60 per cent of women bank managers reported that this was the main obstacle they had to overcome to enter the lower level of management, and almost as many reported that it was the main obstacle to entering the middle level.

Central banks play a crucial role in the financial and economic system of a country. The European Union study shows that women have historically been excluded from central bank decision-making and are just beginning to reach the top positions. Women headed two of the 15 central banks in 1994/1995—in Denmark and Finland. However, four of those banks had no women in the first five levels of decision-making.[57]

Women earn less than men

Although the principle of equal pay for work of equal value has been incorporated in the labour legislation of many countries, in no country for which data are available do women earn as much as men. In manufacturing, for example, in 13 out of 39 countries, women earn up to 20 per cent less than men; in the other countries, the pay differential is even greater. However, the differ-

Time-use surveys in developing countries

Until recently, time-use data were not part of the data-collection programmes of national statistical offices in developing countries. Time-use studies in these countries were mainly case studies of either one locality or a few localities and did not cover a 24-hour day.

However, following the recommendations of the Fourth World Conference on Women held at Beijing in 1995, at least 22 countries—in Africa, Asia, Latin America and the Caribbean—have begun work on national time-use surveys (see list of countries below).[a] Although geographically, economically and culturally diverse, each of these countries has come to consider national time-use surveys an important statistical tool for measuring and valuing paid and unpaid work of women and men, and for increasing the visibility of women's work both at home and in the labour market. Some of the surveys (in Benin, Chad, India and Oman and the pilot studies in Nigeria and South Africa) also aim to improve data collection on women's economic activities, especially in the informal sector. In India, the objectives of the pilot survey also include using these data for skills training, as well as for designing poverty eradication programmes.

A joint project of the United Nations Statistics Division, the United Nations Development Programme (UNDP), and the International Development Research Centre/Canada (IDRC) is studying the methods used in new national time-use surveys to determine which procedures are suitable for collecting time-use data in developing countries; whether time-use data can be collected from illiterate persons using methods from developed countries; and whether the problems of survey methods in developing and developed countries are more similar than previously recognized. The project is also developing guidelines for collecting and analysing time-use statistics in developing countries.

Independent time-use surveys were utilized by approximately half of the countries collecting time-use data for the first time. The other countries collected data through a module on a multipurpose survey, such as a labour force or an income and expenditure survey.

Another tool needed for a time-use survey is a classification of activities of daily life. The existing classifications, based on developed countries, do not identify a set of economic activities that are crucial to livelihood in developing countries, such as production for home use, certain types of home-based work, street vending and other informal sector economic activities. The United Nations Statistics Division\UNDP\IDRC project is also refining and further developing a trial international classification for time-use statistics. One objective of this work is to develop methods of data collection and classification of time-use statistics that can be adapted to the situations in developing and developed countries.[b]

[a] Independent time-use surveys: Cuba, Dominican Republic, India, Mexico, Mongolia, Morocco, Nigeria, Occupied Palestinian Territory, Philippines, the Russian Federation (Komi Republic), South Africa and Thailand. Time-use module in multipurpose household surveys: Benin, Chad, Ecuador, Guatemala, Indonesia, Lao People's Democratic Republic, Nepal, Nicaragua, Oman and Viet Nam.

[b] More detailed information on the methods used in these surveys is available at http://www.un.org/Depts/unsd/timeuse/inter.htm

ential between women's and men's earnings narrowed between 1990 and 1997 in 26 of the 36 countries reporting data for the manufacturing sector, while it remained constant or widened in the remaining 10 countries **(chart 5.23)**.

Pay differentials between women and men vary across occupational groups and countries. In Finland, for instance, the income of female wage and salary earners was, on average, 80 per cent that of men in 1993, while female managers earned 66 per cent of the salary of male managers.[58] In the United Kingdom, women professionals earned 17 per cent less than men in 1996 and women managers earned 27 per cent less than men. In Uruguay, earnings of women managers in the banking and finance sector were as little as 47 per cent of those of men in 1995.[59]

Part-time employment increasing and women majority of part-time workers

There has been an increase in part-time employment relative to full-time employment in the last two decades.[60] Part-time work is particularly important to women, offering them an effective way to divide their time between paid work, household responsibilities and child-rearing. It can facilitate gradual entry into, participation in and retirement from the labour market. However, it is often associated with low professional status, lower pay and fewer or nonexistent career opportunities.

In countries for which data are reported, women represent the large majority of part-time workers, accounting for 80 per cent or more in some cases **(table 5.B)**.

Part-time work is common for women in Western Europe. More than half of employed women work part time in the Netherlands, close to half in Switzerland and more than one third in Iceland, Norway and the United Kingdom. In contrast, 3 to 11 per cent of men work part-time in this region.

Part-time work is also common for women in the developed regions outside Europe (19 to 38 per cent). Though part-time work for men is low in these regions, it is slowly increasing, except in the United States.

Chart 5.23:

Women continue to earn less than men in all countries and areas
Women's wages in manufacturing as a percentage of men's wages

Africa	1990	1992/1997	Developed regions	1990	1992/1997
Egypt	68	74	Australia	82	85
Kenya	73	..	Austria	..	66
Swaziland	73	71	Belgium	75	80
Zambia	73	..	Bulgaria	..	72
			Denmark	85	85
Latin America			Finland	77	79
Brazil	54	54	France	79	79
Costa Rica	74	86	Germany	73	74
El Salvador	94	95	Greece	78	81
Mexico	50	71	Hungary	70	70
Paraguay	66	77	Ireland	69	75
Asia			Italy	83	..
Bangladesh	49	50	Japan	41	..
Cyprus	58	60	Latvia	84	89
China			Lithuania	..	81
Hong Kong SAR	69	61	Luxembourg	62	63
Macao SAR	67	57	Netherlands	77	..
Jordan	57	62	New Zealand	74	78
Malaysia	49	58	Norway	86	87
Myanmar	97	96	Portugal	69	69
Republic of Korea	50	56	Spain	72	..
Singapore	55	60	Sweden	89	90
Sri Lanka	88	85	Switzerland	68	69
Thailand	64	68	United Kingdom	68	72
Turkey	81	99	United States	68	..

Source: Prepared by the Statistics Division of the United Nations Secretariat from *Women's Indicators and Statistics Database (Wistat), Version 4*, CD-ROM (United Nations publication, Sales No. E.00.XVII.4), based on ILO, *Yearbook of Labour Statistics* (Geneva), 1977-1998.

In Eastern Europe, part-time work is less common and differences between women and men workers are less pronounced. In five out of eight of these countries, 10 per cent or fewer women and men workers are employed part-time.

Few countries in the developing regions report data on part-time employment. In these countries the part-time work force is largely female.

More women employed during childbearing years

How to reconcile work outside the home with family responsibilities is the focus of much concern. More women are spending their childbearing and child-rearing years in paid employment **(see section on activity rates over the life cycle)**. The rights of working women during their reproductive years are increasingly being considered in labour legislation and workplace practices have improved; however, the gap between legislation and practice remains wide. Married women with children find it easier to take advantage of career opportunities when employers grant them the flexibility to combine household responsibilities and a career.[61] The ILO has conducted an extensive review of the conventions and practices relating to pregnancy and working women **(see section on maternity leave)**.[62]

Many working mothers still experience unequal treatment in employment at some point during their time in the workforce. Discriminatory practices based on potential or actual maternity are widespread, so much so that some countries have passed, or are considering, legislation prohibiting employers from requiring as a condition of employment a sterilization certificate or a commitment from the employee that she will not become pregnant during the term of her contract.

Maternity leave

The right of the mother to a leave from employment after childbirth and a guarantee that she can resume her job has been recognized internationally since the ILO Maternity Protection Convention was adopted in 1952. This Convention stipulates a standard maternity leave of at least 12 weeks duration. Today, 119 countries meet this standard of 12 weeks or more; in 20 countries, maternity leave is 17 weeks or longer; and 31 countries offer less than 12 weeks of maternity leave **(table 5.C)**.

How maternity leave is implemented and whether granting it is optional or compulsory for the employer can profoundly affect women's actual entitlement. In the United States, it is optional; in other countries there is a mandatory minimum level. In still other

countries, the standard minimum duration of 12 weeks, stipulated as a minimum requirement in the Maternity Protection Convention, is compulsory.

Most women can only take advantage of maternity leave if it is paid. Most countries provide for full payment or close to full payment during maternity leave. However, many countries provide no cash benefits at all. In some countries, benefits are paid only during the first part of the leave or are granted to public employees only **(table 5.C)**.

Where social security systems fund maternity leave, minimum contribution levels may be required to qualify. Part-time and temporary workers may also have difficulty qualifying, and the number of women actually covered varies across countries. Because they work outside the formal sector to which social security is extended, a large proportion of economically active women do not enjoy maternity and medical benefits. Some countries (Ecuador, Morocco and Tunisia) have extended maternity benefits to agricultural workers. Belgium, France, Gabon, Luxembourg and Spain have set up special schemes to cover self-employed women.

Employment protection

Keeping their jobs through pregnancy, childbirth and maternity leave is an essential right of employed women. According to the ILO, 29 countries, mostly in Africa and Asia, prohibit dismissing a worker on maternity leave for any reason. In addition, several countries prohibit dismissal during a period following the employee's return to work. The duration of this prohibition ranges from 30 days after return from leave in Belgium and the Republic of Korea to two years in Mongolia and three years in Belarus and Ukraine.

Termination of employment due to pregnancy is reported even in countries that outlaw the practice. In the United Kingdom, one in eight inquiries received by the Equal Opportunity Commission concerns dismissal due to pregnancy. Women who return to work after childbirth face new obstacles to their career development and are often placed in lower status positions.

Parental leave

Parental leave, which allows employed male and female parents to stay home with their children when needed, is considered an essential component of equal opportunity for women and men who combine parenthood with employment.

In a review of legislation in 138 member countries, the ILO found 36 with legislation governing parental leave. In 25 of them, including nine of the 14 European Union countries with such legislation, this leave is paid.[63] The Nordic countries offer the most generous policy packages to parents, with a high level of compensation for loss of earnings. In Australia, New Zealand and the United States, parental leave, though completely gender neutral, is unpaid.

Most parental leave schemes also provide a guarantee that the employee can return to his or her job after the leave—a guarantee that is indispensable for the scheme to be effective. The length of the leave, the age of the child for which the leave is granted, the flexibility in terms of when leave can be taken and whether the mother and the father can transfer leave to each other are other important components of parental leave legislation. Moreover, it appears that parents are most likely to take leave where it is paid.

Few countries report the number of parents taking parental leave. In countries that do provide this

Toward a more comprehensive knowledge of all forms of work

Currently, our knowledge of work and production within the economies of countries is defined by two main systems: the measurement of economic activities and the estimation of the value of production. Yet the boundary within which these statistics are confined—i.e., the production boundary set by the System of National Accounts (SNA)—limits the comprehensiveness of official statistics on work and the completeness of national accounts estimates. Thus, beyond the issue of gender inequity in the measurement of work, there is some evidence that employment statistics do not cover all work done in the total economic system and that "much of subsistence work and production and all household work and production escape regular statistical measurement".[a]

Within the SNA framework, work[b] may fall either within or outside the production boundary. Work that falls within the SNA production boundary is considered "economic" in labour force statistics, and the person engaged in such activities is recorded as economically active. Work that falls outside the SNA production boundary is considered "non-economic" in labour force statistics, and the person engaged only in such activities is not recorded as economically active. When the amount of households' own-account production of goods is deemed not to be quantitatively important in relation to the total supply of those goods in a country, this production may not be recorded or included in national accounts estimates.[c]

There are different ways in which the various forms of work may be categorized. In the developed countries, the primary interest is to consider both work within the SNA boundary and work outside the SNA boundary. For developing countries, considering the relative difficulties in measurement of activities, the forms of work can be grouped as follows: (a) formal market economy, (b) informal economy, (c) subsistence economy and (d) household economy. The trends and interactions of these segments can only be properly understood if the levels of participation and production are measured regularly. The various forms must also be measured separately in order to maintain the integrity of the long-established system of national accounts. The 1993 SNA recognizes the need for separate measurement and recommends that valuation of production outside the boundaries set for the SNA be undertaken in "satellite" accounts, separate from but consistent with the main SNA estimates.

Work in progress

Efforts to expand coverage of activities of individuals and households, with respect to both the measurement of the quantity of work and the valuation of production, are being undertaken in countries of the developing and developed regions.

Concerning the measurement of work, developed countries have concentrated efforts on time-use surveys that help determine the relative shares of women's and men's time in economic activities and household work. In developing countries, where labour statistics are still inadequate to cover the various forms of work discussed above, efforts focus on the improvement of data collection in the informal sector and subsistence production activities, as well as on the development of time-use surveys, with special focus on methods and classification of activities (see box on time-use surveys in developing countries).

Concerning the valuation of production, methods for satellite accounts are being produced and tested in some countries, with two main areas of interest. Satellite accounts should provide information on the value of households' contribution to the economy, outside the production boundary. In addition, they may help assess the relative contribution of women and men to the economy as a whole as well as to the household sector. Efforts have been undertaken mainly in developed countries and have largely focused on household production activities.

By 1995, Bulgaria, Denmark and Norway had each estimated the value of production outside the SNA production boundary for three points in time and Finland, for two points in time. A study sponsored by the United Nations Development Programme shows that of the 14 countries reported to have carried out time-use surveys by 1995, seven had used these data to estimate the value of non-SNA production (Australia, Bulgaria, Denmark, Finland, France, Germany and Norway).[d] Another cross-national study by OECD in 1995 reviewed methods used to measure household production in selected OECD member countries (Australia, Canada, Denmark, Finland, Germany, New Zealand and Norway).[e]

More detailed review of methods for valuation and development of satellite accounts on household production has been undertaken by the International Research and Training Institute for the Advancement of Women (INSTRAW),[f] covering Canada, Finland and Nepal. The Statistical Office of the European Communities (Eurostat) has proposed a framework for developing satellite accounts of household production based on a review of the experiences of such countries as Germany and the United Kingdom, which have produced household satellite accounts, as well as Australia, Canada, Denmark, Finland, Norway and Sweden, which compile input-output tables for household production.[g]

Methods of valuation

In accordance with the SNA, household production is defined as covering a wide range of productive activities both within and outside the SNA production boundary, including:

- production of agricultural goods by households for their own final consumption;
- construction of a household's own dwellings or other structures for their own use, or engaging in structural improvements or extensions to existing dwellings or structures;

leave, such as Denmark, Norway and Sweden, nearly all eligible families (mostly mothers) take advantage of these plans.

In the majority of countries, parental leave is designed as a family right and can be taken by the mother or the father. However, most men do not take parental leave. In Denmark, 92 per cent of leave-takers in 1996 were women. In Germany, women represented 96 per cent of all parents who took leave in 1995. In Finland, 38 per cent of fathers took leave when the child was born, but only 2 per cent took parental leave. Among mothers in Finland, 99 per cent took both maternal and parental leave.

Some countries (Belgium, Denmark, Greece, the Netherlands and Sweden) have specific measures to encourage fathers to share child-rearing with their partners, such as allotting a non-transferable portion of leave to the father.[64] ■

- production of other goods for their own final use by households; e.g., cloth, clothing, furniture and other household goods and foodstuffs;
- production of housing services by owner occupiers for their own consumption;
- production of domestic and personal services for consumption within the same household; e.g. the preparation of meals, care and training of children, cleaning, repairs etc.[h]

Household production has typically been measured either by time inputs or by outputs. From the time-input side, production is expressed in terms of the number of hours and minutes household members spend on productive household activities. From the output side, the quantities of goods and services produced by household members for their own consumption are valued in monetary terms.

The main sources of data for valuation of household production are time-use surveys, household expenditure surveys, household budget surveys or any other surveys that collect information on household production. Time-use surveys provide estimates of time-inputs, while household expenditure surveys are particularly suited to provide information on intermediate consumption (which consists of the value of goods and services consumed as inputs by the production process).[i]

Since, by definition, household production is not sold, it bears no price. Its valuation has therefore entailed imputation of monetary value to the outputs of the various activities. Only then can production be aggregated and compared to national accounts aggregates—that is, if the outputs are "valued at market price of equivalent market products".[j] This method, referred to as *output-based valuation*, has rarely been used because data on physical output of households are scarce.

The other method, *input-based valuation*, involves valuing labour inputs as well as other inputs, to obtain household production at costs of inputs. However, most studies have only valued the labour cost. Imputing monetary value to household labour inputs has been approached in three ways: the opportunity cost method, the market replacement cost of a "global substitute" and the market replacement cost of "specialized substitutes":

- *Opportunity cost method:* valuing housework time at the wage that household members would expect to receive on the labour market, based on such characteristics as age, sex, qualification, and to the extent that data are available, employment status.
- *Market replacement cost of a "global substitute":* estimated based on the market value of household members' time. Each member's time input into household production is valued at the average wage rate of domestic helpers.
- *Market replacement cost of "specialized substitutes":* different wage rates are applied according to the specific household activity, assuming that different persons would be hired for each category of household task, such as cooking, cleaning, sewing, nursing, etc.

Issues arising from studies of satellite accounts

A major issue with the methods of valuation based on costing labour factors is the fact that women's wages tend to be low, due in part to occupational sex segregation. Consequently, housework done by women is assigned a lower value. In addition, each of these approaches to imputation yields different results. Another issue that needs to be addressed is whether net wages or gross wages are to be used.

Due to differences in wage determination and in time-use data, estimates of household production are not comparable across countries.

Studies on valuation of household production indicate that there is need to (a) collect information on non-SNA activities that have hitherto not been systematically recorded and (b) compile monetary values of households' output compatible with the SNA. While significant progress is being made in time-use methodology (see box on time-use surveys in developing countries), there is limited development in the estimation of households' production. It will be necessary to develop and test the output-based methods of valuation, as well as to ascertain the sensitivity of estimates to different definitions of household production and methods of valuation of input-based household work.

[a] Duncan Ironmonger, "Towards a more comprehensive knowledge of all forms of work: Statistics for the development and monitoring of social and economic policies", paper presented at an expert group meeting on engendering labour force statistics", New York, 1998.

[b] Work includes all productive activities that are performed for another's benefit or for one's own benefit provided that it could be carried out by someone other than the person benefiting from it, while achieving the desired result.

[c] Commission of the European Communities and others, *System of National Accounts, 1993* (United Nations publication, Sales No.E.94.XVII.4), paras. 1.21,1.22, and 6.25.

[d] L. Goldschmidt-Clermont and Elisabeth Pagnossin-Aligisakis, "Measures of unrecorded economic activities in fourteen countries", in UNDP, *Background Papers: Human Development Report 1995* (New York, Oxford University Press).

[e] OECD, *Household Production in OECD Countries: Data Sources and Measurement Methods* (Paris, 1995).

[f] INSTRAW, *Measurement and Valuation of Unpaid Contribution: Accounting through Time and Output* (Santo Domingo, 1995); and INSTRAW, *Valuation of Household Production and the Satellite Accounts* (Santo Domingo, 1996).

[g] Eurostat, "Proposal for a satellite account of household production" (1999).

[h] Commission of the European Communities and others, 1993; op. cit., para. 1.21.

[i] Ibid., para. 6.147.

[j] Goldschmidt-Clermont and Pagnossin-Aligisakis, loc. cit.

Notes

1 ILO, *World Employment Report 1998-99: Employability in the Global Economy: How Training Matters* (Geneva, 1998).

2 Maria Lazrey, ed., *Making the Transition Work for Women in Europe and Central Asia*, World Bank Discussion Paper, No. 411 (1999).

3 UNICEF, *Women in Transition*, MONEE Project Regional Monitoring Report, No. 6 (1999).

4 See for example, Susan Jeokes, "Trade-related employment for women in industry and services in developing countries", United Nations Research Institute for Social Development, Occasional Paper, OP 5 (Geneva, August 1995); Valentine M. Moghadam, "The political economy of female employment in the Arab region", in *Gender and Development in the Arab World: Women's Economic Participation: Patterns and Policies,* Nabil F. Khoury and Valentine Moghadam (London, Zed Books, 1995).

5 United Nations, *Arab Women 1995: Trends, Statistics and Indicators* (New York, 1997).

6 ILO, "Maternity protection at work", International Labour Conference, eighty-seventh session, 1999, report V (1).

7 Ibid.

8 Ibid.

9 Ibid.

10 Peter Auer and Maniàngels Fortuny, A*geing of the Labour Force in OECD Countries: Economic and Social Consequences,* ILO Employment Paper, No. 2000/2.

11 Ibid.

12 ILO, *World Employment 1995: An ILO Report* (Geneva, 1995).

13 ILO, *World Employment 1996/97: National Policies in a Global Context* (Geneva, 1996).

14 ILO, *World Employment Report 1998-99...*

15 World Bank, *Enhancing Women's Participation in Economic Development*, World Bank Policy Paper (Washington, D.C., 1994).

16 Recent data for sub-Saharan Africa are sparse.

17 ILO, *World Employment 1996/97...*

18 Based on a study of 21 OECD countries; see ILO, *World Employment 1996/97...*

19 Data are reported in ILO, *Key Indicators of the Labour Market* (Geneva, 1999), table 3.

20 Based on the International Classification of Status in Employment, adopted by the Fifteenth Conference of International Labour Statisticians in 1993; see ILO, *Bulletin of Labour Statistics*, 1993-2 (Geneva).

21 OECD, *Financing Newly Emerging Private Enterprises in Transition Economies* (Paris, 1999).

22 Izolda Kruitkiene, "SME development in Lithuania", in OECD, *Financing Newly Emerging Private Enterprises in Transition Economies* (Paris, 1999).

23 ILO, "General conditions to stimulate job creation in small and medium-sized enterprises", International Labour Conference, eighty-fifth session, 1997, report V(1).

24 Candida G. Brush, "A resource perspective on women's entrepreneurship research, relevance and recognition", in OECD, *Women Entrepreneurs in Small and Medium Enterprises* (Paris, 1997).

25 See "Introduction" in OECD, *Women Entrepreneurs in Small and Medium Enterprises* (Paris, 1997).

26 Amartya Sen, "Inequality, unemployment and contemporary Europe", *International Labour Review,* vol. 136, No. 2 (1997).

27 Based on regional averages compiled from ILO, *Key Indicators of the Labour Market* (Geneva, 1999), table 11.

28 ILO, *World Employment Report, 1998-1999...*

29 Analysis of regional averages compiled from ILO, *Key Indicators of the Labour Market* (Geneva, 1999), table 10.

30 ILO, *World Employment Report, 1998-1999...*

31 The definition was adopted by the Fifteenth International Conference of Labour Statisticians. See ILO, *Bulletin of Labour Statistics,* 1993-2 (Geneva).

32 The estimates presented in this section are experimental. See "Gender and the informal sector", paper prepared by Jacques Charmes as consultant to the United Nations Statistics Division, 1999.

33 A review of the main findings on home-based workers around the world is contained in Martha Chen, Jennifer Sebstad and Lesley O'Connell, "Counting the invisible workforce: the case of homebased workers", *World Development,* vol. 27, No. 3 (1999).

34 ILO, Convention concerning Home Work, Eighty-third International Labour Conference, Geneva, 1996.

[35] Based on data compiled by Jacques Charmes as consultant to the Statistics Division of the United Nations Secretariat from survey data contained in national reports.

[36] Based on data from national reports contained in "Gender and informal sector", paper prepared by Jacques Charmes as consultant to the Statistics Division of the United Nations Secretariat (unpublished, 1999).

[37] United Nations, *The World's Women 1995: Trends and Statistics* (United Nations publication, Sales No. E.95XVII.2).

[38] For analysis of data from earlier time-use surveys, see United Nations, *The World's Women 1970-1990: Trends and Statistics* (United Nations publication, Sales No. E.90.XVII.3); and United Nations, *The World's Women 1995...*

[39] Based on analysis of data prepared by Andrew Harvey as consultant to the Statistics Division of the United Nations Secretariat from the Multinational Time Budget Archive database, micro-data from country studies and other published reports.

[40] Article 11(c) to (d). The Convention was adopted by the General Assembly in its resolution 34/180 of 18 December 1979; see also chap. 6 below.

[41] ILO, *More and Better Jobs for Women: An Action Guide* (Geneva, 1996).

[42] Richard Anker, "Theories of occupational segregation by sex: an overview", in *International Labour Review*, vol. 136, No. 3.

[43] ILO, *Gender Equality and Occupational Segregation in Nordic Labour Markets* (Geneva, 1998).

[44] The study covered 41 countries, with 50 per cent of the data for the 1990s and the remainder for prior years. Detailed occupational classification, providing 175 occupations per country, formed the basis of the study, which included 17 OECD member countries, four transition economies, seven countries from Asia and the Pacific, six from the Middle East and North Africa, and seven from other developed countries and areas. See ILO, *Gender and Jobs: Sex Segregation of Occupations in the World* (Geneva, 1998).

[45] Anker, loc. cit.

[46] ILO, *Gender and Jobs...*

[47] OECD, *The Future of Female-Dominated Occupations* (Paris, 1998).

[48] Anker, loc. cit.

[49] OECD, *The Future of Female-Dominated Occupations...*

[50] ILO, "Breaking through the glass ceiling: women in management" (Geneva, 1997).

[51] UNICEF, op. cit.

[52] 1999 Catalyst Census of Women Board Directors of the Fortune 1000, accessed at: http://www.catalystwomen.org/press/factswbd99.html.

[53] "Catalyst census finds few women corporate officers", accessed at: http://www.catalystwomen.org/press/release 020800.html.

[54] ILO, "Breaking through the glass ceiling...

[55] Ibid.

[56] Sigrid Quack and Bob Hancké, in cooperation with the European Network, "Women in decision-making in finance" (European Commission, 1997).

[57] Ibid.

[58] Veikkola Eeva-Sisko, "Women and men at the top", *Gender Statistics* (Statistics Finland), 1997:1.

[59] ILO, "Breaking through the glass ceiling...

[60] "Perspectives: part-time work-solution or trap", *International Labour Review*, vol. 136, No. 4, 1997.

[61] European Commission, "Equal opportunities for women and men in the European Union", annual report 1997; and Reed Abelson, "A push from the top shatters a glass ceiling", *The New York Times*, 22 August 1999.

[62] Unless otherwise indicated, the information and discussion in this section are taken from ILO, "Maternity protection at work"...

[63] *New Ways to Work: Parental Leave in European Union Countries* (London, 1998).

[64] Data are reported for temporary parental allowances in Statistics Sweden, *Women and Men in Sweden, 1998*.

Table 5.A:
Unemployment rate

Country or area	Unemployment rate (%), 1991/1997		Country or area	Unemployment rate (%), 1991/1997	
	W	M		W	M
Africa			**Asia** (cont'd)		
Algeria[a]	24.0	26.9	Republic of Korea	2.3	2.8
Botswana	23.9	19.4	Singapore	2.4	2.4
Egypt	24.1	7.6	Sri Lanka[g]	17.6	8.0
Mauritius	13.9	7.8	Syrian Arab Republic	14.0	5.2
Morocco[b]	23.0	15.8	Tajikistan	2.9	2.4
			Thailand	0.9	0.9
Latin America and the Caribbean			Turkey	7.4	6.0
			Uzbekistan	0.5	0.3
Antigua and Barbuda	5.6	6.4			
Argentina	17.6	15.4	**Developed regions**		
Aruba	7.9	5.4	Australia	8.1	8.6
Bahamas	12.0	10.3	Belarus	3.3	2.2
Barbados	22.9	16.5	Belgium	11.5	7.1
Belize	18.6	11.7	Bulgaria	14.1	14.2
Bolivia[b]	4.5	3.7	Canada	9.2	9.2
Brazil[c]	8.8	5.7	Croatia	20.1	14.0
Chile	6.6	4.7	Czech Republic	5.8	3.8
Colombia[d]	15.1	9.8	Denmark	6.4	4.5
Costa Rica	7.5	4.9	Estonia	9.2	10.7
Dominican Republic	28.6	9.5	Finland	15.1	13.8
Ecuador[b]	12.7	7.0	France	14.2	10.8
El Salvador	5.3	9.5	Germany	10.9	8.9
Grenada	12.7	14.6	Greece	14.8	6.2
Guyana	18.1	8.4	Hungary	7.7	9.5
Honduras[b]	3.2	3.2	Iceland	4.5	3.3
Jamaica	23.0	9.9	Ireland	10.3	10.3
Mexico	4.7	2.9	Italy	16.9	9.7
Nicaragua	14.8	12.6	Japan	3.4	3.4
Panama	20.0	11.3	Latvia	14.6	14.3
Paraguay[b]	8.6	7.8	Lithuania	6.9	6.6
Peru[b]	8.9	6.8	Luxembourg	3.6	1.8
Puerto Rico[e]	12.1	14.4	Malta	2.8	5.8
Saint Lucia	19.3	13.8	Netherlands	7.0	4.4
St. Vincent/Grenadines	22.1	18.4	New Zealand	6.7	6.6
Suriname	16.4	7.9	Norway	4.3	4.0
Trinidad and Tobago	21.0	13.2	Poland	13.2	9.5
Uruguay[b]	13.2	8.0	Portugal	8.5	6.6
Venezuela	12.8	9.0	Romania	6.4	5.7
			Russian Federation	9.0	9.6
Asia			San Marino	7.3	1.9
Bangladesh	2.3	2.7	Slovakia[h]	12.5	10.8
China			Slovenia	7.3	7.0
Hong Kong SAR	2.0	2.3	Spain	28.3	15.8
Macao SAR	2.5	3.6	Sweden	7.5	8.3
Cyprus	4.3	2.3	Switzerland	3.9	4.3
Indonesia	5.1	3.3	The FYR of Macedonia	44.5	35.0
Israel[f]	8.8	6.8	Ukraine	8.4	9.5
Pakistan	13.7	4.1	United Kingdom	5.8	8.1
Philippines	8.5	7.5	United States	5.0	4.9

Source: ILO, *Key Indicators of the Labour Market (KILM)* (Geneva, 1999), table 8a. *KILM* table 8a was compiled from the following sources: ILO, *Yearbook of Labour Statistics, 1998* (Geneva, 1998); ILO, *Digest of Caribbean Labour Statistics, 1997* (Port of Spain); and OECD, *Labour Force Statistics, 1976-1996* (Paris).

[a] Excluding unemployed not previously employed.

[b] Urban areas.

[c] Excluding the rural population of Rondônia, Acre, Amazonas, Roraima, Pará and Amapá.

[d] Seven main cities.

[e] Excluding persons temporarily laid off.

[f] Including the residents of East Jerusalem.

[g] Excluding northern and eastern provinces.

[h] Excluding persons on childcare leave.

Table 5.B:
Part-time employment

Country or area	Percentage of adult employment that is part-time				Women's share of part-time employment (%)		Country or area	Percentage of adult employment that is part-time				Women's share of part-time employment (%)	
	1990/1993		1996/1998		1990/1993	1996/1998		1990/1993		1996/1998		1990/1993	1996/1998
	W	M	W	M				W	M	W	M		
Caribbean							**Western Europe** (cont'd)						
Bahamas	14	11	15	11	53	52	France	22	4	25	6	80	79
Barbados	9	6	6	4	54	59	Germany	25	2	30	4	89	86
Jamaica	12	7	10	5	59	59	Greece	12	4	14	5	61	63
Suriname	32	8	24	8	68	61	Iceland	38	7	37	8	82	77
Trinidad and Tobago	21	18	17	14	39	41	Ireland	20	4	27	7	72	73
Central America							Italy	18	4	22	5	71	71
Belize	33	16	38	21	47	42	Luxembourg	19	2	24	2	83	82
Mexico	31[a]	10[a]	30	9	61[a]	64	Netherlands	53	13	55	11	70	78
Asia							Norway	39	7	37	8	83	80
Republic of Korea	6	3	8	3	59	62	Portugal	12	3	17	5	74	73
Turkey	20	5	13	3	63	64	Sweden	25	5	23	7	81	76
Eastern Europe							Switzerland	46	9	48	8	80	83
Bulgaria	2	2	1	1	48	42	United Kingdom	40	5	41	8	85	80
Czech Republic	10	3	10	3	74	74	**Other developed regions**						
Hungary	4	2	8	3	66	71	Australia	36	11	38	14	69	67
Poland	13	9	14	8	54	57	Canada	27	9	29	11	70	70
Romania	17[b]	10[b]	18	12	60[b]	55	Japan	33	9	36	12	71	68
Slovakia	5	2	4	1	73	74	United States	20	8	19	8	68	70
Slovenia	4	3	10	7	53	57							
Latvia	12[a]	12[a]	14	12	48[a]	52							
Western Europe													
Austria	22[a]	3[a]	21	3	84[a]	86							
Belgium	30	5	32	5	80	83							
Denmark	30	10	24	11	72	64							
Finland	10	5	11	6	68	62							

Source: ILO, *Key Indicators of the Labour Market (KILM)* (Geneva, 1999), table 5. KILM table 5 was compiled from the following sources: ILO, *Digest of Caribbean Labour Statistics, 1997* (Port of Spain); OECD-CCNM Labour Market Database; and OECD, *Employment Outlook, June 1998.*

[a] Data refer to 1995.

[b] Data refer to 1994.

Table 5.C:
Maternity leave benefits, as of 1998

Country or area	Length of maternity leave	Percentage of wages paid in covered period	Provider of coverage
Africa			
Algeria	14 weeks	100	Social Security
Angola	90 days	100	Employer
Benin	14 weeks	100	Social Security
Botswana	12 weeks	25	Employer
Burkina Faso	14 weeks	100	S.S. / Employer
Burundi	12 weeks	50	Employer
Cameroon	14 weeks	100	Social Security
Central African Rep.	14 weeks	50	Social Security
Chad	14 weeks	50	Social Security
Comoros	14 weeks	100	Employer
Congo	15 weeks	100	50% Employer / 50% S.S.
Côte d'Ivoire	14 weeks	100	Social Security
Dem. Rep. of the Congo	14 weeks	67	Employer
Djibouti	14 weeks	50 (100 for public employees)	Employer / S.S.
Egypt	50 days	100	S.S. / Employer
Equatorial Guinea	12 weeks	75	Social Security
Eritrea	60 days	..	..
Ethiopia	90 days	100	Employer
Gabon	14 weeks	100	Social Security
Gambia	12 weeks	100	Employer
Ghana	12 weeks	50	Employer
Guinea	14 weeks	100	50% Employer / 50% S.S.
Guinea-Bissau	60 days	100	Employer / S.S.
Kenya	2 months	100	Employer
Lesotho	12 weeks	0	..
Libyan Arab Jamahiriya	50 days	50	Employer
Madagascar	14 weeks	100[a]	50% Employer / 50% S.S.
Mali	14 weeks	100	Social Security
Mauritania	14 weeks	100	Social Security
Mauritius	12 weeks	100	Employer
Morocco	12 weeks	100	Social Security
Mozambique	60 days	100	Employer
Namibia	12 weeks	as prescribed	Social Security
Niger	14 weeks	50	Social Security
Nigeria	12 weeks	50	Employer
Rwanda	12 weeks	67	Employer
Sao Tome and Principe	70 days	100 for 60 days	Social Security
Senegal	14 weeks	100	Social Security
Seychelles	14 weeks	flat rate for 10 weeks	Social Security
Somalia	14 weeks	50	Employer
South Africa	12 weeks	45	Unemployment Insurance
Sudan	8 weeks	100	Employer
Swaziland	12 weeks	0	--
Togo	14 weeks	100	50% Employer / 50% S.S.

Table 5.C (cont'd):

Maternity leave benefits, as of 1998

Country or area	Length of maternity leave	Percentage of wages paid in covered period	Provider of coverage
Africa (cont'd)			
Tunisia	30 days	67	Social Security
Uganda	8 weeks	100 for one month	Employer
United Rep. of Tanzania	12 weeks	100	Employer
Zambia	12 weeks	100	Employer
Zimbabwe	90 days	60–75	Employer
Latin America and the Caribbean			
Antigua and Barbuda	13 weeks	60	S.S. + possible employer supplement
Argentina	90 days	100	Social Security
Bahamas	8 weeks	100	40% Employer / 60% S.S.
Barbados	12 weeks	100	Social Security
Belize	12 weeks	80	Social Security
Bolivia	60 days	100% of nat'l min wage + 70% of wages above min wage	Social Security
Brazil	120 days	100	Social Security
Chile	18 weeks	100	Social Security
Colombia	12 weeks	100	Social Security
Costa Rica	4 months	100	50% Employer / 50% S.S.
Cuba	18 weeks	100	Social Security
Dominica	12 weeks	60	S.S. / Employer
Dominican Republic	12 weeks	100	50% Employer / 50% S.S.
Ecuador	12 weeks	100	25% Employer / 75% S.S.
El Salvador	12 weeks	75	Social Security
Grenada	3 months	100 for 2 months, 60 for 3rd month	S.S. / Employer
Guatemala	12 weeks	100	33% Employer / 67% S.S.
Guyana	13 weeks	70	Social Security
Haiti	12 weeks	100 for 6 weeks	Employer
Honduras	10 weeks	100 for 84 days	33% Employer / 67% S.S.
Jamaica	12 weeks	100 for 8 weeks	Employer
Mexico	12 weeks	100	Social Security
Nicaragua	12 weeks	60	Social Security
Panama	14 weeks	100	Social Security
Paraguay	12 weeks	50 for 9 weeks	Social Security
Peru	90 days	100	Social Security
Saint Lucia	13 weeks	65	Social Security
Trinidad and Tobago	13 weeks	60–100	S.S./Employer
Uruguay	12 weeks	100	Social Security
Venezuela	18 weeks	100	Social Security
Asia			
Afghanistan	90 days	100	Employer
Azerbaijan	18 weeks	..	..
Bahrain	45 days	100	Employer
Bangladesh	12 weeks	100	Employer

Table 5.C (cont'd):
Maternity leave benefits, as of 1998

Country or area	Length of maternity leave	Percentage of wages paid in covered period	Provider of coverage
Asia (cont'd)			
Cambodia	90 days	50	Employer
China	90 days	100	Employer
Cyprus	16 weeks	75	Social Security
India	12 weeks	100	Employer / S.S.
Indonesia	3 months	100	Employer
Iran (Islamic Republic of)	90 days	66.7 for 16 weeks	Social Security
Iraq	62 days	100	Social Security
Israel	12 weeks	75[a]	Social Security
Jordan	10 weeks	100	Employer
Kuwait	70 days	100	Employer
Lao People's Dem. Rep.	90 days	100	Social Security
Lebanon	40 days	100	Employer
Malaysia	60 days	100	Employer
Mongolia	101 days	..	..
Myanmar	12 weeks	66.7	Social Security
Nepal	52 days	100	Employer
Pakistan	12 weeks	100	Employer
Philippines	60 days	100	Social Security
Qatar	40–60 days	100 for civil servants	Agency concerned
Republic of Korea	60 days	100	Employer
Saudi Arabia	10 weeks	50 or 100	Employer
Singapore	8 weeks	100	Employer
Sri Lanka	12 weeks	100	Employer
Syrian Arab Republic	75 days	100	Employer
Thailand	90 days	100 for 45 days then 50% for 15 days	Employer for 45 days, then S.S.
Turkey	12 weeks	66.7	Social Security
United Arab Emirates	45 days	100	Employer
Viet Nam	4–6 months	100	Social Security
Yemen	60 days	100	Employer
Oceania			
Fiji	84 days	Flat rate	Employer
Papua New Guinea	6 weeks	0	..
Solomon Islands	12 weeks	25	Employer
Developed regions			
Australia	1 year	0	..
Austria	16 weeks	100	Social Security
Belarus	126 days	100	Social Security
Belgium	15 weeks	82% for 30 days, 75% thereafter[a]	Social Security
Bulgaria	120–180 days	100	Social Security
Canada	17–18 weeks	55 for 15 weeks	Unemployment Insurance
Croatia	6 months + 4 weeks	..	..
Czech Republic	28 weeks	..	..
Denmark	18 weeks[b]	100[a]	Social Security

Table 5.C (cont'd):
Maternity leave benefits, as of 1998

Country or area	Length of maternity leave	Percentage of wages paid in covered period	Provider of coverage
Developed regions (cont'd)			
Estonia	18 weeks	..	..
Finland	105 days	80	Social Security
France	16–26 weeks	100	Social Security
Germany	14 weeks	100	S.S.to ceiling; employer pays difference
Greece	16 weeks	75	Social Security
Hungary	24 weeks	100	Social Security
Iceland	2 months	Flat rate	Social Security
Ireland	14 weeks	70% or fixed rate[a]	Social Security
Italy	5 months	80	Social Security
Japan	14 weeks	60	Social Security or health insurance
Liechtenstein	8 weeks	80	Social Security
Luxembourg	16 weeks	100	Social Security
Malta	13 weeks	100	Social Security
Netherlands	16 weeks	100	Social Security
New Zealand	14 weeks	0	..
Norway	18 weeks	100, and 26 extra paid weeks by either parent	Social Security
Poland	16–18 weeks	100	Social Security
Portugal	98 days	100	Social Security
Romania	112 days	50–94	Social Security
Russian Federation	140 days	100	Social Security
Spain	16 weeks	100	Social Security
Sweden	14 weeks	450 days paid parental leave: 360 days at 75% and 90 days at flat rate	Social Security
Switzerland	8 weeks	100	Employer
Ukraine	126 days	100	Social Security
United Kingdom	14–18 weeks	90 for 6 weeks, flat rate thereafter	Social Security
United States	12 weeks[c]	0	..

Source: ILO, press release of 12 February 1998 (ILO/98/7).

[a] Up to a ceiling.

[b] 10 additional weeks may be taken up by either parent.

[c] The Family and Medical Leave Act (FMLA) of 1993 provided a total of 12 work weeks of unpaid leave during any 12-month period for the birth of a child and the care of the newborn. FMLA applies only to workers in companies with 50 or more workers.

Table 5.D:
Economic activity

Country or area	Adult (15+) economic activity rate (%)				% women in the adult labour force, 1995/1997	% distribution of the labour force, each sex, 1990/1997						% women among admin. and managerial workers, 1985/1997
	1990		1995/1997			Wage and salaried workers		Self-employed workers		Contributing family workers		
	W	M	W	M		W	M	W	M	W	M	
Africa												
Algeria	19	76	24	76	24	..	..	..	..	..	..	6
Angola	74	90	73	90	46	..	..	..	..	..	..	..
Benin	76	85	75	84	49	3	7	64	54	29[a]	32[a]	..
Botswana	66	84	46	60	47	59	65	8	5	16	18	26
Burkina Faso	78	91	77	90	47	..	..	..	..	..	..	14
Burundi	83	93	83	93	50	..	..	..	..	..	..	13
Cameroon	47	87	48	86	37	..	..	..	..	..	..	10
Cape Verde	43	88	45	88	39	46	58	30	21	3	2	23
Central African Rep.	70	89	69	87	47	..	..	..	..	..	..	9
Chad	66	89	67	88	44	..	..	..	..	..	..	..
Comoros	63	86	63	86	42	..	..	..	..	..	..	..
Congo	58	84	58	83	43	..	..	..	..	..	..	..
Côte d'Ivoire	43	89	44	88	32	..	..	..	..	..	..	10
Dem. Rep. of the Congo	62	85	62	85	43	..	..	..	..	..	..	..
Djibouti	..	..	..	..	..	..	..	..	..	..	..	2
Egypt	27[b]	73[b]	22[b]	73[b]	22[b]	35	55	12	29	36	10	16
Equatorial Guinea	45	90	46	89	36	..	..	..	..	..	..	..
Eritrea	76	87	75	87	47	..	..	..	..	..	..	..
Ethiopia	58	86	58	86	40	5	8	28	59	65	28	8
Gabon	63	84	63	84	44	..	..	..	..	..	..	..
Gambia	69	91	70	90	44	..	..	..	..	..	..	..
Ghana	82	82	81	83	51	..	..	..	..	..	..	..
Guinea	79	88	78	87	47	..	..	..	..	..	..	..
Guinea-Bissau	57	92	57	91	40	..	..	..	..	..	..	..
Kenya	75	90	74	89	46	12	32	17	19	56	30	..
Lesotho	46	86	47	85	37	..	..	..	..	..	..	33
Liberia	54	85	54	84	39	..	..	..	..	..	..	..
Libyan Arab Jamahiriya	21	81	23	78	21	..	..	..	..	..	..	..
Madagascar	70	90	69	89	44	..	..	..	..	..	..	..
Malawi	80	88	79	87	49	..	..	..	..	..	..	8
Mali	73	90	72	90	46	..	..	..	..	..	..	20
Mauritania	65	87	64	87	44	..	..	..	..	..	..	8
Mauritius	35	81	39	80	33	86	79	10	20	4	2	..
Morocco	39	80	40	79	34	81[c]	70[c]	5[c]	23[c]	..	..	..
Mozambique	84	92	83	91	49	..	..	..	..	..	..	..
Namibia	54	82	54	81	41	36	60	20	16	28	10	21
Niger	70	94	70	93	44	..	..	..	..	..	..	..
Nigeria	47	88	48	87	36	..	..	..	..	..	..	6
Reunion	45	67	47	68	43	54	53	5	13	..	..	..
Rwanda	84	94	85[d]	87[d]	56[d]	..	..	..	..	..	..	46
Sao Tome and Principe	..	..	..	..	..	..	..	..	..	..	..	..
Senegal	61	86	61	86	42	..	..	..	..	..	..	..
Seychelles	..	..	..	..	..	..	..	..	..	..	..	29
Sierra Leone	42	85	44	84	36	..	..	..	..	..	..	8

Table 5.D (cont'd):
Economic activity

Country or area	Adult (15+) economic activity rate (%)				% women in the adult labour force, 1995/1997	% distribution of the labour force, each sex, 1990/1997						% women among admin. and managerial workers, 1985/1997
	1990		1995/1997			Wage and salaried workers		Self-employed workers		Contributing family workers		
	W	M	W	M		W	M	W	M	W	M	
Africa (cont'd)												
Somalia	64	88	64	87	43	..	..	..	..	..	..	..
South Africa	46	80	46	79	37	70	78	5	8	..	..	19
Sudan	31	87	33	86	28	..	..	..	..	..	..	..
Swaziland	40	80	41	80	37	..	..	..	..	..	..	15
Togo	53	88	53	87	39	..	..	..	..	..	..	..
Tunisia	33	80	35	79	30	70	71	14	25	15	3	9
Uganda	81	92	81	91	48	7	21	39	62	54	17	14
United Rep. of Tanzania	83	89	83	89	49	..	..	..	..	..	..	..
Western Sahara	..	..	..	..	..	..	..	..	..	..	..	..
Zambia	66	87	66	86	45	..	..	..	..	..	..	6
Zimbabwe	67	86	67	86	45	..	..	..	..	..	..	15
Latin America and the Caribbean												
Antigua and Barbuda	..	..	..	..	..	83	78	15	20	1	1	..
Argentina	29	79	41	76	37	..	..	..	..	..	..	..
Aruba	..	..	..	..	..	94	88	5	12	1	0	..
Bahamas	65	81	67	81	47	86	78	12	19	1	0	26
Barbados	60	76	62	73	49	90	83	9	16	0	0	38
Belize	24	86	34	79	31	75	62	21	34	4	4	..
Bolivia	46	84	56[e]	74[e]	46[e]	43[d]	60[d]	45[d]	35[d]	12[d]	5[d]	24
Brazil	44[b]	85[b]	51	82	40	64[f]	61[f]	22[f]	29[f]	10[f]	6[f]	37[f]
Chile	32	75	35	75	33	..	..	..	..	..	..	19
Colombia	46[b]	80[b]	52[b]	78[b]	44[b]	70[g]	61[g]	28[g]	38[g]	2[g]	1[g]	35
Costa Rica	33[b]	83[b]	36[b]	81[b]	32[b]	74	68	22	29	4	3	27
Cuba	42	75	47	77	38	..	..	..	..	..	..	..
Dominica	..	..	..	..	..	..	..	..	..	..	..	36
Dominican Republic	34	86	38	86	30	65	47	31	48	4	5	28
Ecuador	28	85	49	81	39	46[d]	59[d]	33[d]	38[d]	9[d]	2[d]	26
El Salvador	51	80	41	79	37	41	60	41	30	7	9	25
French Guyana	..	..	..	..	..	..	..	..	..	..	..	..
Grenada	..	..	..	..	..	84	74	12	17	1	2	32
Guadeloupe	53	71	55	72	44	..	..	..	..	..	..	..
Guatemala	28	90	32	88	27	68[h]	73[h]	26[h]	24[h]	5[h]	3[h]	32
Guyana	37	84	40	85	33	53	52	44	38	..	..	..
Haiti	58	82	57	82	43	18	15	57	61	10	11	33
Honduras	34	87	41[b]	88[b]	34[b]	48	46	42	41	11	12	39
Jamaica	62	77	69	81	46	65	55	31	42	4	2	..
Martinique	55	69	57	70	47	..	..	..	..	..	..	..
Mexico	34	84	39	84	34	58	58	23	32	19	10	20
Netherlands Antilles	51	74	52	68	48	92	88	4	9	1	0	48
Nicaragua	40	87	44	86	35	..	..	..	..	..	..	..
Panama	39	79	43[b]	80[b]	36[b]	79	60	18	37	3	4	27
Paraguay	51	83	35	87	29	69	77	25	20	6	3	14
Peru	29	80	55	78	44	33[d]	54[d]	45[d]	40[d]	13[d]	5[d]	23

Table 5.D (cont'd):
Economic activity

Country or area	Adult (15+) economic activity rate (%)				% women in the adult labour force, 1995/1997	% distribution of the labour force, each sex, 1990/1997						% women among admin. and managerial workers, 1985/1997
	1990		1995/1997			Wage and salaried workers		Self-employed workers		Contributing family workers		
	W	M	W	M		W	M	W	M	W	M	
Latin America and the Caribbean (cont'd)												
Puerto Rico	31 [i]	61 [i]	35 [i]	62 [i]	40 [i]	92	81	6	18	1	0	59
Saint Kitts and Nevis	..	..	..	..	..	84	81	13	16	1	1	..
Saint Lucia	..	..	..	..	..	..	..	..	..	..	..	..
St. Vincent/Grenadines	..	..	..	..	..	79	71	18	27	3	2	42
Suriname	30	74	33 [j]	64 [j]	35 [j]	..	..	..	..	..	..	10
Trinidad and Tobago	38	74	47	74	39	77	72	16	24	6	2	42
Uruguay	44	75	47 [d]	74 [d]	43 [d]	74d	71 [d]	19 [d]	26 [d]	4 [d]	1 [d]	28
US Virgin Islands	..	..	..	..	..	88	83	4	11	0	0	49
Venezuela	38	82	41	81	33	70	58	23	34	2	1	24
Asia												
Afghanistan	46	86	48	86	34	..	..	..	..	..	..	..
Armenia	63	76	62	74	48	..	..	..	..	..	..	..
Azerbaijan	52	75	53	74	44	..	..	..	..	..	..	..
Bahrain	29	88	31	87	19	..	..	..	..	..	..	21
Bangladesh	66	88	56	89	38	9	15	8	43	77	17	5
Bhutan	58	91	58	90	39	..	..	..	..	..	..	..
Brunei Darussalam	45	82	48	82	34	..	..	..	..	..	..	17
Cambodia	82	84	76	82	53	..	..	..	..	..	..	..
China	74	86	74	86	45	..	..	..	..	..	..	12 [k]
Hong Kong SAR	47	79	48	76	39	93	84	3	14	2	0	18
Macao SAR	53	84	55	79	44	90	83	5	14	2	0	15
Cyprus	48	81	49	80	38	..	..	..	..	..	..	10 [l]
Dem. People's Rep. of Korea	61	79	62	82	44	..	..	..	..	..	..	..
East Timor	76	89	76	89	44	..	..	..	..	..	..	..
Georgia	56	75	55	73	46	..	..	..	..	..	..	..
India	40	86	41	86	31	..	..	..	..	..	..	..
Indonesia	50	83	53	82	40	24	32	29	52	45	14	17
Iran (Islamic Rep. of)	21	81	25	79	24	..	..	..	..	..	..	2
Iraq	15	75	17	75	18	..	..	..	..	..	..	13
Israel	41	62	46	62	44	90 [m]	80 [m]	9 [m]	20 [m]	1 [m]	0 [m]	19
Jordan	17	76	22	76	21	..	..	..	..	..	..	..
Kazakhstan	61	78	60	76	46	..	..	..	..	..	..	48
Kuwait	38	85	39	79	31	..	..	..	..	..	..	5
Kyrgyzstan	59	74	60	74	47	..	..	..	..	..	..	..
Lao People's Dem. Rep.	74	90	75	89	47	..	..	..	..	..	..	..
Lebanon	24	74	27	76	28	..	..	..	..	..	..	..
Malaysia	45 [n]	82 [n]	47 [n]	81 [n]	37 [n]	72	71	14	25	15	4	16
Maldives	66	84	65	83	42	43	51	44	39	7	4	14
Mongolia	72	85	73	84	47	..	..	..	..	..	..	..
Myanmar	66	89	66	88	44	..	..	..	..	..	..	..
Nepal	56	88	57	86	40	..	..	..	..	..	..	9
Occupied Palestinian Territory	6	66	8	68	10	..	..	..	..	..	..	..
Oman	13	82	16	79	14	..	..	..	..	..	..	..

Table 5.D (cont'd):
Economic activity

Country or area	Adult (15+) economic activity rate (%)				% women in the adult labour force, 1995/1997	% distribution of the labour force, each sex, 1990/1997						% women among admin. and managerial workers, 1985/1997
	1990		1995/1997			Wage and salaried workers		Self-employed workers		Contributing family workers		
	W	M	W	M		W	M	W	M	W	M	
Asia (cont'd)												
Pakistan	29	85	13	82	13	25	35	14	47	62	17	4
Philippines	48	82	49	82	38	41	42	30	40	19	10	35
Qatar	34	94	35	92	13	..	..	..	..	..	..	1
Republic of Korea	47[b]	74[b]	50[b]	76[b]	41[b]	60	65	20	34	20	2	4
Saudi Arabia	15	85	18	82	13	..	..	..	..	..	..	..
Singapore	51	80	51	78	41	93	83	6	17	2	0	36
Sri Lanka	40	79	41	78	36	68[o]	60[o]	16[o]	34[o]	16[o]	6[o]	15[o]
Syrian Arab Republic	24	78	26	78	25	46[p]	50[p]	6[p]	37[p]	35[p]	8[p]	3[p]
Tajikistan	52	74	55	74	44	..	..	..	..	..	..	..
Thailand	76[b]	88[b]	67[b]	82[b]	45[b]	34	41	21	43	44	16	21
Turkey	34	80	28	74	28	25	49	8	39	67	12	6
Turkmenistan	59	78	61	78	45	..	..	..	..	..	..	..
United Arab Emirates	29	91	31	89	13	..	..	..	..	..	..	2
Uzbekistan	59	75	61	74	46	..	..	..	..	..	..	..
Viet Nam	76	85	75	84	49	..	..	..	..	..	..	..
Yemen	28	81	29	82	27	..	..	..	..	..	..	..
Oceania												
American Samoa	..	..	..	..	..	..	..	..	..	..	..	31
Fiji	26	84	32	82	27	..	..	..	..	..	..	9
French Polynesia	..	..	..	..	..	..	..	..	..	..	..	16
Guam	..	..	..	..	..	..	..	..	..	..	..	41
Kiribati	..	..	..	..	..	..	..	..	..	..	..	9
Marshall Islands	..	..	..	..	..	..	..	..	..	..	..	7
Micronesia (Fed. States of)	..	..	..	..	..	..	..	..	..	..	..	9[q]
New Caledonia	..	..	..	..	..	..	..	..	..	..	..	14
Palau	..	..	..	..	..	..	..	..	..	..	..	32
Papua New Guinea	67	88	67	87	42	..	..	..	..	..	..	..
Samoa	..	..	..	..	..	..	..	..	..	..	..	12
Solomon Islands	83	90	82	89	46	..	..	..	..	..	..	3
Tonga	36	76	45	74	39	46	45	31	35	14	18	5
Vanuatu	..	..	..	..	..	..	..	..	..	..	..	13
Developed regions												
Albania	58	83	59	83	41	..	..	..	..	..	..	..
Andorra	..	..	..	..	..	..	..	..	..	..	..	..
Australia	52	75	53	72	43	88	83	11	17	1	1	24
Austria	43	69	46	67	43	87	86	9	12	5	2	22
Belarus	61	76	59	74	49	..	..	..	..	..	..	..
Belgium	37	61	41	61	42	82	81	10	18	8	1	..
Bermuda	..	..	..	..	..	..	..	..	..	..	..	37
Bosnia and Herzegovina	43	76	44	75	38	..	..	..	..	..	..	..
Bulgaria	60	68	58	66	48	..	..	..	..	..	..	31
Canada	59	76	57	73	45	90	88	9	12	1[a]	0[a]	43
Croatia	48	71	48	69	44	..	..	..	..	..	..	24

Table 5.D (cont'd):
Economic activity

Country or area	Adult (15+) economic activity rate (%) 1990 W	1990 M	1995/1997 W	1995/1997 M	% women in the adult labour force, 1995/1997	% distribution of the labour force, each sex, 1990/1997 Wage and salaried workers W	M	Self-employed workers W	M	Contributing family workers W	M	% women among admin. and managerial workers, 1985/1997
Developed regions (cont'd)	W	M	W	M		W	M	W	M	W	M	
Czech Republic	61	74	52	71	44	91	83	9	17	1	0	..
Denmark	62	75	59	72	46	95	88	6	12	0	0	20
Estonia	64	77	53[r]	69[r]	48[r]	97	91	2	8	1	1	..
Finland	64	74	62[r]	71[r]	47[r]	90	81	10	18	1	1	25
France	46	64	47	62	45	..	..	..	..	..	..	10
Germany	44[s]	70[s]	47	68	43	92	87	6	13	2	0	19
Greece	35	66	36	63	39	58	53	19	42	24	5	12
Hungary	48	68	43[b]	60[b]	44[b]	90	82	8	15	2	1	58
Iceland	66	82	68[i]	80[i]	47[i]	89	77	11	23	1	0	..
Ireland	36	69	42	68	39	91	72	8	27	2	1	17
Italy	36[b]	64[b]	35[b]	61[b]	38[b]	77	68	17	29	7	3	54
Japan	50	77	50	78	41	80	84	8	14	12	2	9
Latvia	63	77	52	69	48	82	80	11	15	7	5	..
Liechtenstein	..	..	..	..	..	..	..	..	..	..	..	..
Lithuania	60	75	54	70	47	83	73	15	21	3	7	..
Luxembourg	34	68	38	65	38	..	..	..	..	..	..	12
Malta	23	73	25	72	27	..	..	..	..	..	..	..
Monaco	..	..	..	..	..	..	..	..	..	..	..	..
Netherlands	53[n]	80[n]	51[n]	72[n]	42[n]	90	87	8	13	2	0	17
New Zealand	54	74	57	75	45	86	75	13	24	1	1	55
Norway	62[i]	77[i]	68[i]	78[i]	46[i]	95	89	4	11	1	0	31
Poland	57	75	50	66	46	74	70	20	26	7	4	66
Portugal	51	74	49	67	45	73	71	26	28	2	1	50
Republic of Moldova	61	75	60	73	49	..	..	..	..	..	..	..
Romania	52	69	58	73	46	56	65	17	26	27	9	45
Russian Federation	60	76	59[t]	74[t]	48[t]	..	..	..	..	..	..	..
San Marino	..	..	..	..	..	84	78	13	16	0	0	17
Slovakia	63	75	51	66	45	96	92	4	8	0	0	60
Slovenia	55	71	52	65	46	84	79	8	16	9	5	23
Spain	33[i]	68[i]	38[i]	64[i]	39[i]	79	75	15	24	5	2	12
Sweden	71[i]	77[i]	65[i]	72[i]	47[i]	94	85	5	15	1	0	59[u]
Switzerland	49	79	57	79	44	86	83	9	15	5	1	29
The FYR of Macedonia	49	73	43[v]	67[v]	39[v]	81	78	8	18	11	5	16
Ukraine	57	73	57[b]	69[b]	50[b]	..	..	..	..	..	..	..
United Kingdom	53[i]	75[i]	54[i]	72[i]	44[i]	92	83	7	17	1	0	33
United States	58[i]	76[i]	60[iw]	75[iw]	46[i]	93	91	6	10	0	0	44
Yugoslavia	50	72	50	71	42	..	..	..	..	..	..	..

Sources: For economic activity rate and % women in the labour force (cols. 1-5): ILO, *Key Indicators of the Labour Market (KILM)* (Geneva, 1999), table 1. *KILM* table 1 was compiled from the following sources: ILO, *Yearbook of Labour Statistics, 1998* (Geneva, 1998); ILO, *Economically Active Population, 1950-2010*, fourth edition (Geneva, 1996); and OECD, *Labour Force Statistics, 1976-1996* (Paris). For percentage distribution of the labour force by status in employment (cols. 6-11): ILO, *Key Indicators of the Labour Market* (Geneva, 1999), table 3. *KILM* table 3 was compiled from the following sources: ILO, *Yearbook of Labour Statistics, 1998* (Geneva, 1998); ILO, *Digest of Caribbean Labor Statistics, 1997* (Port of Spain); OECD, *Labour Force Statistics, 1976-1996* (Paris); and ILO, Economic, Labour and Social Indicators Database (Santiago). For percentage women among administrative and managerial workers (col. 12): prepared by the Statistics Division of the United Nations Secretariat from *Women's Indicators and Statistics Database (Wistat), Version 4,* CD-ROM (United Nations publication, Sales No. E.00.XVII.4), based on the following: ILO, *Yearbook of Labour Statistics* (Geneva), various years up to 1992; ILO, LABORSTA database (as of August 1998); national census and survey reports; and national statistical yearbooks.

[a] "Contributing family workers" includes apprentices.

[b] Data are estimated to correspond to standard age groups.

[c] Urban areas. "Wage and salaried workers" includes unpaid family workers and members of producers' cooperatives.

[d] Urban areas.

[e] The data relate to the urban survey conducted in the main departmental capitals of the country.

[f] Excluding the rural populations of Rondônia, Acre, Amazonas, Roraima, Pará and Amapá. Excluding institutional household members.

[g] Seven main cities.

[h] Guatemala City.

[i] For persons aged 16 or over.

[j] The data relate to the districts of Wanica and Paramaribo.

[k] Covering only the civilian population of 30 provinces, municipalities and autonomous regions. Excluding Jimmen and Mazhu islands and persons working for the first time.

[l] Data relate to the government controlled areas.

[m] Including the residents of East Jerusalem.

[n] For persons aged 15 to 64.

[o] Excluding northern and eastern provinces.

[p] Syrians only.

[q] Data refer to Chuuk state only.

[r] For persons aged 15 to 74.

[s] Data for 1990 do not include the former German Democratic Republic.

[t] For persons aged 15 to 72.

[u] The category "administrative and managerial workers" includes clerical and related workers.

[v] For persons aged 15 to 80.

[w] Data are not strictly comparable with 1990 data due to the introduction of revised population controls.

Technical notes

Table 5.A presents statistics on the unemployment rate–i.e., the proportion of the labour force that is unemployed. The unemployed are persons who are currently without work, who are seeking or have sought work recently, and who are currently available for work. The base for these statistics is the labour force (the economically active portion of the population), not the total population. The statistics in table 5.A cover the period from 1991 to 1997 and have been compiled from the International Labour Office's (ILO) *Key Indicators of the Labour Market (KILM)* database.[1]

Table 5.B presents statistics on part-time workers–i.e., persons with jobs whose working hours total less than "full time" (see definition below). The two types of data presented in this table are total part-time employment as a percentage of total employment, calculated separately for women and for men, and the proportion of women among all part-time workers. The statistics refer to two periods, 1990-1993 and 1996-1998, and have been compiled from the *KILM* database.

There is no internationally accepted standard for the minimum number of hours worked per week that would constitute full-time work. The framework is therefore established on a country-by-country basis or in special regional compilations. Many countries have established demarcation points that lie between 30 and 40 hour per week. Other countries classify part-time and full-time workers on the basis of respondents' interpretations of their personal work situations–i.e., whether they view themselves as full-time or as part-time job-holders. In an attempt to make statistics on part-time work comparable across countries, the Organisation for Economic Co-operation and Development (OECD) applied a 30-hour cut-off for distinguishing part-time from full-time workers. Thus, in the OECD data set, one of the main sources of the *KILM* database, persons who work 30 hours or more per week are considered "full-time workers" and those who work less than 30 hours per week are considered "part-time workers".[2]

Table 5.C presents data on maternity leave benefits currently available to women in countries surveyed by the ILO, including the length of time for which benefits are provided, the extent of compensation and the institution responsible for providing the coverage. The data presented was compiled by the ILO, based on information provided by countries as of 1998.

Table 5.D presents statistics on women and men in the economically active population aged 15 or over, the percentage distribution of the labour force by status in employment and the proportion of women among administrative and managerial workers.

Indicators concerning the total economically active population aged 15 or over have been compiled mainly from the *KILM* database,[3] for the latest year for which data are available between 1990 and 1997. The first indicator is the economic activity rate, defined as the proportion of the population aged 15 or over who furnish, or are available to furnish, the supply of labour for production of goods and services in accordance with the System of National Accounts. The second indicator on economic activity is the percentage of women among the total labour force.

Issues concerning statistics on economically active women are discussed in the box entitled "Concepts related to the labour force" in this chapter, and in a box entitled "Counting economically active women" in *The World's Women 1970-1990: Trends and Statistics*. The definition of the economically active population provided by the ILO comprises all employed and unemployed persons, including those seeking work for the first time, employers operating unincorporated enterprises, persons working on their own account, employees, contributing family workers, members of producers' co-operatives and members of the armed forces. In principle, a person who performs such work for as little as one hour per week is considered economical-ly active. ILO's recommended definition also accounts for production of primary products, such as foodstuffs, fetching/transporting water and collecting firewood for own consumption. Certain other non-monetary activities—e.g., construction, major repair and renovation of owner-occupied dwelling—are considered economic activity and persons engaged in such production are regarded as economically active.

Specific elements of the standard concepts differ substantially from country to country (e.g., the choice of reference period and the determination of minimum hours of work and unpaid family work, including production for own consumption), and these differences may result in underestimation of women's participation in economic activity. Moreover, censuses and surveys are seldom conducted regularly and the results in developing regions become available only after several years. Stereotypes held by census and survey interviewers and respondents' own perceptions about what does or does not constitute economic activity may also lead to errors in the reporting and recording of the economic activity, resulting in underestimation of women's economic activity. In addition, in many countries, women are engaged predominantly in those economic activities that are the most difficult to measure, such as subsistence production and informal sector or home-based work.

The indicators on status in employment of the economically active population have been compiled from the *KILM* database[4] and are based on the classification used in population censuses and surveys in most countries. The statistics presented pertain to the period between 1990 and 1997. National classifications often include the following categories: employer, own-account worker, employee, unpaid family worker and member of producers' co-operative. In table 5.D, three status groups are presented: "wage and salaried workers" corresponds to employees–persons who work for a public or private employer and receive remuneration in wages, salary, commission, tips, piece-rates or pay in kind; "self-employed" comprises employers and own-account workers–persons who operate their own economic enterprises or engage independently in a profession or trade; and "contributing family workers" refers to persons who work without pay in an economic enterprise operated by a related person living in the same household. Proportions of these three groups of workers among all workers are presented separately for women and men.

The indicator on administrative and managerial workers is derived from statistics published by ILO in the *Yearbook of Labour Statistics* and supplemented by national sources. According to the International Standard Classification of Occupations, revised edition (ISCO-68), the major group "administrative and managerial workers" includes (a) legislative officials and government administrators and (b) managers. In a few countries, the revised ISCO (ISCO-88) is already in use; in those cases, the category "administrative and managerial workers" includes the following sub-groups: (a) legislators and senior officials; (b) corporate managers; and (c) general managers. The indicator expresses the number of women administrators and managers as a percentage of all workers in this occupational group, and covers the latest year between 1985 to 1997 for which data are available.

---

[1] ILO, *Key Indicators of the Labour Market Database* (Geneva, 1999), table 8a. Explanation of the indicator may also be accessed at: http://www.ilo.org/public/english/employment/strat/polemp/kilm/ind_11.htm.

[2] Ibid., table 5. Explanation of the indicator may also be accessed at: http://www.ilo.org/public/english/employment/strat/polemp/kilm/ind_8a.htm.

[3] Ibid., table 1. Explanation of the indicator may also be accessed at: http://www.ilo.org/public/english/employment/strat/polemp/kilm/ind_1.htm.

[4] Ibid., table 3. Explanation of the indicator may also be accessed at: http://www.ilo.org/public/english/employment/strat/polemp/kilm/ind_5.htm.

CHAPTER 6

Human rights and political decision-making

Some important findings:

- All but 26 States have ratified the Convention on the Elimination of All Forms of Discrimination against Women, making it the second most widely ratified human rights treaty.

- Physical and sexual abuse affect millions of girls and women worldwide— yet are known to be seriously under-reported.

- In some African countries, more than half of all women and girls have undergone female genital mutilation and its prevalence is not declining.

- Women and girls comprise half of the world's refugees and, as refugees, are particularly vulnerable to sexual violence while in flight, in refugee camps and/or during resettlement.

- Despite calls for gender equality, women are significantly under-represented in Governments, political parties and at the United Nations.

The Beijing Platform for Action adopted by the Fourth World Conference on Women identified the lack of respect for, and the inadequate promotion and protection of, the human rights of women as a critical area of concern. The Platform for Action reaffirmed that the human rights of women are an integral part of universal human rights and that full enjoyment of all human rights is critical to women's empowerment and autonomy. It further acknowledged that equality between women and men would benefit society as a whole.

Since the Fourth World Conference on Women, efforts to promote the human rights of women have increased at the international, regional and national levels. Protecting women and the girl child from physical and sexual violence and ensuring women's freedom to participate in politics, both as voters and as representatives, have been central to these efforts.

WOMEN'S RIGHTS AS HUMAN RIGHTS

International bill of rights for women widely ratified

The Convention on the Elimination of All Forms of Discrimination against Women is the most comprehensive treaty on women's human rights and is often described as the international bill of rights for women. It was adopted by the United Nations General Assembly in 1979 and came into force in 1981.

As of 1 April 2000, the Convention had been ratified or acceded to by 165 States parties, making it the second most widely ratified international human rights treaty after the Convention on the Rights of the Child.[1] Twenty-six States have not ratified the Convention, including 17 in Asia and the Pacific **(chart 6.1 and table 6.A)**.

The Convention calls for equality between women and men in the enjoyment of civil, political, economic, social and cultural rights. States that have ratified or acceded to it are obligated to abolish all forms of discrimination, in public and private life, and to ensure that true equality between women and men is realized.

The Convention is the only human rights treaty to assert the reproductive rights of women, particularly access to health care services, including family planning. It recognizes that culture and tradition shape gender roles and family relations, while emphasizing that they should not be used to justify discrimination. Governments that ratify the Convention agree to take all appropriate measures to modify the social and cultural patterns of conduct of women and men, with a view toward eliminating prejudices and customs and all other practices that are based on the idea of the inferiority or superiority of either sex or on stereotypical roles for women and men.

The Convention defines discrimination against women as any distinction, exclusion or restriction made on the basis of sex that has the effect or purpose of impairing or nullifying the recognition, enjoyment or exercise by women, irrespective of their marital status, on a basis of equality of men and women, of human rights and fundamental freedoms in the political, economic, social, cultural, civil or any other field.[2] The articles of the Convention identify specific actions to be taken on behalf of women by States that ratify or accede to the Convention, including eliminating trafficking in women and their exploitation through prostitution; achieving equality in political and public life and international representation, as well as in acquiring, changing and retaining nationality; and assuring equality in the right to education, employment, health, and economic and social benefits, both before the law and in marriage and family life. The Convention also requires States parties to take account of the particular problems of women in rural areas, and to take appropriate measures to eliminate discrimination against them **(see box on implementation of the Convention).**

To monitor its implementation, States that were party to the Convention elected 23 experts to form the Committee on the Elimination of Discrimination against Women (CEDAW). The Committee meets regularly to review progress in countries that have ratified or acceded to the Convention. Governments report to the Committee on the measures they have taken to comply with the Convention one year after becoming party to it, and at least once every four years after that.

The Committee has the authority to make general recommendations on ways to eliminate discrimination against women in areas not specifically included in the Convention. The Committee has used this power to address such topics as the human immunodeficiency virus/acquired immunodeficiency syndrome (HIV/AIDS) and violence against women.

Periodic review of countries' progress is the only designated means of monitoring implementation of the Convention. However, in October 1999, the General Assembly adopted an Optional Protocol to the Convention. The Optional Protocol allows individual women or groups of women who have exhausted domestic remedies to petition the Committee about violations of the Convention by their Governments, and grants the Committee the authority to conduct inquiries into grave or systematic abuses of women's human rights in States that are party to the Convention and the Protocol. As of 3 April 2000, 34 States had signed the Protocol, indicating their intention to ratify or accede **(chart 6.2).**

Violence against women—in all its forms—still pervasive and under-reported

Violence against women is a worldwide problem. In 1993, the United Nations General Assembly adopted the Declaration on the Elimination of Violence Against Women, which defines violence against women as any act of gender-based violence that results in, or is likely to result in, physical, sexual or mental harm or suffering to women, including threats of such acts, coercion or arbitrary deprivation of liberty, whether occurring in public or in private life.[3] The Declaration states that violence against women encompasses physical, sexual and psychological violence occurring in the family and in the general community, including battering, sexual abuse of female children, dowry-related violence, marital rape, female genital mutilation and other traditional practices harmful to women; violence related to exploitation, sexual harassment and intimidation at work, in educational institutions and elsewhere; trafficking in women; forced prostitution; and violence perpetrated or condoned by the state.[4]

In 1994, the Commission on Human Rights appointed the Special Rapporteur on violence against women to examine violence against women, its causes and its consequences. The Fourth World Conference on Women in 1995 identified violence against women as a critical issue and made recommendations to eradicate the problem in its Platform for Action, calling the long-standing failure to protect women's rights and freedoms in this area a matter of concern for all States.[5]

Domestic violence

The term "domestic violence" is given different meanings but is most often used to refer to violence against a woman (physical, sexual or emotional) by an intimate partner, also called "wife abuse" or "wife battering".[6] Physical violence is often accompanied by emotional or psychological abuse and sexual violence.[7]

Until recently, data on domestic violence against women, particularly from developing countries, was largely anecdotal or derived from small ad hoc studies. However, in the last five years many new studies have been undertaken, including a number of national studies, to collect data on violence against women, especially violence by intimate male partners. Data collected from these surveys may underestimate the prevalence of violence against women, and are not comparable for several reasons—e.g., differences in populations included in the surveys and differences in definitions of violence (some surveys only address the most severe forms of violence). The World Health Organization (WHO) has initiated projects to compile existing statistics in an international database and to promote the development and implementation of methodologies for studying violence against women cross-culturally **(see box on WHO efforts to improve data on violence against women)**.

Abuse by a husband or intimate partner is the most common form of violence against women. In national studies in 11 countries, the proportion of women who report having been abused by an intimate partner at some point in their lives ranges from 5 to 48 per cent **(chart 6.3)**. Localized studies in Africa, Latin America and Asia report higher rates of physical violence—up to 58 per cent of women. National survey data show that among women who had been in a relationship during the past year, 3 per cent in Australia and Canada, 6 per cent in South Africa and Switzerland, 7 per cent in the Republic of Moldova and 12 per cent in Nicaragua had been assaulted by an intimate partner. Studies in local areas report higher rates—for example, 30 per cent of women in Managua, Nicaragua, had been assaulted by an intimate partner during the past 12 months.

Physical abuse is often accompanied by sexual and emotional abuse. Among 613 women in Japan who reported having been abused at some point in their lives, 57 per cent had suffered all three types of abuse, while 8 per cent had experienced only physical abuse.[8] A study in Nicaragua found substantial overlap between physical, sexual and emotional violence, with 20 per cent of ever-married women reporting all three kinds of abuse, while less than 2 per cent reported only physical abuse.[9] In Zimbabwe, the number of women who reported forced sex by their partners, in addition to threats and physical assault, was almost three times

as high as the number of women who reported forced sex but had not been threatened or assaulted.[10]

The WHO Database on Violence against Women contains only a few national surveys on the occurrence of sexual violence against women by an intimate partner **(chart 6.4)**. According to these data, 8 per cent of Canadian women have been sexually assaulted in an intimate relationship and 12 per cent of women in Switzerland had an intimate partner who had forced sex or attempted to do so. Other studies of smaller populations found much higher rates of sexual assault and attempted or completed forced sex.

In cases of homicide of women, the perpetrator is most likely to be an intimate partner. One study in Brazil found that 60 per cent of women homicide victims were killed by an intimate partner.[11] According to a study in one province in Canada, a current or former partner commits 61 to 78 per cent of female homicides, and three times more women than men fall victim to homicide by an intimate partner.[12] A local study in the United States shows that intimate partners commit an estimated 30 per cent of homicides of women.[13]

Victims of abuse are reported to be at highest risk of being killed by their abusers during the two months following a legal or physical separation.[14] A woman's risk of being killed by an intimate partner is reported to increase if she tries but fails to separate from him.[15]

In some Southern Asian countries, deaths may be related to the custom of dowry. The phenomenon is probably underestimated, due to the limited information available[16] and to the fact that these deaths are often disguised as kitchen accidents or suicides.[17]

In so-called "honour killings", male family members kill women or girls suspected of behavior regarded as shameful or dishonouring. Under the legislative codes of several countries, such circumstances are considered a valid defence in criminal proceedings, and men who commit this crime are excused or given

---

Implementation of the Convention on the Elimination of All Forms of Discrimination against Women

Since the Fourth World Conference on Women, States that are parties to the Convention have taken action at the national level in various ways:
- Prepared or strengthened national plans of action for the advancement of women;
- Created the post of Secretary of State for Women to coordinate official policies, or formed ministries for women's affairs or assigned gender focal points in already existing ministries;

- Compiled statistics to monitor the impact of policies and programmes on girls and women;
- Added provisions to their Constitutions that guarantee the enjoyment of human rights without discrimination on the basis of sex;
- Adopted legal provisions that guarantee women's economic, social, civil and political rights;
- Introduced law reform and policy change regarding violence against women.

Chart 6.3:

Many women have been physically abused by an intimate partner

Percentage of adult women who have been physically assaulted by an intimate partner, 1991/1999

	Coverage	In past 12 mos.	Ever (in any relationship)		Coverage	In past 12 mos.	Ever (in any relationship)
Africa				**Asia**			
Egypt	National	..	34	Bangladesh	National (villages)	19	47
Ethiopia	Meskanena Woreda	10 [a]	45	China	Hong Kong SAR	10 [d]	..
Nigeria	Not stated	..	31	India	Rural areas in 2 states	..	40 [b]
South Africa	National	6	16	India	6 states	14 [e]	40
Uganda	Lira and Masaka districts	..	41 [b]	Occupied Palestinian Territory	Palestinians	48	..
Latin America and the Caribbean				Philippines	National	..	5
Chile	Santiago	23	..	Thailand	Bangkok	..	20 [b]
Chile	Metro Santiago and Santiago province	..	26 [b]	Turkey	East and South East Anatolia	..	58 [c]
Colombia	National	..	19 [b c]	**Developed regions**			
Mexico	Durango City	..	40	Australia	Metropolitan Melbourne	22 [d f]	..
Mexico	Metropolitan Guadalajara	15	27	Australia	National	3	23
Nicaragua	Leon	27 [d]	52	Canada	National	3 [g]	29 [g]
Nicaragua	Managua	30	..	Canada	Toronto	..	27 [c]
Nicaragua	National	12	28	Republic of Moldova	National	7	14
Paraguay	Western state except Chaco region	..	10 [c]	Switzerland	National	6 [g]	13
Peru	Metropolitan Lima (middle and low income)	31	..	United Kingdom	North London	12 [c]	30 [c]
Puerto Rico	National	..	48 [c]	United States	National	1 [c]	22 [c]

Source: WHO, Database on Violence against Women (as at March 2000).

Note: Data in the last column are lifetime rates, and include any relationship or marriage in adult life.

[a] In past 3 months.

[b] In current relationship only.

[c] Sample group included women who had never been in a relationship and therefore were not in exposed group.

[d] Definition includes throwing objects.

[e] Severe physical violence (hit, kick or beat). Percentage would probably be higher if moderate violence were included.

[f] Respondents were recruited from women visiting medical practitioners' offices or hospital/health care centers.

[g] Physical or sexual contact.

References:

Egypt: *Egypt Demographic and Health Survey 1995* (Cairo, National Population Council and Calverton, Maryland, Macro International, 1995).
Ethiopia: N. Deyessa et al., "Magnitude, type and outcomes of physical violence against married women in Butajira, Southern Ethiopia" (1996), unpublished.
Nigeria: O. Odujinrin, "Wife battering in Nigeria", *International Journal of Gynecology and Obstetrics*, No. 41 (1993).
South Africa: *South Africa: Demographic and Health Survey 1998: Preliminary Report* (South Africa, Department of Health, and Calverton, Maryland, Macro International, 1999).
Uganda: A.K. Blanc et al., *Negotiating*

Reproductive Outcomes in Uganda, (Institute of Statistics and Applied Economics and Calverton, Maryland, Macro International, 1996).
Chile: Santiago: A. Morrison et al., "The socio-economic impact of domestic violence against women in Chile and Nicaragua" (Washington, D.C., Inter-American Development Bank, 1997).
Chile: Metro Santiago and Santiago province: S. Larrain-Heiremans, "Violencia familiar y la situacion de la mujer en Chile" (1993), unpublished.
Colombia: *Colombia, Encuesta National de Demografia y Salud 1995* (Colombia, PROFAMILIA, DHS/Institute for Resource Development, and Calverton, Maryland, Macro International, 1995).
Mexico: Durango City: G. Alvarado-Zaldivar et al., "Prevalencia de violencia doméstica en la ciudad de Durango", *Salud Pública de México,* vol. 40, No. 6 (1998).
Mexico: Metropolitan Guadalajara: J.C. Ramirez Rodriguez et al., "Una espada de doble filo: la salud reproductiva y la violencia doméstica contra la mujer", paper presented at a seminar entitled "Salud reproductiva en América Latina y el Caribe: temas y problemas", Brazil, 1996.
Nicaragua: Leon: M.C. Ellsberg, "Candies in hell: domestic violence against women in Nicaragua" (Umea University, Sweden, 1997).
Nicaragua: Managua : A. Morrison et al., "The socio-economic impact of domestic violence against women in Chile and Nicaragua" (Washington, D.C., Inter-American Development Bank, 1997).
Nicaragua: national: *Nicaragua, Encuesta National de Demografia y Salud 1998* (Calverton, Maryland, Macro International, 1998).

Paraguay: *Paraguay, Encuesta Nacional de Demografia y Salud Reproductiva, 1995-1996* (Centro Paraguaya de Estudios de Población, 1996).
Peru: E. Gonzales de Olarte et al., "Poverty and domestic violence against women in Metropolitan Lima" (Washington, D.C., Inter-American Development Bank, 1997).
Puerto Rico: *Puerto Rico, Encuesta de Salud Reproductiva 1995-1996: Resumen de los Hallazgos* (Universidad de Puerto Rico, and Atlanta, Centers for Disease Control and Prevention, 1998).
Bangladesh: S.R. Schuler et al., "Credit programs, patriarchy and men's violence against women in rural Bangladesh", *Social Science and Medicine*, vol. 43, No. 12 (1996).
China: C.S. Tang, "Wife abuse in Hong Kong Chinese families: a community survey", *Journal of Family Violence*, vol. 14, No. 2 (1999).
India: rural areas in 2 states: S. Jejeebhoy et al., "State accountability for wife-beating: the Indian challenge", *Lancet,* No. 348 (Supplement) (1997).
India: 6 states: IndiaSAFE Steering Committee, *IndiaSAFE Final Report* (Washington D.C., International Center for Research on Women, 1999).
Occupied Palestinian Territory: M.M. Haj-Yahia, "The incidence of wife abuse and battering and some sociodemographic correlates as revealed in two national surveys in Palestinian society" (Ramallah, Palestinian Authority, Besir Center for Research and Development, 1998).
Philippines: "Domestic violence and rape", in *National Safe Motherhood Survey 1993* (Calverton, Maryland, Macro International, 1994).
Thailand: K.L. Hoffman et al., "Physical wife

abuse in a non-western society: an integrated theoretical approach", *Journal of Marriage and the Family*, No. 56 (1994).
Turkey: P. Ilkkaracan et al., "Exploring the context of women's sexuality in Eastern Turkey", *Reproductive Health Matters*, vol. 6, No. 12 (1998).
Australia: Metropolitan Melbourne: D. Mazza et al., "Physical, sexual and emotional violence against women: a general practice-based prevalence study", *Medical Journal of Australia*, vol. 164, No. 1 (1996).
Australia: national: Australia Bureau of Statistics, *Women's Safety: Australia* (Belconnen, Australia, 1998).
Canada: national : K. Rodgers, "Wife assault: the findings of a national survey", *Juristat Service Bulletin*, vol. 14, No. 9 (Canadian Centre for Justice Statistics, 1994).
Canada: Toronto: M. Randall et al., "Sexual violence in women's lives: findings from the women's safety project, a community-based survey", *Violence Against Women*, vol. 1, No. 1 (1995).
Republic of Moldova: F. Serbanescu et al., *Reproductive Health Survey, Moldova 1997*, Final Report (Atlanta, Centers for Disease Control, 1998).
Switzerland: L. Gillioz et al., "Domination masculine et violences envers les femmes dans la famille en Suisse" (Geneva, 1996), unpublished.
United Kingdom: J. Mooney, "The hidden figure: domestic violence in North London" (Middlesex University, 1993).
United States: United States Department of Justice, "Prevalence, incidence, and consequences of violence against women: findings from the national violence against women survey" (Washington, D.C., 1998).

reduced sentences. Several countries are reviewing their criminal and civil codes so as to prevent honour killings, while others have initiated public education campaigns to be carried out in cooperation with non-governmental organizations.[18]

Coerced sex among women and children

Some forms of physical sexual coercion—forced penetration (rape), sexual assault (forced sexual contact), statutory rape and sexual molestation of children—are recognized as crimes by most legal systems. However, rape and sexual assault are generally under-reported crimes. Low reporting is the result of a number of factors, including reluctance to relive the incident and to discuss it with others, fear of reprisal or of damage to one's reputation, shame, and lack of confidence in the ability and willingness of the police and the judiciary system to solve the crime and bring the criminal to justice. Police-based crime statistics are thus of limited use in evaluating the magnitude of this problem.

Although rates are under-reported, it appears that some countries do place priority on compiling rape statistics. The Fifth United Nations Survey of Crime Trends and the Operations of Criminal Justice Systems in 1993 found that the proportion of countries providing statistics for reported rape convictions was higher than for other crimes; 60 per cent of the reporting countries provided statistics for rape convictions, compared to 56 per cent for robbery.[19]

A United Nations Children's Fund (UNICEF) analysis of police- and court-based rape statistics for 12 countries in transition found that the number of rapes reported declined in nine of the countries between 1989 and 1997.[20] UNICEF determined that the decline was the result of reduced reporting of rape rather than a reduction in the number of rapes committed. In half of the countries included in the study, the rate of conviction for rape also fell.

Victimization surveys, the other major source of data on crime, measure a population's experience with crime, and can often provide more reliable data on incidence of sexual victimization. However, the way in which surveys regarding crimes of a sexual nature are administered—for example, how questions are worded and whether other family members are present during the interview—has a substantial effect on survey results.

Questions on sexual assault, including rape, attempted rape and indecent assault, as well as on sexual harassment, were included in the Third International Crime Victim Survey, undertaken in 1996-97. The survey was conducted mainly in urban areas in 11 developed countries, 14 developing countries and 20 countries in transition. The results indicate that 1 to 8 per cent of women in the six cities surveyed in Latin America, 1 to 5 per cent in six cities in Africa and less than 1 per cent to 3 per cent in four cities in Asia had been sexually assaulted. In the survey report, the United Nations Interregional Crime and Justice Research Institute (UNICRI) cautioned that these results help to disclose the "broad", rather than the "true", extent of victimization of women. UNICRI also indicated that, on average, one quarter of attempted rapes and one third of rapes were reported to the police in the countries surveyed.[21]

Sexual abuse during childhood is usually perpetrated by close relatives, teachers or others with authority over the child. According to studies in 19 countries, including 10 national surveys, levels of childhood sexual abuse range from 7 per cent to 36 per cent for girls and from 3 per cent to 29 per cent for boys. Overall, girls were victims of sexual violence 1.5 to 3 times as often as boys.[22] Childhood sexual abuse can have long-term physical and emotional health consequences, and can lead to high-risk sexual behaviours later in life.[23]

In a study in Kingston, Jamaica, of a random sample of 452 girls aged 13 to 14, 17 per cent reported experiencing attempted or completed rape, half of them before the age of 12.[24] A survey of randomly selected ninth grade students in Geneva in 1996 reported that 20 per cent of girls and 3 per cent of boys had experienced at least one incident of sexual abuse involving physical contact.[25]

For a large proportion of women, first sexual intercourse is not consensual. In a survey of women aged 20 to 22 in Dunedin, New Zealand, 7 per cent reported forced first intercourse.[26] Studies of school girls aged 12 to 24 in Kenya and Mozambique in 1993 found that for 8 per cent of the girls interviewed, first intercourse was forced.[27] In a national survey of family growth in the United States in 1995, 9 per cent of women characterized first intercourse as "not voluntary". Respondents who first had intercourse after age 15 and characterized the experience as "voluntary" were then asked to rate the "wantedness" of first intercourse on a scale of 1 to 10 (1 being the lowest); 26 per cent gave a rating lower than 5, with 7 per cent assigning a rating of 1.[28]

Sexual violence against women in situations of armed conflict

During the last century, the burden of armed conflict on civilian populations has increased substantially. Five per cent of World War I casualties, 52 per cent of World War II casualties, and approximately 90 per cent of casualties in conflicts during 1991 were reportedly civilians.[29] In civil wars, the predominant form of conflict in the world today, over 90 per cent of casualties are civilians.[30] Of civilians caught up in the Kosovo conflict, 80 per cent were women and children.[31] The number of civilians who become refugees and internally displaced persons as a result of armed conflict has also increased over the last few decades, and women and children in such circumstances are particularly vulnerable to sexual violence. There is a dearth of sex-disaggregated statistics on the impact of armed conflict but the amount of information available on sexual violence against women is increasing.[32]

The Special Rapporteur of the Commission of Human Rights determined that during the conflict in Rwanda in 1994, rape was systematic and was used as a "weapon" by the perpetrators of the massacres. According to consistent and reliable testimony, rape was the rule rather than the exception. Among those women victimized were: children, the elderly, pregnant women, those who had just given birth, and even corpses.[33]

Human Rights Watch found that rape and other forms of sexual violence were used in Kosovo in 1999 as weapons of war and instruments of systematic "ethnic cleansing". The organization found 96 verifiable

Chart 6.4:
Occurrence of sexual violence against women by an intimate male partner
Percentage of women who have been sexually victimized by a male partner, 1991/1997

	Coverage	In past 12 mos.		Ever (in any relationship)	
		Sexual assault	Attempted/completed forced sex	Sexual assault	Attempted/completed forced sex
Latin America and the Caribbean					
Chile	Santiago	..	9	..	..
Mexico	Durango City	..	..	42	..
Mexico	Metropolitan Guadalajara	15	..	23	..
Nicaragua	Leon	..	..	..	22
Nicaragua	Managua	..	18	..	..
Peru	Metropolitan Lima	..	49	..	..
Puerto Rico	National	..	..	..	6 [a] [b]
Asia					
Occupied Palestinian Territory	Palestinians	38	27 [b]	..	..
Turkey	East and South East Anatolia	..	..	..	52 [a] [b]
Developed regions					
Canada	National	..	..	8	..
Canada	Toronto	..	..	..	15 [b]
Switzerland	National	..	..	..	12
United Kingdom	North London	..	6 [b]	..	23 [b]
United States	National	..	0 [b]	..	8 [a] [b]

Source: WHO, Database on Violence against Women (as at June 1999).

[a] Completed forced sex only.

[b] Study included women who had never been in a relationship and therefore were not in the exposed group.

References:

Chile: A. Morrison et al., "The socio-economic impact of domestic violence against women in Chile and Nicaragua" (Washington, D.C., Inter-American Development Bank, 1997).
Mexico: Durango City: G. Alvarado-Zaldivar et al., "Prevalencia de violencia doméstica en la ciudad de Durango", *Salud pública de México*, vol. 40, No. 6 (1998).
Mexico: Metropolitan Guadalajara: J.C. Ramirez Rodriguez et al., "Una espada de doble filo: la salud reproductiva y la violencia doméstica contra la mujer", paper presented at a seminar entitled "Salud reproductiva en América Latina y el Caribe: temas y problemas", Brazil, 1996.
Nicaragua, Leon: M.C. Ellsberg, "Candies in hell: domestic violence against women in Nicaragua" (Umea University, Sweden, 1997).
Nicaragua, Managua: A. Morrison et al., "The socio-economic impact of domestic violence against women in Chile and

Nicaragua" (Washington, D.C., Inter-American Development Bank, 1997).
Peru: E. Gonzales de Olarte et al., "Poverty and domestic violence against women in Metropolitan Lima" (Washington, D.C., Inter-American Development Bank, 1997).
Puerto Rico: *Puerto Rico, Encuesta de Salud Reproductiva 1995-1996: Resumen de los Hallazgos* (Universidad de Puerto Rico, and Atlanta, Centers for Disease Control and Prevention, 1998).
Occupied Palestinian Territory: M.M. Haj-Yahia, "The incidence of wife abuse and battering and some sociodemographic correlates as revealed in two national surveys in Palestinian society" (Ramallah, Palestinian Authority, Besir Center for Research and Development, 1998).
Turkey: P. Ilkkaracan et al., "Exploring the context of women's sexuality in Eastern Turkey", *Reproductive Health Matters*, vol. 6, No. 12 (1998).

Canada: national : K. Rodgers, "Wife assault: the findings of a national survey", *Juristat Service Bulletin*, vol. 14, No. 9 (Canadian Centre for Justice Statistics, 1994).
Canada: Toronto: M. Randall et al., "Sexual violence in women's lives: findings from the women's safety project, a community-based survey", *Violence Against Women*, vol. 1, No. 1 (1995).
Switzerland: L. Gillioz et al., Domination masculine et violences envers les femmes dans la famille en Suisse" (1996), unpublished.
United Kingdom: J. Mooney, "The hidden figure: domestic violence in North London" (Middlesex University, 1993).
United States: United States Department of Justice, "Prevalence, incidence, and consequences of violence against women: findings from the national violence against women survey" (Washington, D.C., 1998).

The Beijing Platform for Action adopted by the Fourth World Conference on Women states that the absence of adequate sex-disaggregated data and statistics on the incidence of violence makes the elaboration of programmes and monitoring of changes difficult. It recommends the promotion of research and data collection on the prevalence of different forms of violence against women, especially domestic violence, and research into the causes, the nature and the consequences of violence against women and the effectiveness of measures implemented to prevent and redress violence against women.[a]

Following up on the recommendations of the Beijing Platform for Action, the World Health Organization (WHO) assembled a panel of experts to develop a programme to eradicate violence against women.[b] The experts recommended that WHO set up a database on violence against women and women's health, and support international research to explore the dimensions, health consequences and risk factors of violence against women. In response to these recommendations, WHO created a database on violence against women and developed a questionnaire and guidelines for undertaking national surveys.

WHO Violence Against Women Database

The WHO *Violence Against Women Database*[c] brings together data and information from studies of physical or sexual violence against women perpetrated by an intimate partner (or ex-partner).

To identify relevant studies, WHO relies on an extensive global network of non-governmental and governmental organizations, as well as individuals and institutions, to gather difficult-to-access, unpublished literature. Materials are also drawn from the World Wide Web and from the more than 3,500 journals listed in *Medline* and *Sociofile*. To be included, studies must be based on a random or quasi-random sampling and provide a comprehensive description of study methods.

The database bibliography contains numerous articles, reports and qualitative studies. The materials presented in the database, including the bibliography, can be accessed free of charge by developing countries, through a collaboration with POPLINE.[d]

The WHO database also includes information on the health consequences of violence against women, which will be used to produce systematic reviews addressing different health consequences of violence. These and other WHO publications on violence against women will be available on the WHO web site.

WHO multi-country study of women's health and domestic violence protocol[e]

The WHO Multi-country Study of Women's Health and Domestic Violence Protocol aims to:
- Obtain reliable estimates of the incidence and frequency of violence against women in several countries;
- Ascertain the health consequences of domestic violence against women;
- Identify and compare risk and protective factors for domestic violence against women within and between settings;
- Explore and compare the strategies and services used by women who are victims of domestic violence.

In addition, the study has been designed to:
- Ensure that the data will be used to initiate policy change and to develop and test strategies for intervention and for the elimination of domestic violence against women;
- Foster collaboration between policy makers, researchers, and women's organizations working in the field, and develop local research capacity;
- Develop methodologies for measuring violence and its consequences cross-culturally, including the role of violence as a risk factor for a range of health-related problems and the impact of violence on national health care costs.

Obtaining more data on violence against women is critical to improving understanding of the problem. However, the increasing interest in research raises important ethical and methodological challenges. It is essential to enhance disclosure while ensuring that women are not put at risk and that ethical standards are respected. Due to the nature of the topic, issues of safety, confidentiality and interviewer skills are of the utmost importance.[f]

Each country participating in the study collects data from its largest urban centre and from one province that comprises both urban and rural communities. Within each locale, cluster sampling is used to randomly select households, and one woman aged 15 to 45 is randomly selected for interview in each household. The core questionnaire developed by WHO is pre-tested in each country. Training materials for interviewers, supervisors and data entry staff have also been developed.

The active participation of local NGOs is a key factor in successfully applying the research and ensuring the use of the findings for interventions and policy change. The WHO study is being undertaken in collaboration with local institutions.[g] Each in-country team is made up of a local research organization (e.g., a university or centre for population studies) or national statistical office and a local women's organization that deals with issues related to violence against women.

---

[a] See United Nations, Report of the Fourth World Conference on Women, Beijing, 4–15 September 1995 (United Nations publication, Sales No. 96.IV.13), Chap. I, resolution I, annex I.

[b] WHO, "Violence against women", WHO consultation, Geneva 5–7 February 1996.

[c] Information from the Database can also be accessed through the WHO web site at http://www.who.int/violence_injury_prevention/

[d] Population information is available online at http://www.jhuccp.org/popline.

[e] WHO, "Multi-country study of women's health and domestic violence protocol" (WHO/EIP/GPE/99.3).

[f] See WHO, "Putting women's safety first: ethical and safety recommendations for research on domestic violence against women" (WHO/EIP/GPE/99.2).

[g] The participating countries and the national institutions comprising each study team are as follows: **Bangladesh**: International Centre for Diarrhoeal Disease Research and Nariphoko; **Brazil**: Department of Preventive Medicine, Faculty of Medicine and School of Public Health, University of São Paulo, Coletivo Feminista Sexualidade y Saude, Corpo, Recife; **Japan**: School of Social Work, University of Michigan, Department of Population Dynamics Research, National Institute of Population and Social Security Research, Tokyo, Kanagawa Women's Center; **Namibia**: Ministry of Health and Social Services, Women and Child Protection United, Fatatura Hospital Central Bureau of Statistics, National Planning Commission and University of Namibia; **Peru**: Centro de la Mujer Peruana Flora Tristan and Centro de Salud Publica, Universidaad Peruana Cayetano Heredia; and **United Republic of Tanzania**: Muhimibili University College of Health Sciences (planned); **Thailand**: Institute for Population and Social Research, Mahidol University and Foundation for Women, Bangkok. The survey is also being carried out in **Samoa** by the Secretariat of the Pacific Community with UNFPA support.

accounts of sexual assault during the period of the NATO bombing from 24 March to 7 May 1999. Human Rights Watch believes that the documented cases represent only a fraction of the incidents that occurred, in part due to cultural stigma attached to rape and Kosovar women's reluctance to discuss sexual attacks.[34]

During 1998, the Special Rapporteur on violence against women received submissions regarding sexual violence in East Timor by Indonesian security forces. Among the violations reported were sexual violence, rape, forced marriage, forced prostitution and the intimidation of female relatives of suspected activists.[35]

Trafficking and forced prostitution
In a report submitted to the Commission on Human Rights in 2000, the Special Rapporteur on violence against women, noting that there is no universally accepted definition of trafficking, put forward the following working definition: trafficking in persons may be defined as the recruitment, transportation, purchase, sale, transfer, harbouring or receipt of persons by threat or use of violence, abduction, fraud, deception or coercion (including the abuse of authority) or debt bondage for the purpose of placing or holding such person, whether for pay or not, in forced labour or slavery-like practices in a community other than the one in which such person lived at the time of the original act. She also noted that trafficking is used to procure women for sex work, including prostitution; for manual labour in various settings; as well as for intimate relationships, such as marriage or adoption.[36]

Since trafficking is a crime, and therefore carried out clandestinely, comprehensive and reliable statistics are not available. However, a number of recent studies show that trafficking in women is a problem in countries all over the world:
• A recent study of international trafficking in women to the United States, prepared under the auspices of the Center for the Study of Intelligence, estimated that 45,000 to 50,000 women and children are trafficked annually to the United States. Trafficking violations range from slavery or slavery-like treatment of victims to criminal exploitation of smuggled economic migrants, including fair labour and safety standard violations. Charges in major cases of trafficking in women prosecuted in the United States since 1995 include: prostitution (one case with victims from Latin America, and six cases with victims from Asia); stripping and sexual touching (two cases with victims from Eastern Europe); sweatshop labour (two cases with victims from Asia); agricultural slave labour (two cases with victims from Latin America); domestic servitude (two cases with victims from Asia, one case with a victim from Latin America); and other servitude (two

cases with victims from Latin America). Over 150 cases of trafficking were prosecuted between 1996 and 1999 by the Involuntary Servitude Coordinator of the Department of Justice and numerous cases were prosecuted by other units of the Department.[37]
• The International Organization for Migration (IOM) estimates that approximately 50,000 women from the Dominican Republic work in the sex trade, primarily in Austria, Curacao, Germany, Greece, Haiti, Italy, the Netherlands, Panama, Puerto Rico, Spain, Switzerland, Venezuela and some Caribbean countries. Sex work abroad was commonly viewed in the Dominican Republic as an alternative for young impoverished women who were unable to find job opportunities at home.[38]
• An IOM study provides data that suggest that the number of women trafficked to Western Europe from Central and Eastern Europe increased during the early 1990s; in Belgium, the number of victims from Central and Eastern Europe who sought assistance in 1993 was twice as high as in 1991. In the Netherlands between 1992 and 1994, the number tripled. Over three quarters of the victims trafficked to the Netherlands were under age 25 (many were aged 15 to 18), and all were working as prostitutes.[39]
• Another IOM study, based on statistics from the Italian statistical authorities, provides some indication of the scale of trafficking of women for sexual exploitation. In 1994, 737 persons were charged with aiding and abetting, encouraging and exploiting prostitution in Italy. More than a third of those charged were foreigners, the majority from Central and Eastern Europe.[40]
• The Asian Coalition against Trafficking in Women estimates that 200,000 Bangladeshi women have been trafficked to Pakistan over the last 10 years, continuing at a rate of 200 to 400 women each month. In Thailand, 20,000 to 30,000 Burmese women are working as prostitutes through such forms of trafficking as deceptive job placements, abduction and the sale of girls from hill tribes. In Australia, 300 Thai women are trafficked into the country for prostitution each year by at least 10 international crime syndicates.[41]

IOM recently studied the availability and adequacy of statistical and other data on trafficking in 25 countries, including the 15 European Union Member States, Norway, Switzerland, and eight countries of Central and Eastern Europe and the developing world, selected because they are known to be source countries or points of transit. A considerable amount of information on trafficking and sexual exploitation is available—in 15 countries there is at least one research project under way on trafficking and in 10 countries an annual report is prepared on trafficking. However, this information is collected on an ad hoc basis and no single agency or institution coordinates data collection at the national level or facilitates the exchange of data in countries of the European Union. IOM recommends that steps be taken at the international and national levels to create a standard framework for data collection and more effective procedures for data exchange. IOM also cautions that, unless Governments and law enforcement agencies address the problem more vigorously, trafficking will remain a largely under-reported crime.[42]

Actions for change

The Beijing Platform for Action adopted by the Fourth World Conference on Women recommends that Governments adopt and/or implement legislation that emphasizes the prevention of violence against women and the prosecution of offenders, and that they periodically review and analyse the legislation to ensure its effectiveness in eliminating violence. So that women who are victims of violence will not be re-victimized, the Platform for Action urges Governments to maintain a gender perspective when designing policies related to violence against women, and to develop programmes for personnel responsible for implementing those policies to increase their understanding of the causes, consequences and mechanisms of violence against women.[43]

In 1999, Governments were asked to report on their actions to implement the Beijing Platform for Action in the 12 critical areas of concern. A review and appraisal of the implementation of the Beijing Platform for Action was prepared, based on responses to the United Nations Secretariat's questionnaire from 135 countries. Analysis of the reports indicates that a significant number of countries have introduced legislation regarding domestic violence, and some have introduced procedural and evidentiary reforms to ensure that offenders are prosecuted and that victims who survive are protected. Sexual violence against women by their husbands has been criminalized by several countries that did not already have such laws, including Austria, Belarus, Bhutan, Hungary, Mexico, Portugal and Seychelles. However, many countries have yet to introduce effective legal provisions and procedures to address the various forms of violence against women. And legislation in many countries still does not recognize rape in marriage or sexual abuse of children. Of the 35 Organization of American States member countries, 29 have now ratified the Inter-American Convention on the Punishment and Prevention of Violence against Women (the Convention of Belem do Para), 15 of them since the Fourth World Conference on Women. Most of the States parties to this Convention have elaborated legislation regarding violence against women, although many have not recognized marital rape as a criminal offence.[44]

Several Governments have established, or provided NGOs with funding for, services that offer support and assistance to survivors of violence, such as hotlines, counseling services, shelters and crisis centres, and emergency medical providers. Several countries have given assurances that women's non-governmental organizations will receive financial support and be included in the development of Government measures to address violence against women. Several countries have established units within the police force with the primary task of addressing violence against women; in some cases, guidelines and protocols have been introduced. However, this strategy has limitations, and wider training for all police is being pursued.[45]

Several countries have launched public education, awareness and advocacy campaigns to foster recognition of women's human rights, public disapproval of violence against women and acceptance of community responsibility for this violence. In several countries, innovative multimedia "zero tolerance" campaigns have been initiated in an effort to create a community consensus that violence against women is unacceptable.[46]

Despite these efforts, much remains to be done. The root causes of violence against women are poorly understood, and efforts to address violence are often reactive and fragmented. Sufficient resources have not been allocated for measures that address violence, and conflicting values and beliefs about women and their place in the family, the community and society undermine the development and implementation of such measures. Paucity of data and statistics on the various forms of violence against women is another obstacle to its eradication, as such information is required for policy formulation and implementation.

New efforts to eliminate harmful traditional practices

Female genital mutilation (FGM)

Based on the limited data available, it has been estimated that 100 to 132 million girls and women have been subjected to female genital mutilation worldwide. Each year, an estimated 2 million more girls will undergo some form of female genital mutilation. Female genital mutilation is known to be practised in 28 African countries, a few countries of Western Asia and some minority communities in other Asian countries. FGM is also reported among immigrant communities in Europe, North America, Australia and New Zealand.[47]

Female genital mutilation is reported in all Western African countries. Data from national studies show prevalence rates ranging from 5 per cent of women in the Niger to 94 per cent in Mali. At least half of all women have undergone the procedure in the majority of the countries surveyed. Prevalence rates in some countries in Eastern Africa are close to or above 90 per cent. In Central African countries for which data are available, prevalence rates range from 5 per cent in the Democratic Republic of Congo to 60 per cent in Chad. In Egypt, 97 per cent of women had undergone FGM according to a national study carried out by Demographic and Health Surveys (DHS) in 1995 (**chart 6.5**). Data are not available for Asian countries.

Experts identify four different levels of female genital mutilation (**see sidebar**). Type I and II represent about 80 per cent of all cases, while infibulation (type III), the most severe type of mutilation, represents 15

per cent of cases. [48] The procedure is usually carried out with rudimentary tools and in unsafe conditions, by either the elderly women of the village or the traditional birth attendant. In urban areas, wealthy families enlist the aid of health personnel, although WHO and other international organizations have repeatedly condemned the medicalization of the procedure. In Egypt and the Sudan, medical professionals perform an increasing number of these operations, according to recent DHS surveys.[49]

In spite of medical risks and serious and certain physical and psychological damage, the practice continues and many women support their daughters undergoing it. The reason most often given for this decision is to maintain social acceptance and to protect girls' reputations. In some communities, only women who have undergone infibulation are considered virgins. Where prevalence is high, as in Egypt, Mali and the Sudan, DHS surveys find that more than 70 per cent of women say that they support the practice of female genital mutilation. Younger women's opinions tend to parallel older women's. Opposition to female genital mutilation is relatively high only in the Central African Republic and Eritrea—56 and 39 per cent of women, respectively, favour discontinuation of the practice. In general, opposition appears to be substantially higher among women with higher education and those who live in urban areas. However, DHS findings indicate that even women who oppose the practice choose to have their daughters undergo FGM because of strong community pressure or the influence of older family members.[50]

It is often assumed that the practice is confined to particular social groups or to less educated families, particularly in rural areas. However, DHS data suggest that, in countries where the practice is widespread, a girl's level of education and whether her family resides in an urban or rural area have little effect on whether she will undergo FGM. In Egypt, 100 per cent of

Chart 6.5:

The traditional practice of female genital mutilation is prevalent in many African countries

	Coverage	Estimated prevalence of FGM (%), 1991/1998
Africa		
Benin	Not stated	50
Burkina Faso	Not stated	70
Cameroon	Southwest and far north provinces	20
Central African Republic	National	43
Chad	Three regions	60
Côte d'Ivoire	National	43
Dem. Rep. of the Congo	Not stated	5
Djibouti	Not stated	98
Egypt	National	97
Eritrea	National	95
Ethiopia	25 regions	85
Gambia	Limited study	80 [a]
Ghana	Upper East region and migrant settlements in Accra	30 [a]
Guinea	Not stated	50
Guinea-Bissau	Limited survey	50
Kenya	National	38
Liberia	Not stated	60
Mali	National	94
Mauritania	Not stated	25
Niger	National	5
Nigeria	Not stated	50 [a]
Senegal	National	20
Sierra Leone	Not stated	90
Somalia	Not stated	98
Sudan	National	89 [b]
Togo	Not stated	50
Uganda	Not stated	5
United Rep. of Tanzania	National	18

Sources: For Central African Republic, Côte d'Ivoire, Egypt, Eritrea, Kenya, Mali, Niger, Sudan and United Republic of Tanzania: Demographic and Health Surveys country reports (Columbia and Calverton, Maryland, Macro International, 1990-1998) and Dara Carr, *Female Genital Cutting* (Calverton, Maryland, Macro International, 1997); for other countries: WHO, "Female genital mutilation information kit" (1996), compiled from Fran Hosken, *The Hosken Report: Genital and Sexual Mutilation of Females*, fourth revised edition (Lexington, Massachussetts, WIN NEWS, 1993) and Nahid Toubia, *Female Genital Mutilation: A Call for Global Action* (New York, Women Ink., 1993).

Note: Data for some countries are based on small studies or anecdotal information.

[a] Data refer to 1985/1987.

[b] Data refer to 1989-1990

women with no education and 91 per cent of those with secondary education had undergone female genital mutilation. In Eritrea, the corresponding figures were 95 and 92 per cent, and in Mali, 94 and 90 per cent. In the Sudan, prevalence is higher among women who received secondary education than among those with no education—98 and 83 per cent, respectively.[51]

In the Central African Republic, Côte d'Ivoire, Kenya and the Niger, where overall prevalence rates are relatively low, education makes a difference. Prevalence rates for women with secondary education are half or less those of women with no education. Urban residence only appears to make a difference in Kenya, the Niger and the United Republic of Tanzania, countries where the practice is less widespread. [52]

Recent DHS surveys found almost no decline in rates of female genital mutilation, especially where overall prevalence is high. The only countries where prevalence rates have declined, slowly but continuously, are the Central African Republic, where fewer women aged 20 to 24 than women aged 45 to 49 had undergone FGM—43 and 53 per cent, respectively— and Kenya, where the corresponding figures were 32 and 48 per cent.[53]

*International and national actions
to eliminate female genital mutilation*
Harmful traditional practices, including female genital mutilation, have been brought to the attention of the international community through the efforts of the United Nations, its specialized agencies, funds and programmes, and civil society, including non-governmental organizations. In April 1997, WHO, UNICEF and the United Nations Population Fund (UNFPA) issued a joint statement on female genital mutilation in which they expressed their support of the efforts of Governments and communities to promote and protect the health and development of women and children and outlined strategies to eliminate female genital mutilation. The United Nations General Assembly has adopted several resolutions in which it has called on Governments to eradicate the practice.[54]

The Committee on the Elimination of Discrimination against Women has also called on Governments to eliminate female genital mutilation, as it constitutes a threat to women's health and well-being. Several countries have introduced specific legislation aimed at the eradication of female genital mutilation and other harmful practices, and have launched, or made efforts to continue, education and awareness campaigns to promote alternative rites of passage. Among countries that have adopted legislative measures to address the practice of female genital mutilation are Burkina Faso, Côte d'Ivoire, Djibouti, Egypt, Ghana, Guinea, Senegal, the United Republic of Tanzania and Togo. In Eritrea, recent civil reforms have banned female genital mutilation and early marriage.[55] Several countries with large immigrant communities that practise female genital mutilation, including Australia, Canada, New Zealand, the United Kingdom and the United States, have also introduced legislation to ban the practice.

In Africa, parliamentarians, Government ministers and members of the Inter-African Committee on Traditional Practices Affecting the Health of Women and Children (IAC) adopted the Ougadougou Declaration at a workshop for members of the West African Economic and Monetary Union, held in May 1999. The Declaration calls for the adoption of national legislation condemning female genital mutilation, and for the establishment of special services to control the migratory flow of circumcisers. The Organization of African Unity (OAU) First Ministerial Conference on Human Rights, held in Mauritius in April 1999, also urged African States to work toward the elimination of discrimination against women and the abolition of cultural practices that dehumanize or demean women and children.[56]

Women and girls represent
half of refugee populations
As of 1 January 1999, the population of concern to the Office of the United Nations High Commissioner for Refugees (UNHCR) was 21.5 million persons, including 11.5 million refugees **(see sidebar on definitions of population of concern to UNHCR)**.[57] Data by sex are available for only 4.2 million refugees assisted by UNHCR, roughly one third of the total refugee population; women comprise 50 per cent of the group **(see box on incorporating data on women in refugee statistics)**. Available data indicate that women represent 53 per cent of refugees in Eastern Europe, 51 per cent in Asia, and 50 per cent in Africa. In Latin America and the Caribbean, 47 per cent of refugees are women **(chart 6.6)**.

The available evidence from registries of refugees suggests that the female refugee population varies according to the reason for the refugee flow. In the case of mass population displacement caused by conflicts, women represent over half of the refugee population. For instance, mass registration of refugees in Georgia and the Federal Republic of Yugoslavia in 1996 found that 56 and 53 per cent, respectively, were women.[58]

Women make up a smaller proportion of asylum applicants—15 per cent in Italy in 1992, and a third in the Czech Republic, the Netherlands and Switzerland in 1995/1996. A little over a third—38 per cent—of asylum applicants in Canada in 1993 and in Sweden in 1997 were women. Most asylum

**Female genital
mutilation (FGM)**[a]

Female genital mutilation constitutes all procedures which involve partial or total removal of the external female genitalia or other injury to the female genital organs, whether for cultural or any other non-therapeutic reasons.
The levels of severity include:
• Type I: Excision of the prepuce with or without excision of part or all of the clitoris.
• Type II: Excision of the prepuce and clitoris together with partial or total excision of the labia minora.
• Type III: Excision of part or all of the external genitalia and stitching/narrowing of the vaginal opening (infibulation).
• Type IV (Unclassified): includes pricking, piercing, or incision of clitoris and/or labia; stretching of clitoris and/or labia; cauterization by burning of clitoris and surrounding tissues; scraping of the vaginal orifice or mutilation of the vagina; introduction of corrosive substances or herbs into the vagina to cause bleeding with the aim of tightening or narrowing the vagina; any other procedure that falls under the definition of FGM.

[a] Source: WHO, "Female genital mutilation: information kit" (WHO/FRH/WHD/96.26).

applicants are young males who leave refugee camps or their country of origin, often to seek work; in many cases, women follow later.[59]

Data for the end of 1998 suggest that the composition of refugee populations in camps is different from that of refugee populations in urban areas. In urban areas, women and girls often represent a smaller proportion of refugees—36 per cent in Latin America and 41 per cent in Africa. Europe is the only region where a majority of urban refugees are women and girls—55 per cent—but this regional average is affected by the large proportion of women and girls (61 per cent) among urban refugees in Croatia. Children under age 5 are also a smaller share of refugees in urban areas—9 per cent, compared to 14 per cent of the overall refugee population.[60]

In contrast, refugee camps are typically composed of families, and women comprise about 50 per cent of the population. The percentage of children under age 5 is higher in refugee camps than in urban areas. The common assumption that these

camps only contain women and children, however, is not borne out by available data. The proportions of women and men aged 18 or over in refugee camps are roughly equal.[61]

Women and girls often become refugees as a result of violence, including sexual violence. They remain vulnerable to sexual violence during flight, in refugee camps, in countries of asylum and resettlement, and during and after repatriation. Studies have found that refugee women and girls are often forced to engage in sexual activity in return for food or other necessities.[62] In response, UNHCR has issued guidelines for Governments and refugee camp staff on the protection of refugee women, as well as more specific guidelines on how to prevent and respond to sexual violence against women.[63]

Governments have increasingly recognized the importance of providing physical and psychological support for refugee women, particularly those who have suffered abuse, and several have established units that offer such support. Other Governments have set out to provide basic health care, education and economic opportunities for refugee women, many of whom are heads of household. Support has also been provided for grass-roots empowerment and economic security projects for women affected by conflict, including widows and the displaced. Identity papers are provided for undocumented persons, allowing women and men to exercise rights that were denied them while they were displaced.

UNHCR also set up programmes to address the needs of women who are returning from exile. For instance, Rwandan women members of parliament who returned from exile were trained in drafting gender-equality legislation. Another UNHCR project, Rwanda Women's Initiative, aims to enhance women's human rights and ensure their full integration in Rwandan society and to reduce sexual abuse. In Liberia, UNHCR supports the protection of returnee widows who face discriminatory inheritance laws. In Iran, Kenya, Malawi and the United States, UNHCR programmes have included education on women's rights for both refugee women and men.[64]

Women's participation in planning and implementing programmes for refugees is reportedly limited, in part due to cultural norms and women's lack of skills and self esteem. UNHCR programmes in Bulgaria,

Definitions of population of concern to UNHCR[a]

Refugees: persons recognized as refugees under the 1951 United Nations Convention relating to the Status of Refugees or its 1967 Protocol, the 1969 Organization of African Unity Convention Governing the Specific Aspects of Refugee Problems in Africa, persons recognized as refugees in accordance with the UNHCR statute, persons granted humanitarian status and those granted temporary protection.

Returned refugees or Returnees: refugees who have repatriated voluntarily to their place of origin and who remain of concern to UNHCR for a limited period after their return (two years for statistical purposes).

Asylum-seekers: persons whose applications for asylum are pending in the asylum procedure or who are otherwise registered as asylum-seekers.

Other categories: certain groups of internally displaced, including returned internally displaced; certain groups of war victims; certain nationals of the former Soviet Union whose nationality is undetermined and who have not established a national bond with any of the countries which emerged following the dissolution of the Soviet Union, etc.

[a] UNHCR, Refugees and Others of Concern to UNHCR: 1998 Statistical Overview (Geneva, July 1999).

Chart 6.6[✛]:

Available data show that there are generally as many women as men among UNHCR-assisted refugees

Region of asylum	UNHCR-assisted refugees, 1998	
	Total number (thousands)	% women
World	4 226	50
Africa	2 168	50
Northern Africa	168	51
Sub-Saharan Africa	2 000	50
Latin America and the Caribbean	35	47
Caribbean	1	16
Central America	29	50
South America	4	33
Asia	1 966	51
Eastern Asia	293	48
South-eastern Asia	4	30
Southern Asia	1 338	52
Central Asia	4	53
Western Asia	327	46
Oceania[a]	4	45
Developed regions		
Eastern Europe	54	53

Source: Prepared by the Statistics Division of the United Nations Secretariat from UNHCR, *Refugees and Others of Concern to UNHCR: 1998 Statistical Overview* (Geneva, 1999).
[a] Data for Papua New Guinea only.

> ✛ In this and subsequent charts, regional and subregional averages are unweighted (i.e., the averages do not take into account the size of the individual countries' populations) and are based only upon available data for that region (see page xi for fuller explanation).

Liberia, Slovenia, Uganda and Western Asia have addressed these problems and enabled women to participate effectively in managing the refugee community.

Gender-related persecution

The 1951 Refugee Convention extends legal protection to refugees who have a well-founded fear of being persecuted for reasons of race, religion, political opinion or membership in a social group, but fails to include those who fear persecution on the basis of sex, sexuality or gender. Since 1985, UNHCR has sought to ensure adequate protection for women, particularly in cases of gender-based persecution, such as sexual violence in conflict situations, forced abortion, forced sterilization, forced female genital mutilation, or severe discrimination as a result of transgressing social mores.

Several States have formulated guidelines for evaluating gender-related asylum claims. A growing number of countries, including Australia, Canada, France, the United Kingdom and the United States, have granted women refugee status on grounds of gender-based persecution, including fear of female genital mutilation, forced marriage, forced abortion and domestic violence. Rape and other forms of sexual violence have also been determined to constitute persecution when perpetrated or condoned by State officials.

POLITICAL DECISION-MAKING

The Convention on the Elimination of All Forms of Discrimination against Women emphasizes the importance of equal participation of women with men in public life. The Convention builds on the Universal Declaration of Human Rights, which includes the right to take part in the conduct of public affairs, either by voting for, or running as, a candidate for election, and on the International Covenant on Civil and Political Rights, which asserts the right of all people to self-determination. States that are parties to the Convention are obligated to ensure women equal

---

Incorporating data on women in refugee statistics

Over the last decade, there is a growing recognition of the need for statistics on refugees. Rather than an "undifferentiated mass of people with identical needs and capacities". refugees are increasingly seen as individuals with individual needs and resources. In particular, women refugees have different needs and experience conflict and displacement in different ways from men. This makes data by sex and data on female-headed households particularly important.

Obtaining demographic information on refugees is difficult for a variety of reasons, including:

- In emergency situations, it is generally difficult to make a reliable estimate, especially when life-saving interventions take priority;
- Populations move in and out refugees camps, often without notifying UNHCR;
- Figures may become quickly outdated as sudden arrivals and departures occur; natural demographic changes within the refugee population are not always properly recorded;
- UNHCR can only count refugees with whom it comes in contact on the basis of its mandate;
- Only a few receiving countries maintain a refugee register recording all changes in the refugee population;
- Generally only the inflow of refugees is recorded, while naturalization, departures, emigration, and cessation of refugee status are not recorded.

The different and sometimes conflicting interests of countries of origin, countries of destination, refugee populations and humanitarian agencies can have an effect on the accuracy of statistics. Finally, UNHCR and other offices collecting data on refugees use different definitions of "refugee". Inconsistency is compounded by the occasional inclusion of "internally displaced persons", as well as by shifting borders in countries of origin and destination.

However, accurate statistics on the refugee population and its characteristics—such as sex, age, ethnic origin, or household structure—are needed to provide effective protection and assistance. Also, when refugee populations wish to return to their homeland, even more detailed statistics on place of origin, occupation and education are needed to plan and implement effective repatriation and reintegration. As noted by the non-governmental organization Médecins sans Frontières, without registration, refugees have no rights and families cannot be reunified. During the 1999 Kosovo crisis, the identification, registration and documentation of refugees was considered a top priority.

UNHCR has initiated important work for the improvement of refugee statistics in the early 1990s. The agency now produces regularly updated and refined registration guidelines that provide field staff and operational partners with registration tools and approaches that can be adapted to various situations. Other measures include training agency and government staff stockpiling of registration kits, appointing two registration officers in Africa to provide technical expertise and coordination, and establishing a roster of UNHCR staff with skills and experience in refugee registration. Since the early 1990s, UNHCR has consolidated, analysed and published refugee statistics on a regular basis.

In addition, the United Nations Statistical Commission has made the reporting of statistical information on refugees an integral part of the measurement of international migration flows. The most recent set of Recommendations on Statistics of International Migration (revision 1) have expanded guidelines related to refugees over what was included in the earlier set of recommendations.

---

[a] Based on Jeff Crisp, "Who has counted refugees? UNHCR and the politics of numbers", New Issues in Refugee Research, Working Paper, No. 12 (June 1999).
[b] United Nations, *Recommendations on Statistics of International Migration*, revision 1 (United Nations publication, Sales No. E.98.XVII.14).

access to, and equal opportunities in, political and public life, including the right to vote and to be eligible for election. States are also obligated to ensure that women have equal opportunities to represent their Governments at the international level, and to participate in the work of international organizations.[65]

Formal limitations to women's access to suffrage and election still exist in a few countries with a Parliamentary system of government, such as Kuwait and the United Arab Emirates. Practical limitations exist in many countries for both women and men, although they sometimes affect women more than men.[66] In other countries, notably Namibia, Samoa and South Africa, voting and standing for election are recently acquired rights for many women and they have only been able to exercise these rights in one or two general elections.

Women vastly under-represented in political parties

Women are rarely represented in the higher echelons

Chart 6.7:

Women are under-represented in national parliaments everywhere, although women's representation has improved significantly in some regions

Percentage women among parliamentarians in Single or Lower chambers of national parliament

	1987	1995	1999
World Average	9	9	11
Africa			
Northern Africa	3	4	3
Sub-Saharan Africa	7	9	10
Latin America and the Caribbean			
Caribbean	9	11	13
Central America	8	10	13
South America	7	9	13
Asia			
Eastern Asia	18	12	13
South-eastern Asia	10	9	12
Southern Asia	5	5	5
Central Asia	..	8	8
Western Asia	4	4	5
Oceania	2	2	3
Developed regions			
Eastern Europe	26	9	10
Western Europe	14	18	21
Other developed regions	7	12	18

Source: Prepared by the Statistics Division of the United Nations Secretariat from data provided by the Inter-Parliamentary Union.

Note: Data for 1987 are based on the sex distribution of parliamentary seats from the last election held between 1982 and 1987. For 1995 and 1999, data refer to the sex distribution as of 1 July 1995 and 1 September 1999, respectively. Data shown for the latter two dates reflect changes, if any, after the most recent election prior to the given date, such as results of by-elections or replacements following a parliamentarian's resignation or death.

of political parties.[67] Without such representation, it is difficult for women to influence party policy, or to assume ministerial duties if the party gains ascendancy in government.

In 1996, the Inter-Parliamentary Union (IPU) gathered information on women's representation in the governing bodies of political parties and in senior posts: party leader (President or First Secretary), deputy leader, parliamentary group leader, and party spokesperson.[68] Among 871 parties in 80 countries, 585—67 per cent—had no women in their governing bodies. Only 11 per cent had a woman President or First Secretary, and 19 per cent had a woman deputy President or deputy First Secretary. Women represented 8 per cent of parliamentary group leaders and 9 per cent of party spokespersons.[69]

Some parties, generally at women's instigation, have introduced a quota system in governing bodies, either by requiring that a designated percentage of party leaders be women or by instituting a rule, written or implicit, that calls for a balance. In a number of countries of Latin America and the developed regions, parties have also established similar quota systems for candidates in legislative elections.

Women's parliamentary representation still very low

National parliaments

Gender parity in parliamentary representation is still far from being realized. Globally, the representation of women in Single or Lower chambers of parliament, which averaged 9 per cent in 1987 and again in 1995, rose to 11 per cent in 1999. The proportions of women in Single or Lower chambers of parliament increased slightly between 1987 and 1995 in most regions, but sharp declines in Eastern Europe and Eastern Asia affected the overall proportion (chart 6.7).

In Northern Africa, Oceania and Southern, Central and Western Asia in 1999, less than 10 per cent of parliamentarians[70] were women. No women were in national parliaments in Djibouti, Jordan, Kuwait, the United Arab Emirates and four small countries in Oceania (table 6.A and chart 6.7).

In sub-Saharan Africa in 1999, 10 per cent of parliamentarians were women, on average. In most countries of sub-Saharan Africa, women's representation was below 10 per cent (below 5 per cent in Chad, Equatorial Guinea, Ethiopia, Gambia, Kenya, Lesotho, Mauritania and Swaziland), but there are important exceptions: in South Africa, 30 per cent of parliamentarians were women; in Mozambique, 25 per cent; in Seychelles, 24 per cent; and in Namibia, 22 per cent (table 6.A).

Among developing regions in 1999, the highest percentages of women parliamentarians were recorded in Latin America and the Caribbean and in Eastern and South-eastern Asia. In Latin America and the Caribbean, on average, 13 per cent of parliamentarians were women. In seven of the 29 countries with data, women comprised less than 10 per cent of parliamentarians. The highest representation for women in the region was in Argentina and Cuba, where 28 per cent of parliamentarians were women (chart 6.8).

Women held at least 20 per cent of parliamentary seats in some countries of Eastern and South-eastern Asia, including China, the Democratic People's Republic of Korea, the Lao People's Democratic Republic and Viet Nam (table 6.A).

Women's parliamentary representation was highest in the developed regions. In 1999, in countries of Western Europe, 21 per cent of parliamentarians were women, and in the developed regions outside Europe, 18 per cent. The Nordic countries and the Netherlands had the world's highest representation—women accounted for more than a third of parliamentarians, as high as 43 per cent in Sweden. In the developed regions outside Europe, women's representation was higher than 20 per cent, except in the United States, where 13 per cent were women, and in Japan, where 5 per cent were women (table 6.A). In countries of Eastern Europe, on average, 10 per cent of parliamentarians were women.

Regional parliamentary assemblies

Women's representation increased in the two regional parliamentary assemblies that are elected by direct suffrage: the Central American Parliament and the European Parliament. In the Central American Parliament, the proportion of women elected increased from 10 per cent in 1991 to 15 per cent in 1996.

Chart 6.8:

In only 16 countries is women's representation in national parliaments above 25 per cent
Percentage women among parliamentarians[a], as of August 1999

Africa		Developed regions	
South Africa	30	Austria	26
		Denmark	37
Latin American and the Caribbean		Finland	37
		Germany	31
Argentina	28	Iceland	35
Cuba	28	Netherlands	36
		New Zealand	29
Asia		Norway	36
Viet Nam	26	Sweden	43

Source: Inter-Parliamentary Union.

[a] Single or Lower chambers of national parliaments.

In the European Parliament, the share of women increased from 20 per cent in 1989 to 30 per cent in 1999. In the 1999 elections to the European Parliament, the proportion of women elected increased considerably in a number of countries but decreased in others. All three Nordic countries in the European Parliament elected fewer women in 1999 than in 1994: Denmark, where the percentage of women among elected representatives decreased from 44 to 38; Finland, from 63 to 44; and Sweden, from 45 to 41.

Women largely excluded from executive branches of government

Countries around the world have different executive arrangements. Most have a President, a Prime Minister, and a Cabinet, but the authority of the President, the Prime Minister and the Cabinet varies among countries and over time within the same country.

Heads of State and Government

Since 1974, when Argentina became the first State to elect a woman President, only 17 States have elected a woman President (see box on heads of State or Government). Women have been elected head of State seven times in San Marino, a small State with a system of co-regency for six-month periods, and twice in Ireland, which has a republican system with a five-year presidential mandate.

The first woman Prime Minister took office in Sri Lanka in 1960. Since then, women have been Prime Minister in 22 States—four times in Sri Lanka, three times in Norway, and twice in Bangladesh, India and Pakistan.

Ministries

Women are still under-represented in decision-making positions in government cabinets. However, there is some evidence of improvement. In 1998, on average, 8 per cent of the world's cabinet ministers were women; compared to 6 per cent in 1994 (see sidebar on ministerial and sub-ministerial positions).[71] In 1998, there were 45 countries in which women held no ministerial positions, compared to 59 countries in 1994. Women held neither ministerial nor sub-ministerial positions in 13 countries in 1998, compared to 26 in 1994 (table 6.A and chart 6.9).

Between 1994 and 1998, the number of countries where women held at least 15 per cent of ministerial positions increased from 16 to 28, and the number of countries where women held at least 20 per cent of ministerial positions increased from 8 to 16 (table 6.A and chart 6.10). Sweden has the highest proportion of women ministers and, as of 1999, is the only country with more women than men ministers. After the 1994 elections in Sweden, women held 52 per cent of ministerial positions.[72] Their share dropped below parity

Chart 6.9:

In 13 countries there were no women in either ministerial or sub-ministerial positions in government as of January 1998

Africa
Somalia
Sudan

Asia and Oceania
Afghanistan
Iraq
Lao People's Democratic Republic
Lebanon
Micronesia (Fed. States of)
Myanmar
Qatar
Saudi Arabia
United Arab Emirates
Yemen

Developed regions
Monaco

Source: *Women's Indicators and Statistics Database (Wistat), Version 4,* CD-ROM (United Nations publication, Sales No. E.00.XVII.4), based on data compiled by the Division for the Advancement of Women of the United Nations Secretariat.

Ministerial and sub-ministerial positions
Ministerial level includes: ministers, Secretaries of State, heads of central banks and of agencies in the Cabinet. Sub-ministerial level includes: deputy and vice ministers or their equivalent, permanent secretaries or their equivalent, and deputy permanent secretaries or their equivalent, such as directors and advisers.

Chart 6.10:

In only 16 countries did women hold at least 20 per cent of ministerial positions in 1998

Percentage of ministerial positions filled by women, January 1998

Africa	
Gambia	29
Mali	21
Seychelles	33

Latin American and the Caribbean	
Barbado	27
Dominica	20
Ecuador	20

Oceania	
Palau	20

Developed regions	
Austria	20
Denmark	41
Finland	29
Ireland	21

Developed regions (cont.)	
Netherlands	28
Norway	20
Sweden	43
United Kingdom	24
United States	26

Source: Prepared by the Statistics Division of the United Nations Secretariat from *Women's Indicators and Statistics Database (Wistat), Version 4*, CD-ROM (United Nations publication, Sales No. E.00.XVII.4), based on data compiled by the Division for the Advancement of Women of the United Nations Secretariat).

Note: Ministerial positions include ministers, secretaries of State, heads of central banks and of agencies in the Cabinet.

in 1998, but increased again in 1999 to the world's highest representation, 55 per cent.[73]

Most ministerial and sub-ministerial positions are still held by men around the world. In 1998, women held fewer than 5 per cent of ministerial-level positions, on average, in Asia and Northern Africa. The average was slightly higher but still at or below 10 per cent in sub-Saharan Africa, Latin America and Eastern Europe. The average exceeded 10 per cent only in the Caribbean, Western Europe and the developed regions outside Europe **(chart 6.11)**.

Women generally hold a greater percentage of sub-ministerial level posts than ministerial-level posts. However, in some countries where women are relatively well represented at the ministerial level, their representation at the sub-ministerial level is lower **(table 6.A and chart 6.11)**.

Women's representation in leadership positions, whether ministerial or sub-ministerial, is generally higher in social ministries and law and justice ministries than in economic and political ministries. Women hold over 10 per cent of ministerial posts in all fields in the Caribbean and in developed regions outside Europe and in nearly all fields in Eastern

Chart 6.11:

In Governments, women are still poorly represented at both ministerial and sub-ministerial levels

Percentage of positions held by women

	January 1994		January 1998	
	Ministerial level	Sub-ministerial level	Ministerial level	Sub-ministerial level
Africa				
Northern Africa	2	4	3	6
Sub-Saharan Africa	6	7	8	10
Latin America and the Caribbean				
Caribbean	8	17	11	23
Central America	10	11	6	15
South America	5	6	10	14
Asia				
Eastern Asia	2	1	..[a]	..[a]
South-eastern Asia	3	3	4	7
Southern Asia	5	2	4	3
Cental Asia	3	4	5	5
Western Asia	2	1	2	3
Oceania	5	5	5	10
Developed Regions				
Eastern Europe	3	6	8	14
Western Europe	16	11	16	14
Other developed regions	11	19	12	21

Source: Prepared by the Statistics Division of the United Nations Secretariat from *Women's Indicators and Statistics Database (Wistat), Version 4*, CD-ROM (United Nations publication, Sales No. E.00.XVII.4), based on data compiled by the Division for the Advancement of Women of the United Nations Secretariat.

Note: Ministerial level includes ministers, secretaries of State, heads of central banks and of agencies in the Cabinet; Sub-ministerial level includes: deputy and vice ministers or their equivalent, permanent secretaries or their equivalent, and deputy permanent secretaries or their equivalent, such as directors and advisors.

[a] Average not shown because data are available for only one country.

Europe and Western Europe (chart 6.12).

Though goals unmet, women making gains in United Nations professional staff

Since 1985, the United Nations General Assembly has set goals for increasing women's representation among the professional staff of the United Nations. The first goal, to achieve 30 per cent representation by 1990, was met in 1991. In December 1998, the General Assembly reaffirmed the goal of 50/50 gender distribution by the year 2000 in all categories of posts within the United System. Although statistics show some improvement, the goal is still far from being met. Women represented 39 per cent of professional staff on geographical appointments as of November 1999, an increase from 34 per cent in 1995 (chart 6.13).

Women in the United Nations have lower representation at the higher levels. Women comprised 48 per cent of the junior professionals but only 21 per cent of senior management in 1999. Of 21 Under-Secretary-Generals, two were women. Although the rate of progress is slow, the representation of women at the senior professional level has improved—from

25 percent in 1995 to 33 per cent in 1999.

Women's representation among professional staff in the specialized agencies of the United Nations at the end of 1998 was 32 per cent, and among senior managers, 16 per cent, both lower than in the United Nations Secretariat. However, among the specialized

Chart 6.13:

Although increasing, women's share of senior management positions in the United Nations is still small
% women among professional staff in the United Nations

	1980	1995	1999
All professionals	19	34	39
Junior profesionals	41	48	48
Mid-level professionals	20	37	40
Senior professionals	7	25	33
Senior managers	5	17	21

Source: Reports of the Secretary-General on the composition of the Secretariat (A/35/528 and A/50/540) and on the improvement of the status of women in the Secretariat (E/CN.6/2000/4).

Note: Data relate to professional staff in posts subject to geographical distribution. Junior professionals refer to staff at the P-1 and P-2 levels; mid-level professionals to P-3 and P-4; senior professionals to P-5 and D-1; and senior managers to D-2, Assistant Secretary-General and Under-Secretary-General.

Chart 6.12:

Women are often better represented in ministerial posts in social and law and justice ministries
Percentage of positions[a] held by women, by ministry, as of January 1998

	All ministries	Chief executive	Economic	Law and Justice	Social	Political
Africa						
Northern Africa	6	3	3	10	11	0
Southern Africa	15	17	9	0	23	15
Rest of sub-Saharan Africa	9	5	5	7	17	5
Latin America and the Caribbean						
Caribbean	19	26	11	16	29	18
Central America	13	10	11	15	17	1
South America	12	9	8	22	20	8
Asia						
South-eastern Asia	6	3	6	1	8	3
Southern Asia	4	4	3	0	4	2
Central Asia	4	2	5	20	4	1
Western Asia	3	1	3	9	6	0
Oceania	9	5	7	2	15	4
Developed regions						
Eastern Europe	12	12	12	17	18	7
Western Europe	13	7	8	21	17	13
Other developed regions	20	23	16	19	28	14

Source: Prepared by the Statistics Division of the United Nations Secretariat from *Women's Indicators and Statistics Database (Wistat), Version 4*, CD-ROM (United Nations publication, Sales No. E.00.XVII.4), based on data compiled by the Division for the Advancement of Women of the United Nations Secretariat.

Note: Eastern Asia not shown because data are available for only one country.

[a] Both ministerial and sub-ministerial positions.

Women heads of State or Government[a]

Country	Presidents	Years in office
Argentina	Maria Estela Martinez de Péron	1974-1976
Bolivia	Lydia Gueiler Tejada	1979-1980
Finland	Tarja Halonen	2000-
Germany (former Dem. Rep. of)	Sabine Bergmann-Pohl	1990
Guyana	Janet Jagan	1997-1999
Haiti	Ertha Pascal Trouillot	1990-1991
Iceland	Vigdis Finnbogadottir	1980-1996
Ireland	Mary Robinson	1990-1997
	Mary McAleese	1997-
Latvia	Vaira Vike-Freiberga	1999-
Liberia	Ruth Perry	1996-1997
Malta	Agatha Barbara	1982-1987
Nicaragua	Violeta Barrios de Chamorro	1990-1996
Panama	Mireya Moscoso	1999-
Philippines	Corazon Aquino	1986-1992
Sri Lanka	Chandrika Kumaratunge	1994-
Switzerland	Ruth Dreifuss	1999

Country	Prime Ministers	Years in office
Bangladesh	Begum Khaleda Zia	1991-1996
	Sheikh Hasina Wajed	1996-
Bulgaria	Reneta Indzhova	1994
Burundi	Sylvie Kinigi	1993-1994
Canada	Kim Campbell	1993
Central African Rep.	Elisabeth Domitien	1974-1976
Dominica	Mary Eugenia Charles	1980-1995
France	Edith Cresson	1991-1992
Guyana	Janet Jagan	1997
Haiti	Claudette Werleigh	1995-1996
India	Indira Gandhi	1966-1977; 1980-1984
Israel	Golda Meir	1969-1974
Lithuania	Kazimiera Prunskiene	1990-1991
New Zealand	Jenny Shipley	1997-1999
	Helen Clark	1999-
Norway	Gro Harlem Brundtland	1981; 1986-1989; 1990-1996
Pakistan	Benazir Bhutto	1988-1990; 1993-1996
Poland	Hanna Suchocka	1992-1993
Portugal	Maria de Lourdes Pintasilgo	1979-1980
Rwanda	Agathe Uwilingiyimana	1993-1994
Sri Lanka	Sirimavo Bandaranaike	1960-1965; 1970-1977; 1994-
	Chandrika Kumaratunge	1994
Turkey	Tansu Çiller	1993-1996
United Kingdom	Margaret Thatcher	1979-1990
Yugoslavia	Milka Planinc	1982-1986

agencies, women have been better represented in organizations headed by women: in UNICEF, women make up 48 per cent of staff and 39 per cent of senior managers; in UNFPA, 47 per cent of staff and 39 per cent of senior managers; in the World Food Programme (WFP), 40 per cent of staff and 22 per cent of senior managers; in UNHCR, 38 per cent of staff and 14 per cent of senior managers.[74] Other agencies where women have relatively high representation are the United Nations Development Programme (UNDP), where women are 38 per cent of staff and 21 per cent of senior managers, and the United Nations Educational, Scientific and Cultural Organization (UNESCO), 39 per cent of staff and 20 per cent of senior managers. Women were best represented in senior management in the Pan American Health Organization and the Joint United Nations Programme on HIV/AIDS; in both organizations women comprised 50 per cent of senior managers. Latest data for 2000 show that women constituted 50 per cent of the total staff and 60 per cent of senior managers in UNFPA.[75] ■

Source: Inter-Parliamentary Union and Torild Skard, "Women leaders—leaders for women?" (book in preparation).

Note: San Marino has a system of co-regency for six-month periods. The following women served as head of state: Maria Lea Pedini in 1981, Gloriana Ramocchini in 1984 and 1989-90, Edda Ceccoli in 1991-1992, Patricia Busignani in 1993, Rosa Zafferani in 1999, and Maria Domenica Michelott in 2000.

[a] Excluding Queens and Governors-General.

Notes

1 In addition, New Zealand ratified the Convention in 1985 on its own behalf and on behalf of the Cook Islands and Niue.

2 Convention on the Elimination of All Forms of Discrimination against Women, United Nations Treaty Series, vol. 1249, No. 20378.

3 General Assembly resolution 48/104.

4 Ibid.

5 See United Nations, *Report of the Fourth World Conference on Women, Beijing, 4-15 September 1995* (United Nations publication, Sales No. 96.IV.13), chap. I, resolution I, annexes I and II.

6 In some cases, the term "domestic violence" also includes violence by other family members. For the purposes of this section, domestic violence is used to mean violence against women by intimate (male) partners or ex-partners.

7 United Nations, *Violence against Women in the Family* (United Nations publication, Sales No. E.89.IV.5).

8 M. Yoshihama et al., "Physical, sexual and emotional abuse by male intimates: experiences of women in Japan", *Violence and Victims,* vol. 9, No. 1 (1994).

9 M.C. Ellsberg, "Candies in hell: domestic violence against women in Nicaragua" (Umea University, Sweden, 1997).

10 C. Watts et al., "Strengthening the health sector response to women experiencing violence in Zimbabwe" (1997).

11 S.G. Diniz et al., "Gender violence and reproductive health", *International Journal of Obstetrics and Gynecology,* vol. 63, No. 1 (1998).

12 M. Crawford et al., "Women killing: intimate femicide in Ontario 1974–1990", unpublished (1991).

13 J. Arbuckle et al., "Safe at home? domestic violence and other homicides among women in New Mexico", *Annals of Emergency Medicine,* vol. 27, No. 2 (1997).

14 D. Ellis et al., "Rethinking estrangement, interventions and intimate femicide", *Violence Against Women,* vol. 3, No. 6 (1997).

15 Crawford, loc. cit.

16 R. Fischbach et al., "Domestic violence and mental health: correlates and conundrums within and across cultures", *Social Science and Medicine,* vol. 45, No. 8 (1997); J. Heise et al., "Violence against women, the hidden burden", World Bank discussion paper (Washington, D.C., 1994).

17 D. Ellis et al., loc. cit.; L. Akanda et al., "Women and violence: a comparative study of rural and urban violence against women in Bangladesh" (Dhaka, 1985); F. Shaheed, "The experience in Pakistan", in M. Davies, ed., *Women and Violence: Realities and Responses Worldwide* (London, Zed Books, 1994).

18 See report of the Secretary-General on traditional or customary practices affecting the health of women (A/54/34) para. 15.

19 G. Howard and G. Newman, "Rape: the most reported crime by countries in the United Nations Criminal Justice System", United Nations, *Global Report on Crime and Justice* (New York, Oxford University Press, 1999).

20 UNICEF, *Women in Transition,* Monitoring Report, No. 6 (Florence, 1999).

21 Anna Alvazzi del Frate, *Victims of Crime in the Developing World,* UNICRI publication, No. 57 (Rome, 1998).

22 D. Finkelhor, "The international epidemiology of child sexual abuse", *Child Abuse and Neglect,* vol. 18, No. 5 (1994); Center for Health and Gender Equity, "Marital health and behavioural outcomes of sexual abuse: data summary" (Takoma Park, Maryland, 1999).

23 K. Fiscella et al., "Does child abuse predict adolescent pregnancy?", *Pediatrics,* vol. 101 (1998); H. Grimstad et al., "Abuse history and health risk behaviors in pregnancy", *Acta obstetrica et gynecologia,* vol. 77 (1998); D.G. Kilpatrick, "A 2-year longitudinal analysis of the relationships between violent assault and substance use in women", *Journal of Consulting and Clinical Psychology,* vol. 65 (1997); W. Pederson et al., "Alcohol and sexual victimization: a longitudinal study of Norwegian girls", *Addiction,* vol. 91, No. 4 (1996).

24 S.P. Walker et al., "Nutritional and Health Determinants of School Failure and Dropout in Adolescent Girls in Kingston, Jamaica" (International Center for Research on Women, 1994).

25 D. Halpérin et al., "Prevalence of child sexual abuse among adolescents in Geneva: results of a cross-sectional survey", *British Medical Journal,* vol. 312 (1996).

26 N. Dickson et al., "First sexual intercourse: age, coercion, and later regrets reported by a birth cohort", *British Medical Journal,* vol. 316 (1998).

27 "Ending violence against women", *Population Reports,* vol. XXVII, No. 4 (Johns Hopkins University, 1999).

28 J. Abma et al., "Young women's degree of control over first intercourse: an exploratory analysis", *Family Planning Perspectives,* vol. 30, No. 1 (1998).

29 Judith Gardam and Michelle Jarvis, "Reviewing the Beijing Platform for Action: What has been achieved at the international level for women in armed conflict?", *Columbia Human Rights Law Review,* vol. 31, No. 3; Report of the Expert of the Secretary-General, Ms. Graça Michel, on the impact of armed conflict on children (A/51/306); C.A. Palmer and A.B. Zwi, "Women, health and humanitarian aid in conflict", *Disasters,* vol. 22, No. 3 (1998).

30 Gardam and Jarvis, loc. cit.; Michel, loc. cit.

31 UNICEF, *Women in Transition...*

32 Gardam and Jarvis, loc. cit.; Michel, loc. cit.

33 See report on the situation of human rights in Rwanda (E/CN.4/1996/68) paras. 16 and 17.

34 Human Rights Watch report entitled "Rape as a weapon of ethnic cleansing".

35 Report of the Special Rapporteur on violence against women, its causes and consequences (E/CN.4/1998/54).

36 Report of the Special Rapporteur on violence against women, its causes and consequences, on trafficking in women, women's migration and violence against women (E/CN.4/2000/68).

37 Amy O'Neill Richard, *International Trafficking in Women to the United States: A Contemporary Manifestation of Slavery and Organized Crime,* monograph (Center for the Study of Intelligence, 1999).

Notes (cont'd)

38 IOM, *Trafficking in Women from the Dominican Republic for Sexual Exploitation* (June 1996).

39 IOM, *Trafficking and Prostitution: The Growing Exploitation of Migrant Women from Central and Eastern Europe* (May 1995).

40 IOM, *Trafficking in Women to Italy for Sexual Exploitation* (June 1996).

41 IOM, "Prostitution in Asia increasingly involves trafficking", *Trafficking In Migrants*, No. 15 (Geneva, June 1997).

42 IOM, "Analysis of data and statistical resources available in the EU member states on trafficking in humans, particularly in women and children for purposes of sexual exploitation: a project of the International Organisation for Migration (IOM) for the European Commission's STOP programme: final report", unpublished.

43 United Nations, *Report of the Fourth World Conference on Women...*

44 United Nations, Report of the Secretary-General on the review and appraisal of the implementation of the Beijing Platform for Action (E/CN.6/2000/PC/2).

45 Ibid.

46 Ibid.

47 WHO, "Female genital mutilation: information kit" (WHO/FRH/WHD/96.26).

48 Ibid.

49 Dara Carr, *Female Genital Mutilation* (Calverton, Maryland, Macro International, 1997).

50 Ibid.

51 Ibid.

52 Ibid.

53 Ibid.

54 For example, resolutions 53/117 and 54/133.

55 Statement of the Inter-African Committee at the fifty-fifth session of the Commission on Human Rights.

56 See CONF/HR/DECL (I), para. 6.

57 UNHCR, *Refugees and Others of Concern to UNHCR: 1998 Statistical Overview* (Geneva, July 1999).

58 UNHCR, "Asylum in Europe: arrivals, stay and gender from a data perspective", paper prepared for a regional population meeting, organized by the Economic Commission for Europe, the Government of Hungary and the United Nations Population Fund, Budapest, 7–9 December 1998.

59 Ibid.

60 UNHCR, "Statistics and registration: a progress report" (EC/50/SC/CRP.10).

61 Ibid.

62 Report of the Special Rapporteur on violence against women, its causes and consequences (ECN.4/1998/54).

63 UNHCR, "Guidelines on the protection of refugee women" (Geneva, 1991); and UNHCR, "Sexual violence against refugees: guidelines on prevention and response" (Geneva, 1995).

64 UNHCR, "1999 global appeal and a woman's lot", *Refugees Magazine*, No. 111 (Spring 1998).

65 The section on political decision-making is based largely on a report entitled "Women and politics" prepared IPU.

66 IPU, *Women and Political Power*, Reports and Documents Series, No. 19 (Geneva, 1992).

67 Ibid.

68 See IPU study entitled "Men and Women in Politics: Democracy Still in the Making", Reports and Documents Series, No. 28 (1997).

69 Information on party leadership (president and deputy president), group leaders and spokespersons was available for smaller groups of parties–from 388 to 418 parties.

70 All references to women in national parliaments pertain to Single and Lower chambers of parliament.

71 Average percentages were calculated by the Statistics Division of the United Nations Secretariat on the basis of percentage women in ministerial positions for all countries for which data are available.

72 United Nations, *The World's Women 1995: Trends and Statistics* (United Nations publication, Sales No. E.95.XVII.2).

73 Data on women in the executive were provided by IPU.

74 Calculated by the Statistics Division of the United Nations Secretariat from ACC, Personnel statistics (ACC/2000/PER/R.10), forthcoming.

75 Based on statistics provided by UNFPA to the Office of the Special Adviser on Gender Issues and Advancement of Women.

Table 6.A
Women in public life

Country or area	% parliamentary seats in Single or Lower chamber occupied by women			% women in decision-making positions in government				Year of ratification of CEDAW[a]	Whether national plan of action provided to the UN Secretariat[b]
				Ministerial level		Sub-ministerial level			
	1987	1995	1999	1994	1998	1994	1998		
Africa									
Algeria	2	7	3	4	0	8	10	1996 [a]	Yes
Angola	15	10	15	7	14	2	10	1986 [a]	Yes
Benin	4	8	6	10	13	0	5	1992	..
Botswana	5	9	9	6	14	6	20	1996 [a]	Yes
Burkina Faso	..	4	8	7	10	14	10	1987 [a]	Yes
Burundi	9	..	6	7	8	0	0	1992	Yes
Cameroon	14	12	6	3	6	5	6	1994 [a]	..
Cape Verde	12	8	11	13	13	9	50	1980 [a]	Yes
Central African Republic	4	4	7	5	4	17	6	1991 [a]	..
Chad	..	16	2	5	0	0	6	1995 [a]	..
Comoros	0	0	..	0	7	0	0	1994 [a]	..
Congo	10	2	12	6	6	0	0	1982	Yes
Côte d'Ivoire	6	5	8	8	3	0	3	1995 [a]	..
Dem. Rep. of the Congo	5	5	..	6	..	7	..	1986	..
Djibouti	0	0	0	0	0	3	3	1998 [a]	..
Egypt	4	2	2	4	6	0	4	1981	Yes
Equatorial Guinea	3	8	4	4	4	0	5	1984 [a]	..
Eritrea	..	21	15	7	5	13	6	1995 [a]	Yes
Ethiopia	<1	5	2	10	5	10	16	1981	Yes
Gabon	13	6	8	7	3	12	9	1983	..
Gambia	8	..	2	0	29	7	17	1993	..
Ghana	..	8	9	11	9	12	9	1986	Yes
Guinea	..	7	9	9	8	8	20	1982	Yes
Guinea-Bissau	15	10	10	4	18	19	16	1985	..
Kenya	2	3	4	0	0	4	9	1984 [a]	Yes
Lesotho	..	5	4	6	6	21	15	1995 [a]	..
Liberia	6	6	..	5	8	0	6	1984 [a]	..
Libyan Arab Jamahiriya	..	..	..	0	7	0	0	1989 [a]	..
Madagascar	1	4	8	0	19	4	8	1989	..
Malawi	10	6	8	9	4	9	4	1987 [a]	Yes
Mali	4	2	12	10	21	0	0	1985	Yes
Mauritania	..	0	4	0	4	6	6	..	..
Mauritius	7	3	8	3	..	7	..	1984 [a]	..
Morocco	0	1	1	0	0	0	8	1993 [a]	Yes
Mozambique	16	25	25	4	0	9	15	1997 [a]	Yes
Namibia	..	18	22	10	8	2	17	1992 [a]	Yes
Niger	..	4	..	5	10	19	8	1999 [a]	Yes
Nigeria	..	..	..	3	6	11	4	1985	Yes
Rwanda	13	17	17	9	5	10	20	1981	..
Sao Tome and Principe	12	7	9	0	0	20	33	..	..
Senegal	11	12	12	7	7	0	15	1985	Yes
Seychelles	16	27	24	31	33	21	16	1992 [a]	..
Sierra Leone	..	..	6	0	10	2	11	1988	..
Somalia	4	..	..	0	0	0	0	..	..
South Africa	2	25	30	6	..	2	..	1995 [a]	..

Table 6.A (cont'd):
Women in public life

Country or area	% parliamentary seats in Single or Lower chamber occupied by women			% women in decision-making positions in government				Year of ratification of CEDAW [a]	Whether national plan of action provided to the UN Secretariat [b]
				Ministerial level		Sub-ministerial level			
	1987	1995	1999	1994	1998	1994	1998		
Africa (cont'd)									
Sudan	8	8	5	0	0	0	0	..	Yes
Swaziland	4	3	3	0	6	6	16	..	Yes
Togo	5	1	..	5	9	0	0	1983 [a]	..
Tunisia	6	7	7	4	3	14	10	1985	Yes
Uganda	..	17	18	10	13	7	13	1985	Yes
United Republic of Tanzania	..	11	16	13	13	4	11	1985	Yes
Zambia	3	7	9	5	3	9	12	1985	Yes
Zimbabwe	11	15	14	3	12	25	6	1991 [a]	Yes
Latin America and the Caribbean									
Antigua and Barbuda	0	5	..	0	0	44	41	1989 [a]	..
Argentina	5	22	28	0	8	3	9	1985	Yes
Bahamas	4	8	15	23	17	35	44	1993 [a]	..
Barbados	4	11	..	0	27	16	20	1980	..
Belize	4	3	7	6	0	13	17	1990	Yes
Bolivia	3	11	12	0	6	8	11	1990	Yes
Brazil	5	7	6	5	4	11	13	1984	Yes
Chile	..	8	11	13	13	0	8	1989	Yes
Colombia	5	11	12	11	18	6	27	1982	Yes
Costa Rica	11	14	19	10	15	9	21	1986	Yes
Cuba	34	23	28	0	5	9	11	1980	Yes
Dominica	10	9	9	9	20	38	33	1980	..
Dominican Republic	8	12	16	4	10	14	16	1982	..
Ecuador	1	4	17	6	20	0	6	1981	Yes
El Salvador	7	11	17	10	6	7	29	1981	Yes
Grenada	13	20	..	10	14	14	43	1990	..
Guatemala	7	8	13	19	0	7	15	1982	..
Guyana	37	20	18	12	15	25	22	1980	..
Haiti	8	..	4	13	0	10	14	1981	Yes
Honduras	8	7	9	11	11	22	17	1983	Yes
Jamaica	12	12	13	5	12	17	22	1984	Yes
Mexico	11	14	17	5	5	5	7	1981	Yes
Nicaragua	15	16	10	10	5	8	13	1981	..
Panama	6	8	..	13	6	15	5	1981	Yes
Paraguay	2	3	3	0	7	3	6	1987 [a]	Yes
Peru	6	10	11	6	10	11	23	1982	Yes
Saint Kitts and Nevis	7	0	13	..	0	..	15	1985 [a]	Yes
Saint Lucia	0	0	11	8	10	0	7	1982 [a]	Yes
Saint Vincent and the Grenadines	5	10	5	0	10	0	14	1981 [a]	..
Suriname	8	6	16	0	5	0	16	1993 [a]	..
Trinidad and Tobago	17	19	11	19	14	13	19	1990	Yes
Uruguay	4	7	7	0	7	5	14	1981	..
Venezuela	4	6	13	11	3	0	7	1983	Yes

Table 6.A (cont'd):
Women in public life

Country or area	% parliamentary seats in Single or Lower chamber occupied by women			% women in decision-making positions in government				Year of ratification of CEDAW [a]	Whether national plan of action provided to the UN Secretariat [b]
				Ministerial level		Sub-ministerial level			
	1987	1995	1999	1994	1998	1994	1998		
Asia									
Afghanistan	..	..	..	0	0	0	0	..	..
Armenia	..	..	..	3	0	2	5	1993 [a]	..
Azerbaijan	..	2	12	5	10	0	5	1995 [a]	..
Bahrain	..	..	..	0	0	0	1	..	Yes
Bangladesh	9	11	9	8	5	2	0	1984 [a]	Yes
Bhutan	2	0	2	22	0	0	8	1981	..
Brunei Darussalam	..	..	..	0	0	0	6	..	Yes
Cambodia	21	6	8	0	..	7	..	1992 [a]	Yes
China	21	21	22	6	..	4	..	1980	Yes
Cyprus	1	4	5	7	0	4	4	1985 [a]	..
Dem. People's Rep. of Korea	21	20	20	0	..	2	..	..	Yes
Georgia	..	6	7	0	4	3	6	1994 [a]	Yes
India	8	8	8	3	..	7	..	1993	Yes
Indonesia	12	12	..	6	3	1	1	1984	Yes
Iran (Islamic Republic of)	1	3	5	0	0	1	1	..	Yes
Iraq	13	11	6	0	0	0	0	1986 [a]	Yes
Israel	8	9	12	4	0	5	9	1991	Yes
Jordan	0	1	0	3	2	0	0	1992	Yes
Kazakhstan	..	..	12	6	5	0	2	1998 [a]	Yes
Kuwait	0	0	0	0	0	0	7	1994 [a]	Yes
Kyrgyzstan	..	5	1	0	4	9	3	1997 [a]	Yes
Lao People's Dem. Rep.	..	9	21	0	0	5	0	1981	..
Lebanon	..	2	2	0	0	0	0	1997 [a]	Yes
Malaysia	5	8	8	7	16	0	13	1995 [a]	Yes
Maldives	2	6	6	5	6	6	11	1993 [a]	Yes
Mongolia	25	4	8	0	0	0	0	1981	Yes
Myanmar	..	..	..	0	0	0	0	1997 [a]	Yes
Nepal	6	..	6	0	3	0	0	1991	..
Oman	..	..	..	0	0	2	4	..	Yes
Pakistan	9	2	2	4	7	1	1	1996 [a]	Yes
Philippines	9	9	12	8	10	11	19	1981	Yes
Qatar	..	..	..	0	0	3	0	..	Yes
Republic of Korea	3	2	4	4	..	0	..	1984	Yes
Saudi Arabia	..	..	..	0	0	0	0	..	..
Singapore	4	4	4	0	0	4	8	1995 [a]	Yes
Sri Lanka	..	5	5	3	13	6	5	1981	..
Syrian Arab Republic	9	10	10	7	8	0	0	..	Yes
Tajikistan	..	3	3	3	6	7	6	1993 [a]	..
Thailand	3	6	6	0	4	2	7	1985 [a]	Yes
Turkey	1	2	4	5	5	0	17	1985 [a]	Yes
Turkmenistan	..	18	18	3	4	0	0	1997 [a]	..
United Arab Emirates	0	0	0	0	0	0	0	..	Yes
Uzbekistan	..	6	6	3	3	5	13	1995 [a]	..
Viet Nam	18	18	26	5	0	0	5	1982	Yes
Yemen	..	1	1	0	0	0	0	1984 [a]	Yes

Table 6.A (cont'd):
Women in public life

Country or area	% parliamentary seats in Single or Lower chamber occupied by women			% women in decision-making positions in government				Year of ratification of CEDAW [a]	Whether national plan of action provided to the UN Secretariat [b]
				Ministerial level		Sub-ministerial level			
	1987	1995	1999	1994	1998	1994	1998		
Oceania									
Fiji	2	4	11	10	10	6	16	1995 (a)	Yes
Kiribati	0	0	5	..	..	..	..	..	..
Marshall Islands	..	3	..	8	0	13	13	..	..
Micronesia (Fed. States of)	..	0	0	0	0	11	0	..	..
Nauru	..	..	0	..	..	..	..	..	..
Palau	..	0	0	..	20	..	17	..	..
Papua New Guinea	0	0	2	0	0	0	8	1995 (a)	..
Samoa	4	4	8	..	7	..	12	1992 (a)	..
Solomon Islands	0	2	2	5	6	0	8	..	..
Tonga	0	3	..	..	..	..	..	..	..
Vanuatu	4	2	0	7	0	0	7	1995 (a)	Yes
Developed regions									
Albania	29	6	5	0	11	0	13	1994 (a)	..
Andorra	..	4	7	..	18	..	67	1997 (a)	..
Australia	6	10	22	13	14	23	17	1983	Yes
Austria	11	23	26	16	20	5	4	1982	Yes
Belarus	..	..	..	3	3	5	10	1981	Yes
Belgium	8	12	23	11	3	15	6	1985	Yes
Bosnia and Herzegovina	..	4	..	0	6	6	7	1993 (d)	..
Bulgaria	21	13	11	0	..	13	..	1982	Yes
Canada	10	18	21	14	..	20	..	1981	Yes
Croatia	..	6	8	4	12	6	20	1992 (d)	Yes
Czech Republic	..	10	15	0	17	0	14	1993 (d)	Yes
Denmark	29	33	37	29	41	11	12	1983	Yes
Estonia	..	13	..	15	12	3	17	1991 (a)	..
Finland	32	34	37	39	29	17	13	1986	Yes
France	7	6	11	7	12	12	12	1983	Yes
Germany	..	26	31	16	8	5	5	1985	Yes
Greece	4	6	6	4	5	8	7	1983	Yes
Hungary	21	11	8	0	5	6	12	1980	..
Iceland	21	25	35	15	8	3	7	1985	..
Ireland	8	13	12	16	21	15	8	1985 (a)	Yes
Italy	13	15	11	12	13	16	9	1985	Yes
Japan	1	3	5	6	0	8	3	1985	Yes
Latvia	..	15	17	0	7	5	27	1992 (a)	..
Liechtenstein	7	8	4	17	14	0	20	1995 (a)	Yes
Lithuania	..	7	18	0	6	6	11	1994 (a)	Yes
Luxembourg	12	20	17	9	17	11	16	1989	Yes
Malta	3	2	9	0	0	0	8	1991 (a)	Yes
Monaco	11	6	22	0	0	0	0	..	..
Netherlands	20	31	36	31	28	10	8	1991	Yes
New Zealand	14	21	29	8	8	17	31	1985	Yes
Norway	34	39	36	35	20	49	24	1981	Yes
Poland	20	13	13	7	17	12	9	1980	Yes

Table 6.A (cont'd):
Women in public life

Country or area	% parliamentary seats in Single or Lower chamber occupied by women			% women in decision-making positions in government				Year of ratification of CEDAW [a]	Whether national plan of action provided to the UN Secretariat [b]
				Ministerial level		Sub-ministerial level			
Developed regions (cont'd)	1987	1995	1999	1994	1998	1994	1998		
Portugal	8	9	13	10	10	5	11	1980	Yes
Republic of Moldova	..	5	9	0	0	6	15	1994 [a]	Yes
Romania	34	4	7	0	8	0	10	1982	Yes
Russian Federation	..	13	10	0	8	3	4	1981	Yes
San Marino	10	12	13	17	0	43	30	..	..
Slovakia	30	15	13	5	19	16	23	1993 [d]	Yes
Slovenia	..	14	8	5	0	13	19	1992 [d]	..
Spain	9	16	22	14	18	0	4	1984	Yes
Sweden	32	40	43	30	43	4	24	1980	Yes
Switzerland	14	18	21	17	17	0	8	1997 [a]	Yes
The FYR of Macedonia	..	3	8	8	9	13	23	1994 [d]	..
Ukraine	..	4	8	0	5	0	3	1981	..
United Kingdom	6	10	18	9	24	7	19	1986	Yes
United States	5	11	13	14	26	26	33	..	Yes
Yugoslavia	..	3	5	..	5	..	12	1982	..

Sources: For parliamentary seats occupied by women: IPU; for women in decision-making positions in government: *Women's Indicators and Statistics Database (Wistat), Version 4*, CD-ROM (United Nations publication, Sales No. E.00.XVII.4), based on compilations prepared by the Division for the Advancement of Women of the United Nations Secretariat; for year of ratification of the Convention on the Elimination of All Forms of Discrimination against Women and information on national plans of action: Division for the Advancement of Women.

Note: Two dots (..) indicate that data are not available; for CEDAW column, two dots indicate that the State has not ratified or acceded to the Convention as of March 2000.

[a] Refers to the year that the Convention on the Elimination of All Forms of Discrimination against Women was ratified. The note (a) next to the year indicates accession to the Convention; the note (d) indicates succession to the Convention. As of March 2000, Afghanistan, Sao Tome and Principe, and the United States have signed but not ratified, acceded or succeeded to the Convention.

[b] "Yes" means that the country or area has, as of April 2000, provided to the United Nations Secretariat its national action plan or strategy for the implementiation of the Beijing Platform for Action.

Technical notes

Table 6.A presents indicators on women's representation in national legislative bodies and in top-level decision-making positions in government. It also gives, for each country, the year of ratification of the Convention on the Elimination of All Forms of Discrimination against Women, and whether a national plan of action for the implementation of the Beijing Platform for Action has been submitted to the United Nations Secretariat. The statistics on parliamentarians are based on data provided to the Inter-Parliamentary Union by national authorities. These statistics, updated regularly, are available in http://www.ipu.org/wmn-e/classif.htm. Data on women in decision-making positions in Government are based on compilations prepared by the Division for the Advancement of Women of the United Nations Secretariat from the 1994 and 1998 issues of *World-wide Government Directories.*

The percentage of parliamentary seats occupied by women presented in table 6.A was calculated only for the lower chamber in countries with a bicameral assembly. Data for 1987 are based on the sex distribution of parliamentarians in the last election held between 1982 and 1987. Data for 1995 and 1999 are based on the sex distribution as at 1 July of the corresponding year, and reflect changes, if any, after the most recent election prior to that date, such as results of by-election or replacements following a parliamentarian's resignation or death.

A decision-making position in Government is defined as a position at the level of minister or the equivalent, deputy or assistant minister or the equivalent, secretary of State or permanent secretary or the equivalent and deputy of State or director of government or the equivalent. In table 6.A, "ministerial level" includes persons at the level of minister or the equivalent, while "sub-ministerial level" includes the rest of the positions enumerated above.

Information on the year of ratification of the Convention is provided by the Division for the Advancement of Women of the United Nations Secretariat, as is information on national plan of action.

The information on the Convention provided in table 6.A is as of March 2000. The Convention is the first international treaty embodying the civil, political, social, economic and cultural rights of women. It therefore covers the full range of issues related to the role and position of women in public and private life and establishes the obligations of States Parties to ensure the full development and advancement of women. It should be noted that many countries that have ratified and put in force the Convention have entered reservations. Conversely, some countries that have not entered reservations continue to permit practices that contravene particular provisions of the Convention.

The column on the national plan of action indicates whether a country has submitted a national action plan for the implementation of the Beijing Platform for Action, to the United Nations Secretariat, as of 4 April 2000. Governments committed themselves in the Platform for Action to developing implementation strategies and plans of action, and the majority of countries have provided their national action plans or strategies to the Secretariat. Many of the plans were prepared in cooperation with non-governmental organizations and other relevant actors. Only a few national action plans established comprehensive, time-bound targets and benchmarks or indicators for monitoring, and most national action plans made no reference to sources of financing for the actions identified.

◼ ANNEX I

Fourth World Conference on Women

Strategic objective H.3 of the Beijing Platform for Action[a]
Generate and disseminate gender-disaggregated data and information for planning and evaluation

Actions to be taken
By national, regional and international statistical services and relevant governmental and United Nations agencies, in cooperation with research and documentation organizations, in their respective areas of responsibility:

(a) Ensure that statistics related to individuals are collected, compiled, analysed and presented by sex and age and reflect problems, issues and questions related to women and men in society;

(b) Collect, compile, analyse and present on a regular basis data disaggregated by age, sex, socio-economic and other relevant indicators, including number of dependants, for utilization in policy and programme planning and implementation;

(c) Involve centres for women's studies and research organizations in developing and testing appropriate indicators and research methodologies to strengthen gender analysis, as well as in monitoring and evaluating the implementation of the goals of the Platform for Action;

(d) Designate or appoint staff to strengthen gender-statistics programmes and ensure coordination, monitoring and linkage to all fields of statistical work, and prepare output that integrates statistics from the various subject areas;

(e) Improve data collection on the full contribution of women and men to the economy, including their participation in the informal sector(s);

(f) Develop a more comprehensive knowledge of all forms of work and employment by:

i. Improving data collection on the unremunerated work which is already included in the United Nations System of National Accounts, such as in agriculture, particularly subsistence agriculture, and other types of non-market production activities;

ii. Improving measurements that at present underestimate women's unemployment and underemployment in the labour market;

iii. Developing methods, in the appropriate forums, for assessing the value, in quantitative terms, of unremunerated work that is outside national accounts, such as caring for dependents and preparing food, for possible reflection in satellite or other official accounts that may be produced separately from but are consistent with core national accounts, with a

view to recognizing the economic contribution of women and making visible the unequal distribution of remunerated and unremunerated work between women and men;

(g) Develop an international classification of activities for time-use statistics that is sensitive to the differences between women and men in remunerated and unremunerated work, and collect data disaggregated by sex. At the national level, subject to national constraints:

i. Conduct regular time-use studies to measure, in quantitative terms, unremunerated work, including recording those activities that are performed simultaneously with remunerated or other unremunerated activities;

ii. Measure, in quantitative terms, unremunerated work that is outside national accounts and work to improve methods to assess and accurately reflect its value in satellite or other official accounts that are separate from but consistent with core national accounts;

(h) Improve concepts and methods of data collection on the measurement of poverty among women and men, including their access to resources;

(i) Strengthen vital statistical systems and incorporate gender analysis into publications and research; give priority to gender differences in research design and in data collection and analysis in order to improve data on morbidity; and improve data collection on access to health services, including access to comprehensive sexual and reproductive health services, maternal care and family planning, with special priority for adolescent mothers and for elder care;

(j) Develop improved gender-disaggregated and age-specific data on the victims and perpetrators of all forms of violence against women, such as domestic violence, sexual harassment, rape, incest and sexual abuse, and trafficking in women and girls, as well as on violence by agents of the State;

(k) Improve concepts and methods of data collection on the participation of women and men with disabilities, including their access to resources.

---

[a] Reproduced from *Report of the Fourth World Conference on Women, Beijing, 4-15 September 1995* (United Nations publication, Sales No. 96.IV.13), Chap. I, resolution 1, annex II, chap. IV.H, para. 206.

Countries, areas and geographical groupings

Africa

Northern Africa
Algeria
Egypt
Libyan Arab Jamahiriya
Morocco
Tunisia
Western Sahara

Sub-Saharan Africa
Angola
Benin
Botswana
Burkina Faso
Burundi
Cameroon
Cape Verde
Central African Republic
Chad
Comoros
Congo
Côte d'Ivoire
Democratic Republic of the Congo
Djibouti
Equatorial Guinea
Eritrea
Ethiopia
Gabon
Gambia
Ghana
Guinea
Guinea-Bissau
Kenya
Lesotho
Liberia
Madagascar
Malawi
Mali
Mauritania
Mauritius
Mozambique
Namibia

Niger
Nigeria
Reunion
Rwanda
Sao Tome and Principe
Senegal
Seychelles
Sierra Leone
Somalia
South Africa
Sudan
Swaziland
Togo
Uganda
United Republic of Tanzania
Zambia
Zimbabwe

Latin America and the Caribbean

Caribbean
Antigua and Barbuda
Aruba
Bahamas
Barbados
Cuba
Dominica
Dominican Republic
Grenada
Guadeloupe
Haiti
Jamaica
Martinique
Netherlands Antilles
Puerto Rico
Saint Kitts and Nevis
Saint Lucia
Saint Vincent and the Grenadines
Trinidad and Tobago
United States Virgin Islands

Central America
Belize
Costa Rica
El Salvador
Guatemala
Honduras
Mexico
Nicaragua
Panama

South America
Argentina
Bolivia
Brazil
Chile
Colombia
Ecuador
French Guiana
Guyana
Paraguay
Peru
Suriname
Uruguay
Venezuela

Asia

Eastern Asia
China
　Hong Kong Special Administrative Region
　Macao Special Administrative Region
Democratic People's Republic of Korea
Mongolia
Republic of Korea

South-eastern Asia
Brunei Darussalam
Cambodia
East Timor
Indonesia
Lao People's Democratic Republic

Malaysia
Myanmar
Philippines
Singapore
Thailand
Viet Nam

Southern Asia
Afghanistan
Bangladesh
Bhutan
India
Iran (Islamic Republic of)
Maldives
Nepal
Pakistan
Sri Lanka

Central Asia
Kazakhstan*
Kyrgyzstan*
Tajikistan*
Turkmenistan*
Uzbekistan*

Western Asia
Armenia*
Azerbaijan*
Bahrain
Cyprus
Georgia*
Iraq
Israel
Jordan
Kuwait
Lebanon
Occupied Palestinian Territory
Oman
Qatar
Saudi Arabia
Syrian Arab Republic
Turkey
United Arab Emirates
Yemen

Oceania
American Samoa
Fiji
French Polynesia
Guam
Kiribati
Marshall Islands
Micronesia (Federated States of)
Nauru
New Caledonia
Palau
Papua New Guinea
Samoa
Solomon Islands
Tonga
Vanuatu

Developed regions

Eastern Europe
Albania*
Belarus*
Bosnia and Herzegovina*
Bulgaria*
Croatia*
Czech Republic*
Estonia*
Hungary*
Latvia*
Lithuania*
Poland*
Republic of Moldova*
Romania*
Russian Federation*
Slovakia*
Slovenia*
The former Yugoslav Republic
  of Macedonia*
Ukraine*
Yugoslavia*

Western Europe
Andorra
Austria
Belgium
Denmark
Finland
France
Germany
Greece
Iceland
Ireland
Italy
Liechtenstein
Luxembourg
Malta
Monaco
Netherlands
Norway
Portugal
San Marino
Spain
Sweden
Switzerland
United Kingdom of Great Britain
  and Northern Ireland

Other developed regions
Australia
Bermuda
Canada
Japan
New Zealand
United States of America

---

* Included in the category "countries in transition".

STATISTICAL SOURCES

1 Center for Reproductive Law and Policy, *The World's Abortion Laws 1999*, wall chart.

2 Inter-Parliamentary Union (IPU), *Women in Parliaments 1945–1995: A World Statistical Survey*, Reports and Documents Series, No. 23, and updates provided by IPU.

3 International Labour Office, *Key Indicators of the Labour Market* (Geneva, 1999).

4 _____, Labour Statistics Database (LABORSTA), as at August 1998.

5 _____, *Yearbook of Labour Statistics*, 1970–1999 (Geneva).

6 International Labour Organization, "More than 120 nations provide paid maternity leave", press release, 12 February 1998 (ILO/98/7).

7 Joint United Nations Programme on HIV/AIDS and World Health Organization, *Report on the Global HIV/AIDS Epidemic, June 1998* (Geneva).

8 _____, *AIDS Epidemic Update* (December 1999).

9 League of Arab States, Pan-Arab Project for Child Development (PAPCHILD), Maternal and Child Health Surveys. PAPCHILD is a regional research programme initiated in 1988 by the League of Arab States with the collaboration of the Arab Gulf Programme for the United Nations Development Organizations, the United Nations Population Fund, the United Nations Children's Fund, the World Health Organization and the Statistics Division of the United Nations Secretariat. The results of participating countries' surveys are published by the League of Arab States and the collaborating agency in each country in country reports.

10 Macro International, Demographic and Health Surveys (Calverton and Colombia, Maryland). The Demographic and Health Surveys (DHS) are a project funded primarily by the United States Agency for International Development to conduct national sample surveys on fertility, family planning and maternal and child health. More than thirty countries have participated in DHS. The results are published by Macro International in individual country reports and in its Comparative Studies series. Data cited from DHS were compiled from these reports.

11 South Pacific Commission, *Pacific Island Populations*, revised edition (Noumea, New Caledonia, 1998).

12 United Nations, reports of the Secretary-General on the composition of the Secretariat, 1980 (A/35/528) and 1995 (A/50/540), and on the improvement of the status of women in the Secretariat, 2000 (E.CN.6/2000/4).

13 _____, *Demographic Yearbook*, 1973–1997, and demographic statistics database, as at January 1999, unpublished.

14 _____, *First Marriage: Patterns and Determinants*, Statistical Papers, Series R, No. 76 (ST/ESA/SER.R/76).

15 _____, *Patterns of First Marriage: Timing and Prevalence*, Statistical Papers, Series R, No. III (ST/ESA/SER.R/III).

16 _____, *Women's Indicators and Statistics Database (Wistat), Version 4*, CD-ROM (United Nations publication, Sales No. E.00.XVII.4).

17 _____, *World Abortion Polices 1999*, wall chart (United Nations publication, Sales No. E.99.XIII.5, 1999).

18 _____, *World Contraceptive Use 1998*, wall chart (United Nations publication, Sales No. E.99.XIII.4).

19 _____, "Trends in total migrant stock by sex", revision 4, data set in digital form (POP/1B/DB/98/4).

20 _____, *World Population Monitoring 1999: Population Growth, Structure and Distribution* (United Nations publication, Sales No. XIII.4).

21 _____, *World Population Prospects: The 1998 Revision*, vol. I, *Comprehensive Tables* (United Nations publication, Sales No. E.99.XIII.9); vol. II, *The Sex and Age Distribution of the World Population* (United Nations publication, Sales No. E.99.XIII.8); and supplementary tabulations entitled "Age patterns of fertility, 1995–2050", "Mortality indicators for older persons" and "Survivors to exact ages, 1990–2050", data set in digital form.

22 _____, *World Urbanization Prospects: The 1999 Revision*, "Percentage of the population living in urban areas", data set in digital form (POP/DB/WUP/Rev.1999/1/F2).

23 United Nations Children's Fund, *Child Malnutrition: Country Profiles* (New York, 1993) and underweight statistics database (as at December 1998), unpublished.

24 _____, *Monitoring Eastern Europe*, MONEE Project database (Florence, International Child Development Centre, 1999).

25 _____, *The State of the World's Children 2000* (New York, 2000).

26 United Nations Educational, Scientific and Cultural Organization (UNESCO), *Compendium of Statistics on Illiteracy*, Statistical Reports and Studies, No. 31 (Paris, 1990).

27 _____, *Statistical Yearbook*, 1986–1998 (Paris) and updates provided by UNESCO.

28 Office of the United Nations High Commissioner for Refugees, *Refugees and Others of Concern to UNHCR: 1998 Statistical Overview* (Geneva, 1999).

29 World Health Organization, "Coverage of maternity care: a listing of available information", fourth edition (WHO/RHT/MSM/96.28) (Geneva, 1997).

30 _____, Global Database on Child Growth and Malnutrition, accessed at http://www.who.int/nutgrowthdb, as at April 1999.

31 _____, "The tobacco epidemic: a global public health emergency", *Tobacco Alert*, special issue (1996).

32 _____, WHO database on violence against women, as at March 2000.

33 _____, *World Health Report 1998: Life in the Twenty-first Century, A Vision for All* (Geneva, 1998).

34 *Worldwide Government Directory*, 1994 and 1998 (Washington, D.C., Belmont).

Note Additional data were provided by the Division for the Advancement of Women of the United Nations Secretariat, the Statistics Division of the Economic Commission for Latin America and the Caribbean and the Statistical Office of the European Communities.